New Mind and Christianity

Love is the New Mind, the New Law is Love

[blank page]

New Mind and Christianity

Love is the New Mind, the New Law is Love

Love is patient, kind, forgiving, full of joy and goodness, faithful, hopeful, gentle, not jealous, not arrogant, not unbecoming: love seeks good and shuns evil. It's the new law.

by

Walter R. Dolen

President of the Becoming-One Church

Becoming-One Publications

2015 Revised Edition
This edition supersedes all previous editions

This work is a corrected and enlarged version of a 1970-71 non-published work and the 1977, 1989 and 2000 published works.
(Since the 2000 edition an Introduction was added and changes made to the Old Mind/Other Mind chapters, the Reason Why chapter and other minor changes; this book was previously called, *New Minds Papers*

Cover photo and graphics by W. Dolen & others
used with permission
[Wikimedia Commons & Corel]

Printed and Published in the USA
April 2023 Printing

ISBN13: 978-1-61918-0246
(Trade Cloth)

ISBN13: 978-1-61918-000-0
(Trade Paper)

Other formats:
ISBN13: 978-1-61918-009-3
(iBook)
also in other e-book formats (Kindle, etc.)

Becoming-One Publications
Pennsylvania
becoming-one.org/books.htm
b1publ.com

NM: Table of Contents

Documentation

When you see, "The God, all in all" (1 Cor 15:28), it means that this is a quote from the New Testament letter called First Corinthians, chapter 15, verse 28. If you see "2 Cor" it would mean the *second* letter of the Corinthians. If you see "2 Cor 11:4" it would mean we quoted from the second letter of the Corinthians, the 11th chapter, and the 4th verse. But sometimes you will see a documentation such as "(1 Pet 2:4)" after a sentence that has no quotes. This kind of documentation is used in order to *support* the previous sentence or sentences, or to *point out other similar or related views* of the previous sentence or sentences, or to *add new light* to the previous sentence or sentences.

When you see reference to "**NM7**" it means more information can be found in *New Mind Papers*, **Part 7**.

When you see reference to "**nm7**" this means more information can be found in **paragraph 7** of the *New Mind Papers*.

NM	= *New Mind and Christianity (aka, New Mind Papers)*
GP	= *God Papers* (aka: *My God is the Becoming-One*)
PR	= *Prophecy Papers* (aka: *Prophecy*)
CP	= *New Chronology Papers*
cf or cf.	= Confer or compare
p. or pp.	= page or pages
w/	= with

Introduction

New Law

Love is patient, kind, forgiving, full of joy and goodness, faithful, hopeful, gentle, not jealous, not arrogant, not unbecoming; love shuns evil and seeks good. Love is the new law and is what Real Christianity must be in order to be Christ's church. In this book we go into great detail about this. However, others only see the negativity of religion. Mark Twain[1] was disillusioned with Christianity and religion because he only saw the paradoxes and the hell-damnation of religiosity. So he wrote the following in a book not published until after his death:

> "A God who could make good children as easily as bad, yet preferred to make bad ones; who could have made every one of them happy, yet never made a single happy one; who made them prize their bitter life, yet stingily cut it short; who gave his angels eternal happiness unearned, yet required his other children to earn it; who gave his angels painless lives, yet cursed his other children with biting miseries and maladies of mind and body; who mouths justice and invented hell - mouths mercy and invented hell - mouths Golden Rules, and forgiveness multiplied by seventy times seven, and invented hell." [Mark Twain, *The Mysterious Stranger*, Chap. 11]

This perception of the inexplicable paradoxes and negativity found in religion, or the emphasis upon such, is one-sided and unfair, for such negativity was superseded by Christ's teaching on Love.

Jesus Christ, for whom Real Christianity is named, changed the way some perceived God. Unfortunately, Jesus' teaching was taken over by those who didn't understand and they changed Christ's teachings of forgiveness and love into the teachings of hell and damnation. Because of this, we are forced to review in detail the doctrines of Christianity because the negativity of the world has been interjected into religion, not only Christianity, but all religion. This projects something about man's mind in this age, which we call the old mind. But Christ announced a new mind, a new spirit, and a new commandment – the commandment of love. Originally this book was

---

[1] A pen name for Samuel Clemens, one of America's best know writers

called the *New Mind Papers* because the new mind was the mind of love, not hate. We think our new title for this book more reflects and projects the real essence of Real Christianity, as taught by Jesus Christ. This book is comprehensive: we cover all the important doctrines found in the Bible about Real Christianity and attempt to negate the misguided teachings of religiosity.

Before we start examining Real Christianity, let me give you some of the premises for my belief.

I believe God did create the universe and here are a few reasons why I do

Law. The evolutionary theory always starts with, and assumes, the eternal existence of laws like those of mass, energy, motion, gravity, conservation, chemical bonding and so forth. Laws, in and of themselves, *are* systematic order and project intelligence and power outside of the law itself. The genetic code of life found in DNA also projects high intelligence and power. *How can* the *code of DNA evolve* or any law such as gravity or chemical bonding evolve? How can any code or law itself have any power? What gives a code power? I am speaking about the code itself, the order of the elements within the code. How can the *arrangement* of the code itself have power? The apparent connection between the code and its effect on a body or plant projects, or strongly suggests some kind of force or power *behind* the law. The code itself doesn't do anything, just as the letters in this book don't do anything by themselves. If you change the arrangement of the letters of the code or a word, it has a different result or may not have any. A seed grows into a certain kind of flower, not because of the code per se, but because of the power behind the code. The basic laws of the universe must have come from somewhere and the power behind these laws must have some connection to the law. Evolution has yet to explain the source of the power behind the universal laws. Science can only *describe* gravity (through mathematical formulas) and partially *describe* the code of life, but it has no idea how the power of gravity works or how or where the code of DNA gets its power. I believe that God, as described in the *God Papers*, is the creator and power behind all universal laws. And I believe it is more naive to believe in a cosmic soup theory (evolution) than in a powerful God, although I agree that common descriptions of God are naive and do not explain the paradoxes pertaining to God.

Beginning. Radioactivity and laws of thermodynamics indicate there was no eternity of matter and it corollary: there was a beginning of matter. If matter always existed, without a starting point, then the "life" period of the radioactive elements would have long ago run its course and the whole universe would be the same temperature (thermodynamic laws). The radioactive elements would have run down and there would not be any radioactive elements left; the whole universe should be the same temperature. Thus, there was a *beginning* of matter, and it wasn't that long ago, since there are still radioactive elements. The "science" of evolution cannot explain energy or matter or its source nor will it ever because it has no witnesses and has no real explanation for their beginning. A mathematical description of energy doesn't explain it, it only describes what it does in a quantitative manner in *our* solar system. God created matter and energy and in some way God is matter and God is energy as we attempt to explain in our book pertaining to God (*God: God is the Becoming-One*).

Life. The relative harmonic-symbiosis of the ecosystems, from the biochemical cell to the earth-sea-heavens, projects design. There is a co-operation, interaction and mutual dependence among life forms; one species cannot live well, or at all, without mutual-beneficial interaction of the whole: the flowers need the birds and insects for pollination in order to continue to exist and vis versa; the seed needs its DNA, the dirt with its nutriments, water and the power behind the DNA for it to grow. Our bodies need a heart, lungs, liver, intestines and so forth in order to exist: we need our whole factory of body parts and a compatible earth in order to live. The whole cannot live without the parts; the parts cannot exist without the whole. The theory of evolution maintains that life is arbitrary, for life came from a hit and miss adventure ("natural selection" or "mutation," etc.). If life is arbitrary, then the universe would be filled with the inferior products of this evolutionary process, and the inferior and half-made life-forms would greatly outnumber the surviving species. There should be fossils of the inferior products of the evolutionary process in all strata, in the rocks everywhere. In other words, the rejections of the evolutionary process should be polluting the universe. Where are the fossils of these inferior life-forms? For that matter, where are the masses of missing links in the evolutionary process? Where? Life came from God, not from the mindless soup of evolution.

The Proof. The big bang theory and other theories need to explain where the material and energy for the big bang theory came from. God, the all powerful Being, by definition, must have always been there, or else there is nothing and we are nothing and so this dialogue doesn't exist. Either the all powerful god of Evolution (mindless soup) was there at the beginning or the all powerful Being was there. Of course we cannot prove God by definition, but there is a way to settle this disagreement:

- The evolutionists can prove the universe came into existence through evolution by physically demonstrating evolution. For example, a new species being spontaneously 'created' before our eyes, or at very least finding the massive amount of missing links in the fossils record and logically explaining where laws get their power;

- The believers in the God can prove to others that there is an all powerful God by people seeing God create a new heaven and earth or by seeing God resurrect the dead back to life. Such is the prophecy recorded in the Bible: all will see the resurrection of the dead and the creation of the new heaven and earth, as apparently the angels witnessed the creation of the present universe at the beginning of the present heaven and earth.

Bible: Is the Bible Reliable?

Typical Criticism

Three Tests to Give

Christianity, Judaism and Islam base their belief and knowledge of God on information found in the Bible. The non-believers think the Bible is too legendary and therefore cannot be the word of God. To the disbeliever the Bible is full of exaggerated stories orally passed on through generations.

Bible's Rich Metaphorical Word Usage

The Bible is a historical document that includes poetry and a rich use of figures of speech. The Bible uses similes, "his eyes were as a flame of fire" (Rev 1:14). The Bible uses metaphors, "tell that fox" (Luke 13:32). The Bible uses metonyms, "if the house be worthy" (Mat 10:13). The Bible uses synecdoches, "all the world should be taxed" (Luke 2:1). The Bible uses personifications, "the earth mourns and fades away" (Isa 24:4). The Bible uses apostrophes, "O death, where is thy sting?" (1Cor 15:55) The Bible uses hyperboles, "the light of the sun shall be sevenfold" (Isa 30:26). The Bible uses allegories, "this Hagar is Mount Sinai in Arabia."(Gal 4:24) The Bible uses parables, "behold, a sower went forth to sow" (Mat 13:3). The Bible also uses irony, riddles, and fables (1Kings 18:27; Rev 13:18; and Judg 9:8 ff & 2Kgs 14:9 ff). So we see that the Bible is rich in its use of language. (The serpent did not literally speak to Eve, only figuratively did the serpent speak to Eve.) Yes, the Bible does have a few fables, riddles and metaphorical serpents talking within its pages. The Israelis were creative writers. Figures of speech are used to draw attention and interest to the meaning of the words, and to aid in the remembrance of the text. A text of poetry is easier to remember than a boring academic document. The fact that the Bible used colorful word usage to convey its message does not mean it does not convey a truthful picture of history and important philosophical and theological messages from God. It may just as well mean that God used man's colorful ways of expression to convey his word so as to better brand the message into the mind of man. Figures of speech can also breed misunderstanding if the hearer/reader takes literally a story that was only meant to teach a lesson. Trees clapping their hands and snakes talking are metaphorical, not literal.

Bible, an Ancient Text with Abundance of Details

The Bible's history goes back thousands of years. Especially in the last hundred and seventy years, archeology has confirmed facts recorded in the Bible that previously had no other confirmation. In comparison to other ancient writings, the Bible is as accurate, if not more accurate than any other historical document in the world (See my *Chronology Papers*). Most ancient historians give a skewed view to make their ethnic group look better than they did in reality. Not so with the writers of the Bible. They wrote, not only of the glory, but of the foibles of their people.

The Bible is filled with specific place names, proper names, topographical descriptions, descriptions of ancient customs and nations, descriptions of ancient artifacts, temples, religions, and human behavior. Until the last couple of centuries the skeptics used to call many of the nations, cultures, and customs described in the Bible – myth, or just oral traditions that had lost their truth. But archaeological finds have helped to alleviate some of this skepticism.

The Bible has the oldest manuscripts of any large ancient document to attest to its ancient origins. The intra-cohesiveness of these old manuscripts helps to indicate that today's Bible may very well reflect truthfully the original documents.[1] But of course, we have no *original* documents for the Bible or any other ancient document, except those written on stone. Remember there were no copy machines when the manuscripts of the Bible were handed down. The copying of manuscripts was done by hand. Because it is almost impossible to copy a large document without some mistakes, there are some variations between the ancient manuscripts and today's, but most of these variations concern different spelling of words or omission of words or words or phrases that were added by scribes so as to clarify the meaning of the text.

Criticism

Typical criticism: The Bible is a mythological book that contains orally transmitted myths that were passed down through generations until about the time of Ezra who compiled most of the Old Testament. Moses did not write five books of the Bible because for one thing, there were few in his day who could write: the Hebrews used oral tradition and/or he was illiterate and so could not write it.

---

[1] My study helped to prove this to me

First about Moses: I don't see anywhere in the Bible where it specifically says that Moses wrote every single word of the first five books of the Bible. Of course he compiled sections from other writings and placed them within his books. He may have had scribes helping him; Jeremiah had a scribe to help him. I don't see in the Bible where it states specifically who actually penned each book. I also don't see any proof that Moses did not know how to read or write, after all, he was brought up by the Pharaoh's daughter in the palace, so of course, he was taught to read and write. The general criticisms are sometimes petty, merely trying to find fault, and not giving the author the benefit of the doubt. While others' criticism seems to be mere scholarly exercises, although they do point out apparent paradoxes in the text and in its depiction of the Hebrew God. Books like Richard Simon's, A Critical History of the Old Testament [1682,English Trans., (archive.org)], seem to be anti-Hebrew in tone by attempting to prove that the caretakers of the Hebrew text made many mistakes in copying, while the Isaiah scroll from the Dead Sea Scrolls is proof of the immense care they took in preserving the Hebrew Bible. To make his case Simon seems to point out every trivial criticism he could think of (the text repeats itself too many times, the text uses synonyms, it wasn't written in a style he appreciates or understands, laws are written with different words at different places within the text and so forth).

The general criticism is not that solid especially when we examine archaeological finds of the last few centuries. For example, the Ebla tablets, discovered in the 1970's prove that there was written text before Moses at least back to about 2250-2000 BC (see my Chronology Papers). In the 1975 season over 15,000 tablets were found, about 18,000 complete clay tablets were eventually found. The language of the tablets was Sumerian script and the Eblaite language, the earliest known Semitic language. Personal names, geographic names, lists of animals, professions, names of officials, vocabularies, sacrificial systems, rituals, proverbs, hymns, and so forth were found. Most of the tablets dealt with economic matters such as bills of sale, receipts, tariffs, contracts of sale, etc. Among the tablets were copies of treaties, one was between Asshur and Ebla. Asshur is mentioned in the 10th chapter of Genesis. The language of Ebla was Semitic and the closeness to Hebrew is striking. The vocabularies were the oldest found so far in history, about 500 years earlier than any previously known. There are tablets with case law on them. This proves that hundreds of years before Moses there was written law. Moses didn't invent law, he merely put it in a Hebrew form. What is unique about Moses's law is the patterns in it and its God. These tablets named the five cities of the plain mentioned in the book of Genesis of the Bible, proving these cities were not mythological. The tablets reflect the culture of the patriarchal period and even mention people's names that appear in the book of Genesis. (see Beld, Hallo, and Michalowski, *The Tablets of Ebla: Concordance and Bibliography*, 1984; Giovanni Pettinato, *The Archives of Ebla, 1981*; Clifford Wilson, *Ebla Tablets*, 1977; etc.)

Because these tablets were found in Syria near the modern city of Aleppo, apparently the information that ties these tablets to the Hebrews is being censored by Syria because of the fear of giving any credence to the Jews' rights to the ancient land of Israel.

Three Tests

There are three tests we can use to determine the reliability of the Bible. **(1) Bibliographical Test**: Not having the original documents of the Bible, how reliable are the copies we have? **(2) Internal Evidence Test**: Is the written record credible? **(3) External Evidence Test**: Does other historical material confirm or deny the material in the Bible?

Bibliographical Test

How reliable are the copies we have in regard to the number of manuscripts and the interval of time between the original and the surviving copy? Concerning New Testament manuscripts there are about 22,000 copies of manuscripts with at least partial contents of the New Testament. The closest ancient work next to the Bible is the Homer's *Iliad* (700?? BC), but it only has about 643 manuscripts. Such works as Aristotle (*c.* 340 BC) have only about five manuscripts for any one of his works, the earliest copy is dated about 1100 AD, about 1400 years after he lived and wrote his work. The history of Thucydides (*c.* 460-400 BC) has just eight manuscripts and the earliest copy is from about 900 AD. Pliny the Younger's History has only 7 copies, the earliest copy from about 850 AD. Plato's work has only 7 copies, the earliest from about 900 AD. Livy's work has only 20 copies. Contrariwise the New Testament manuscripts are about 22,000 in number, with one of the earliest (John Ryland MSS) dating from about 130 AD, about a century after Christ. The *Chester Beatty Papyri* located in the Beatty Museum in Dublin has three manuscripts containing major parts of the New Testament. Two of these papyri manuscripts are dated in the second half of the third century (250-300 AD). But manuscript ^{p46}, which was originally dated about 200 AD has since been dated to 100 AD on paleographical grounds (*Biblica* 69:2 [1988], pp. 248-257). "Paleography (literally, old writing) is the study of the manuscripts themselves rather than the text they contain. In attempting to date manuscripts, paleographers are especially concerned with the script, i.e., the style of the letters used. We have so many papyri from Egypt that a definite progression in the style of script from one period to the next can be seen" (Darrell Hannah, "New Testament Manuscripts," *Bible Review*, Feb. 1990, p. 7). [Some of this paragraph's info was taken from Josh McDowell, *New Evidence that Demands a Verdict*, 800 pages, 1999.]

Until the discovery of the Dead Sea Scrolls the oldest Old Testament manuscript was dated about 900 AD. This was about a 1300-1400 year gap from when the Bible was completed. Because of the reverence for the scriptures, the Jewish community went to great lengths in making new copies of the Old Testament as accurate and perfect as humanly possible. "Besides recording varieties of reading, tradition, or conjecture, the Massoretes undertook a number of calculations which do not enter into the ordinary sphere of textual criticism. They numbered the verses, words, and letters of every book. They calculated the middle word and the middle letter of each. They enumerated verses which contained all the letters of the alphabet ... These trivialities ... had yet the effect of securing minute attention to the precise transmission of the text; and they are but an excessive manifestation of a respect for the sacred Scriptures..." (Frederic Kenyon, *Our Bible and the Ancient Manuscripts*, 1941). Because of this meticulous care of the Jewish caretakers of the Bible, it has been believed the Bible copies were highly accurate. The Dead Sea Scrolls helped to confirm this belief.

The Dead Sea Scrolls are made up tens of thousands of inscribed fragments from over 900 texts. The texts can be divided into three groups: Biblical manuscripts (copies from the Hebrew Bible) make up about 40% of the total; Apocryphal texts, which make up about 30% of the total; and Sectarian manuscripts. They are dated from about 150 BC to 70AD. One complete scroll of the Old Testament book of Isaiah was found among the Dead Sea Scrolls. According to Gleason Archer, the Isaiah scroll "proved to be word for word identical with our standard Hebrew Bible in more than 95% of the text, but in 1QIs[b] [a partial text about 1/3 of Isaiah], (ca. 75 B.C.) the preserved text is almost letter for letter identical with the Leningrad Manuscript. The 5% of variation consisted chiefly of obvious slips of the pen and variations in spelling" (Gleason Archer, *A Survey of the Old Testament*, 1994, p. 29).

Internal Evidence Test

When you analyze the Bible itself you must be fair. To use what some call Aristotle's dictum:[1] "the benefit of the doubt is to be given to the document itself, and not arrogated by the critic to himself." You should not assume fraud or error unless you find contradictions of known fact.

> "Giving "benefit of the doubt" until further evidence is uncovered and investigation undertaken is hardly incompatible with a healthy skepticism. Extreme incredulity is no more inherently virtuous or useful than extreme credulity. Indeed both represent a mindset not conducive to honest and fair examination of a particular claim....

> It is no coincidence that atheists, and skeptics come down on the side of the burden of proof falling upon the document while Conservative Christian scholars come down on the side of the burden of proof falling to the critic.... the burden of proof issue often says more about the person examining a particular text than about the text itself. It often reveals the presuppositions and philosophical assumptions of the contemporary historian.

> "Those who accept the empirical claims of a historical text bear the burden of proof just as much as those who assert their falsehood; in the absence of such proof we should suspend judgment. Empirical uncertainty thus forms the middle ground between the claim that empirical claims are certainly true and the claim that empirical claims are certainly false." [Jeff Lowder][2]

The biggest problem that the secular intellectuals find with scriptures is God and his supernaturalness. According to their system of thinking any supernaturalness is automatically thrown out. But at the same time the magic of evolution, the cosmic non-intelligent soup that by some miracle created the universe, is not thrown out. This is the result of a mindset. The writers of the New Testament were eyewitnesses (Luke 1:1-3; John 19:35; 1 John 1:3; 2 Peter 1:16; etc). They spoke

---

[1] I could find no evidence that Aristotle actually said this, but the idea is still worthy to note.

[2] www.theologyweb.com, June 22, 2003, by markg

to others who were eyewitnesses (Acts 2:22; 26:24-28; etc.). At first they did not believe in Christ's resurrection, and admitted this very thing in their writings (Mark 16:11; Luke 24:11, 25; John 20:24-29). But later they saw the resurrected Christ and believed (Luke 24:48; John 20:19-20; Acts 1:8; 2:24,32; 3:15; 4:33; 5:32; 10:39, 41; 13:31; 22:15; 26:16; 1 Cor 15:4-9, 15; 1 John 1:2). Later many of them died because of this belief (Acts 7:58-60; 9:1; Rev 6:11; Heb 11:35-12:1). Tradition has it that 11 of the apostles were martyred for their belief. If it was all a lie, if they made it up, why did they allow themselves to die for it? Even when they lived they gained nothing materially from their belief. They must therefore have believed it because they *saw* the things they wrote about.

Sir William Ramsay, one of the great archaeologists, is another witness to the Bible's accuracy:

> "He was a student of the German historical school that taught that the Book of Acts was a product of the mid-second century A.D. and not the first century as it purports to be. After reading modern criticism about the Book of Acts, he became convinced that it was not a trustworthy account of the facts of that time (A.D. 50) and therefore was unworthy of consideration by a historian. So in his research on the history of Asia Minor, Ramsay paid little attention to the New Testament. His investigation, however, eventually compelled him to consider the writing of Luke. He observed the meticulous accuracy of the historical details, and his attitude toward the Book of Acts began to change. He was forced to conclude that 'Luke is a historian of the first rank ... this author should be placed along with the very greatest of historians.'" (J. McDowell, *He Walked Among Us*, p. 110)

More could be said on the internal evidence, but we will let other books speak on this matter (see book lists below).

External Evidence Test

Does other historical material confirm or deny the testimony in the Bible? For one thing the names and descriptions of kings, cities, geography, customs, events, wars, and so forth are well attested and confirmed by secular findings such as archeology. In our *Chronology Papers* we give some evidence of this. The books in the book list below as well as the evidence and books referenced within these books also attest to this. Joseph P. Free, in his *Archaeology and Bible History*, said "Archaeology has confirmed countless passages which have been rejected by critics as unhistorical or contradictory to known facts" (p.1). Read the many books available on this subject.

The following short list of books will help you in your search:

- Josh McDowell, *New Evidence that Demands a Verdict*, 800 pages, 1999

- F.F. Bruce, *The New Testament Documents: Are They Reliable?*, 2009

- Josh McDowell & Bill Wilson, *He Walked Among Us: Evidence for the Historical Jesus*, 1988, 2011

- Merrill F. Unger, *Archaeology and the Old Testament*, 1954, 2009

- J. Pritchard, *Ancient Near Eastern Texts Relating to the Old Testament*, 1969, 2010

- Jack Finegan, *Archaeological History of the Ancient Middle East*, 1979, 1996

Duality of the Bible

Type and Antitype

Visible Projects Invisible

More Examples

Look to the Higher Meaning

There is a way to read the Bible for spiritual truth

For God speaks once, yet twice, though people do not perceive it (Job 33:14)

Before I found this way or method of reading the Bible, the book was like an enigma to me as it was and is to many others. The method has to do with the duality of meaning in the Bible: one a physical meaning; one a spiritual meaning. All of the sections in this book, *God*, and most of my other religious writings project and rely on the duality of the Bible in order to explain it's higher meaning. If there is a secret in understanding the Bible, it is the duality of the Bible – the type and antitype of the Bible. There are events and words in the Bible that have dual meanings. One meaning is the physical meaning; the other meaning is the spiritual meaning. The physical meaning is the typical rendition. The spiritual meaning is the antitypical rendition. Of course I wasn't the first to see this duality, many other writers, including Paul of the New Testament, have pointed to this duality. If there is a secret to reading the Bible, this is it.

Type and Antitype

The duality of the Bible consists of "types" and "antitypes." A "type" is an event, person, thing, or symbol in the Bible that represents some Spiritual Truth. The Spiritual Truth is the antitype of the type. For example, in the Old Testament it describes the Passover lamb. In the New Testament it tells us the True or Real Passover lamb is Jesus Christ (1 Cor 5:7). The Old Testament's Passover lamb is a type of the New Testament's Passover lamb, which is Jesus Christ (see "God's Appointed Times" paper [NM16]). The Old Testament's Passover foreshadowed the New Testament's Passover.

Paul of the New Testament, in his letter called Hebrews, tried to explain the duality of the Bible. He didn't use the word "duality" when he tried to explain it, but nevertheless he was explaining the duality of the Bible. Paul in Hebrews speaks of a "sanctuary that is a copy and shadow of what is in heaven. This is why Moses was warned when he was about to build the tabernacle: 'See to it that you make everything [in the tabernacle] according to the pattern shown you on the mountain.'" (Hebrews 8:5; Ex 25:9, 40) Paul is saying that the tabernacle that Moses built was a *pattern* of the tabernacle in heaven. What does this mean?

When you see the word "heaven" used in the Bible, you can think of it as *spiritual*, for both "heaven" and "spiritual" are used interchangeably in the Bible (compare "heaven" and "spiritual" in 1 Cor 15:44-49). Thus Paul is saying that Moses made his tabernacle (the physical one) according to the pattern of the heavenly or spiritual tabernacle.

Paul explains that Christ didn't go into the physical tabernacle, but the "true tabernacle" or the "more perfect tabernacle that is not man-made," "for Christ did not enter a man-made sanctuary that was only a copy of the true one; He entered heaven itself [the spiritual dimension itself], now to appear for us in God's presence" (Hebrews 8:2; 9:11, 24). The physical tabernacle built by Moses was merely a copy of the Real or True tabernacle. Paul tells us that "the law [much of the Old Testament is called the law] is only a shadow of the good things that are coming — not the realities themselves" (Heb 10:1). The law and things of the Old Testament were merely shadows of the good things, the real things, to come. The Old Testament and the things in it are only the *types* of the *antitypes*. The antitype being the Real and True — the Spiritual fulfillment of the type. Paul tells us that the things written in the Old Testament were *types* or *examples* for us, that is, types or examples for us Real Christians (1 Cor 10:11).

Visible projects the Invisible

Paul tells us that the invisible qualities of God can be understood by the things that God has made. (Rom 1:19-20) And in our papers you will see how many aspects of this world, like males and females, which God made, are types of the antitype. Marriage, being born, women, water, stars, and so forth all have a higher meaning: they all have a Spiritual meaning; they are all types of the Real or True, which is the antitype. For example, "stars" are representative of angels (see Rev 1:20). And even "water" foreshadows the Spirit (John 7:38-39)

More Examples

Female and Male Language; Type and Antitype Language

The two sexes use the same language and understand the same language in slightly different ways. The same words or sentences have different meanings to each sex (*Male/Female Language*, by Mary Ritchie Key, 1996) because of their biosocial differences (see my Sex Difference book). Just as women and men can get two different meanings from the same words (a sex/gender difference), people also understand the Bible in two different ways: its physical and its Spiritual meaning. In all my books pertaining to the Bible I manifest this and attempt to explain this phenomenon.

Even New Testament rituals like water baptism are types of the antitypes. Water baptism represents spiritual baptism. (see "Baptism Paper" [NM4]) All of the Bible projects its duality through its language of type and antitype. This includes the Old as well as the New Testament. Even the physical creation is representative of a higher or spiritual meaning (Rom 1:20). The physical creation (the type) is representative of the spiritual creation (the antitype). For example the days of the week are seven. The week was instituted right after the creation (see Genesis, chapter 1). But this week is a type. It represents the antitypical week. The Bible gives a few hints that to God a day is like a 1000 years or a 1000 years like a day (2 Pet 3:8; Ps 90:4). Therefore in the duality of the Bible, the physical week (seven days of the week: the type) is representative of the Spiritual 7,000 year week (the antitype). Even such things as "salt" and "light" have higher or antitypical meaning (Matt 5:13-16). "Clean" and "unclean" have a higher meaning (Matt 15:2,11,15-20). "Yeast" has a higher meaning (Matt 16:5-12).

Look to the Higher Meaning

We are to look for the higher meanings or Spiritual meaning of scripture *vis a vis* merely the earthly things (Col 3:1-2; Phil 3:19-20; 1 Cor 15:44-49). In my study I found that the typical and antitypical meanings are a check onto each other and helps to verify the accuracy of the Bible's transmission from the original text to us.

Walter, 2012

Mindset Paper

Ptolemy's Theory

Brain Cell Problem

We are born into a world of traditions. The traditions that we are born into have sets of rules, written and non-written. We are taught or influenced by our parents, teachers, environment, mind(s), the language(s) we speak, and our biology to believe in certain things and act in certain ways. From this we form a belief system, or mindset. A "mindset" is a perceptual set. Through this set we perceive the world. A mindset acts like a filter. It filters out any mental conceptions or realities that do not fit our mindset.

The word "liberal" means something different to a liberal than to a conservative. The word "communist" means something different to a communist than to a capitalist. The word "Catholic" means something different to a Catholic than to a Protestant. The word "evolution" means something different to an evolutionist than to a creationist. A peaceful countryside, where a nuclear plant is planned, means something different to environmentalists than to the owner or builder of the nuclear plant.

A person who does not know anything about the game of baseball who overhears someone talking about Smith "stealing" second base, may think that Smith committed a crime. As our knowledge and background filters our perception of the words, "Smith *stole* second base," so too with almost everything else. Words sometimes have different meaning to different people; words often times have *shades* of different meaning to different people.

Ptolemy's Mathematical-Geocentric Theory

One of the biggest examples of a mindset was the geocentric theory in which the earth was the center of the universe. The geocentric theory is the idea that the earth is the center of the universe while the sun, moon, planets, and stars made a complete revolution around the earth each day. This theory was represented well by Claudius Ptolemy. Claudius Ptolemy's work commonly known as the *Almagest* was actually called "Mathematical Systematic Treatise" in the Greek version because it was a mathematical system. Ptolemy believed that mathematics was the highest form of science:

"that only mathematics can provide sure and unshakeable knowledge to its devotees, provided one approaches it rigorously.

For its kind of proof proceeds by indisputable methods, namely arithmetic and geometry" (G.J. Toomer, *Ptolemy's Almagest*, p 36).

Today the public makes light of the *Almagest* by thinking of it as some naive theological or church backed doctrine. But instead it was the most scientific work of its day containing abundant mathematical proof with tables and charts, with premises from Greek philosophy, not church doctrine. "One of the most influential scientific works in history, and a masterpiece of technical exposition in its own right" (G.J. Toomer, p. vii). Yes, today the geocentric theory seems preposterous, since after all, we know that the earth is not the center of the universe, and in fact that the earth makes one revolution around the sun each year. We believe this even though it *appears* (empirical evidence) from our eyesight that the sun, planets, and stars revolve around the earth each day.

Ptolemy and his Treatise

"His name was Claudius Ptolemaeus ... he lived from approximately A.D. 100 to approximately A.D. 175, and that he worked in Alexandria, the principal city of Greco-Roman Egypt, which possessed, among other advantages, what was probably still the best library in the ancient world.... As is implied by its Greek name, ... , 'mathematical systematic treatise,' the Almagest is a complete exposition of mathematical astronomy as the Greeks understood the term" (Toomer, p. 1). By the "fourth century (and probably much earlier), when Pappus wrote a commentary on it, the Almagest had become the standard textbook on astronomy which it was to remain for more than a thousand years.... It was dominant to an extent and for a length of time which is unsurpassed by any scientific work except Euclid's *Elements*.... " (Toomer p. 2-3)

"Ptolemy called his principal work on astronomy the Great System (*Megale Syntaxis tes Astronomias*, later known as *Almagest* from the Arabic translation). This somewhat arrogant title was fully justified, for he had examined every problem in astronomy, and solved every one with Euclidean precision. Ptolemy created the first complete scientific system — a structure so vast and coherent that not even the comprehensive mind of an Aristotle could have conceived it, let alone worked it out.

"Toward the solution of the chief problem, the apparently irregular velocities of the planets, he made a crucial discovery. Ptolemy drew an overlapping circle near Apollonius' circle.... The second circles came to be known as Ptolemy's epicycles. From the center of the epicycle the motion around Apollonius' eccentric circle appeared to be uniform.

The system was extremely complicated, but it worked; Ptolemy could use it to calculate any future position of Mars... Ptolemy could justly boast that he had laid the keystone of Greek astronomy.... Mathematically speaking, this was true; henceforth, everything was calculable.... The planets now traveled in loops, that is to say, around an imaginary point that for unknown reasons itself revolved around the Earth.... (Rudolf Thiel, *And There was Light*, trans. by Richard and Clara Winston, pp. 49-51).

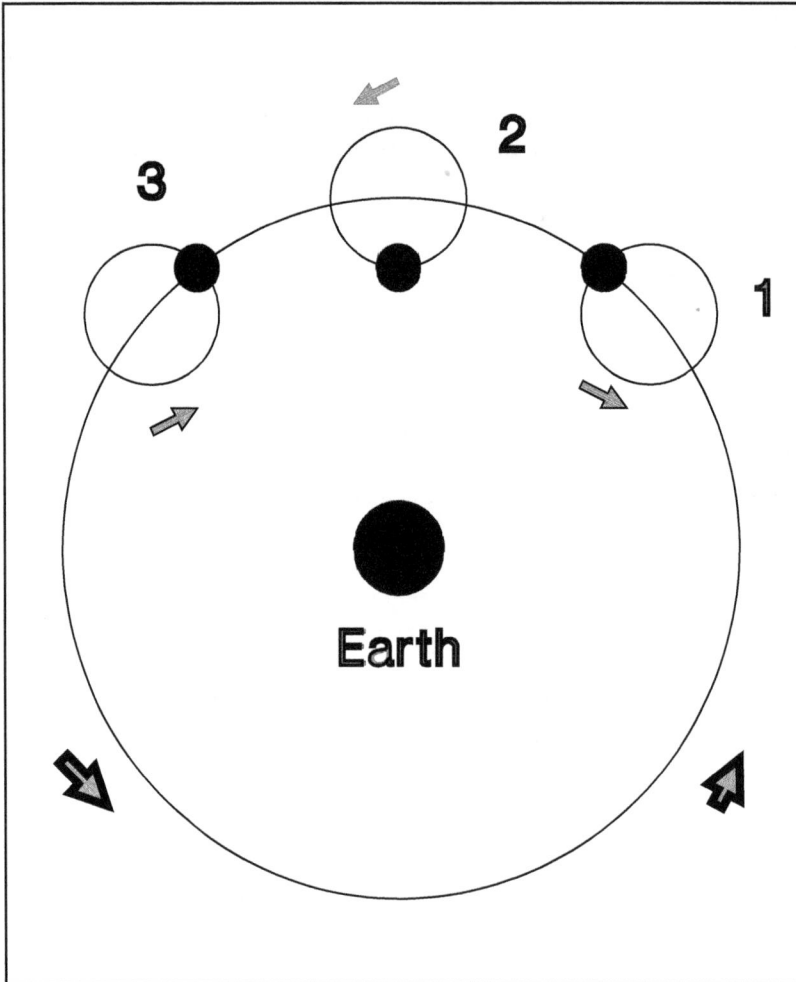

Graphic by Walter R. Dolen

Ptolemy's system had the earth as the center with the stars, moon, planets, and even the sun circling the earth each day. Ptolemy used the wrong and illusionary concept of epicycles to explain the apparent movement of the planets in the night. He further used mathematics to predict the future movement of planets. His system worked to a remarkable degree. It had a mathematical system to back it up. His book was well written and seemed quite logical. After all even today the planet, sun, moon, and stars do *apparently* circle the earth. Ptolemy system made sense out of wandering stars (planets). It predicted future positions of planets. It was the great system. It lasted for almost 1500 years. Apparently it was the perfect system. It was backed by mathematics. It was apparently backed by observation. But it was wrong. How wrong can you be to think that the massive sun circles the earth *each* day? But because of the prevailing mindset Ptolemy remained king. A mindset can be very compelling. It rules all. Since 1984 English readers have been able to read Ptolemy's work, as translated by G.J. Toomer, *Ptolemy's Almagest*. In this translation you can see the apparent logic to the whole work. You can see the massive amount of tables, observations, and mathematics to back Ptolemy's theory.

How can a work so logical, based on so many observations, and backed up by mathematics be wrong? It was wrong because it was based on some faulty thinking (the enormous sun going around the smaller earth would have to move at an unbelievable rate), because Ptolemy was a charlatan that cheated on his mathematical figures and cheated on his observations (Newton, *The Crime of Claudius Ptolemy*), and because he had a mindset that told him that all heavenly objects were perfect and god-like, they moved in perfect circles, he thus placed epicycles into his system:

> "The heaven is spherical in shape, and moves as a sphere; the earth too is sensibly spherical in shape ... in position it lies in the middle of the heavens very much like its center.... [Toomer, p.38] The following considerations also lead us to the concept of the sphericity of the heavens....[p. 39] We think that the mathematician's task and goal ought to be to show all the heavenly phenomena being reproduced by uniform circular motions.." (p. 140).

Ptolemy got his mindset about the orbits having to be perfect circular orbits from the Greeks such as Aristotle:

"There must be some substance which is eternal and immutable....
But motion cannot be either generated or destroyed, for it always
existed.... But there is no continuous motion except that which is
spatial, and of spatial motion only that which is circular... There are
other spatial motions – those of the planets – which are eternal
(because a body which moves in a circle is eternal...).... for the
nature of the heavenly bodies is eternal (Aristotle, *Metaphysics* Book XII
[Loeb Classical Lib. No. 287], pp. 141 & 155).

Ptolemy was so overly influenced by the Grecian philosophy that he
fabricated a mathematical system to help prove his preposterous belief:
"We think that the mathematician's task and goal ought to be to show all
the heavenly phenomena being reproduced by uniform circular motions."
(Toomer, p. 140)

Today math is used extensively to "prove" likewise absurd theories.
They do not appear preposterous to most today only because of today's
mindsets which filter reality. Mathematics are wrongly used today in the
scientific age. Today mathematics are blinding otherwise intelligent
people into believing in paradoxical and nonsensical theories on the
cosmos, physics, and biology. Today much of what is called science exists
inside of a mindset.

Mindset, A Brain Cell Problem

The main problem with a mindset occurs when you try to
communicate with someone with a different mindset. Sometimes it is
almost impossible. A Catholic trying to convert a Protestant has a terrible
time trying to communicate his point of view, and vice versa. Many times
even trying to communicate your different point of view will be met with
a harsh reaction and sometimes even a violent reaction. Why?

One book tried to explain this. Daniel Cohen, in a 1982 book, called
Re:Thinking, put it this way:

"Once a pattern — an idea or belief — becomes fixed in our neurological
pathways, it is extremely hard to alter it. The more basic the belief, the more we
refer to it in our thoughts, the more well worn is that particular neural pathway
— and thus the harder it is to change the idea, even when it is wrong" (p. 70).

"Our memories and beliefs are stored in our brains in the form of nerve cell
patterns. When you argue with someone you are pitting your nerve cell patterns
against his. The beliefs and opinions you hold are not the result of some abstract
intellectual process. They are the result of your total life experience. But your
opponent's beliefs and opinions are the same. For both of you, changing these
deeply held beliefs is hard and painful." (p. 118).

With our mindset we see only what our mindset allows us to see. It
acts like a filter and filters out any pattern not belonging to the sets of
rules we have etched in our brain cells.

"Love is patient, love is kind. It does not envy, it does not boast, it is not proud. It is not rude, it is not self-seeking, it is not easily angered, it keeps no record of wrongs. Love does not delight in evil but rejoices with the truth" [1Cor 13:4-7].

NM 1: What is a Christian?

Christian Doctrine
Physical v. Spiritual Meaning
What is a Christian?
How does one know he is a Christian?
What can one expect as a Christian?
Other names for Christians?

NM1 Abstract

In this book we put forth the doctrines of the Bible as we found them, taking into consideration the type and antitype found throughout scripture. What we are doing is attempting to simplify various doctrines of Christianity. In this paper we give short renditions as to what is a Christian, how one becomes one, what one can expect as a Christian, and so forth, thus setting the stage for the rest of this work.

Christian Doctrine

nm1 » In the New Testament of the Bible you can read about many important subjects. Significant subjects such as heaven, hell, sin, law, freedom, miracles, death, resurrection, immortality, predestination, the kingdom of God, and so forth are spoken about throughout the New Testament of the Bible. These subjects and others have to do with our very life, our souls, and our future. These subjects are very important and we cannot permit tradition to dictate to us concerning these subjects. We must test and analyze our views to see if they are correct. If they are not we must correct them. We must take charge of our storehouse of beliefs; we must correct our false beliefs; we must become sound in our knowledge.

Many Opinions

nm2 » But there are many opinions on all of these subjects, and it is difficult to find the truth. There are so many who claim to hold the truth. There are so many traditions, so many teachers, so many differing beliefs. There is confusion on how one is baptized, on the soul, and on the other doctrines of Christianity. There are the liberal Christians, the conservative Christians, and many other classifications.

Doctrines as Found in the Bible

nm3 » In this book we will put forth the real doctrines of the Bible as we found them. It is up to you the reader to prove or disprove what is presented in these papers. Only you can make the decision for yourself. That is, only you *should* make the decision for yourself. Do not let tradition or the authorities of your church or your science prevent *you* from making your own decision.

Physical Meaning versus Spiritual Meaning

nm4 » The mistakes in Christian doctrine were made because of the lack of knowledge of the pattern manifested in the Bible and the inability to see these patterns. In the "Duality Paper" we have spoken briefly about this Biblical pattern. Those making mistakes are only looking at the physical meaning or typical meaning of scripture instead of the higher meaning or Spiritual meaning. We are to worship God in Spirit (John 4:24). We are to look away from the physical to the Spiritual for the true meaning of God's word (see the "Duality Paper"). If we take or understand Jesus Christ's words only in a typical or physical manner we will not understand what he was trying to tell us. Not only this, but we will dramatically misunderstand him. When Jesus spoke about eating his body (John 6:53-56) he was speaking in a Spiritual way (see John 6:63). But if we only take Jesus' words in their literal, or simple, or physical meaning, we will drastically misunderstand him like many of his disciples did at that time (John 6:60-61). When some of Christ's disciples heard him, they mistakenly thought he was advocating cannibalism, a hideous crime against mankind, instead of encouraging the *spiritual* eating of his body. To eat or drink Jesus Christ in a Spiritual way is to *Spiritually* eat and drink his Spiritual body, or that is, "eat" his Spirit or "drink" his Spirit. Being baptized with God's Spirit, or eating Christ's Spirit, or drinking Christ's Spirit, and so forth are all signifying one thing – having God's Spirit or the New Mind. To have God's Spirit is to have the power to do good works. But if we only take the physical or typical meaning of scripture we will not understand the Spiritual words. We must look to the higher or Spiritual meaning of scripture or we will not understand.

What is a Christian?

nm5 » There is a direct relationship between Christianity and the New Mind. We call the Spirit of God the New Mind. You are a Christian when and only when you have the New Mind. Christianity is not Christianity without the New Mind. If you have the New Mind you are a Christian. But what is a Christian? Is a Christian someone who only goes to a Christian church? Can a Christian go to church? Are all Christian churches in reality, Christian? Are all who call themselves Christians in reality Christians?

nm6 » A Christian is a believer in Jesus Christ. Yet not only is he a believer, he is also a doer of what Christ did (James 1:22). Christians follow in Christ's way (1Peter 2:21). When Christians follow Christ, they are following God because God was manifested in Christ (1Tim. 3:16). God cannot sin (1John 3:9). Christ didn't sin (2Cor. 5:21). God's behavior was manifested in Christ. God and Christ the man behaved the same. Therefore God was manifested in Christ the man's behavior. God is love (1John 4:8). And Paul said: "love does not work any ill to its neighbor, so love is the fulfilling of the law" (Romans 13:10). To follow Christ is to follow God. Since God is love, then to follow God is to follow love. "Love is patient, love is kind. It does not envy, it does not boast, it is not proud. It is not rude, it is not self-seeking, it is not easily angered, it keeps no record of wrongs. Love does not delight in evil but rejoices in the truth. It always protects, always trusts, always hopes, always perseveres. Love never fails" (1Cor. 13:4-8, NIV).

New Man versus Old Man

nm7 » The main difference between a Christian and others is that Christians follow after love to the degree of power they were given to follow after love. All Christians in the old age never get close to the level of Jesus Christ's love because Christ was given the full power. Love is a system of behavior that is quite different than the system of behavior we observe around us today. Christians belong to the New Age with its New Mind. Today, Christians are New Age People who live in the old age. The old age is the present age with its confusion and hate. The New Age is the Kingdom of God with its system of love.

How Does One Become a Christian?

nm8 » To become a Christian you must have the Spirit or Mind of God, that is, the New Mind. To receive this New Mind, you must be Spiritually baptized into the Name of the Father, Son, and Holy Spirit (NM 4).

How Does One Know He Is a Christian?

nm9 » You know you are a Christian if you have the New Mind. There is another mind, the old mind, that works in the old age (see NM 21). We can see the power of the old mind working in the old age every day. The confusion of this world comes from the old mind. But when we receive the New Mind we begin to see the difference in our thinking. Instead of getting flash-thoughts concerning evil things, we begin to get flash-thoughts concerning the beautiful and good things. With the New Mind we get flash-thoughts that help us to begin to be patient, kind, truthful, hopeful, trustful, etc. You know you are a Christian when you have the New Mind. And you can *prove* you have the New Mind by your new behavior. If you have a new behavior that is more in keeping with the way of love, then you can be sure you have been given the New Mind (see "Proof Paper" [NM 10]).

What Can One Expect As a Christian?

nm10 » When you are a Christian you have the Spirit of God, the New Mind. You see matters from a different viewpoint. You have put on the New Mind which is being renewed in knowledge, and thus you are a new person in God (Col 3:10; Rom 12:2). You begin to understand that no one thing is bad in itself (Rom 14:14; 1Tim 4:4), but only wrong activity is bad (Prov 8:13). As a Christian you begin to do to others as you would like them to do to you (Rom 13:8-10). A new Christian begins to change and to do things differently, for he has a New Mind with a new attitude.

nm11 » But because Christians are changed, others around them will notice this transformation (1Peter 4:4). Because mankind as a whole feels threatened when others do not believe as they do, a Christian can expect to be disliked by people, even those of his own family (John 15:18-19; Mat 10:34-37). But a Christian is to be peaceful and try as much as possible to keep the peace. But at times because true Christians do not run after twisted things as much as others, the people belonging to this age will not like Christians.

nm12 » Besides receiving the New Mind (Spirit) a Christian will also receive the life in and throughout the first 1000 years of the coming kingdom of God. Read the paper entitled, "Reward for Christians" [NM 11] for more details.

What Are Other Names For Christians?

nm13 » In the Bible Christians are called:

- the Israel of God (Gal 6:16);
- the sheep (John 10);
- the holy temple (Eph 2:21);
- Jews, meaning Spiritual Jews (Rom 2:29);
- the Lamb's wife (Rev 21:9);
- Christ's wife (Rev 19:7);
- the 144,000 (Rev 14:3; 5:9-10);
- virgins (Rev 14:4);
- Zion (Heb 12:22);
- New Jerusalem (Rev 21:2);
- The body of Christ (Rom 12:4-5; 1Cor. 12:27);
- the church of the first born (Heb 12:23);
- the first fruits (Rev 14:4);
- saints (Eph 1:1);
- little children (1John 2:13; 5:21);
- living sacrifices (Rom 12:1);
- the holy nation (1Peter 2:9); etc.
- and many other names

Simplify Doctrine

nm14 » What we will be doing in the rest of this book is to simplify doctrines by examining in detail the scriptures on the doctrines. The main aspect of what we will be doing is showing you about Jesus Christ's Spirit, the New Mind, and the fruits or effects of the New Mind. The Bible speaks on many different subjects such as repentance, baptism, grace, and so forth. We will see what these subjects have to do with the Spirit of God and the effects of having this Spirit.

NM 2: On The Church of God

What is the Church?
Church Separate from the World?
Church is in Christ's Spiritual Body
How is the Church One?
How can Christians be of Christ's Flesh?
What is the Church Founded Upon?
Can the Church make any Law?
Behavior of those in the Church
Physical Organization for the Spiritual Church?
Is the Physical Church the Spiritual Church?
Doctrinal Errors?
False-Shepherds over the Church?

NM2 Abstract

In this paper we give Biblical definitions as to what the Church is, who or what it is founded upon, whether or not Churches can make just any church law or ruling, what should be the behavior of Church members, and consider the problem of doctrinal errors or false-shepherds over the Church.

What Is The Church?

nm15 » The word "church" comes from a Greek word that means, "called out." Those of the Church are called out from the world, or the way of the world: "Come out from among them, and be you separate" (2Cor 6:17). "Come out of her [Babylon] my people" (Rev 18:4).

nm16 » The word "virgin," which the Church is Spiritually called (Rev 14:4), is translated from the Greek word *parthenos*, which literally means, "one put aside." That is, the Church, the Spiritual wife of God (Rev 19:7), is put aside from the way of the world. Also the word "saint," which is used to describe those in the Church of the New Testament, is translated from the Greek word *hagios*, which means, "set apart." Those in the Church are set apart from the world. They are set-apart by God (see "Predestination Paper"[NM 8]). It is God who puts people in the Church (see Acts 2:47).

nm17 » Christ when he was praying to his Spiritual Father spoke about those of the Church: "Holy Father, keep them in your own NAME, which you have given me, that they may be one, as we are ... I have given them your word, and the world hates them, because they are not of the world, even as I am not of the world. I pray not that you should take them out of the world, but that you should keep them from evil. They are not of the world even as I am not of the world" (John 17:11, 14-16). Therefore those of the Church are Spiritually called out of the world, and are separate from it even though they are physically still in it. How are they apart from the world?

Church Separate From The World?

nm18 » They are apart from the world because they have the set-apart Spirit, or as some translations have it, the Holy Spirit. This set-apart Spirit, or Holy Spirit is the Spirit of God, or of Christ because Christ is God (John 20:28). The Spirit of God is the New Mind (cf Rom 12:2; Eph 4:23; Rom 6:4; 7:6). And those of the Church have the Spirit of God in them (Rom 8:9-11, 14-16).

nm19 » The one main thing that makes you a member of the body or Church of Christ is that you must have the Spirit of God (1Cor 12:12-13). "There is one body, and one Spirit ... One God and Father of all, who is above all, and through all, and in all" (Eph 4:4, 6). "For through him [Christ] we both have access by one Spirit unto the Father" (Eph 2:18). This one kind of Spirit is the Spirit in the body of Christ, which is the Church (1Cor 12:4, 13).

Church is in Christ's Spiritual Body

nm20 » Those in the Church are in the collective body of Christ, and are the collective body of Christians. "For as the body is one, and has many members, and all the members of that one body, being many, are one body; so also is Christ. For in one Spirit are we all baptized into one body, whether we be Jews or Gentiles, whether we be bond or free; and have been all made to drink into one Spirit ... Now you are the body of Christ, and members in particular" (1Cor 12:12-13, 27).

nm21 » Therefore, you are in the Church, or in the body of Christ, when you are in the Spirit of God (you have the New Mind), or when you have the Spirit of God in you (Rom 8:14-16).

nm22 » Those in the Church are the members of Christ's body, and Christ is "the *head* over all things to the church, which is his body" (Eph 1:22, 23).

- Christ is the head of the body, and we are the members of his body (1Cor 12:27).

- "Christ is the head of the church: and he is the savior of the body," as "the husband is the head of the wife" (Eph 5:23).

- We are the wife of Christ, and the bride of the lamb (Rev 19:7). Christ is the lamb of God (John 1:29).

- Those in the Church are the sheep, and Christ is the shepherd (John chap 10).

- Those in the Church are the branches, Christ is the root of the vine (John 15).

- Those in the Church are the stones of the building, Christ is the chief cornerstone (1Pet 2:5; Eph 2:19-22).

- Those in the Church are of the kingdom of priests, and Christ is the High Priest (Rev 1:6; 1Pet 2:5-9; Heb 3:1; 5:1-10).

How Is The Church One?

nm23 » There is only one body of Christ, one Lord, one Faith, one Baptism (Eph 4:4-5). There is only one Church, with one baptism, one faith, one Lord. The Church is not many different groups. The Church is ONE group, ONE body with ONE Spirit. Those with the Spirit of God, that New Mind, are the people of the ONE true Church with the one baptism, one faith, and one Lord.

nm24 » The Church is made up of people who have the Spirit of God inside them leading them into the way of harmony. It is the Spirit that sets people apart from the world. It is the Spirit that makes people one. "For in one Spirit are we all baptized into one body" (1Cor 12:13). With this same Spirit we receive the gifts of the Spirit (1Cor 12:4). These gifts of the Spirit are "love, joy, peace, long-suffering, gentleness, goodness, faith" (Gal 5:22). When we have this one Spirit, we have the same gifts or fruits from this Spirit, "according to the measure of the gift of Christ" (Eph 4:7). These gifts are given "for the edifying of the body of Christ: till we all come into the unity of the faith" (Eph 4:11-13).

How Can Christians Be of Christ's Flesh?

nm25 » When we have the Spirit we are in the Church, and "we are members of his body, of his flesh, and of his bones" (Eph 5:30).

nm26 » When we are Spiritually baptized into the body of Christ, we are baptized into it by the one Spirit of God (1Cor 12:13). Those who have been baptized into the body of Christ, "have been baptized into Christ have put on Christ" (Gal 3:27). When one is Spiritually baptized into Christ, "there is neither Jew nor Greek, there is neither bond nor free, there is neither male nor female: for you are one in Christ Jesus" (Gal 3:28). These are one in Christ because they "have been all made to drink into one Spirit" (1Cor 12:13). They are one in the sense that they have the one Spirit. Males are still males in the physical sense. Females are still females in the physical sense. But they are one in the Spiritual sense because they have the one true Spirit of God. "And if you are Christ's, then you are Abraham's seed, and heirs according to the promise" (Gal 3:29). Christ was a descendant of Abraham (Luke 3:34, 23), he was of the seed of Abraham. Therefore when we are in Christ's body (his Church) we too are the descendant of Abraham, we are of the promised seed of Abraham because we have "that holy Spirit of promise, which is the evidence of our inheritance" (Eph 1:13, 14). Because we are of the seed of Abraham, we are also of the Flesh of Christ (Eph 5:30), we are of Israel, we are of the Spiritual "Israel of God" (Gal 6:16).

Who Or What Is The Church Founded Upon?

nm27 » Christ said, "and I say also unto thee, that you are Peter, and upon this the rock I will build my church" (Mat 16:18). Now the Roman Catholic Church has used this verse incorrectly to say that Christ built his Church on the foundation of Peter. The word "Peter" comes here from a Greek word that means, "stone" or "rock." But the sentence reads, "you are Peter and upon this *the* rock I will build my Church." Who is *the* rock Christ was speaking about here? Was it Peter, or was it THE ROCK? Which rock is the Church founded upon?

> "For through him we both have access by one Spirit unto the Father. Now therefore you are no more strangers and foreigners, but fellow citizens with the saints, and of the household of God; And are built upon the foundation of the apostles and prophets, Jesus Christ himself being the chief corner *stone*" (Eph 2:18-20).

nm28 » It is Christ who is the chief foundational stone, or rock. Christ is "the stone which the builders disallowed, the same is made the head of the corner, and a stone of stumbling, and a rock of offense" (1Pet 2:7-8). Christ is God (John 20:28, see *God Papers*). And God is the ROCK (Deut 32:4; Psa 18:2, 31). It is God, or Christ who is the head Rock of the Church, He is the foundation, the chief foundation, not Peter. Peter is just one of the "living stones" of the Church (1Pet 2:5; Eph 2:20), he is not the main foundation. Therefore the "rock" spoken about in Matthew 16:18 is God, not Peter.

Can Churches Make Any Law They Wish?

nm29 » Note Matthew 16:19. Many churches tell their flock that this verse gives them the right to make laws on their own, and that such laws are binding. This is wrong! Notice, "and I will give unto you the keys of the kingdom of heaven: and whatsoever you shall bind on earth shall be bound in heaven" (Mat 16:19). And from the *Twentieth Century New Testament* translation: "whatever you forbid on earth will be held in Heaven to be forbidden." Now IF this translation is correct, it is saying the earthly can tell the heavenly what is right or what is wrong. But this is contrary to all the Bible. It is the heavenly that shows the earthly what is right, not vice versa. In the prayer which Jesus asked us to pray in like manner, Jesus said to ask our Father: "your wish be done in the earth, as it is in heaven" (Mat 6:10). The Church is only to bind on earth things that have already been bound in the heavenly sense. *The Church can only bind things on earth that reflect the heavenly or spiritual sense or spiritual dimension*.

What Was The Bible In Christ's Day?

nm30 » The only Bible they had during the time of Christ and shortly thereafter was the Old Testament scripture. Paul's letters to the Church of God were merely letters explaining the Old Testament promises in light of the things of Jesus Christ. When the Bereans searched the scriptures, they searched the Old Testament (Acts 17:10-11). But today the Christian Bible is the Old and New Testaments of the Bible. The Christian Bible includes the inspired material of the apostles.

How Many Are To Become Members of The Church?

Few Saved Now; All Later

nm31 » Everyone will become members of the Church before the plan of God is completed, but up to the Messiah's return only the few will be saved (see "All Saved Paper" [NM 13]). "Wide is the gate, and broad is the way, that leads to destruction, and many there be which go in thereat: because narrow is the gate, and narrow is the way, which leads unto life, and *few* there be that find it" (Mat 7:13-14). Many will go into aeonian destruction, for it is the many who are misled. "And Jesus answered and said unto them, Take heed that no man mislead you. For many shall come in my name, saying, I am Christ, and shall mislead many." It is the confusion of Satan that has misled the whole world (Rev 12:9). Most will be misled. In fact all have been, for those who learn of the Way were themselves at one time deceived. It is only the *few* who will be given the Spirit which leads them into all the truth (Mat 7:14 & John 16:13). But as we will see in these papers all will receive the Spirit in the Great Last Spiritual Day of Creation, thus all will be saved eventually.

What Is The Behavior of Those In The Church?

nm32 » Since those in the Church are Christians in the truest sense, then they behave as Christians should behave, not like most so-called Christians behave in this age. This book, *New Mind Papers*, manifests that true Christians follow the law or system of love. They follow it according to the degree of Spiritual power given them. All Christians produce much Spiritual fruit (see paper, "Prove Paper" [NM 10] and the "Freedom and Law" [NM 17]).

Physical Organization for the Spiritual Church?

nm33 » As the Church was shown organized physically in the book of Acts, so too the Church may be at times physically organized since the days of the book of Acts. Christ said that the Church would be scattered: "I will smite the shepherd, and the sheep shall be scattered" (Mark 14:27). Christ said since they persecuted him, they would persecute the Church (John 15:20). And in Acts 8:1 it reads, "and at that time there was a great persecution against the Church which was at Jerusalem; and they were all scattered abroad throughout the regions of Judah and Samaria, except the apostles." So the Church was scattered from Jerusalem and throughout the known world as Paul's letters indicated.

nm34 » But even though Paul's epistles showed they were scattered, some came nevertheless together in certain cities throughout the world. The Church of Acts had a center at Jerusalem, and was physically organized and did send out teachers from Jerusalem throughout the world. But Jerusalem was destroyed by the invading Roman troops, and tradition has it that the apostles were killed about 40 years after Christ died. Thus, according to the records available today, at that time at least a center of the physically organized Church ceased, yet the Spiritual Church didn't cease since the Church is Spiritually organized through the medium of the Spirit. As long as there is one person on earth with God's Spirit, the New Mind, there is the Church of God.

nm35 » After the center in Jerusalem of the Church was destroyed about 40 years after Christ was killed, more than likely the Church was physically organized in some way many times again over the years. But there does not need to be a physically organized Church on earth in order for there to be a Church of God on earth. The Church of God is made up of those who have the New Mind or the Spirit of God, irrespective of whether there is or isn't a physically organized Church. We can never say with any certainty that any physically organized church, after the Apostles died, was indeed the Church. Even in the physical churches organized by the Apostles, real Christians were put-out (3John 1:9-10). To repeat: the Church is Spiritual and various physical churches cannot in this age be identified with any certainty as being the Church.

Is a Physical Church *the* Spiritual Church?

nm36 » To be in the Church is to have the Spirit. Yet Jude wrote of "certain men who crept in unawares, who were before of old ordained to this the judgement, ungodly men, turning the grace of our God into loose conduct, and denying the only Lord God, and our Lord Jesus Christ" (Jude 4). "These are they who separate themselves, sensual, having not the Spirit" (Jude 19). This shows there were some physically in the Church who didn't have the Spirit of God (see Gal 2:4).

nm37 » Also 1John 2:18-19 shows that some left the Church because they weren't of the Church. But in some cases the true Christians were forced out of the physical churches in certain areas of the world (see 3John 1:9-10). This was prophesied by Christ (see Luke 6:22). There will even be false teachers among the physical church (2Pet 2:1). Therefore not all in a physically organized Christian Church are of the Spirit of God.

Find the True Physically Organized Church?

nm38 » The best indication that you have found it is by the behavior of the people in the church. Are the people following Spiritually the law of love? Or is the Church merely serving a social function? Whatever, we must be careful of how we judge. We must remember that there may be more non-Christians in a physical church than true Christians with the New Mind. Therefore be careful how we judge.

What About Doctrinal Errors of Churches?

nm39 » When errors of doctrine are brought forward, the Church will admit the error, as Peter admitted one of his (Gal 2:11-14), and as all those with the New Mind should admit their errors when reproved (Job 33:27; Prov 28:13; 1John 1:8-9).

nm40 » Some reasons for error in doctrine may be mistranslations of the Bible, or non-Spiritual leaders, or lack of the Bible or parts of the Bible. There will be errors until Elijah comes (Mat 17:10-11).

nm41 » In Ezekiel 34 it shows that the shepherds of Israel are false shepherds. This is dual: (1) it speaks of false shepherds over physical Israel; and (2) it speaks of false shepherds over Spiritual Israel. But God says, "I will deliver my flock from their mouth" (Ezek 34:10). Therefore it is possible for false shepherds to actually mislead some or many in the true Church, and this could be a reason for doctrinal error. In the truest sense it indicates the other-mind that remains in the minds of Christians in the old age. This evil mind continues to attempt to mislead Christians and sometimes succeeds.

False Shepherds Over The True Church?

nm42 » We will now discuss the scripture about false shepherds 'over' the True Church. Peter wrote about false teachers among Christians (2Pet 2:1). But in order to understand this further we must know that the scripture is dual, with a typical and antitypical fulfillment. Now, or near the end of the age all prophecy will be fulfilled that has seemed to fail previously:

- "Son of man, what is that proverb that you have in the land of Israel, saying, The days are prolonged, and every vision fails? Tell them therefore, Thus says the Lord GOD; I will make this proverb to cease, and they shall no more use it as a proverb in Israel; but say unto them, The days are at hand, and the effect of every vision" (Ezek 12:22-23).

Now the time is close at hand (see, the "End of the Age"[PR7]). Therefore all prophecy will be fulfilled soon.

nm43 » In the scriptures it indicates that over physical Israel false shepherds would rule at various times. And throughout the history of Israel there were evil leaders over Israel and its congregation. Since the New Testament Church is the antitypical Israel ("Israel of God," Gal 6:16), then Spiritual Israel will have false shepherds misleading it at different times.

nm44 » In Ezekiel 34, it pictures "the shepherds of Israel that do feed themselves" (v. 2). God continues to the false shepherds,

"You eat the fat, and you clothe you with the wool, you kill them that are fed: but you feed not the flock. The diseased have you not strengthened, neither have you healed that which was sick, neither have you bound up that which was broken, neither have you brought again that which was driven away, neither have you sought that which was lost; but with force and with cruelty have you ruled them" (Ezek 34:3-4).

nm45 » Among these false shepherds is the idolatrous or worthless shepherd. Zechariah 11:16-17 tells of this worthless shepherd:

> "For, lo, I will raise up a shepherd in the land, which shall not visit those that be cut off; neither shall seek the young one, nor heal that which is broken, nor feed that which stands still: but he shall eat the flesh of the fat, and tear their claws in pieces. Woe to the idolatrous shepherd that leaves the flock! the sword shall be upon his arm, and upon his right eye: his arm shall be clean dried up, and his right eye shall be utterly darkened."

Spiritually speaking, this means the worthless shepherd will not have the right (good) side or good eye; he will not have the Spirit of God. In the truest sense this scripture and others like it point to Satan and his spirit of evil (the other-mind).

nm46 » Ezekiel 44 projects to us some more details on these false shepherds:

- And you shall say to the rebellious, even to the house of Israel, Thus says the Lord GOD; O you house of Israel, let it suffice you of all your abominations, In that you have brought into my sanctuary strangers, uncircumcised in heart [without God's Spirit], and uncircumcised in flesh [without the flesh of Christ, Eph 5:30], to be in my sanctuary [Church], to pollute it, even my house, when you offer my bread [Spiritual], the fat and the blood, and they have broken my covenant because of all your abominations. And you have not kept the charge of mine holy things: but you have set keepers of my charge in my sanctuary for themselves ... And the Levites that have gone away far from me, when Israel went astray, which went astray away from me after their idols; they shall even bear their iniquity. Yet they [the non-Spiritual Levites] shall be ministers in my sanctuary [Church], having charge at the gates of the house, and ministering to the house ... Because they ministered unto them before their idols ["idols in their heart," Ezek 14:3], and · caused the house of Israel [Church] to fall into iniquity, therefore have I lifted my hand against them, says the Lord GOD, and they shall bear their iniquity (Ezek 44:6-12).

nm47 » In verse 13 it says these uncircumcised shall not come near to minister, but verse 14 says they *do*, yet verse 15 speaks of the "sons of righteous" ("Zakok") that keep charge in God's Church. Thus, both the Spiritual and non-Spiritual ministers have "ruled" over the Church. Yet Ezekiel 34 and Zechariah speak of the idolatrous shepherd misruling the sheep with other false shepherds. But God said in Ezekiel 34:10 that he will deliver his flock from the false shepherds' mouth. And Ezekiel 13:23 says the same thing: "for I will deliver my people out of your hand: and you shall know that I am the LORD." It is/was Jesus Christ that delivers his people, the Spiritual Israel, out of the hands of the false shepherds, by overcoming Satan and giving the New Mind to the New Israel. It is with the New Mind that the New or Spiritual Israel is defeating and will defeat the other-mind and its evil power.

nm48 » In Ezekiel 13 and 14 it describes antitypically some things about these false ministers. They "prophesy out of their *own* hearts," but they call it the word of God: "hear you the word of the LORD" (Ezek 13:2). They see visions of peace for the Church, Spiritual Jerusalem (Ezek 13:16). But Christ prophesied of trouble within the Church (Luke 21:12, 16; Mark 13:9, 12; Mat 24:9-10). And Revelation 2:10 says the Church will have tribulation.

nm49 » In Ezekiel 9:6 it says God will begin to destroy the abomination of Israel at his sanctuary (see verses 4-11). He will begin with the elders of the Church (last part of Ezek 9:6). Three shepherds will be cut off in a month or new moon (Zech 11:8). Again this speaks of the destruction of the spiritual abomination that was in old Israel – the old mind or other-mind – through the power of the New Mind. The old evil spiritual shepherds who ruled over Israel were and are being destroyed by the New Mind that was given to Jesus Christ and Jesus Christ is now giving the New Mind or Spirit to the New Israel (see the "Seed Paper" [PR1] and the *God Papers*).

NM 3: Repentance

NM3 Abstract

In this paper we examine what real repentance is, how many will repent, and who it is that gives repentance. Do we repent on our own or does God give us the power to repent?

nm50 » The New Testament of the Bible speaks of repentance. People are warned to repent for the kingdom of heaven is near (Mat 3:2). People are asked to repent and be baptized or converted (Acts 2:38; 3:19). The repentance the Bible is talking about here is a changed mind. To repent is to change your mind. The Greek word which was translated into our English "repent" is *metanoeo*, which means "to have another mind," or "to change your mind," or to think anew. When the Bible says to repent it speaks to those with the old mind, that evil mind of the old age. To repent is to change your mind. The way those with the old mind change their mind is to receive the New Mind. *To repent then is to change minds.* To repent is to change from the old mind with the evil spirit to the New Mind with the good Spirit.

All To Repent

nm51 » God wants all to come to repentance (2Peter 3:9). In other words, God wants all to have a changed mind. In the paper entitled, "All Saved" [NM 13], we show how all the creation will be freed from the old mind and old cosmos and given life in the new cosmos. The life in the new cosmos will be with the New Mind, the changed mind from the old evil mind.

Repentance Is a Gift From God

nm52 » It is God who *gives* us a changed mind (Acts 5:31; 11:18; 2Tim 2:25). Paul confirms this, "Or do you despise the riches of his goodness and forbearance and long-suffering, not knowing that the goodness of God leads you to repentance" (Romans 2:4). Paul's own changed mind came through God's power, not Paul's power (Acts 9:1-18).

Result of Repentance

nm53 » The result of a changed mind is a new attitude towards God. Paul taught that people "should repent and turn to God, doing works worthy of repentance" (Acts 26:20). Paul did earnestly testify "both to Jews and Greeks repentance toward God and Faith toward our Lord Jesus Christ" (Acts 20:21). Jesus taught, "repent and believe in the gospel" (Mark 1:15). Those with a changed mind believe in the good news of Christ (the gospel), they have turned to God, they do works worthy of their changed mind, they have faith toward Christ, etc.

nm54 » Repentance is also for the sending away ("remission") of sins (Luke 24:47). When you repent you are converted toward the blotting out of sins (Acts 3:19). And it is this repentance that leads to salvation (2Cor. 7:10).

How Does God Give Repentance?

nm55 » As Romans 8:7-9 shows us, it is through God's Spirit that mankind's attitude changes from the way of death towards the way of life. This Spirit of God is a gift from God (1Thes. 4:8; 2Cor. 1:22; 5:5; Romans 5:5; Acts 2:38). With this gift of the Spirit we receive the fruits or effects of this Spirit. "But the fruit of the Spirit is love, joy, peace..." (Gal. 5:22). It is through God's free gift of the Spirit of God that mankind's mind changes from the old mind to the New Mind. In this age the gift of this New Mind is given to those who were predestinated before the world began to receive the New Mind in the old age (see "Predestination Paper" [NM 8]).

NM 4: Baptism: Physical & Spiritual

Christian Baptism
Water Baptism v. Spiritual Baptism
Spiritual Baptism
Baptized in the Name
In the Name of Christ?

NM4 Abstract

In this paper we learn that there are two kinds of baptisms. One is the physical and is only symbolic. The other is Spiritual baptism in which we are put into the Name of the true God. John the Baptist who only baptized with water predicted the Spiritual baptism.

Christian Baptism

nm56 » The baptism of Christians is the baptism of the Spirit of God. Baptism means to *dip*, *immerge*, or *submerge*. To be baptized with the Spirit is to be submerged into the Spirit. To be baptized with the Spirit is another way of saying you are sealed with the Spirit or that you have received the Spirit, or that you have put on the New Mind, or that you have received the Promise, or that you have the New Life, etc. When you are baptized with the Spirit, you have the New Mind of Love that thinks the positive thoughts of the Spirit of the True God. When you are baptized with the Spirit you are in the body or assembly of Jesus Christ, you are a part of the BeComingOne, which is the True Oneness. When we are baptized with the Spirit our old life is put to death and we are raised up into the New Life (see Rom 6:4). Baptism with the Spirit is different from baptism with water. Baptism with the Spirit is a gift from the True God given to those in this age who were predestinated before the world began to receive the Spirit or New Mind in this age (see "Predestination Paper" [NM 8]). All will eventually be Spiritually baptized (see "All Saved Paper" [NM 13]).

Baptism With Water versus Baptism With Spirit

nm57 » It was John the Baptist who baptized with water. In John's own words: "I indeed baptize you in water to repentance. But He [Jesus] who is coming after me is mightier than I ... He shall baptize you in the Holy Spirit and in fire" (Mat 3:11). Again John's words: "I baptize with water" (John 1:26). John baptized with water, but it was He who was coming after John who would baptize with the Spirit (John 1:26-33). And in Jesus Christ's own words after He was resurrected from the dead: "And gathering them together, He commanded them not to leave Jerusalem, but said, Wait for the promise of the Father which you heard from Me. For John indeed baptized with water, but you shall be baptized in the Holy Spirit not many days after this" (Acts 1:4-5). And while Jesus Christ's followers were waiting in Jerusalem the Promise did come in the form of the Spirit (Acts 2:1-47). Now the Promise is the Holy Spirit: "the Promise of the Holy Spirit from the Father" (Acts 2:33). This Promise was not only to Christ but to "as many as the Lord our God shall call" (Acts 2:39). It is the baptism with the Spirit that counts, not baptism with water. "Water" is merely a symbolic representation of Spirit. When Christ spoke of water he meant the Spirit (see John 7:38-39). Remember here and remember always: look at the higher or Spiritual meaning.

nm58 » John the Baptist's baptism with water prefigured Christ's baptism with the Spirit. As water cleans the body, so does the Spirit clean the body. Water cleans in a physical way, but the Spirit cleans in a Spiritual way. When we are cleansed with the Spirit our minds are cleansed from the dirt of the other-mind, that old twisted mind of the old age. The baptism of John was the baptism with water. This water baptism does not bring with it the Holy Spirit, or the New-Mind (note Acts 18:24-19:6). The Spirit of God comes with the baptism of the Spirit. When one is submerged into the Spirit, he takes on the Spiritual reality. When one is baptized in physical water, he is only cleansed physically. We are to look to the higher and Spiritual meaning in the Bible in order to learn the Truth. Water can only clean physically, but the Spirit cleans Spiritually.

nm59 » Now we see in certain verses in the New Testament of the Bible where some of the early disciples used water to baptize (Acts 8:36-38). Even after some received the Holy Spirit Peter had some baptized with physical water (Acts 10:44-48). The reason for this was because at that time they did not understand fully the power of God and that it is the Spiritual reality that counts not the physical types of the Spiritual reality. The early leaders gradually learned that physical rituals such as water baptism and circumcision were not the important things (see "Freedom and Law Paper"[NM 17]). The old laws of the Old Testament were done away with. They were merely types of the True Reality (Heb 10:1; see the "Freedom and Law Paper" [NM 17]).

Spiritual Baptism

nm60 » Christians are baptized with the Spirit (Acts 1:5; 1Cor 12:13). "For by one Spirit also we were baptized into one body" (1Cor 12:13). Christians are in the body of Christ. On the Pentecost the first Christians were filled with the Holy Spirit "suddenly" (Acts 2:4,2). And again later, "Even while Peter was speaking these words, the Holy Spirit fell on all those hearing the word" (Acts 10:44). "And as I began to speak, the Holy Spirit fell upon them also, even as on us in the beginning. And I remembered the word of the Lord saying, John indeed baptized with water, but you shall be baptized with the Holy Spirit" (Acts 11:15-16). God saves people through "the washing of regeneration and renewing of the Holy Spirit, which He poured out on us richly through Jesus Christ our Savior" (Titus 3:5-6). It is the Spiritual washing of the Spirit of God that Spiritually cleans people, not the physical water. *In the True Church of God there is no need or requirement for water baptism.* Water baptism is merely a physical ritual that represents a Spiritual truth. As water baptism cleans the physical body, so does Spiritual baptism clean the Spiritual body in a Spiritual way. Physical ritual does not free anyone from the mad cosmos we live in. It is the Spiritual gift from God, the Spirit of God, that gives us the freedom. There is no certain set of words (magic) that gives us True Life (such as, "I baptize you in the name of the ... "). There are no physical rituals that give us Life. True baptism is Spiritual baptism not water baptism.

Baptized *into* Christ's Name & Spiritual Body

nm61 » When Christians are Spiritually baptized they are baptized *into* Christ's body (1Cor 12:13). They are baptized into Christ (Rom 6:3; Gal 3:27). They are baptized into his Name (Mat 28:19-20; Acts 2:38; 8:16; 10:48; 19:5).

Baptized Into The Name of Christ?

nm62 » What does it mean to be Spiritually baptized into the NAME of Christ? In the Bible many times a name signifies something about that person. Thus, "Jesus" signifies that Christ is the Savior, for "Jesus" means, *savior*. When one is baptized *into* the NAME of Christ he takes on the NAME of Christ. Since a name describes characteristics of someone, then if one is put into a name, he is actually being put into the characteristics of that person. Allegorically, when a woman marries, she is married into a name. She becomes a part of the family. If the family is rich she shares in the riches. A person baptized into Christ's NAME takes on the NAME and characteristics of Christ. The person is married into Christ's NAME in a sense. In fact women are allegorical to the Church (Eph 5:21-32). Christ is going to marry this woman (Church) allegorically at his physical return (Rev 19:7). Those baptized into the NAME of Christ take on his NAME and some of his characteristics. They become Christians; they receive his Spirit. You are a Christian only when you have the Spirit of God (Rom 8:9, 14).

Baptized into the Name of the Father, Son, and Holy Spirit

nm63 » "Baptize them into the Name of the Father, and of the Son, and of the Holy Spirit" (Mat 28:19). When you are baptized are you baptized into three names or one Name? When you are in Christ, you are in his Father because Christ is in his Father (John 14:11). Since Christ's Father is God, when you are in the Father you are in God – you are a child of God. When you are in Christ's NAME you are in the NAME of God because Christ came in the NAME of God (John 5:43; 10:25; 12:13; Luke 13:35; 19:38; Mat 21:9; John 17:11). When you are Spiritually baptized into Christ, you are baptized into the Name of God the Father, for Christ is in God the Father (John 14:11). You thus become a part of the Coming Oneness (see, *God Papers*).

nm64 » The Spirit of God and the Spirit of Christ are the same thing, "for in one Spirit are we all baptized into one body ... and have been made to drink into one Spirit" (1Cor 12:13). This one Spirit is the Spirit of God. But when you are baptized you receive the Holy Spirit (Acts 2:38; 10:47; 11:16; Mark 1:8; Acts 1:5). The Holy Sprit is the Spirit of God, the Spirit of Christ. Everyone who is a Christian has the Holy Spirit of God. When one is baptized into the NAME of Christ, he receives the Spirit of God, that is, the Spirit of Christ, that is, the Holy Spirit, for Christ is God (John 20:28; Jude 25) and has God's Name (John 5:43; 10:25; 12:13; Luke 13:35; 19:38; Mat 21:9; John 17:11; see *God Papers*). "The Father, the Word, and the Holy Spirit are one" (1John 5:7) because they are the same One Spirit, the Holy Spirit of God the Father. You are not baptized into three names, but into the very NAME of God.

In the Name of Christ?

nm65 » Acts 2:38 is one place where it speaks of being baptized in the NAME of Christ. The word translated "in" is a Greek word that can mean, *in* or *among*. Thus it could as easily be translated, "and be baptized every one of you *among* the name of Jesus Christ." When one is baptized into the NAME of Christ he is also baptized *among* those belonging to Christ.

nm66 » Notice that those "in the name" or "among the name shall cast out demons" (Mark 16:17). Those who have the Spirit of power, God's Spirit, will be in the body of Christ, will be among the others who are in Christ. And it is those in Christ or among his body members that will cast out the demons, or the other-minds. (*Some* had that power; others will do it at the Messiah's return when all demons will be cast out of mankind's mind.) Paul speaking to Christians said, "you are the body of Christ, and members in particular" (1Cor 12:27). When people do things "in the name of Christ," they do these things while they are among or in Christ. That is, they do these things because they have the Spirit which puts them in the NAME of Christ.

nm67 » When you are in the NAME of Christ:

- you are saved (Acts 4:12);

- you have life (John 20:31);

- you are justified (1Cor 6:11);

- you preach boldly (Acts 9:27, 29);

- you may do signs and wonders (Acts 4:30);

- devils ['other minds'] are subjected to you (Luke 10:17); etc.

NM 5: Begotten, Born – the Difference

Difference between Born & Begotten
Pregnant Woman Metaphor
Born of Flesh, Born of Spirit
Fleshly Body, Spiritual Body
Greek Word, *gennao*, and its ambiguity

NM5 Abstract

In this paper we show you the difference between being born of God and being begotten of God. There are Biblical verses that use the metaphor of the pregnant woman (Church) giving birth at the coming of God to set up the kingdom on earth. Before Christ's coming Christians are like babies in the Church's womb waiting to be born. A Greek word that can mean either begotten or born has added to the misinformation on this subject.

Difference Between Born & Begotten

nm68 » Christ spoke about being born again (John 3:5-6). When one is baptized in the Spirit that person receives, or is sealed with the Spirit of God. At that time he becomes a child of God (Rom 8:14). One aspect of this has been overlooked by most. That is, there is a difference between being *born* of God and being *begotten* of God. We need to know the difference. The Bible speaks of both. In short we will find that when one is Spiritually baptized, he is begotten of God. But when one is resurrected to God, he is born of God. Let's explain this.

Pregnant Woman Metaphor

nm69 » The Church is pictured allegorically as a woman or wife of Christ (Eph 5:22-32). But further it is pictured as a "mother of us all" (Gal 4:26; cf "Jerusalem" in Rev 21:2, 9). Yet it is pictured as a pregnant mother (Rev 12:1-2, 4). And in Isaiah 66:6-8 it pictures this woman in labor pains ready to bring forth. The time setting here is when the Lord will recompense or repay his enemies which is the day of the Lord or on the day of God's wrath (Isa 66:6; see "God's Wrath Paper" [PR4]). This woman, or Church, brings forth a whole nation at once (Isa 66:8). This whole nation is a holy nation (1Pet 2:9) of *born* children of God as we will see.

nm70 » This pregnant woman is allegorical to the Church. Inside her womb are her children, a whole nation of children (Isa 66:8). But before one is born of a woman, he is begotten or conceived inside her womb. And in Revelation 12:1-2, 4 it pictures the Church allegorically as a pregnant woman ready to deliver (Rev 12:2). This pictures the Church ready to be born of God with the dragon (who is Satan, Rev 12:9) waiting "for to devour her child as soon as it was born." This is the "day of trouble" for the Church. See the papers on God's Wrath to understand this "day of trouble."

nm71 » In the Bible it speaks about people being born of God or begotten of God (1John 2:29; 3:9; 5:1; 5:4; 5:18). Some people teach being born of God as some heartfelt feeling. They do not take it literally; thus they do not understand God's plan. Being born of God is not just a feeling in the heart.

Born of Flesh, Born of Spirit

nm72 » Christ the man said during his ministry that, "except a man be born of water and of the Spirit, he cannot enter into the kingdom of God. That which is born of the flesh is flesh; and that which is born of the Spirit is Spirit" (John 3:5-6). In verse 8 of John 3 he makes an allegory between Spirit and the wind and says as one cannot see the wind so also he cannot see the spirit. As we just quoted Christ, "except a man be born of water and of the Spirit, he cannot enter into the kingdom of God." Thus since Spirit is invisible, when one is born of God he is invisible. Yet there are verses where the resurrected Christ as God was also flesh and blood (Luke 24:39). Yes, Christ was born of flesh, he was a son of mankind (Gal 4:4). Thus, "that which is born of flesh is flesh" (John 3:6). But Christ is a son of God also (Rom 1:4). Thus when Christ was resurrected he was born of God and became Spirit. Therefore as spirit he could become invisible as he did after he was born of God (Luke 24:31).

Fleshly Body, Spiritual Body

nm73 » The resurrected Christ is a son of God, and a son of man. Once he was born of flesh; those born of flesh are flesh (John 3:6). Once he was born of God by a resurrection (Rom 1:4); those born of Spirit are Spirit (John 3:6). Christ the God is flesh and Spirit. He has two essences, he has two bodies. Christ the God as a son of man has a fleshly body, "there is a fleshly body" (1Cor 15:44). But as a son of God he has a Spiritual body, "there is also a spiritual body" (1Cor 15:44). The resurrected Christ has two bodies, or two essences – a spiritual and a fleshly essence. Scripture does not say that when one is born of God he loses his fleshly body. No it says they are made immortal (1Cor 15:52-55). And as Christ is, so shall all born of God be, for He is the first born of many brethren (Rom 8:29). Scripture indicates those born of God will be like Christ, "we shall be like him" (1John 3:2). "The Lord Jesus Christ who shall change our vile body, that it may be fashioned like unto his glorious body" (Phil 3:20, 21).

Greek Word, *gennao*, Ambiguity of

nm74 » But not only was Christ born of the flesh and born of the Spirit, he was also begotten of the flesh (inside Mary's womb) and begotten of the Spirit (while he was in his first fleshly state). Christ not only was born of flesh, he was also begotten of flesh. Christ not only was born of Spirit, he was also begotten of the Spirit. But because of the vagueness of a Greek word many do not understand this. The word translated born in many English translations comes from the Greek word, *gennao*. In contrast, this Greek word can mean either to *beget* or to be *born*. In the English language we have two separate words for the process of being begotten and being born. But the Greek word *gennao* can be used to mean either being begotten or being born. Because of this there is ambiguity when translating *gennao* into English.

nm75 » Being begotten is the same as being conceived, or fertilized, or impregnated. To be begotten is to be conceived. An egg-cell is begotten by a sperm cell. This is being begotten. Once begotten an egg-cell grows inside the womb of its mother. Allegorically, a Christian is begotten by the Spirit of God and grows Spiritually inside the womb of the Church, their heavenly mother, or Spiritual mother.

nm76 » But after the egg-cell has grown inside the mother's womb it is born of mankind. Allegorically, after a Christian is begotten, he grows Spiritually in the Church's womb until he is born of God. Isaiah 66:6-8 pictures the Christians all at once being born of God. This will happen at the last trumpet (1Cor 15:52-55; Rev 11:15). This is the time of Christ's physical return (1Thes 4:15-18).

nm77 » Therefore because the New Testament was written in Greek, and because in Greek there is a word that can express two different processes or stages of birth, and because this Greek word (*gennao*) was used in verses to express either "begotten" and/or "born," and because many of those who translated the Bible didn't understand God's plan; then the translators sometimes mistranslated "born" where they should have translated "begotten" and vice versa. And because of this vagueness of the Greek word *gennao* many people today do not understand what it means to be begotten or born of God. (Many places, if not all places, where *gennao* is used, can be and should be understood in the sense of begotten and/or born.) See "Last War and God's Wrath" PR5, in its Notes for more information or details on "begotten" and "born."

NM 6: Body, Soul, Spirit, and Immortality
Soul
Immortal Soul?
Spirit

NM6 Abstract

In this paper we look at what scripture says about the body, soul, and spirit. There is a difference between all three. The scriptures indicate that the soul is not the spirit of man, but tradition mixes these two different things. When some today speak of the soul, what they mean is the spirit. This causes confusion since the soul can die (it is mortal), but the spiritual element cannot die (it is immortal).

Soul

nm78 » *To help clarify*: in this paper we are not referring to the "soul" in the sense that it is used today in music or art ("he has soul"), or as a synonym for emotion or passion or feelings or spiritual depth or mind or psyche, or in any other way except as the word soul is used in the Bible (old and new testaments). In context with the Bible, what does the soul have to do with the body or with the spirit? What is the body? What is the soul? What is the spirit? And is the soul immortal? There is much confusion about what a soul is and if it is immortal. The view of Catholics, many Protestants, and some Jews is that the soul is immortal. From *This is the Faith*, written by the former Archbishop of Liverpool, Dr. Richard Downey, we see the Catholic view on the soul:

> Man ... has a body and a soul ... it is a spirit, immortal, and endowed with intelligence and free will. Soul is not just another word for spirit. Animals have souls, but their souls are not spirits. Only man's soul is a spirit; in man is the only kind of spirit that is a soul.... There is an obvious difference between a living human body and a corpse. That difference is the soul." (pp. 21-22)

As we will see from scripture there are several assertions here that are wrong. First the soul is not a spirit, second it is not immortal, and third its free will is limited under the absolute free will of God. You will not find immortality connected to the soul in scripture, but you will find

Satan telling Eve that she is immortal (Gen 3:4; serpent = Satan, Rev 12:9). So how do the Catholics "prove" that the soul is immortal?

> "Scripture is full of proof that the soul of man is spiritual and immortal. 'The Lord God formed man of the slime of the earth and breathed into his face the breath of life; and man became a living soul' (Gen 2:7)

> The souls of the just are in the hand of God, and torment of death shall not touch them. In the sight of the unwise they seemed to die .... but they are in peace .... their hope is full of immortality." (Wis 3:1-4)

These two quotes are under the heading, "What Does Scripture Say?," and are the two main verses used by the author to prove his assertion. The first quote of Genesis 2:7 says nothing about the soul being immortal. The second, even though it is not from the Bible, does not say the soul is immortal, but that man has hope of immortality. Of course they have hope of immortality because of the resurrection. The other scriptures quoted by the author speak of the hope of immortality because of the resurrection or the immortality given through the Spirit. The author substitutes the *hope* of immortality for mankind with mankind's mortality, and mixes the soul with the spirit. The hope of immortality is not the same as immortality; soul and spirit are not one and the same. Let's see what the scripture actually says about the body, soul, spirit, and immortality.

Man is a Living Soul

nm79 » In the Bible the word soul is translated from the Hebrew word *nephesh* (נֶפֶשׁ) and from the Greek word *psuche* (ψυχῆς). From Genesis we see what a soul is:

- "And Jehovah God formed the man, dust from the ground, and breathed into his nostrils breath of life; and man became a living soul." (Gen 2:7)

With the help of God man became a living soul. Man was formed from the dirt of the ground. Man is earthly. Then Jehovah [YHWH] breathed into man the breath of life and he became a living soul. In context with the other scriptures in Genesis, chapters 1 and 2, we see that Jehovah first made man's body, and second he made man a living soul when and because Jehovah breathed into him. It took the breath of Jehovah to make man a living soul. The living soul is not just a body: it is a body with God's breath in it.

God has a Soul

nm80 » Although theologians call it anthropopathy even God has a soul according to Bible:

- DBY Leviticus 26:11 And I will set my habitation among you; and **my soul** shall not abhor you;

- DBY Leviticus 26:30 And I will lay waste your high places, and cut down your sun-pillars, and cast your carcases upon the carcases of your idols; and **my soul** shall abhor you.

- DBY Isaiah 42:1 Behold my servant whom I uphold, mine elect {in whom} **my soul** delighteth! I will put my Spirit upon him; he shall bring forth judgment to the nations. [Compare with Mat 12:18.]

- DBY Jeremiah 5:9 Shall I not visit for these things? saith Jehovah, and shall not **my soul** be avenged on such a nation as this?

- DBY Jeremiah 6:8 Be thou instructed, Jerusalem, lest **my soul** be alienated from thee; lest I make thee a desolation, a land not inhabited.

- DBY Ezekiel 23:18 And she discovered her whoredoms, and discovered her nakedness; and **my soul** was alienated from her, like as **my soul** was alienated from her sister.

- DBY Zechariah 11:8 And I destroyed three shepherds in one month; and **my soul** was vexed with them, and their soul also loathed me.

- DBY Matthew 12:18 Behold my servant, whom I have chosen, my beloved, in whom **my soul** has found its delight. I will put my Spirit upon him, and he shall shew forth judgment to the nations. [Compare with Isa 42:1.]

- DBY Hebrews 10:38 But the just shall live by faith; and, if he draw back, **my soul** does not take pleasure in him.

   (Lev 26:11, 30; Isa 42:1; Jer 5:9; 6:8; Ezek 23:18; Zech 11:8; Mat 12:18; Heb 10:38)

Jesus became or was the soul of God (Mat 12:18; see *God Papers*).

Animals also have Souls

nm81 » Not only does mankind, and God, have souls, so do animals. The following verses in Hebrew show that animals have a soul (*nephesh* or *psuche*) also:

- DBY Genesis 1:20 And God said, Let the waters swarm with swarms of living **souls**, and let fowl fly above the earth in the expanse of the heavens.

- DBY Genesis 1:21 And God created the great sea monsters, and every living **soul** that moves with which the waters swarm, after their kind, and every winged fowl after its kind. And God saw that it was good.

- DBY Genesis 1:24 And God said, Let the earth bring forth living **souls** after their kind, cattle, and creeping thing, and beast of the earth, after their kind. And it was so.

- DBY Genesis 1:30 and to every animal of the earth, and to every fowl of the heavens, and to everything that creepeth on the earth, in which is a living **soul**, every green herb for food. And it was so.

- DBY Genesis 2:19 And out of the ground Jehovah Elohim had formed every animal of the field and all fowl of the heavens, and brought {them} to Man, to see what he would call them; and whatever Man called each living **soul**, that was its name.

- DBY Genesis 9:10 and with every living **soul** which is with you, fowl as well as cattle, and all the animals of the earth with you, of all that has gone out of the ark -- every animal of the earth.

- DBY Genesis 9:12 And God said, This is the sign of the covenant that I set between me and you and every living **soul** that is with you, for everlasting generations:

- DBY Genesis 9:15 and I will remember my covenant which is between me and you and every living **soul** of all flesh; and the waters shall not henceforth become a flood to destroy all flesh. 16 And the bow shall be in the cloud; and I will look upon it, that I may remember the everlasting covenant between God and every living **soul** of all flesh that is upon the earth.

- DBY Leviticus 11:10 but all that have not fins and scales in seas and in rivers, of all that swarm in the waters, and of every living **soul** which is in the waters -- they shall be an abomination unto you.

- DBY Revelation 8:9 and the third part of the creatures which were in the sea which had life [**soul**] died; and the third part of the ships were destroyed.

  (Gen 1:20, 21, 24, 30; 2:19; 9:10; 9:12, 15, 16; Lev 11:10; Rev 8:9; etc.)

Many English Bibles have translated the word "creature" or "life" for soul or *nephesh* or *psuche*. In the *BeComingOne Bible* we have translated *nephesh* or *psuche* into soul consistently.]

Souls Can Die

nm82 » According to the official Catholic view the soul is immortal:

Lateran Council of 1513

"Whereas some have dared to assert
concerning the nature of the reasonable soul
that it is mortal, we, with the approbation of
the sacred council do condemn and reprobate
all those who assert that the intellectual soul is
mortal, seeing, according to the canon of Pope
Clement V, that the soul is [...] immortal [...]
and we decree that all who adhere to like
erroneous assertions shall be shunned and
punished as heretics."

But contrary to the Catholic view, scripture indicates that souls can die. The following verses indicate that souls are destructible:

- DBY Genesis 17:14 And the uncircumcised male who hath not been circumcised in the flesh of his foreskin, that **soul** shall be cut off from his peoples: he hath broken my covenant.

- DBY Genesis 37:21 And Reuben heard {it}, and delivered him out of their hand, and said, Let us not take his life [**soul**].

- DBY Exodus 12:15 Seven days shall ye eat unleavened bread: on the very first day ye shall put away leaven out of your houses; for whoever eateth leavened bread from the first day until the seventh day -- that **soul** shall be cut off from Israel.

- DBY Leviticus 7:20 But the **soul** that eateth the flesh of the sacrifice of peace-offering which is for Jehovah, having his uncleanness upon him, that **soul** shall be cut off from his peoples.

- DBY Leviticus 24:17 And if any one smiteth any man mortally [kills any **soul**], he shall certainly be put to death.

- DBY Numbers 23:10 Who can count the dust of Jacob, and the number of the fourth part of Israel? Let my **soul** die the death of the righteous, and let my end be like his!

- DBY Numbers 31:19 And encamp outside the camp seven days; whoever hath killed a person [**soul**], and whoever hath touched any slain; ye shall purify yourselves on the third day, and on the seventh day, you and your captives.

- DBY Numbers 35:30 Whoever shall smite a person mortally, at the mouth of witnesses shall the murderer be put to death; but one witness shall not testify against a person [**soul**] to cause him to die.

- DBY Deuteronomy 19:6 lest the avenger of blood pursue the manslayer, while his heart is hot, and overtake him, because the way is long, and smite him mortally [slay his **soul**]; whereas he was not worthy of death, since he hated him not previously.

- DBY Joshua 2:13 that ye will let my father live, and my mother, and my brethren, and my sisters, and all that belong to them, and deliver our **souls** from death.

- DBY Judges 5:18 Zebulun is a people {that} jeoparded their lives [**souls**] unto death, Naphtali also, on the high places of the field.

- DBY 1Kings 19:4 And he himself went a day's journey into the wilderness, and came and sat down under a certain broom-bush, and requested for himself that he might die; and said, It is enough: now, Jehovah, take my life [**soul**]; for I am not better than my fathers.

- BY Job 36:14 Their **soul** dieth in youth, and their life is among the unclean.

- DBY Psalm 22:29 All the fat ones of the earth shall eat and worship; all they that go down to the dust shall bow before him, and he that cannot keep alive his own **soul**.

- DBY Psalm 78:50 He made a way for his anger; he spared not their **soul** from death, but gave their life over to the pestilence;

- DBY Isaiah 55:3 Incline your ear, and come unto me; hear, and your **soul** shall live; and I will make an everlasting covenant with you, the sure mercies of David.

- DBY Jeremiah 4:10 And I said, Alas, Lord Jehovah! surely thou hast greatly deceived this people and Jerusalem, saying, Ye shall have peace; whereas the sword reacheth unto the **soul**.

- DBY Ezekiel 13:19 And will ye profane me among my people for handfuls of barley and for morsels of bread, to slay the **souls** that should not die, and to save the **souls** alive that should not live, by your lying to my people that listen to lying?

- DBY Ezekiel 22:27 Her princes in the midst of her are like wolves ravening the prey, to shed blood, to destroy **souls,** to get dishonest gain.

- DBY Matthew 2:20 Arise, take to {thee} the little child and its mother, and go into the land of Israel: for they who sought the life [**soul**] of the little child are dead.

- DBY Matthew 10:28 And be not afraid of those who kill the body, but cannot kill the **soul**; but fear rather him who is able to destroy both **soul** and body in hell.

- DBY Matthew 26:38 Then he says to them, My **soul** is very sorrowful even unto death; remain here and watch with me.

- DBY Mark 3:4 And he says to them, Is it lawful on the sabbath to do good or to do evil, to save life [**soul**] or to kill? But they were silent.

- DBY Mark 14:34 And he says to them, My **soul** is full of grief even unto death; abide here and watch.

- DBY Luke 6:9 Jesus therefore said to them, I will ask you if it is lawful on the Sabbath to do good, or to do evil? to save life [a **soul**], or to destroy {it}?

- DBY Luke 17:33 Whosoever shall seek to save his life [**soul**] shall lose it, and whosoever shall lose it shall preserve it.

- DBY John 10:15 as the Father knows me and I know the Father; and I lay down my life [**soul**] for the sheep.

- DBY John 12:25 He that loves his life [**soul**] shall lose it, and he that hates his life [**soul**] in this world shall keep it to life eternal [aeonian].

- DBY Acts 3:23 And it shall be that whatsoever **soul** shall not hear that prophet shall be destroyed from among the people.

- DBY Romans 11:3 Lord, they have killed thy prophets, they have dug down thine altars; and I have been left alone, and they seek my life [**soul**].

- DBY Hebrews 10:39 But we are not drawers back to perdition, but of faith to saving {the} **soul**.

- DBY James 5:20 let him know that he that brings back a sinner from {the} error of his way shall save a **soul** from death and shall cover a multitude of sins.

- DBY Revelation 8:9 and the third part of the creatures which were in the sea which had life [**soul**] died; and the third part of the ships were destroyed.

- DBY Revelation 12:11 and they have overcome him by reason of the blood of the Lamb, and by reason of the word of their testimony, and have not loved their life [**souls**] even unto death.

- DBY Revelation 16:3 And the second poured out his bowl on the sea; and it became blood, as of a dead man; and every living **soul** died in the sea.

  (Gen 17:14; 37:21; Ex 12:15; Lev 7:20; 24:17; Num 23:10; 31:19; 35:30; Deut 19:6; Joshua 2:13; Jud 5:18; 1Kings 19:4; Job 36:14; Psalms 22:29; 78:50; Isa 55:3; Jer 4:10; Ezek 13:19; 22:27; Mat 2:20; 10:28; 26:38; Mark 3:4; 14:34; Luke 6:9; 17:33; John 10:15; 12:25; Acts 3:23; Rom 11:3; Heb 10:39; James 5:20; Rev 8:9; 12:11; 16:3; etc.)

nm83 » That souls can die is absolutely clear in the Hebrew or Greek as well as the *BeComingOne Bible* and other more literal Bibles. Sometimes English translations leave out soul from the translation as in Judges 16:30 where it should read: "And Samson said, Let my soul die...." Sometimes English translations have life instead of soul as in John 10:15.

nm84 » The following verses indicate that there can be dead souls:

- DBY Leviticus 21:11 Neither shall he come near any person [**soul**] dead, nor make himself unclean for his father and for his mother;

- DBY Leviticus 22:4 Whatsoever man of the seed of Aaron is a leper, or hath a flux, he shall not eat of the holy things, until he is clean. And he that toucheth any one that is unclean by a dead person [**soul**], or a man whose seed of copulation hath passed from him;

- DBY Numbers 5:2 Command the children of Israel, that they put out of the camp every leper, and every one that hath an issue, and whosoever is defiled by a dead person [**soul**]:

- DBY Numbers 6:11 And the priest shall offer one for a sin-offering, and the other for a burnt-offering, and make an atonement for him, for that he sinned by the dead person [**soul**]; and he shall hallow his head that same day.

    (Lev 21:11; 22:4; Num 5:2; 6:11; etc.)

[In some translations "body" or "dead" = soul; see Hebrew text.]

Two Meanings of a Dead Soul

Because there is a type and antitype to the Bible, there are two meanings to dead souls, the physical and the spiritual:

- Those who lose the breath of life become dead

- Those with the breath (or spirit) of Satan are dead

Immortal Soul: Satan's Lie

nm85 » Even though mankind will in the future become immortal, the above scripture indicates that the soul is not now immortal. The idea that the soul is now immortal did not come from the Bible. The false idea that humans in this age have immortal souls came from Satan's first lie. Satan's lie occurred right after God said that man would die if they ate from the tree of knowledge of good and evil (Gen 2:16-17):

- And the serpent said unto the woman, Ye shall not surely die. [Gen 3:4]

This idea of the immortality of the soul continued through the Greeks, Babylonians, Egyptians, Romans, and so forth. Of course these cultures got this idea of the immortality of the soul from the power of Satan which feeds mankind false and destructive information (NM 21). From this theologians down through the years have interjected this false idea into the doctrines of Christianity and other religions.

Salvation of the Soul

nm86 » From Genesis 2:7 we know that a body can be a soul, if it has breath in it. From other scripture mentioned above we see that any living and breathing body, even an animal's body, is called a soul. Also we know from the scripture referred to above that a soul can be destroyed and can die and so can be called a dead soul. Thus in this age mankind's soul is *not* immortal. This is why the Bible talks about the *salvation* of the soul (1Pet 1:9; Heb 10:39; 1Thes 5:23; Luke 21:19; James 5:20) and talks about going from mortality to immortality (1Cor 15:53-54; Rom 8:11; 2Cor 5:4). The idea of the immortal soul came from the influence of Satan, the Greeks, and other ancient peoples. But although the soul is *not* immortal, there is one aspect of man that is immortal. That immortal aspect is the spirit.

Spirit

nm87 » As shown in this book and in the *God Papers* spirits are immortal, and there is a particular spirit for each and every person. For clarification you must read the books: *New Mind Papers* and the *God Papers* [aka *God*]. For now let it be said that there is an immortal aspect to mankind, and it has to do with man's own spirit. Spirits are immortal; souls can and do die. What most religions do is mix-up the nature of the spirit with the nature of the soul. Our soul is not our spirit; our spirit is not our soul. This mix-up began at the time of Adam and Eve (Gen 3:4) and still causes confusion today. If the translators had only consistently translated the Hebrew *nephesh* and the Greek *psuche* into soul we would not have as much confusion. Of course the reason they didn't translate these words consistently is because of their mindset which made them twist the scriptures to force their incorrect ideas into the text of the Bible.

Note: Remember that in Genesis 2:7 Jehovah "breathed" into man the "breath" of life. In the English version of the Old Testament the word "breath" is translated from either the Hebrew word *neshamah* or *ruah*. These words differ slightly in meaning, both signifying sometimes "wind" or sometimes "breath." The word translated into "breath" in Genesis 2:7 is the Hebrew word *neshamah*. Both Hebrew words, *neshamah* and *ruah* are translated as "spirit" in various places in the English translations of the Bible. This means that the book of Genesis could just as well have been translated showing God breathing into man a spirit. This is just another example of duality (type and antitype) of the Bible. As it turned out both senses are true: God breathed a breath of air into man; God also breathed a spirit into man. See *New Mind* 22 for more information on this. But that spirit was not the soul of man.

NM 7: Age Paper

Eternal & Forever in the Bible
Contradictions
Aeonian Meaning in Harmony with Scripture
Context Argument One
Context Argument Two
Paradox: All Saved; Evil Damned Forever
Two Ages: One Ends; One Does Not End
Why Misusage of Word
Review and Further Arguments
Everliving or Agelasting?: Rosetta Stone

NM7 Abstract

One of the biggest mistakes in traditional Christianity is the mistranslation of two words into "eternal" that actually mean aeon or age. From this mistake came the eternal hell and punishment for those who never had the chance to learn about Christ or who simply did not believe in him. Not only this, but from this mistake we get such nonsense as, sacrifices for eternity, slaves for eternity, time before eternity, more than one eternity, and other such impossibilities. In this paper we refute the best arguments from Augustine and others. This paper is a key to unlocking the truth that has been hidden behind this mistranslation.

Eternal & Forever in the Bible

nm88 » Do you know that *eternal* and *forever* in most translations of the Bible are incorrectly translated from words that mean **age?** Since the early fifth century AD and probably long before, this major inaccuracy in translation has filtered and shaded most doctrines of the Bible.

Olam & Aionios

nm89 » In the Old Testament the Hebrew *olam* [עוֹלָם] is the most common word translated to English as 'forever.' In the New Testament the Greek *aionios* [αἰώνιός] is the most common word translated to English as 'forever' or 'eternal.' From Young's *Analytical Concordance to the Bible* and Strong's *Exhaustive Concordance of the Bible* we see the proof that the words 'everlasting' and 'forever' were most often translated to English (KJV) from the Hebrew *olam* or the Greek *aionios*.

nm90 » Even though most translations of the Bible incorrectly translate the Hebrew *olam* or the Greek *aionios* in scripture, there are translations that correctly use them. Translations such as Young's *Literal Translation of the Holy Bible* and Rotherham's *The Emphasized Bible* do use 'age' or 'age-abiding' instead of 'forever.' You will find that in our papers we use the words 'age' or 'agelasting' or 'aeonian' instead of the inaccurate 'forever' or 'everlasting' or 'eternal.' Why do most translations use *forever, everlasting*, and *eternal* (or comparable words in other languages) while we use 'age' or 'agelasting' or 'aeonian'?

Vague Time Period

nm91 » We will show in this paper that the Hebrew *olam* means age or agelong or an eon of indefinite length, and that the Greek *aion* and its adjective *aionios* mean an age of unknown length or agelong or aeonian. The main and only real meaning of these words is an *age or eon of unknown length*. The words in and of themselves tell us nothing about duration, or the beginning or end of the age. In context they *may* indicate "an age (of foreverness)" when it is speaking of an age that will not end, an endless age. But here they only indicate "an age (of foreverness)" by auxiliary words that clarify their normal vague meaning: the word 'age' by itself never tells us the length of the age or the beginning or end of the age. Without auxiliary words that specify its length, the word 'age' or 'eon' is always unclear as to its length.

Damning, Unforgiving Mindset

nm92 » But there is a desire in mankind that wants and needs to believe that the Hebrew *olam* and the Greek *aionios* mean forever or eternal, and because of this they ignore the doctrine of forgiveness and the great all powerfulness of God. The desire has turned into a mindset.

nm93 » This mindset traps mankind into paradoxes that make God contradictory and impotent. Mankind has its 'hell' theories where a supposedly good, forgiving, and almighty God puts humans in a hell-fire that somehow burns their fleshly body for ever and ever: their god does not terminate their life, he tortures them forever. They say, "those who don't believe or commit themselves to Christ, are damned forever." But all one has to do is to translate *olam* and *aionios* into 'agelong' or 'aeonian,' as we did in the *BeComingOne Bible*, and many of the great paradoxes of Biblical doctrine will end. But this isn't easy for many. They *insist* on holding on to their tangled doctrines.

nm94 » I once believed in this distortion. But once I learned of the mistranslation in 1969 it was obvious that major doctrines of the Bible were being taught incorrectly. There is a large difference between the word age and the word forever. Age normally indicates limits (most ages have beginnings and/or ends), but forever and eternal always indicate no limits and no end. In this paper we will go into much more detail on the mistranslated words *olam* and *anionios*, which are incorrectly translated into 'forever,' 'everlasting,' and 'eternal.' This is very important.

Contradictions

nm95 » First let's look at some paradoxical translations caused by the incorrect translation of *olam* and *aionios*. If we translate these words correctly there are no paradoxes.

Sacrifices Forever?

nm96 » Some sacrifices, offerings, and rituals of the Old Testament were *olam* or *aionios* sacrifices. (Note: Lev 3:17; 6:18; 7:36; 10:9, 15; 16:29; 17:17; 23:14; 24:3; Num 10:8; 15:15; 18:8; 19:10; etc.) If *olam* or *aionios* mean forever or eternal why are these sacrifices, offerings, and rituals not now being performed? They are not still being performed because they were for an age, not forever. Christ abolished them by his perfect sacrifice (Heb 10:10-14).

Circumcision Forever?

nm97 » If *olam* or *aionios* means forever or eternal why are not Christians following this *olam* or *aionios* covenant of circumcision:

- "My covenant shall be in your flesh for an *olam* [or *aionios*] covenant" (Gen 17:13).

If *olam* or *aionios* mean forever or eternal, how can anyone unbound such a regulation? Of course *olam* and *aionios* only mean age, thus the reason Christians are no longer bond by physical circumcision (note Acts 15:5-29; 1Cor 7:18-19; Gal 5:1-4, 6; Col 3:11).

Slaves Forever?

nm98 » If *olam* or *aionios* mean forever or eternal, then according to the law of the Old testament, some can be made slaves forever or for eternity (Lev 25:46; Deut 15:17). Of course there are no forever slaves: *olam* and *aionios* do not mean forever, they speak of an age.

Before Eternity?

nm99 » If *aionios* means forever or eternal how could there have been any time *before* eternity, "before the times of eternities [*aionion*, plural of *aionios*]" (Greek text, 2Tim 1:9)?

More Than One Eternity?

nm100 » Is there more than one eternity? *If* the Greek *aionios* or the Hebrew *olam* mean eternal, then according to 2Tim 1:9 there was a time before *eternitieS*. How can there be more than one eternity. There are at least two other places in the Greek New Testament that has *aionios* in its plural form:

- "But the things invisible are *aionia*" (2Cor 4:16). [This Greek *aionia* is the plural form of aionios (*Analytical Greek Lex.*, Zondervan)..]

- "Which God, who cannot lie, promised before times of *aionion*" (Titus 1:2). [According to the Lexicon *aionion* here is in its plural form.]

nm101 » The Hebrew word *olam* is also translated forever or everlasting. *Olam* is also found in its plural form in such verses as in Isaiah 26:4; 45:17; Psa 77:6; 145:13. Is there more than one eternity? Of course not.

nm102 » The Greek *aionios* and the Hebrew *olam* are speaking about an age or ages of secret or hidden or unknown time lengths. We can only ascertain the time periods of each *olam* and *aionios* by other words in context that explain to us what age the Bible is speaking about. The words *olam* or *aionios* in and of themselves tell us nothing about the duration, or the beginning or the ending of the age. We only know that the age of Satan will end because of scripture. We only know the new and coming age of the True God will *not* end because of scripture. And we can know through scripture that there are ages within the great age of God just as there are ages within Satan's age.

Never Die?

nm103 » In John 8:51 and verse 52 we see contradictions: "If a man keep my saying, he shall never see death. Then said the Jews unto him [unto Jesus], Now we know that you are possessed of a demon. Abraham is dead, and the prophets; and you say, If a man keep my saying, he shall never taste of death." And in John 11:26 we see a similar contradiction: "And whosoever lives and believes in me shall never die."

nm104 » In this translation Christ seems to say that if one kept his words and believed in him that such a person would *never* die. But by reading the New Testament we know that those who do keep his word and that do believe in him do die. A contradiction? No! It is a mistranslation.

nm105 » The English word "never" in these verses was mistranslated. It should have been translated as follows: "no not death should he behold into the age" – John 8:51; "no not should he taste of death into the age" – John 8:52; "no not [anyone believing] should die into the age" – John 11:26. Double negatives in Greek adds emphasis to the negative. "No not" can be translated "absolutely not." Thus "absolutely not should anyone who believes in Christ die into the age."

nm106 » These scriptures speak about an *age* and that into that age or in that age those who believe in Christ (those who keep his word) will not, absolutely not, die. This great age begins with the 1000 year age as other scripture indicates (see *Reward for Christians* [NM 11]). When we translate *aion* literally these scriptures make sense. But when we translate it as some *think* it ought to be translated we come up with contradictions. In the above three scriptures "never" was mistranslated for the Greek words that literally meant "no not" and "age."

David's Throne Forever?

nm107 » If *olam* or *aionios* mean forever or eternal, then David and Solomon's thrones should have lasted forever (1Kings 9:5; 2Sam 7:12-13, 16). Of course this kingdom of David and Solomon lasted only for an age. It is the Spiritual Seed of David that will establish the kingdom in the endless age or endless *olam* or *aionios*.

Cities and Land Destroyed Forever?

nm108 » If *olam* or *aionios* mean forever or eternal, then there are cities and lands that forever or for eternity will be in ruins (Isa 25:2; 32:14; Ezek 26:21; 27:36; 28:19; Jer 18:15; 25:9, 12; 49:13, 33; 51:26, 62; Ezek 35:9; etc.). But this cannot be true because when Jesus Christ returns to the earth, the earth will be renewed and eventually created totally new (Rev 21:5; Psa 104:30; Isa 61:4; Ezek 36:10-11; Amos 9:14; etc.). Of course, since *olam* or *aionios* only indicate an age, these cities and lands will not be forever ruined, but will be renewed and the people of these former cities will be resurrected.

Present Earth Forever?

nm109 » In such places as Eccl 1:4 and Psa 104:5 it speaks about the earth standing for *olam* or *aionios*. But Christ said that heaven and earth would pass away (Mat 24:35; Mark 13:31; Luke 21:33). The present earth stands not forever, but for an *olam* or *aionios*, that is, it stands for an age. But after that age it will be totally created new (Rev 21:5).

Land Forever?

nm110 » If *olam* or *aionios* means forever or eternal, then Israel would have continually and forever possessed the land (Note Gen 13:15; see Greek trans.). But if *olam* or *aionios* means agelong, the Genesis 13:15 promise means that Israel would possess the land during an age. This is what happened: physical Israel did possess the land for an age – not forever. The true higher meaning of this scripture is that the Spiritual Israel will possess the land during the age (*olam*) of the True God.

Aeonian or Agelasting Meaning in Harmony With Scripture

nm111 » When the Greek *aion*, its adjective *aionios*, and the Hebrew *olam* are translated anything but age or aeonian or agelasting, contradictions occur in scripture. But when these words are correctly translated a clear meaning is projected to the reader. In all our papers on doctrine we always use the correct translation of these words because it is the best way to translate these words. And because throughout our papers and in the BeComingOne Bible we have translated "aeonian" as it should be translated, we project to you the mercy of God and the great plan of the God. The True God is not a damning forever God. Our God is a God of love and forgiveness. He punishes, but He also will eventually save all. See our paper "All Saved" [NM 13] for there are many scriptures in the Bible where it says that *all* will eventually be saved. There is/was a purpose for evil. There is hope for all.

Hebrew Meaning of *Olam*

nm112 » In Hebrew, the language of the Old Testament, the Hebrew word most often translated "forever" or "everlasting" is *olam*.

[or *alam*, Strong's # 5956 & # 5957; *'owlan*, #5769; *'eylowm*, # 5865; see also *'ad*, # 5703. Note that the word is spelled in Hebrew differently at different times because of prefixes and suffixes attached to it.]

From the *Hebrew and Chaldee Lexicon* by Gesenius, it shows that the Hebrew word *olam* (Strong's # 5956) has the meaning of a hidden age or hidden time specifically "hidden time, long."

nm113 » From the *Analytical Hebrew and Chaldee Lexicon* by Benjamin Davidson (Pub., by Zondervan, 1970), it shows that the Hebrew word *olam* means a hidden time or secret time or age.

nm114 » This word was first used in the Bible to describe the hidden or secret age that Adam and Eve missed because of their sin: "and live into *olam*" (Gen 3:22). Its basic meaning concerns a hidden or secret age, or simply an age of unknown length. At the time Genesis 3:22 was spoken, Adam and Eve were only alive a short while. At that time Adam and Eve did not and could not understand time. Time is something one learns to understand through living in time. See "Reason Why" paper [NM 19] to understand how one learns.

Greek Meaning of *Aion*

nm115 » In Greek, the language of the New Testament, the Greek words most often translated "forever" or "everlasting" or "eternal" are *aion* or *aionios*. (Note: both of these words are spelled somewhat differently in the New Testament text depending on the usage in the sentence.)

nm116 » From Thayer's *Greek-English Lexicon of the New Testament*, the Greek word *aion* is said to mean age or a human lifetime.

nm117 » From *The Analytical Greek Lexicon* (Pub. Zondervan), the Greek word *aion* is said to mean "a period of time of significant character; life; an era; an age."

nm118 » From William F. Arndt and F. Wilbur Gingrich's *A Greek-English Lexicon of the New Testament*, the meaning of *aion* is "time, age."

nm119 » From the Lexicons in Young's and Strong's concordances, the Greek word *aion* also is indicated as meaning an age or time.

nm120 » From Wuest's *Word Studies*, Volume 8, *Studies in the Vocabulary*, under "world," we see concerning *aion* the following:

- "*Aion* which comes from *aio* [it is debatable whether *aion* came from *aio*] 'to breathe,' means 'a space or period of time,' especially 'a lifetime, life.' It is used of one's time of life, age, the age of man, an age, a generation." And in the same place, "as to *aion*, the papyri speak of a person led off to death, the literal Greek being 'led off from *aion* life.' A report of a public meeting speaks of a cry that was uttered by the crowd, namely, 'The Emperors forever' (*aion*). It is also found in the sense of 'a period of life.'"

nm121 » In the Greek translation of the Old Testament, *aion* was used for *olam* in such verses as Psa 90:2: "from everlasting to everlasting … "; Hebrew has it: 'from olam to olam; and Greek has it: "from the aion until the aion;" the literal text of the *Emphasized Bible* has it: "from age unto age";

Meaning of *aionios*

nm122 » The Greek word *aionios* is merely an adjective that comes from the root *aion*. While *aion* means "age," *aionios*, being an adjective, means "agelasting," or "aeonian," or "agelong." When the *Septuagint* was translated, the translators used in many cases the Greek word *aionios* for the Hebrew word *olam*.

nm123 » For example the Greek *aionios* was used for the Hebrew *olam* in Genesis 13:15: "For all the land which you see I will give to you, and to your seed during *olam*."

nm124 » Or again in Genesis 3:22: "And now, lest he put forth his hand and also take from the tree of life and eat and live into *olam* [Greek *aiona*]."

nm125 » And again, "Every man child among you shall be circumcised ... my covenant shall be in your flesh for an *olam* [or *aionion*] covenant" (Gen 17:10, 13).

nm126 » Thus, from the above scripture and many others, we see the Greek *aionios* must be a synonym for the Hebrew word *olam*. To ascertain the meaning of *aionios* we can look to the meaning of *olam*. As shown above *olam* means basically a hidden or secret age or time. Thus *aionios* also must mean a hidden age or time or an unknown age or time. And so it is, the basic meaning of *aionios* is an indeterminate time or age. The word *aionios* can be translated as "agelasting" or "aeonian" or "agelong." It speaks of an age which has an unknown length and which begins and ends at an unknown time.

nm127 » From William Barclay's *New Testament Words* we note the following concerning the Greek word *aionios*. Barclay says *aionios* is an adjective formed from the noun *aion*. "In classical Greek this word *aion* has three main meanings. It means a *life-time* . . .. Then it comes to mean an *age*, a *generation*, or an *epoch* . . . But then the word comes to mean a *very long space of time*." Then Barclay's goes on and tries to say that the "strange" word *aionios* somehow means *eternal* and gives some examples from Plato to back up his contention.

Magic Word

nm128 » One question will do here. How can an adjective that came from a word that means age, come to mean eternal? It would be comparable to the word "some" (i.e. some of time) coming to mean "all" (i.e. all of time). You cannot correctly use the adjective of *age*, which is agelasting or aeonian, as if it meant forever. The whole idea that *aionios* means eternal or everlasting is ludicrous. It is a lie. It is magical in an evil way. That lie has twisted scripture, and has made true doctrine in the Bible almost impossible to see. It has put a blindfold over peoples' eyes.

Aionios in Context

nm129 » Barclay gives a few examples of Plato using *aionios* as if it meant eternal.

- ■ "The most significant of all the Platonic passages is in the *Timaeus* 37d. There he speaks about the Creator and the universe which he has created, 'the created glory of the eternal [aionios] gods.'"

To Barclay, for some reason, because Plato used *aionios* in connection with "gods," it is some kind of proof that *aionios* means eternal. According to this reasoning since God ("gods") is eternal, then *aionios* must mean eternal. But this overlooks the fact that, yes, God in someway was/is perpetual (His power, Rom 1:20), but also God may in some sense also be or relate to an aeonian (aionios) time. Just because the word *aionios* is used in connection with "gods" does not give it the meaning of eternal. Furthermore, what do Plato's writings have to do with our God and the definition of His "eternalness"? Plato was speaking in the above example about *gods*, not God. Plato's writings were not inspired by God: they are full of myth and faulty thinking.

nm130 » Others like Barclay try to make the adjective *aionios* ("agelasting"), which comes from the noun *aion* ("age"), mean "forever," "everlasting," and "eternal." They say *aionios* means "eternal" because in context of its usage it is used as if it literally means "everlasting." They call the Greek word *aionios*, "strange." And to me it is strange that a word that is derived from a word that means "age" should somehow mean "everlasting."

nm131 » We will give you hereafter two of their "best" arguments in favor of the idea that *aionios* means "everlasting," and then we will refute their wrong reasoning. These same arguments were used by Augustine in the fourth-fifth century AD (see below).

Context Argument One

Aionios God; *Olam* God

nm132 » This argument deals with the usage of *aionios* in connection with God. We will only examine this argument of context by referring to the relevant Biblical text usage. To try and say *aionios* means eternal because Plato or Aristotle seems to use it that way is off the mark. We are only interested in how the Bible uses the word *aionios*, not how some Greek philosopher seems to use it.

nm133 » Romans 16:26: "the *aionios* God." Romans 16:26 speaks of the aeonian God or the God of the aeonian time. Notice that Genesis 21:33 speaks of the God of *olam* and Isaiah 40:28 speaks of the God of *olam*. These verses were translated by the Greek *aionios* in the Greek text. Somehow this usage of *aionios* (or *olam*) is proof positive to many that *aionios* means "everlasting." But the Greek word *aionios* is simply an adjective that comes from the noun *aion*, which means age. The literal meaning of *aionios* is "aeonian" or "agelong." The book of Romans is speaking about one aspect of God. Somehow God is "aeonian." Of course since God is Spirit (John 4:24), and since spirits or angels do not die (Luke 20:36), then God will not die. God is immortal (1Tim 1:17). God's power and Godship was/is/will-be continuous (Rom 1:20, Greek *aidios*). But Romans 16:26 tells us that in some way God is aeonian.

nm134 » In one aspect God *is* aeonian. The true God is aeonian in the respect that He rules through Jesus Christ as King of kings beginning in the age of 1000 years (Rev 19:16; 20:4). In this present age in which I write, the god of the world is a false one, the god of this age is the one called Satan by the Bible (2Cor 4:4). Satan is an agelasting god ruling in the old age. Satan is the power of death. The true God (His Good Spirit) does not rule this old age and that is the reason this age is so twisted. The true God through Jesus Christ rules beginning in the aeonian time, the 1000 year age. This is an aeonian aspect of God. Of course, since God's agelong (*olam* or *aionios*) kingdom will not end (Dan 2:44; 7:14; Luke 1:33), then this new aeonian kingdom (see Greek text, 2Peter 1:11) and rule will never end. It is an endless age, but it does have a beginning at the coming of Jesus Christ (Rev 11:15). Therefore it is an aeonian rulership. The word *aionios* (or *olam*) by itself means agelong, but the new and coming age belonging to God will not end like most ages because other clarifying words tell us that this special age, unlike ages before it, will not end (Luke 1:33; Dan 2:44; 7:14; Isa 9:6-7). It also can be said that the new age began in one sense at Christ's first presence or coming.

Greek Words that Mean Forever

nm135 » If Paul wanted in Romans 16:26 to describe God as the everlasting God or the endless God, Paul had many other Greek words to use to say this. Paul could have used *akatalutos*, which means "indissoluble." Paul could have used *atelestos*, which means "endlessness." Or Paul could have used *aperantos*, which also means "endless," as he used this word in 1Tim 1:4. But Paul did not use these words or other Greek words or phrases because he did not want to use them, for he was simply mentioning in Romans 16:26 that some aspect of God is "aeonian." God is a lot of things, and one of these is that he is in a certain way "aeonian." God belongs to the new never ending age – God's age or God's *olam* or *aion*. God is God of *olam* or God of *aionios*, He is the God of the new, great, never ending age. We know it is a new great and never ending age, not by the word *olam or aionios*, but by **other** words and sentences because *olam* and *aionios* speak only of a vague or undefined age, not a forever age.

nm136 » In some translations of the Old Testament, it has "eternal God" in Deuteronomy 33:27, but this should be translated "ancient God" or "God of old." This mistranslated word is strong's # 6924, *qedem*. In some translations of Genesis 21:33 and Isaiah 40:28 it has "everlasting God," but should be translated "*olam* God" or "God of *olam*." This means that God belongs or pertains to *olam* or the hidden age of the future first mentioned in Genesis 3:22.

Context Argument Two

Aionios Life and Punishment

nm137 » The second argument of context which Augustine cleverly articulated back in the early fifth century AD (413-26), in his *City of God* (trans. W.M. Green, The Loeb Classical Library, 1972), deals with two items: one is punishment, and the other is life. In Augustine's time some were teaching that the *aionios* punishment would end. Augustine in book 21 of his *City of God* was in part arguing against this position.

nm138 » Augustine translates the word *aionios* from scripture into the Latin, *aeternus* and *aeternitas*. These Latin words are related to the Latin *aevum*, which in turn is related to the Greek *aion* (cf. *Oxford Latin Dict.*, 1968, p. 74, col. 2, under *aeternus*, "[aevvm + -ternvs]").. Augustine knows that these words can mean longlasting, with the possibility of an end.

Thus Augustine must emphasize in his writings that he is not speaking of the Latin, *aeternus*, in the sense of a long period, but in the sense of eternal, a period without end. Notice Augustine's own words, translated from Latin:

■ The term "eternal," as applied here, does not refer to a long period of time (*aetas*) lasting through many ages, but still at some time bound to end.[1] Rather, as it stands written in the gospel, "of his kingdom there shall be no end.[Luke 1:33]"
(*City of God*, book 22, part 1; page 173)

[1] The words "eternal" and "eternity," from Latin *aeternus*, *aeternitas*, are related to *aevum*, which means both "unending time" and "a period of time"; for the second meaning the commoner word is *aetas*. Augustine seeks to make it clear that the "eternal" happiness of the saints is unending happiness, that is, an unending immortality for each individual (text of editorial footnote 1 on p. 173).

And from the *Oxford Latin Dictionary*, 1968, we see that:

■ *aetas* means

1. The number of years one has lived, one's age. 2. Period or time of life. 3. A person or person of a particular age or period of life, an age group. 4. a. youth. b. old or advancing age; greater age. 5. The whole period of a man's life, the mortal span, one's lifetime, an age. 6. Human life and all that goes with it. 7. The passage or lapse of time. 8. The time or period to which a person or thing belongs, an era, age; the duration of this as a unit of time, a generation.

■ *aevum* means

1. time of life. 2 a generation. 3. age.

nm139 » Thus, even in his time, Augustine knew that *aionios* meant agelong or longlasting, thus he reasoned by context:

■ Then what sort of reasoning is it, to take the eternal [*aeternum*] punishment of the wicked as a fire of long duration and believe that eternal [*aeternam*] life is without end? For Christ said in the very same place, including both in one and the same sentence: "So these will go into eternal [Lat., *aeternum*; Greek *aionios*] punishment, but the righteous into eternal [Lat., *aeternam*; Greek, *aionios*] life." [Mat 25:46] If both are eternal, then surely both must be understood as "long," but having an end, or else as "everlasting," without an end. For they are matched with each other: in one clause eternal punishment, in the other eternal life. But to say in one and the same sentence: "Eternal life shall be without end, eternal punishment will have an end," is utterly absurd. Hence, since the eternal life of the saints

will be without end, eternal punishment also will surely
have no end, for these whose lot it is. [book 21, part 23; p. 113]

nm140 » Augustine finds a place in the Bible where the Greek *aionios*
is used to speak both of the punishment of sinners and the reward of
the saints (Mat 25:46). But because all Christians think and know that
their 'reward' is immortality, an everlasting life, and since in one
sentence *aionios* describes the life for the righteous, and the
punishment for evil, then according to this argument, *aionios* must
mean forever, at least in context. This may seem logical, but in context
of other scriptures it is not logical.

All Made Alive

nm141 » Notice one sentence where it shows that since all die, all
will be saved:

From Paul's resurrection chapter we read:

- For as in Adam ALL die, even so in Christ shall ALL be
  made alive (1Cor 15:22; see Rom 5:14-18; Psa 82:7-8).

In this one sentence we have "all" repeated twice. Most believe the
first "all," that is, because of Adam's sin *all* die. Most do *not* believe the
second "all," that is, because of Christ *all* will be made alive.

nm142 » What is meant in 1Corinthians 15:22 by "be made alive"?
Does it mean be made alive (resurrected) and thereafter be killed in
some kind of hell-fire? In context what does it mean to "be made
alive"?

- "For since by a man came death, by a man also came the
  resurrection of the dead. For as in Adam all die, so also in
  Christ *all* shall be made alive. But each in his own order"
  (1Cor 15:21-23, NASB).

nm143 » Here it speaks of the resurrection of the dead. All shall be
made *alive*, but not at the same time. There is an *order* to the "all shall
be made alive." In context this resurrection has something to do with
"the resurrection of the dead."

nm144 » As we clearly show in our papers, 'All Saved' and 'Does All
Mean All?,' there are three orders or ranks of resurrection. The first
was Jesus Christ. The second will be the Christians at Christ's second
coming. The third and final resurrection will be at the *end* of creation
when the universal resurrection of all others occur. This will not be a
resurrection to death, but one to life. Please read these two papers so
as to begin to see the truth about the universal resurrection to life.
Also read the "Reason Why" [GP 7] paper in the *God Papers* to

understand the need for the present age of confusion. There is hope for all. All will be given the good Spirit and the good mind.

But they forget...

nm145 » According to those who say *aionios* means "everlasting," those who do evil in this age will go away to serve an everlasting punishment because they did not bring God into their lives. And also according to these same people, those who do good in this age and/or those who accept God in this age will be given everlasting life. But they forget that it is God who gives the power for people to be good, to repent ("change one's mind"), to receive God's Spirit, and so forth (see the rest of this book, *New Mind Papers*, for documentation). Thus, simply, those who will be damned for everlasting punishment, as some assert, will be damned merely because God did not give them the power to save themselves. What these people are saying is that God is discriminating wrongly against some: he saves some forever through his grace; he damns others forever by not giving them his grace.

Paradox: All Eventually Saved; Evil Damned Forever

nm146 » The answer is not as Augustine argues, that all does not mean all (Book 21, part 24). Augustine needlessly throws in more confusion by alleging that 'all' does not mean 'all.' But the real answer negates the confusion. The answer to the paradox is that *aionios*, an adjective of *aion* (which is a word that means *age*), means aeonian, and that 'all' means 'all.' The *aionios* punishment the Bible speaks about is *age*lasting. There is an agelasting or aeonian punishment for many, not an everlasting punishment. Notice the following scriptures concerning the *aionios* (aeonian) punishment or judgment.

Aeonian or Agelasting Punishment.

nm147 » There is an agelasting fire: "And if your hand or your foot offend you, cut them off, and cast them from you: it is better for you to enter into life lame and crippled, rather than having two hands or two feet to be cast into the *aionios* fire" (Mat 18:8).

nm148 » At the physical return of the Messiah some people will burn in the fire (caused by the Last War) which is to last for an age. This fire was meant for the other-mind, our spiritual adversary, and his spiritual friends: "Then shall he say also unto them on the left hand, Depart from me, you cursed, into *aionios* fire, prepared for the devil and his angels" (Mat 25:41).

nm149 » This *aionios* fire is an *aionios* punishment: "And these shall go away into *aionios* punishment" (Mat 25:46). As shown in the

"Thousand Years and Beyond Paper" [NM 15] this fire is mainly for the twisted spirits of Satan because people can't live in fire. People die in fire. But with this fire many will die. Their punishment is death from the fire. But the twisted spirits will be punished in the fire because they can't die in it.

nm150 » This *aionios* fire, this *aionios* punishment is an agelasting destruction away from the glory of the Lord in his 1000 year rule: "The Lord Jesus shall be revealed from heaven with his mighty angels, In flaming fire taking vengeance on them that know not God, and that obey not the good-news of our Lord Jesus Christ: Who [those not knowing God] shall be punished with *aionios* destruction from the presence of the Lord, and from the glory of his power" (2Thes 1:7-9).

Aeonian or Agelasting Life versus Immortal Life

nm151 » Now the Bible speaks of an *aionios* life, thus an *age*lasting or aeonian life. As shown in the "Reward for Christians" paper [NM 11] this age-life begins at the beginning of the 1000 year rule of Christ the God. Of course, since this coming new age will never end, the *aionios* life continues after the 1000 years. There are at least 44 scriptures mentioning the *aionios* life and other scripture mentioning the age-life for those who are in God (see the Englishman's Greek Concordance under *aionios*; See "Reward for Christians Paper" [NM 11] and other papers for more detail on this *age*lasting "life."). When one is resurrected in the resurrection at Christ's coming, he/she will receive immortal life *and* he/she will live during an *aionios* period of 1000 years, *and* will also live after that 1000 year age into the next age or endless period of time since he/she will be immortal. It is possible for someone to live in the aeonian life and be mortal for those physically born during the 1000 years will be mortal. There is a difference between immortal life and aeonian life as explained in the *Reward for Christians* paper [NM 11].

Two Ages: One Ends; One Does Not End

Old Age

nm152 » There are two main ages. There is Satan's age of confusion with its spirit of confusion. There is the True God's age of harmony with its Spirit of harmony. Matthew 12:32 speaks about the present age (*aion*) and about the coming age. The KJV translates *aion* as "world." In Matthew 13:22 it speaks about, "the care of this *aion* [KJV, "world"], and the deceitfulness of riches." In Matthew 13:39-40 it speaks about "the end of the world," that is the end of the age (*aion*). There is a certain "wisdom" of this age or aion (1Cor 2:6). There are certain children of this age (Luke 16:8; 20:34 - KJV "world"). These children are of the devil (Mat 13:38-40). There is a god of this age or *aion* (2Cor 4:4; KJV, "world"). People fight "against the rulers of darkness of this age [*aion*]" (Eph 6:12).

New Age

nm153 » Scripture indicates that the end of this wicked age comes at the beginning of the new age – at Jesus Christ's coming. (Mat 13:38-40; 24:3-31; 2Thes 2:1, 8; Rev 11:15; 12:10-11; 20:1-5; Dan 2:44; 7:17-18, 25-27; see "Beast Paper" [PR2, PR3], "God's Wrath Paper" [PR4], etc.)

nm154 » There is a coming age at the end of the old wicked age. Such scriptures as Mark 10:30; Luke 18:30; 20:35; Eph 1:21 in the Greek text indicate this. This New Age (*aion*) or agelasting (*aionios*) period under God's Spirit will not end as Luke 1:33, Dan 2:44, and Dan 7:14 indicate. But during this endless age their will be the 1000 year age in which some will be punished. After this age there is another short age called the Great Last Day (see "Thousand Years and Beyond Paper" [NM 15] and others).

Why Misusage of these Words?

nm155 » There could easily be a book written on the story behind the misusage of *olam* and *aionios*. One reason was some of the early fathers of the Catholic Church such as Augustine relied too heavily on the Greek literature especially Plato's to obtain doctrine instead of relying on Biblical scripture. Augustine used the faulty Greek text of the Old Testament instead of the inspired Hebrew text (*City of God*, book 18, chapter 43). Some of the very arguments used by Augustine to "prove" that *aionios* means eternal (*City of God*, book 21, chapters 23, 10-22, 9; etc.) are used today by theologians and preachers to "prove" that *aionios* means eternal (Berkhof's *Systematic Theology*, "The Duration of their Punishment," p. 736; etc.).

nm156 » We should no longer take our doctrine on the God and His ages from Plato or the other Greeks. The truth is found in the Bible, not Greek literature. Do read all our papers on Christianity to better understand the age plan of God.

Review And Further Arguments for the Use of *Age*lasting or Aeonian

nm157 » The Issue:

- The misuse of the words "forever," "everlasting," and "eternal" instead of the correct usage of "age" or "aeonian."

nm158 » The Question:

- Why do Christians teach of an "everlasting" damnation (death or punishment) when the very word "everlasting" from which these Christians obtain their doctrine is a mistranslation according to reliable Biblical aids?

Explain to me why Christians use the traditional mistranslation of the Hebrew word *olam* and the Greek word *aionios* instead of the inspired meaning of these words?

Significance:

nm159 »

- The great importance of using the correct translation is that it opens up highly important truths of the Bible. If one takes the literal meaning of these words every place they appear in the Bible, an "age" plan of God is projected.

Further Response to the Arguments of Context

nm160 »

1. *The use of the context argument in the English language.*

   One way to disprove the context argument is to try and use the English word "age" to mean "everlasting" or "eternal." This can *not* be reasonably done.

2. *The quantity of misusage of the Hebrew and Greek words for age.*

   If the context argument is correct then why should the great majority of the original words, that mean "age" in Hebrew and Greek be translated to mean "forever"? It would be more reasonable if most of the original words were translated with their literal meaning instead of their evolved "context" meaning.

3. *Why didn't the writers of the Bible use other words or phrases in Greek that meant everlasting or eternal?*

   If the context argument is correct, in that the Greek word that means "age" should be read "forever" because of the context, then *why* didn't the original writers use other Greek words or phrases that literally meant "forever" when they were writing? No, they used words that meant literally *age*lasting because they were speaking of an *age*lasting time not an everlasting time. The writers of the

Bible were referring to the time of *olam* that Adam and Eve missed by their sin (Gen 3:22).

4. *The dubiousness of writers using two different languages using words that literally mean "age" which they intended to be understood by their readers to mean "everlasting."*

The fact that the two main original languages of the Bible have words that mean "agelasting," which are said to mean "everlasting" because of their usage in context, helps to rule out the argument of context. Maybe, just maybe, *one* language could use a word that literally means "agelasting" in context so as to mean "everlasting." But both of the languages used words that literally meant "*age*lasting" to describe the agelasting reward and agelasting punishment of Christians and non-Christians because they were speaking of an *age*-time reward and punishment not an everlasting reward and punishment.

5. *The dubiousness of most of the 40 or so writers of the Bible using words that literally meant "age" which they meant to be understood by their readers to mean "everlasting."*

Maybe some of the writers would use words that mean "agelasting" in context to mean "everlasting," but surely not most of them.

6. *On the passages such as Romans 16:26 where if taken literally God would be an agelasting God in some aspect.*

Now there are many other places where it indicates that God is in someway an eternal God. God is in a sense eternal – His Power. But in another sense he is also an *age*lasting God. He is an agelasting God because His age begins in the coming 1000 years of the Kingdom of God. This is the age when God is King of kings, this is the age wherein God will rule all. In the present age God is not the God of the world, for Satan is now that god (2Cor. 4:4). The new age of the true God will not end (Luke 1:33; Dan 2:44; etc.). The new age is different from the age of Satan, for Satan's age will end when God's age begins.

7. *On the reward for Christians – agelasting life.*

Christians live the agelasting life as servant-rulers under Christ, but since they also are made immortal at the beginning of the 1000 year age (1Cor 15:52-54), then they live on forever after that 1000 year age (see "Reward for Christians" paper [NM 11]). This 1000 year age is an age within an age or within the great age or great ages. The great age is the *olam* or *aion* of God, and this new age of ages will not end (Luke 1:33; Dan 2:44; 7:14; Isa 9:6-7).

Everliving? or Ageliving

Rosetta Stone: Egyptian Holy or Hieroglyphic Script.

nm161 » The error of turning words that mean age into everlasting is not confined to the Bible. Of some interest is the translation of the Egyptian hieroglyphic signs into "everliving." On the Rosetta Stone certain hieroglyphs were translated into, "everliving." On the Rosetta Stone there are two languages: Egyptian and Greek. The Egyptian language is cut into the stone in two different kinds of characters: (1) Hieroglyphic characters were used for state and ceremonial documents that were intended to be seen by the public; and (2) Demotic characters, were "the conventional, abbreviated and modified form of the Hieratic character, or cursive form of hieroglyphic writing, which was in use in the Ptolemaic Period" (E.A. Wallis Budge, *The Rosetta Stone*, Ares Publishers; Chicago:1980, reprint of 1922 work, p. 2). The Greek portion of the inscription was cut into the stone in ordinary uncials. "The inscription on the Rosetta Stone is a copy of the Decree passed by the General Council of Egyptian priests assembled at Memphis to celebrate the first commemoration of the coronation of Ptolemy V. Epiphanes, king of all Egypt" (p. 7). This coronation of Ptolemy to king of Egypt took place about 196 BC. "The original form of the Decree is given by the Greek section, and the Hieroglyphic and Demotic versions were made from it" (p. 7).

Greek/English Translation of "Everliving"

nm162 » In Budge's *The Rosetta Stone*, he has the translation of the Greek into English. On lines 4, 8, 37, 49, and 54 of the translation he has the Greek *aionobioy* translated into "everliving." But this Greek word is made up of two parts. The Greek *aion* is the word for "age" or "era." The Greek *bioy* is the genitive singular for *bios*, which means "life" or "living." Thus this Greek word means "age-living" or "era-living" or in a sense "long-living." This word does not mean everliving.

Copic Translation of "Eternity"

nm163 » Quoting Budge from page 6,

- it was therefore guessed that the next sign [the next part of the hieroglyphic signs translated into "everliving"] meant "ever." Coptic again showed that one of the old Egyptian words for "ever, age, eternity," was Djet, and as we already know that the phonetic value of the second sign in the word is T, we may assume that the value of [sign] is DJ.

Budge attempts to show in another way through a Coptic word that a certain hieroglyphic sign means "everliving." But notice this Coptic word means, "ever, age, eternity." Here it is again, the mixing of the word age with eternity. But as we see using the Greek translation of the Rosetta Stone, this sign reads "age-living" or "long-living" or "era-living." Remember the original was written in Greek and the Egyptian translation was taken from the Greek.

Egyptian's "Everlastingness," "Eternity," or "Millions of Years"

nm164 » In Budge's, *The Gods of the Egyptians*, this **same** hieroglyphic sign mentioned on page 6 of Budge's, *The Rosetta Stone*, is translated as either "ever" or "everlastingness" (Vol 1, pp 54-55, line 521). But also note that the hieroglyphic sign, *heh*, is translated "eternity" in line 520 of this same book. Yet,

- "according to Dr. Brugsch the name Heh is connected with the word which indicates an undefined and unlimited number, *i.e., heh*, when applied to time the idea suggested is "millions of years," and Heh is equivalent to the Greek αιων [*aion*]" (Budge, *The Gods of the Egyptians*, Vol 1, p. 285).

Thus, the sign, *heh*, is wrongly translated as "eternity" and sometimes translated "millions of years," but is equivalent to the Greek *aion*, which we have seen in this paper means an age of undefined time.

To Conclude

nm165 » Not only was the Bible mistranslated, but what we are manifesting here is that one should be very careful when reading translations in general. There is a bias against translating words or signs that mean "age" correctly. They prefer the hyperbolic mistranslations of "forever," "everlasting," or "eternity." Be careful.

The Saying, "To the Age"

nm166 » A saying that goes back to ancient time is, "long live the king." Or in the Bible it has it:

- "let live my lord king David to *olam*" (1Kings 1:31)

- "the king to *olam* live" (Neh 2:3)

- "king to *alam* live" (Dan 2:4; 3:9; 5:10; 6:6, 21)

nm167 » As we have learned in the "Age Paper" [NM 7] *olam* or *alam* means a hidden age or time. It in fact is that great age of the kingdom of God promised since the garden of Eden after mankind lost the right to "live to *olam*" (Gen 3:22, see Hebrew). The Hebrew preposition *el*, which means to or towards or into, is connected in the above verses with the Hebrew *olam* or *alam*, thus our translation of "to *olam*" or "to (the) age." Throughout my life I have heard the saying "til kingdom come" or "to kingdom come." These sayings are versions of the Bible's 'to *olam*,' that is, to (the) age of the kingdom.

Examples in the NT

KJV Revelation 20:10 And the devil that deceived them was cast into the lake of fire and brimstone, where the beast and the false prophet *are*, and shall be tormented day and night for **ever and ever**.

YLT Revelation 20:10 and the Devil, who is leading them astray, was cast into the lake of fire and brimstone, where {are} the beast and the false prophet, and they shall be tormented day and night--to the **ages of the ages**.

GNT Revelation 20:10 καὶ ὁ διάβολος ὁ πλανῶν αὐτοὺς ἐβλήθη εἰς τὴν λίμνην τοῦ πυρὸς καὶ θείου ὅπου καὶ τὸ θηρίον καὶ ὁ ψευδοπροφήτης, καὶ βασανισθήσονται ἡμέρας καὶ νυκτὸς εἰς τοὺς <u>αἰῶνας τῶν αἰώνων</u>.

NM 8: Predestinated: Called and Chosen

Many are Called, Few are Chosen
Christians are Predestinated
God Chooses
Predestinated to Destruction?
Two Groups
Losing God's Spirit?
Chosen are Called
Are you Predestinated?

NM8 Abstract

Why are many called, but few chosen? Why does the Bible say that Christians are predestinated if there is no predestination? And if there is predestination, how can God damn anyone forever who was predestinated to do evil? Predestination is a difficult subject for anyone who believes in the false translation we corrected in NM7. When you understand the mistranslation of the Bible corrected in NM7, you will understand how there can be a logical doctrine of predestination.

nm168 » The doctrine of Predestination has been twisted and turned by those who do not understand the great power of God. What is the Biblical definition of "predestination," being "called," and being "chosen"? There is a difference between being just called or invited to the kingdom of God than being called, chosen, and predestinated. Let's define these three words found in the King James Version. These words were translated from Greek words which were inspired to be written through the power of God (2Pet 1:20-21).

- *Predestination* (#4309, from 4253 & 3724) means, to be marked off beforehand.

- *Chosen* (#1588 & 1586; O.T. #977) means, to be laid out or chosen or select.

- *Called* (#2821, 2822, 2564) means, to be invited.

Many are Called but Few are Chosen

nm169 » There is a difference between being just called and being chosen, "for many are called but few are chosen" (Mat 22:14; 20:16). Many are called or invited to God's kingdom, but few are chosen for that kingdom. Many will be invited to be in the new reality of God, but few will be in it at its beginning. In fact near the end of the age of Satan's kingdom (the old age) all will be invited to the kingdom of God (see Mat 24:14; Mark 16:15; Psa 19:4; Col 1:23), but few are chosen. We notice that at Christ's coming "they that are with him are called, and chosen, and faithful" (Rev 17:14). We need to know what the Bible means by being chosen, and being predestinated.

Father Chose Before the Foundation of the World

nm170 » "According as He [the Father] has *chosen us* in him [Christ] *before the foundation of the world* [cosmos], that we should be holy and without blame before him in love: Having *predestinated* us unto the adoption of children by Jesus Christ to Himself, according to the good pleasure of His [the Father's] will" (Eph 1:4-5). "In whom also we have obtained an inheritance, being *predestinated according to the purpose of Him* who works all things after the counsel of His own will" (Eph 1:11).

Chosen <u>Before</u> the Cosmos

When scripture says that God chose or predestinated before the foundation of the world (Eph1:4-5; 1Pet 1:19-20), since the word "world" is from the Greek *kosmos*, this means God predestinated <u>before</u> the creation (cosmos), <u>before</u> good (as we know it), <u>before</u> evil (as we know it), <u>before</u> law (as we know it), and consequently <u>before</u> sin (as we know it).

nm171 » The ones chosen, thus, were chosen by the Father "before the foundation of the world," and these chosen were predestinated to "the adoption of children [of God] through Jesus Christ." And these predestinated to be children of God were predestinated "according to the good pleasure of His [God's] will."

Foreknown, Predestinated, Called, Justified & Glorified

nm172 » "And we know that all things work together for good to them that love God, to them who are called according to his purpose. For those he did *foreknow*, he also did *predestinate* to be conformed to the image of his Son, that he [His son] might be the first-born among many brethren. Moreover those he did *predestinate*, them he also *called*: and those he called, them he also *justified*: and those he justified, them he also *glorified*" (Rom 8:28-30).

nm173 » We see that those predestinated, God also did foreknow. Now from Ephesians 1:4-5 we see that the chosen are predestinated and that they were predestinated before the world began. And here in Romans 8:29 we see God foreknew those who are "predestinated to be conformed to the image of his Son," or to be a child of God. And we see

(Rom 8:28) that those called according to God's purpose are the ones who were foreknown and predestinated.

nm174 » Then in Romans 8:30 we see those predestinated are called or invited. Called for what? They are called "according to his [God's] purpose" (v. 28). Now those called (who were predestinated) are justified (v. 30). As we see in the paper on justification [NM 18] those justified are those who have God's Spirit or the new mind.

Christians Are Predestinated

nm175 » Thus, those *chosen*, were chosen before the world began (Eph 1:4). And these are predestinated to be children of God (Eph 1:5). And those chosen and predestinated are called according to God's purpose (Rom 8:28). Also these were foreknown and predestinated to conform to the image of Christ (Rom 8:29). We also see those chosen, predestinated, foreknown, and called are justified (Rom 8:30). From the paper on justification (see "Other Papers" section [NM 18]) we know that those justified have become real Spiritual Christians. And in Romans 8:30 we see that those justified "he also glorified." Hence, real Christians are the ones chosen, predestinated, and called. This is confirmed in God's word:

- "*Elect* [chosen] according to the *foreknowledge* of God the Father, through sanctification of the Spirit, unto obedience and sprinkling of blood of Jesus Christ: Grace unto you, and peace, be multiplied" (1Pet 1:2).

- "But we are bound to give thanks always to God for you, brethren beloved of the Lord, because *God has from the beginning chosen you* to salvation through sanctification of the Spirit and belief of the truth" (2Thes 2:13).

- "Who has saved us, and called us with a *holy calling*, not according to our works, but according to his own purpose and grace, *which was given us in Christ Jesus before the world began*" (2Tim 1:9).

- "But *you are a chosen generation*, a royal priesthood, a holy nation, a peculiar people; that you should show forth the praises of him who has *called you* out of darkness into his marvelous light" (1Pet 2:9).

nm176 » Furthermore, the word *elect* (#1588 &1589) used to describe Christians in the New Testament means "chosen;" and *Saint* (#6918) means "set apart" or "sacred." The real Christians were set apart, chosen, and predestinated before the world began as the above scriptures clearly indicate. And now the chosen are being called or invited.

Christians Predestinated for Good

nm177 » Notice the real Christians were "created in Christ Jesus unto good works, which God has before ordained that we [Christians] should walk in them" (Eph 2:10). Christians were not predestinated to be free to do anything, but to do good works. The very proof that one is a Christian is that he does good works (see "Proof Paper" [NM 10]).

God Chooses

nm178 » Hear what Christ says: "you have not chosen me, but I have chosen you, and ordained you" (John 15:16). No one can choose to follow Christ, unless Christ has chosen them. Yet Christ only does the will of his Father (John 6:38). Christ chooses what his Father chose for him. Is this confirmed anywhere else in the Bible? "No man can come to me, except the Father which has sent me draw him" (John 6:44).

nm179 » The only way to follow Christ is Spiritually with the aid of God's Spirit (John 4:23-24). "Jesus says unto him, I am the way, the truth, the life: no man comes unto the Father, but by me" (John 14:6). No one comes to the Father's Spirit (see verses 5-10) except through Christ. One comes to the Father's Spirit through Christ, but it is God who chooses (Eph 1:4-5). Although Christ also chooses, he chooses only what his Father wills (John 6:44). One can only come to the Father's Spirit if the Father draws that one to himself through Christ.

God Draws To Himself Through Grace

nm180 » And how does the Father draw one to himself through Christ? "But when it pleased God ... called me [Paul] by his grace" (Gal 1:15). Now grace is merely a free spiritual gift of God. One form of grace is Faith (1Cor 12:9). And it is through the medium of this Faith of God's Spirit (Gal 5:22; Eph 2:8) that God baptizes his chosen.

nm181 » No man can come to Christ or choose Christ unless God the Father draws him through his grace. "All that the Father gives me shall come to me" (John 6:37). And, "Holy Father, keep them in your own name which you have given me, that they may be one, as we are" (John 17:11). It is God the Father that gives the chosen to Christ (Eph 1:3-4; John 17:11; John 6:44), and no one can come to Christ unless the Father has chosen them (John 6:44; Eph 1:4-5). What does this mean?

nm182 » These scriptures mean exactly what they say! None can come to Christ to be a Christian unless they were chosen before the foundation of the world. One, if he was not predestinated to be a Christian, cannot come to Christ's body or Church.

Marriage as a type

nm183 » God has made the physical to be a type of the Spiritual or the true reality (Rom 1:20). The physical marriage between man and woman prefigured the true marriage – the marriage of Christ to his wife, the Church (Rev 19:7). Now, who traditionally has chosen the bride? – the man. Yet it was traditional that the man only chose a bride that was acceptable to his parents. In fact the parents usually chose the bride for him. It was the parents who made the arrangements for their children (Gen 21:21; 24:3-4). God the Father was the parent of Christ. And in God's Word it says that God the Father has chosen those who will be in the Spiritual marriage to Christ. The physical arrangements for marriage prefigured the true arrangement that God the Father made before the beginning of the cosmos, the Spiritual wedding of his Son to his Son's wife – the Church. It is the real Christians who are chosen and predestinated to be the Spiritual wife of Christ. Only those chosen, will be married to Christ. Is this confirmed yet again in God's word?

Predestinated to Destruction?

nm184 » "Has not the potter power over the clay, of the same lump to make one vessel unto honor, and another unto dishonor? What if God, willing to show his wrath, and to make his power known, endured with much long-suffering the vessels of wrath fitted to destruction. And that he might make known the riches of his glory on the vessels of mercy, which he had before prepared unto glory" (Rom 9:21-23). The potter is God as such verses as Jer 18:6 and Isa 45:9 show. But what is being said here?

nm185 » God has prepared from the same lump of clay: vessels of destruction and vessels of mercy, and the latter were before prepared unto glory? Has God prepared some for destruction? In Jude 4 it speaks of those "who were before of old ordained to this condemnation, ungodly men." And, "the LORD (Jehovah) has made all things for himself; yea, even the wicked for the day of evil" (Prov 16:4). "Even to them which stumble at the word, being disobedient: whereunto also they were *appointed*" (1Pet 2:8).

nm186 » We have already shown you that real Christians were chosen and predestinated before the foundations of the world to become Christians unto good works. Now we see that the others were prepared for destruction. But remember, God predestinated everything <u>before</u> the creation, thus before time (as we know it), before good (as we know it), before evil (as we know it), before law (as we know it), and thus before sin (as we know it).

nm187 » The true Christians are "not appointed as to wrath, but to obtain salvation by our Lord Jesus Christ" (1Thes 5:9). "I make peace, and create evil: I the LORD [Jehovah] do all these things" (Isa 45:7). Are we to take these words literally? If you do not, you have nothing to base your faith on. One cannot read and believe one part of the Bible and then pass over another part. Let's look closer at this apparent problem.

Two Groups

nm188 » The Bible clearly speaks of two groups of people: the "dead" and the "living," the children of the devil and the children of God, the children of wrath and the children of light, and so forth. One group is identified with God and his way. These belong to the "living." The other group follows the way of destruction. These belong to the "dead." The group that follows God's way are the vessels of mercy. The other group are the vessels of wrath. One was appointed to salvation; the other group was appointed to wrath (1Thes 5:9). They were appointed before the foundation of the world as Ephesians 1:4 and Jude 4 tells us. Now those chosen to be Christians are created "unto good works" (Eph 2:10). In fact it can be proven that doing good works is a proof of one's own Christianity (see "Proof Paper" [NM 10]). The chosen group of God does good works as opposed to the other group which follows in the ways of confusion. Now is this fair that one group is set up one way and the other group another way?

Is God fair?

nm189 » Is God fair? Can God predestinate one group to mercy and another group to wrath and still be fair?

- "So then He has mercy on whom He desires, and He hardens whom He desires. 19 You will say to me then, 'Why does He still find fault? For who resists His will?' 20 On the contrary, who are you, O man, who answers back to God? The thing molded will not say to the molder, 'Why did you make me like this,' will it?" (Rom 9:18-20)

- "Shall the clay say to him that fashions it, What are you doing? or to your work, He has no hands? Woe unto him that says unto his father, What are you doing? or to the woman, What have you brought forth?" (Isa 45:9-10)

- "Yet the children of your people say, The way of the Lord is not equal. O you house of Israel, I will judge you every one after his ways" (Ezek 33:17, 20; see 18:30).

nm190 » God judges man according to man's ways, according to his works, according to his behavior. This means that those who do evil will destroy the world by their own behavior (See PR4 to PR6) and their own destruction will judge them (NM24). Each group was prepared before the cosmos began either to do good works, or to do the works of confusion. This means they were predestinated <u>before</u> good (as we know it), <u>before</u> evil (as we know it), <u>before</u> law (as we know it), and <u>before</u> sin (as we know it). You cannot accuse God of sin for something done before there was law or even a cosmos.

Seven Days to Finish the Creation

nm191 » Also the type and antitype nature of the Bible teaches us that we are now in the midst of a creation process. God is now creating, and has yet to finish. Look at the typical creation mentioned in the book of Genesis. First God created the universe in seven days: actively working for six days (Gen 1:1-31), but also in some way finishing the creation on the seventh day (Gen 2:2). Accordingly, it will only be on the antitypical seventh day that God's real work will be complete (NM15; NM16; NM26). As we learn in other parts of this book, there are seven 1000 year periods or days wherein God is creating the knowledge of good and evil, the knowledge of time, the knowledge of peace, the knowledge of paradise and other important spiritual things. Therefore it will not be until the end of the seventh 1000 year period that mankind will be atoned, and consequently be brought back into the great God. All at the beginning went out of God, but all by the end of creation will be brought back into God. This is called the Great Cycle (NM13, "Three Divisions"). We are now in the midst of a creation process, and therefore anything being created in it is not yet done. The creation will only be good at the end of the creation process, when all are back into God (1Cor 15:28), when only the One God is in the truest sense, good (Mat 19:17, see Greek text). God is only One, when all come back into the God (1Cor 15:28; GP6). Even the scriptures about Jesus Christ being now at the right side of God (Psa 110:1; Acts 2:32-35; Heb 2:7-10) tell us that all things are not yet under Christ, but all will be: "But now we see not yet all things put under him" (Heb 2:8). The creation is not yet finished in the truest sense. All must be under Christ, then, and only then, will all be back in God, so that God will be all in all, so that, God will be ONE. When the antitypical creation is finished, no one can accuse God of being partial, for as we see in NM13 and GP6, God will bring all back into God, so that God will be all in all (1Cor 15:28). The creation is similar to a clay pot, and God is the potter forming the pot. When the potter is making the pot there is waste (vessels of wrath), but God is perfect and will not waste any material in the process of making the pot. God will pick up the clay discarded on the ground and reintroduce it back into the clay pot, so all will be in the pot (new creation). As we cannot blame the potter for any spillage, until he has totally completed his work, we also cannot blame God for any temporary waste, until he has finished all in all.

nm192 » Read the "Reason Why" paper [NM 19] to understand *why* God did such a thing. Also, after you read the *God Papers* you will understand that God the Father gave all his power to his Son, Jesus Christ. Jesus Christ is our God and he has done no wrong. Jesus Christ is now the right side of God's power. If Jesus Christ is the right side, who is the left side? In the *God Papers* we prove that the left side of God is the evil facet of God (Isa 45:7) that was predestinated by God before law and before sin, and thus we cannot find fault with God over this matter. God who is *all* powerful even has power over evil, for he somehow has created evil (Isa 45:7). We cannot speak of this in detail here. We cover the left side of God in the *God Papers*. It should be noted here that predestination was done <u>before</u> the creation, thus before law and sin.

Both Groups Exercise Each Other

nm193 » It is true that there are two groups on the earth today. One group is appointed to God and one group is appointed to Satan. Each group is against the other as the law of confusion is against the law of love. Each is exercising the other. Satan's way and his group are allowing the world to learn of evil. God's group has come out of the other group, and they have a changed attitude towards the world's way. And God's group is now learning of good through God's Spirit given to them. God has granted one group mercy. These are the vessels of mercy (Rom 9:23). It is through the vessels of mercy that all will eventually learn of good through the kingdom of God or the rulership of God. All will eventually be saved (see "All Saved Paper" [NM 13]). Each group is now using each other in order to produce the knowledge of good and evil (see the *God Papers*).

nm194 » All people in this old age are, or were, in Satan's group, but to the predestinated vessels of mercy, God has given mercy by allowing them to see the true light. The vessels of Satan's group are vessels from the same lump of clay but are fitted to destruction – aeonian punishment (Mat 25:46). The vessels of God's group are the vessels of mercy who will have aeonian life while the other group has aeonian death away from the glory of the millennium (2Thess 1:9; see *Last Judgment*).

nm195 » Can any of Satan's group become through any effort of their own a part of God's group? "No man can come to me, except the Father which has sent me draw him," answers Christ (John 6:44). "Consider the work of God: for who can make straight, which he made crooked? ... that which is crooked cannot be made straight" (Eccl 7:13; 1:15). Spiritually, only God can make the crooked things straight (Isa 42:16).

Losing God's Spirit?

nm196 » Can a Christian return completely to Satan's group after he has turned to God? "And grieve not the holy Spirit of God whereby you are sealed unto the day of redemption" (Eph 4:30; see Isa 59:21).

nm197 » Can one lose the New Mind or Spirit of God after he has received it? The following scriptures tell us no!

- "Of them which you gave me I have lost none" (John 18:9).

- "All that the Father gives me shall come to me; and him that comes to me I will in no way cast out" (John 6:37).

- "And this is the Father's will which has sent me, that all which he has given me I should lose nothing, but should raise it up again at the last day" (John 6:39).

- "No man can come to me, except the Father has sent me draw him: and I will raise him up at the last day. It is written in the prophets, and they shall be all taught of God. Every man therefore that has heard, and has learned of the Father, comes unto me" (John 6:44-45). That is, all that learns Spiritually or hears Spiritually will come to Christ.

- "And when he puts forth his own sheep he goes before them, and the sheep follow him: for they know his voice" (John 10:4).

- "My sheep hear my voice, and I know them, and they follow me: and I give unto them aeonian life; and they shall *not* be destroyed for the age, neither shall any man pluck them out of my hand. My Father, which gave them to me, is greater than all; and no one is able to pluck them out of my Father's hand" (John 10:27-29).

nm198 » Notice that Jesus said no one could take those chosen out of his Father's hand – that means a chosen one himself has no power to change his predestination:

■ "While I was with them in the world, I kept them in your NAME, which you have given me, and I have kept, and none of them is lost, but the son of perdition; that the scripture might be fulfilled" (John 17:12).

nm199 » If Christ was not lying when he said he lost none, then Judas was not a chosen one of God the Father. That is, Judas was not chosen to salvation, but to wrath.

Chosen Are Called

nm200 » Those chosen, predestinated before the world began are called: "and the sheep follow him: for they know his voice" (John 10:4). Further, "all that the Father gives me shall come to me" (John 6:37).

nm201 » Why are there *many* called, but *few* chosen? (Mat 22:14) For the whole world is invited or called to the kingdom of God (Mat 24:14; Mark 16:15; Psa 19:4; Col 1:23), but only a few of these were predestinated and chosen to begin that kingdom. It is those who are of the chosen who hear the words of the calling and understand (John 10:4, 27).

Predestinated: Are You to Live in The 1000 Years?

nm202 » Are you one of the called, predestinated, and chosen to live in and throughout the New Age during the first 1000 years? Your proof is in your good works. If one is not doing works of the Spirit then they do not have the New Mind or Spirit of God (see "Proof Paper" [NM 10]).

Why Have Some Been Chosen?

nm203 » "I returned, and saw under the sun, that the race is not to the swift, nor the battle to the strong, neither yet bread to the wise, nor riches to men of understanding, nor yet favor to men of skill; but *time and chance happens to them all*" (Eccl 9:11). "For you see your calling, brethren, how that not many wise men according to the flesh, not many mighty, not many noble, are called: But God has chosen the foolish things of the world to confuse the wise; and God has chosen the weak things of the world to confuse the things which are mighty; And the base things of the world, and things which are despised, has God chosen, yea, and things which are not, to bring to nought things that are: *That no flesh should boast in his presence*" (1Cor 1:26-29).

nm204 » Those chosen where chosen by time and chance, and were mostly from the unwise in the ways of the world. And these were chosen for good works (Eph 2:10).

NM 9: Free Will versus Predestination

God Predestinates All Things
Free Will
Free Will v. Happiness
Self-righteousness and Free Will
Job Seemed Upright
God Answers Job
Way to Wisdom and Knowledge
God Does All

NM9 Abstract

If there is predestination, how can there be free will? Or, if there is free will, how can there be predestination? We learned about predestination in NM8. There is ample scripture that tells us that God in some way is all powerful and is our creator. Knowing this, in this paper we will learn that true free will is impossible when you have a creator who made us and is making us into what he wishes us to be. We will also study the book of Job in order to better understand this subject.

Many Predestination Scriptures: Most Still Believe in Free Will

nm205 » Many refuse to believe in predestination even though the scripture clearly teaches that the God has predestinated everything to be as it was, as it is, and as it will be. They believe in "free will." In this paper we will contrast the "free will" scriptures and arguments against the predestination scriptures.

nm206 » In the paper, "Predestination: Called and Chosen" [NM 8], we saw many of the predestination scriptures. Some are chosen to mercy; some are chosen even to wrath. Christians were chosen and predestinated for good while others were chosen for wrath and evil. There is a reason for this.

God Predestinates All Things

nm207 » God in someway has predestinated, chosen, elected, ordained, set apart beforehand, or set in motion before the cosmos, before good, before evil, before law, and thus before sin:

- The nation of Israel [Deut 7:7-8; 10:15; 1Sam 12:22; Psa 135:4]

- Jacob versus Esau [Mal 1:2-3; Rom 9:11-13]

- The Christians [Eph 1:4-5,11; Acts 10:41; Rom 8:28-29; 1Thes 5:9; 2Thes 2:13; 2Tim 1:9; 1Pet 5:10]

- The Church [Acts 2:47; 1Pet 1:2; 2John 1:2]

- The Christ [1Pet 1:19-20; 2:6; Isa 42:1; Luke 24:26-27; see *All the Messianic Prophecies of the Bible*, by Lockyer; etc.]

- Christ's death [Acts 4:27-28; 2:23; 3:18; 1Pet 1:19-20]

- The results of sin [Gen 2:7; 3:16-19; Rom 5:12; 6:23

- Nations and their leaders [Jer 18:7, 9; 1:10; Acts 17:26; Job 12:23-25; Dan 4:28-35; 2:44-45; 7:14]

- Individuals (and nations from some of these individuals) [Paul, 2Tim 1:1,11; Gal 1:15-16]

- Esau [Mal 1:2-3]

- Jacob [Mal 1:2-3]

- Pharaoh [Rom 9:17]

- Samson [Judges 13:3-5]

- Solomon [2Sam 7:12-1-3; 1Chron 22:6-19]

- Josiah [1Kings 13:2]

- Jeremiah [Jer 1:5]

- Cyrus [Isa 45:1]

- John the Baptist [Luke 1:13-17]

- Judas Iscariot [Acts 1:16-17]

- Jesus, see "Seed Paper" [PR1]

- Elijah [Mal 4:5; Mat 11:14; Luke 1:17; Mark 9:12]

- Noah, Abram or Abraham, Isaac, Pharaoh's butler, Joseph, Aaron, Angel of Yehowah, Korah, Dathan & Abiram, Moses, Judah, Simeon, Levi, Reuben, Zebulun, Issachar, Naphtali, Dan, Benjamin, Gideon, Manoah's wife, Ahab, Elisha, Jonah, etc (see *Encyclopedia of Biblical Prophecy*, by Payne, "Summary A & B").

- Vessels of wrath and of mercy [Rom 9:21-23]
- All those appointed to wrath, evil, condemnation, wickedness, etc. [Rom 9:21-23; Jude 1:4; Prov 16:4; 1Pet 2:8; see "Predestination Paper" (NM 8)]
- All generations [Isa 41:4]
- The future [Isa 41:4, 22, 26; 44:7; 46:9-11]

God Predestinates: Summary

- "Known unto God are all his works from the beginning of the world." [Acts 15:18]
- "God makes all things." [Eccl 11:5]

nm208 » God can and does predestinate all things because He is all knowing (1John 3:20; Psa 147:5), because he is all powerful (Gen 17:1; Rev 1:8; 4:8; 15:3), and because he creates all (Eccl 11:5; 2Chron 20:6; Eccl 11:5). God has even in some sense created evil (Isa 45:7; see *God Papers*). But God has promised that before the end he will make all that is crooked or dark – straight or light (Isa 42:16; 1Cor 15:24-28; see "All Saved Paper" [NM 13]). God will make the lamb live with the wolf (Isa 11:6, spiritual meaning, see *God Papers*). The answer to the paradox of the God creating evil, yet being Good, is explained in the *God Papers*. There is an answer to this.

Free Will

nm209 » But what about "free will"? Much of the "free will" doctrine comes from the Greeks and other ancients. In the truest sense of the word, no one is *free*, except God. It is God's will that will be done over and above all others' will (Isa 46:10-11; Acts 15:18). Since from the beginning God has through his power created all things with the laws concerning these things (Eccl 11:5; James 4:12; Isa 33:22), then all are limited by these laws. We have physical limitations. We can only run so fast, climb so high, or live so long. We have mental limitations. We can only think or concentrate on one thing at a time, while God can think on a million, a billion, a trillion ... things at one time. His mind is not limited like ours. There is some freedom within these laws. God could have limited our minds and ability so as to make it impossible for us to sin. But God gave us the apparent "freedom" to choose to sin (Gen 2:16-17; Deut 30:19-20). But if we choose sin, then there are evil results for this sin (Gen 2:17; Deut 28:15ff). And if we "choose" not to sin then there will be certain "rewards" (Deut 28:1-2ff). God judges solely by our ways or behavior (Ezek 18:20, 25, 30). If mankind kills those of mankind, then some of mankind will be killed (Rev 13:10; Gen 9:6).

Do we have Free Will?

No Power or Knowledge to Choose Good

nm210 » But do we have free-will? Did Israel have free-will? Do we have the power to choose not to sin? Did Israel have the power or freedom to choose not to sin?:

- "Moses summoned all the Israelites and said to them: 'Your eyes have seen all that the LORD did in Egypt to Pharaoh, to all his officials and to all his land. With you own eyes you saw those great trials, those miraculous signs and great wonders. **But to this day the LORD has not given you a mind that understands or eyes that see or ears that hear**.'" (Deut 29:2-4, NIV)

Israel, in fact, did not have the mind to understand. Mankind cannot please God (Rom 8:7-8). They cannot understand or please God because they do not have the power of the Spirit to see, and thus do not truly have the freedom to choose. Israel and mankind are blind. They have been limited. They cannot see the truth.

nm211 » Does mankind in this old age have the freewill to do good?

- "Because the carnal mind is enmity against God; for it is not subject to the law of God, nor indeed can be. **So then, those who are in the flesh cannot please God**" (Rom 8:7-8, NKJV).

Good Spirit Has the Power to Choose Good

nm212 » It is only when mankind gets the New Mind (the Spirit) that he understands and is able to choose the good:

- "And the LORD your God will circumcise your heart and the heart of your descendants ... that you may live" (Deut 30:6, NKJV).

- "In him you were also circumcised with the circumcision made without hands, by putting off the body of the sins of the flesh, by the circumcision of Christ" (Col 2:11).

- "For we are the circumcision, who worship God in Spirit . . ." (Phil 3:3).

- "These things we also speak, not in words which man's wisdom teaches but which the Holy Spirit teaches, comparing spiritual things with spiritual. But the natural man does not receive the things of the Spirit of God, for they are foolishness to him; nor can he know them, because they are spiritually discerned" (1Cor 2:13-14).

Those with the circumcised heart, the true circumcision of Christ, that is, the Spirit, can see and choose the good things of the Spirit of God.

Reasons For No Real Freedom to Choose Good

nm213 » There are some reasons for mankind and angelkind not having the power or freedom to choose good over evil:

nm214 »

- **Lack of Spirit.** Adam and Eve did not have the New Mind and therefore did not have the ability of obeying God (see "Old Mind Paper" [NM 20-21]). It is through the Spirit of God (the New Mind) that mankind is given the gifts of goodness (Gal 5:22-23). It is through the first sinner, Satan & his lie (Gen 3:4; John 8:44), that sin entered the world through the willingness of man (Gen 3:4-12; Rom 5:12).

nm215 »

- **Lack of Knowledge.** Mankind and angelkind at the beginning did not have the *knowledge* of good and evil. It was only after mankind ate from the tree of *knowledge* of good and evil that mankind and angelkind began to know about evil, and thus were, also in a manner, learning about good (see "Old Mind Paper" [NM 20-21], "Reason Why" paper [NM 19], and the *God Papers* [GP 7]). So in part and in one sense, the ignorance of both Satan and mankind led to the first sin.

nm216 »

- **God Created With Limitations.** But it was God's power that made all, with its limitations and abilities. And all that we are, or all that we have, comes from outside of us: "For what makes you differ from another? And what do you have that you did not receive? Now if you did indeed receive it, why do you glory as if you had not received it?" (1Cor 4:7) The lack of positive goodness on Satan and mankind's part was because God did not *give* Satan or mankind his own Good Spirit.

Freewill v. Happiness

nm217 » But if God at first gave mankind and angelkind (specifically Satan) his goodness, then how would we come to appreciate the goodness, how would we understand good, if we had never lived in an evil place? *If God had given us goodness and the environment of paradise (peace and harmony) at first with immortal life, we would never have been happy.* In order to be happy, in order to know good, in order to know peace, in order to know harmony, in order to know pleasure, in order to know life, we MUST first know unhappiness, evil, war, disharmony, pain and death. The very basic Law of Knowledge tells us that (see "Reason Why" paper [NM 19] and the *God Papers* [GP 7]). God has no pleasure in our present evil (Heb 10:8), He, of course, did not want or desire the evil period (sacrifice), but he knew that we first must suffer in order to know the Good and to be able to enjoy paradise. God by creating evil (Isa 45:7), in a sense through Satan, was creating good, because according to the Law of Knowledge:

> "Particularly, in the case of opposite qualities (good and evil) you must know *both* qualities to know either: you must compare each with the other to know either." (NM19)

Evil a Mistake?

nm218 » Since God is all powerful, He is in the last analysis responsible for evil. God did not make a mistake when he allowed evil through Satan. God created all and He knew what would happen when he created the universe and all that was in it. God at some time did create the angel Satan, although at first Satan did not appear as the evil Satan until God stated a law (see "Old Mind Paper" [NM 21]). Satan has not gone beyond what he was allowed to do (note Job 1:12; 2:6; see below). Satan's evil came about because he lacked the knowledge of good and evil and because he did not have the good Spirit. See and read all of the *God Papers* carefully to understand the paradox of God's goodness and his creating of evil through Satan. In this age for certain we can say that Satan is the power behind evil, and that God is the power behind good, but in a sense it is the God who has created evil (Isa 45:7), by predestinating evil before creation, before law (as we know it), and before sin (as we know it).

Self-righteousness and Freewill

nm219 » Those who do not believe in the Biblical doctrine of Predestination are in reality saying that their "good" behavior is because *they* are somehow doing this "good" through their *own* striving and thus are "qualifying" for or "earning" a reward – the kingdom of God (heaven, paradise, eternity, etc.). *They* are being good, thus will reap *their* just reward. They say or imply that their witnessing, or tithing, or going to church, or giving to the poor, or eating the right foods, or believing in the right doctrines are their means to their reward – God's Kingdom or paradise. They think (at least subconsciously) that they *deserve* God's good reward because of their apparent good behavior. They are being righteous through their own efforts: they are *self*-righteous. Let's study Job and his *self*-righteousness to understand why self-righteousness is wrong and to understand its connection to the freewill doctrine.

Job

Job Seemed Upright

nm220 » Job was a rich man from the land of Uz. "And this man was perfect and upright, and fearing God, and turning away from evil" (Job 1:1).

Satan against Job

nm221 » But Satan went against Job to test him with trials to see if he would still love God (1:6-12). After a great loss to his sheep, camels, servants, and sons and daughters (1:13-19), "Job rose up and tore his robe, and shaved his head. And he fell on the ground and worshiped. And he said, I came naked out of my mother's womb, and naked I shall return. Jehovah gave, and Jehovah has taken away. Blessed be the name of Jehovah. *In all this Job did not sin, nor charge wrong to God*" (1:20-21).

nm222 » To continue from the book of Job:

- Again a day came when the sons of God came to present themselves before Jehovah. And Satan also came among them to present himself before Jehovah. And Jehovah said to Satan, From where have you come? And Satan answered Jehovah and said, "From going to and fro in the earth, and walking up and down in it." And Jehovah said to Satan, "have you set your heart on My servant Job, that there is none like him in the earth, a perfect and upright man, fearing God, and turning away from evil? And he is still holding to his integrity, although you incited Me against him, to destroy him for nothing." And Satan answered Jehovah and said, "Skin for skin. Yea, all that a man has he will give for his life. Put out Your hand now and touch his bone and his flesh, and he will curse You to Your face." And Jehovah said to Satan, "Behold, He is in your hand; but save his life." And Satan went out from the presence of Jehovah. And he struck Job with bad burning ulcers from the sole of his foot to the top of his head. And he [Job] took a broken piece of pottery with which to scrape himself. And he sat down among the ashes. And his wife said to him, "Are you still holding fast to your integrity? Curse God and die!" But he said to her, "You speak as one of the foolish women speaks. Indeed shall we receive good at the hand of God, and shall we not receive evil?" In all this Job did not sin with his lips (Job 2:1-10).

nm223 » Then three of Job's friends came to him after hearing about his troubles: "They sat on the ground with him for seven days and seven nights. No one said a word to him, because they saw how great his suffering was" (Job 2:11-13).

nm224 » But after this Job "cursed the day of his birth" (Job 3:1). "why did I not perish at birth, and die as I came from the womb? ... I have no peace, no quietness; I have no rest, but only turmoil" (Job 3:11, 26; see 3:1-26).

Charge: Job Suffered Because He Sinned

nm225 » In chapter 4 to 36 Job's friends Eliphaz, Bildad, and Zophar gave discourses that suggested that Job's suffering was *only* because Job had sinned against God:

- Consider now: who, being innocent, has ever perished? Where were the upright ever destroyed? As I have observed, those who plow evil and those who sow trouble reap it (Job 4:7-8).

- Blessed is the man whom God corrects; so do not despise the discipline of the Almighty (Job 5:17).

- When your [Job's] children sinned against him [God], he gave them over to the penalty of their sin. [Job's children were destroyed by a natural disaster (Job 1:5, 18)]

- If you are pure and upright, even now he [God] will rouse himself on your behalf (Job 8:4,6).

- You [Job] say to God, My beliefs are flawless and I am pure in your sight ... If you put away the sin that is in your hand and allow no evil to dwell in your tent ... [then] you will surely forget your trouble ... Life will be brighter than noonday (Job 11:4, 14, 16, 17).

- All his days the wicked man suffers torment (Job 15:20).

- The lamp of the wicked is snuffed out (Job 18:5).

- A flood will carry off his house, rushing waters on the day of God's wrath. Such is the fate God allots the wicked (Job 20:28-29).

- Is it for your piety that he rebukes you and brings charges against you? Is not your [Job] wickedness great? Are not your sins endless? (Job 22:4-5)

- Submit to God and be at peace with him in this way prosperity will come to you (Job 22:21).

- Evil, a Mistake? How then can a man be righteous before God? (Job 25:4)

Job answered these charges: 'I am blameless'

nm226 »

- Teach me, and I will be quiet; show me where I have been wrong (Job 6:24).

- If I have sinned, what have I done to you, O Watcher of men? Why have you made me your target? (Job 7:20)

- How then can I dispute with him [God]? ... though I were innocent, I could not answer him (Job 9:14-15).

- Although I am blameless ... (Job 9:21)

- I loathe my very life ... I will say to God: Do not condemn me, but tell me what charges you have against me. Does it please you to oppress me, to spurn the work of your hands, while you smile on the schemes of the wicked? (Job 10:1-3)

- Though you know that I am not guilty . . . (Job 10:7)..

- If I sinned ... If I am guilty – woe to me (Job 10:14, 15).

- Now that I have prepared my case, I know I will be vindicated. Can anyone bring charges against me? If so, I will be silent and die (Job 13:18-19).

- How many wrongs and sins have I committed? Show me my offense and my sin (Job 13:23).

- My face is red with weeping, deep shadows ring my eyes; yet my hands have been free of violence and my prayer is pure (Job 16:16-17).

- Though I cry, 'I've been wronged!' I get no response (Job 19:7).

- I have kept to his way without turning aside (Job 23:11).

- As surely as God lives, who has denied me justice, the Almighty, who has made me taste bitterness of soul (Job 27:1). [Here Job accuses God of denying him justice.]

- I will never admit you [his friends] are in the right; til I die, I will no way deny my integrity. I will maintain my righteousness ... (Job 27:5-6).

- ...He will know that I am blameless (Job 31:6).

- Job runs through his list of his righteousness (see Job 31:1-40).

- But the text says, "So these three men stopped answering Job, because *he was righteous in his own eyes*" (Job 32:1).

Charge: Job Is Saying God Is Unjust

nm227 » Elihu, who had listened to the exchanges between Job and his three friends, answered correctly Job's cries:

- Job says, "I am innocent, but God denies me justice. Although I am right, I am considered a liar; although I am guiltless, his arrow inflects an incurable wound" (Job 34:5-6).

- For he says, "It *profits* a man nothing when he tries to please God" (Job 34:9).

- Therefore, O man of heart, listen to me; far be it from God to commit iniquity; and the Almighty, to do wrong. For He repays man's work to him; and according to a man's way.

Surely God will not do wickedly, nor will the Almighty pervert justice (Job 34:10-12).

■ He punishes them for their wickedness ... . They cause the cry of the poor to come before him ... But if he [God] remains silent, who can condemn him (Job 34:26, 28-29).

■ Job speaks without knowledge, his words lack insight, Oh, that Job might be tested to the utmost for answering like a wicked man. To his sins he adds rebellion (Job 34:35-37).

■ Yet you ask him. "What *profit* it to me, and what do I gain by not sinning?" (Job 35:3)

■ He [God] does not answer when men cry out because of the arrogance of the wicked (35:12).

■ So Job opens his mouth with empty talk; without knowledge he [Job] multiplies words (Job 36:16).

■ God is mighty, but does not despise men; he is mighty, and firm in his purpose (Job 36:5).

■ The godless in heart harbors resentment (Job 36:13).

■ How great is God – beyond our understanding (Job 36:26).

■ In his justice and great righteousness, he does not oppress (Job 37:23).

God Answers Job

nm228 » After this Jehovah answered Job "out of a whirlwind" stating some of his great power (see Job 38:1-40:7; and see Job 40:9-42:1) and then adding:

■ Would you discredit my justice? Would you condemn me to justify yourself? (Job 40:8)

Job Repents

nm229 » Job's reply to God:

■ I know that you [God] can do all things; no plan of yours can be thwarted. You asked, "Who is this [Job] that obscures my counsel without knowledge?" Surely I spoke of things I did not understand, things too wonderful for me to know (Job 42:2-3).

- My ears had heard of you but now my eyes have seen you.
  Therefore I despise myself and repent in dust and ashes
  (Job 42:5-6).

Job's Self-Righteousness

nm230 » Job was declared righteous *before* his hard testing by Satan
(1:1). Sometime after Job's friends mourned with him, and after Satan
tested Job the second time, Job did not recognize God's all mightiness –
that it is God who, in the truest sense, gives and takes away (Although,
immediately after the second testing by Satan, Job did verbally
recognize this. – Job 2:10). According to the text, Job did not do any
wrong until sometime after Satan tested him for the second time. And
because Job had done no wrong before Satan's testing, Job thought that
he was being punished unjustly and was challenging God to prove or
show his sin. Job incorrectly thought like his friends, that *only* those
who did wrong suffered in this present life ("Only those who do wrong
do not have expensive cars, houses, goods. Those who are righteous
have physical rewards in this life."). But suffering comes in this life to
the righteous as well as the unrighteous (see below). Therefore Job in
declaring his own righteousness was projecting his own *self-*
righteousness, and thus denying God's *all* mightiness. Everything that
man is comes from God. And everything that man gains or suffers
comes from God:

- "Shall we receive good at the hand of God, and shall we not
  receive evil? In all this Job did not sin with his lips" (Job
  2:10).

Job a Prostitute?

nm231 » Furthermore, besides Job's self-righteousness, he acted like
a prostitute:

- What *profit* is it to me, and what do I gain by not sinning?
  (Job 35:3; 34:9)

nm232 » If you are righteous, if you are of the good, you do not
behave honorably for rewards – for profit or gain – you behave
honorably because you are righteous, because you are of the good and
hate all evil. If you hate evil you do not want any part of it even if you
are apparently not physically rewarded for good. (Christ is an
example: He never sinned, but died because of His good behavior,
without any apparent reward before His death.) In the truest sense of
the word, Job was *not* righteous, when he acted *apparently* righteously
before his testing by Satan, because afterward he showed his real color

– his prostitute mind: "Where is my reward for being good" (cf. Job 34:9; Job 35:3). Satan's testing merely brought out the evil in Job.

nm233 » But Job finally *saw* God and understood that God does *all* things (Job 42:2-6). There is a reason for evil and suffering even though it might not be understood by most men in this age (Job 36:26). God does all things (Job 12:10-25; 42:2). God is just (Job 34:10; 37:23). If God allows evil it is for a just and noble purpose (Job 4:8-9; 11:7; 37:23; Rom 8:28; see "Reason Why" paper [NM 19] and the *God Papers*). Satan does not interfere with God's purpose, for Satan can only do what God allows (Job 42:2; 1:12; 2:6; Isa 46:9-11; 55:11; Psa 115:3).

Way to Wisdom and Knowledge

nm234 » Although the book of Job does not reveal the purpose of God allowing evil and suffering it says something that implies the answer:

- There is a mine for silver and a place where gold is refined .... But where can wisdom be found? Where does understanding dwell? *Man does not comprehend its worth* .... It cannot be bought with the finest gold, nor can its price be weighted in silver .... Where then does wisdom come from? Where does understanding dwell? .... God understands the way to it and he alone knows where it dwells .... He [God] looked at wisdom and appraised it; he confirmed it and tested it. And he said to man, the *fear* of the Lord – that is wisdom, and to shun evil is understanding (Job 28:1,12-13,15, 20,23,27-28, see Hebrew for verse 28 "Lord" = *Adonay* # 136, which is in a plural form).

nm235 » Notice there is wisdom in the *fear* of the Lord (Job 28:28) or the fear of the LORD (Prov 1:7) and to shun evil is understanding (see Prov 1:7). When you *fear* the Lord, who does *all* things, even in someway creating and predestinating evil, then there is wisdom. And when you shun evil or hate evil there is understanding. But you must know evil to shun it or hate it. The only way you can know evil is to learn about it. The only way to learn about evil is to live in a time of evil. Thus, God saw the great *worth* of wisdom (wisdom is the fear of the Lord & to shun or hate evil – Prov 8:13), thus He created evil (Isa 45:7) by predestination before creation and sin through Satan (Job 1:7-12; 2:2-7) so that mankind could learn to hate evil and thus obtain wisdom and understanding. Therefore, God allowed man to take from the tree of *knowledge* of good and evil for a higher purpose (see "Reason Why" paper [NM 19] and the *God Papers* [GP 7]).

nm236 » *False common thinking*. Job and his friend projected the common thinking that *only* the evil ones are supposed to suffer, and that if you do good you will be rewarded in this life or age. Their thinking says that there is *profit* for being good in this age.

nm237 » ***Both the good and the evil suffer***. But scripture clearly shows those with good behavior also suffer (note Christ's human life; see Hebrews chapter 11; Rom 8:17; 1Pet 3:14, 17; 4:1; etc.). Of course, the evil ones are also suffering for their sins and the spiritual evil ones will suffer in the 1000 years (Job 15:20; 31:3; note "Thousand Years and Beyond Paper" [NM 15]). Those who do good suffer because they live in an evil environment. The world is under the influence of the evil mind – the other-mind. Therefore and thereby, the whole creation is now suffering (Rom 8:22).

nm238 » But the common mistaken thinking of Job and his friends, is the kind of thinking that ignores the many predestination scriptures *and* ignores the many scriptures that clearly indicate that the God does all and gives all. We have looked at some of the predestination scriptures, now let us look at the scriptures that indicate that the God does all.

God Does All

nm239 »

- First, God is Almighty – He has ALL the power. "I am Almighty God." (Gen 17:1; Rev 15:3; etc.)

- In His All mightiness God creates ALL. "God who makes all things." (Eccl 11:5; Gen 1:1; Jer 10:16)

- In God's creating, God creates good. "I make alive ... I heal ... I make peace ... the LORD [YHWH] is good to all: and his mercies are over all his WORKS." (Deut 32:39; Isa 45:7; Psa 145:9; Gen 1:31)

- God even predestinates some to good. (Rom 9:21-23; Eph 1:4-5; etc.; see "Predestination Paper" [NM 8])

- But somehow in God's all powerfulness, He creates evil. "I kill ... I wound ... and create evil." (Deut 32:39; Isa 45:7)

- God even predestinates some to evil. (See Romans 9:21-23; Jude 1:4; Prov 16:4; 1Pet 2:8; see "Predestination Paper" [NM 8])

- Yet God will in the future make ALL THINGS NEW. "I make all things new." (Rev 21:5; Isa 65:17)

- And then ALL WILL BE IN GOD. "Then the end ... the last enemy that shall be destroyed is death ... that God may be all in all." (1Cor 15:24-28; "All Saved Paper" [NM 13]; etc)

- ■ God even gives:
  - ● the Spirit (Gal 4:6; 1Cor 12:1 ff)
  - ● repentance (Acts 5:31; 11:18; 2Tim 2:25)
  - ● grace (Rom 11:5-6; 15:15)
  - ● salvation (Tit 3:5-7)

nm240 » *In summary*, anything that you are (whether you are good or evil) is from outside of you:

- ■ "For who makes you different from anyone else? What do you have that you did not receive? And if you did receive it, why do you boast as though you did not?" (1Cor 4:7)

nm241 » We receive all from God, even our good works are from God's predestination – he *gave* us our ability to do good (the Spirit), he gave us the physical body in order to do this good, he gave us a place (the earth) to do good, he gave us the physical energy to do good, and he gave us a time of evil so that there could be good, for without evil there could never have been good because evil and good are comparative qualities (see "Reason Why" paper [NM 19] and the *God Papers* [GP 7]). What, then, is there to boast about?

nm242 » See the "Proof Paper" [NM 10] to understand why Christians run the race, why they continue to try to do good even though they were predestinated. When you are predestinated to evil, you do not know it. When you are predestinated to good, your good works are your *proof*, but God gives you the power. When you are predestinated for good, you do good essentially because you hate evil and love the good, and because you have no desire for evil, not for some kind of reward you may receive for good behavior.

See also "Reward for Christians Paper" [NM 11] and "According to Works Paper" [NM 12].

NM 10: Proof Paper

Prove Yourself
What Kind of Faith?
God's Spirit in All Christians
Christ the Vine
Keep the Commandments
Christians do no Sin Willfully
Tests to Prove Yourself
Lose Salvation?
More Tests to Give Yourself
Prove Yourself

NM10 Abstract

There is a physical faith; there is a Spiritual faith. Can you prove what kind of faith your have? How do Christians "keep the commandments"? Can Christian lose salvation? Give yourself the test.

Proof of Being a Christian: Prove Yourself

nm243 » How does one know he is a Christian? We know that one is a Christian when one has a changed attitude away from the ways of this age and towards the ways of the coming age. We know that a true Christian has the New Mind, which is the Spirit of God, and that this New Mind makes the Christian behave in a more positive manner. The main difference between a Christian and non-Christian is the fact that a Christian has the Spirit of God in himself. How does one know he really has the New Mind or Spirit of God? How do you know? How can we tell if we have the New Mind or not?

nm244 » The word of God, the Bible, tells us to "prove all things."(1Thes 5:21) Is there a way to prove one's Christianity, to prove to oneself, whether one is a Christian?

nm245 » "Prove yourselves, whether you are in the faith; prove your own selves" (2Cor 13:5). God says through Paul's words, "prove yourselves"! Prove what? – whether you are in the faith. What faith? What kind of faith?

What Kind of Faith?

nm246 » "What does it profit, my brethren, though a man say he has faith, and have not works? can faith save him? ... show me your faith without your works, and I will show you my faith by my works ... But don't you know, O vain man, that faith without works is dead?" (James 2:14, 18, 20) Faith without good works is dead. "For as the body without the Spirit is dead, so faith without works is dead also" (James 2:26). Thus, we see there is a faith that is dead because there are no good works with this dead faith.

nm247 » Is this dead faith, the faith spoken about when, through Paul, God says?: "Prove yourselves, whether you are in the faith; prove your own selves" (2Cor 13:5). No, God is not talking about dead faith, for to continue: "Know you not your own selves, how that Jesus Christ is in you, if not you are reprobates?" Those not in the faith, who have not Christ in them are reprobates. What are reprobates according to the Bible?

Reprobates

nm248 » People who are reprobates must have a reprobate's mind. Paul defines a reprobate mind:

- "And just as they did not see fit to acknowledge God any longer, God gave them over to a depraved mind, to do those things which are not proper, 29 being filled with all unrighteousness, wickedness, greed, evil; full of envy, murder, strife, deceit, malice; *they are* gossips." (Rom 1:28-29)

A reprobate mind does the opposite of good works. When God tells us to prove if we are in the faith, he is not speaking of dead faith belonging to the class of people called reprobates by God. By the way, the word translated "reprobate" is from a Greek word which means worthless.

nm249 » Those of the dead faith are those who "profess that they know God; but in works [they do works of reprobates, Rom 1:28-29] they deny him, being abominable, and disobedient, and unto every good work reprobate" (Titus 1:16).

nm250 » Those of the dead faith, do reprobate works; "they profess that they know God; but in works they deny him" (Titus 1:16). Those reprobates say (profess) that they know God, but they have the dead faith that does not do good works (James 2:20).

Law Keeper: Truth in Them

nm251 » "He that says he abides in him [Christ] ought himself also to walk, even as he [Christ] walked" (1John 2:6). How did Jesus walk? Jesus said, "I have kept my Father's commandments" (John 15:10).

What are his Father's commandments?

nm252 » What are Jesus Christ's Father's commandments? When Jesus Christ was on earth before his death, he was under the laws and commandments of the Old Testament. Christ kept these laws perfectly (not the add-on laws of the Rabbis). But now the law or system of love is in effect and this is the law or commandment that Christians keep. Please see the "Freedom and Law Paper" [NM 17] for more information on the system of love and God's laws.

Truth in them

nm253 » To continue, "He that says I know him, and keeps not his commandments, is a liar, and the truth is not in him" (1John 2:4). What is this "truth" that is not in him (the reprobate) who does not keep God's commandments? – "the *Spirit* of Truth," "the *Spirit* is Truth" (John 14:17; 1John 5:6). Hence, those who say they know Christ (1John 2:4), and those who say they abide in Christ (1John 2:6) ought to walk in God's commandments (1John 2:6; John 15:10). If they do not keep the commandments, then those who say they are in Christ and know Christ are liars, if they do not keep the commandments (1John 2:4). These reprobates do not have the Spirit of truth in them. By putting these verses together we can see that those who say they know and are in Christ (they call themselves Christians), but who do not keep God's commandments of love are liars. They are not Christians according to God's Word. And they are not Christians, for the *Spirit* of God or the *Mind* of God isn't in them.

nm254 » "Whosoever transgresses, and abides not in the doctrine of Christ [words of Christ, which are the words of God, John 17:14, 17], has not God. He that abides in the doctrine of Christ, he has both the Father and the Son" (2John 9). Whoever sins and does not keep the doctrines of God has not God, but he that keeps God's Word does have both God the Father and Christ in them. What does it mean to have the Father and the Son?

God's Spirit in All Christians

nm255 » "You Father, art in me, and I in you ... I am in my Father, and you [speaking of Christians] in me, and I in you" (John 17:21; 14:20). "One God and Father of all, who is above all, and through all, and in you [Christians] all" (Eph 4:6). What does it mean here about God in Jesus, Jesus in God, Christians in Christ, Jesus in Christians, and God the Father in all?

nm256 » "For as the body [the Church – 1Cor 12:27; Eph 4:4; 5:23-32; Col 1:24; Rom 12:4-5] is one, and has many members, and all the members of that one body [Church], being many, are one body: so also Christ. For by one Spirit are we all baptized into one body [Church] ... and have been all made to drink into one Spirit" (1Cor 12:12-13). Here it pictures the Church of God, which has one Spirit that all spiritually drink from. The Spirit or New Mind is in all the body. When Jesus says his Father is in him and he in his Father, that Christians are in him and he in Christians, and that God is in all, he is merely saying that God the Father's Spirit or Mind is in all – "all made to drink into one Spirit." Romans 8:9, 10-11, 14-16 reiterates this: to be the son of God one must have God's Spirit dwelling in him. Thus, "the body [Church] without the Spirit [of God] is dead" (James 2:26).

nm257 » Now we can better understand the verse: "whosoever transgresses, and abides not in the doctrine of Christ, has not God" (2John 9). Thus, those who go against the doctrines of love do not have God's Spirit or God's Mind. But "he that abides in the doctrine of Christ, he has the Father and the Son" (2John 9). He that has God's Spirit that is common to the Father and Son (John 14:10, 20) does abide in the doctrine of Christ. "He that says, I know Him ["I'm a Christian, I believe in him"], and keeps not his commandments, is a liar, and the truth [God's Spirit, 1John 5:6] is not in him" (1John 2:4). Thus, those who do not keep God's commandments are not Christians, they are liars because they do not have God's Spirit. Conversely, those who follow God's commandments are Christians and have God's Spirit (end of 2John 9). Those who are Christians will walk as Christ walked (1John 2:6). Yes, "and he that keeps His commandments dwells in Him, and He in him" (1John 3:24). The Spirit or Mind of God makes you in Christ, and Christ in you.

Christ The Vine

nm258 » In John 15:1-8 it pictures the body of Christ or the Church of God as a vine, with the branches as the members of the Church, and the root as Christ (See also Rom 11:13-24, "root" is Christ – Rev 22:16). Jesus says, "every branch in me that bears not fruit he [God] takes away" (John 15:2). Let's stop here. Now since this vine is metonymical for the Church, we know that the fruit this branch should bear is the fruit of God's Spirit: "love, joy, peace," etc (Gal 5:22). Thus, God takes away the branch that does not produce love, joy, peace, and so on. We know from 1Cor 13:4-7 that love is patient, kind, envies not, is not puffed up, rejoices in truth, and so on. Hence, the branch that does not produce fruit, is the one who does not produce good works of God's commandments, for "love is the fulfilling of the law" (Rom 13:10).

nm259 » Notice that Jesus says this branch that does not do good works or that does not produce fruit is in Him, but notice what Christ does not say: that Christ is in this branch. This is very significant! Why?: for "he that says he abides in Him ought himself so to walk, even as he [Christ] walked" (1John 2:6). He that says he is in his vine [his body, God's Church] should walk as Christ walked. He that says he is in Christ ought to produce fruit. "He that says he is in the light [God is light, 1John 1:5], and hates his brother, is in darkness even until now" (1John 2:9). Those who say they are in Christ but who hate their Spiritual brother, are in Satan (darkness) even until now. These are in Satan's church, not in God's if they hate the Spiritual brother: "The man that wanders out of the way of understanding shall remain in the congregation of the dead" (Prov 21:16). Notice they remain or rest (Hebrew) in the church of the dead, they do not go back to it when they wander, but remain or rest in it – "is in darkness even until now" (1John 2:9).

nm260 » "He that says, I know Him, and keeps not His commandments, is a liar, and the truth [God's Spirit, 1John 5:6] is not in him" (1John 2:4). If the Mind of truth is not in them, they are not Christians.

nm261 » "But whoso keeps his word, in him verily is the love of God perfected: hereby know we that we are in Him" (1John 2:5). Those in Christ know they are in Him when they keep his word.

nm262 » Hence, the branch taken away for not bearing fruit (John 15:2) was never in Christ (in the vine), for the proof that you are in Him is that you produce fruit [keep his Word – 1John 2:5; keep his commandments –1John 2:4; walk like Christ – 1John 2:6; not hate your brother –1John 2:9]. You know you are in Christ when you produce the fruit of the Spirit (Gal 5:22-23). Those in Christ, and Christ in them, have what is in

Christ. They have God's Spirit and Mind. And those in Christ and Christ in them do produce the fruit of love.

nm263 » "And every branch that bears fruit, he purges ["cleans"] it, that it may bring forth more fruit ... abide in me, and I in you. As the branch cannot bear fruit of itself, except it abide in the vine; no more can you, except you abide in me. I am the vine, you are the branches: He that abides in me, and I in him, the same brings forth much fruit: for apart from me you can do nothing" (John 15:2, 4-5). Notice it says abide in me, and I in you. As explained previously, those in Christ and with Christ in them are in the Spirit of God, are in the body of Christ and drink in the same Spirit (1Cor 12:12-13; John 14:10, 20). The branch that was in Christ (John 15:2), did not produce fruit, because Christ was not in the branch. Verse 2 only says that it was in Christ, the verse did not say Christ was in the branch. This branch, in other words, *says* it is in Christ or in the Church, but the fact that it does not produce fruit means it was never in Christ.

nm264 » Now we see those in Christ, and Christ in them do produce much fruit (John 15:5). And it adds, that one can't do anything if it is apart from Christ, that is, apart from the Church because it does not have God's Spirit. One does produce much fruit if the Spirit is in him. "If you keep my commandments, you shall abide in my love" (John 15:10). "God is love" (1John 4:8, 16). "God" can be used metonymically here for love: "If you keep my commandments, you shall abide in my God." When one keeps the commandments he is in God, and God is in him. "And he that keeps His commandments dwells in Him, and He in him" (1John 3:24). Those in God, and God in them, produce much fruit of the Spirit (John 15:5, 8, 16). "The Head [Christ is the Head – Eph 1:22], from which all the body [Church] by joints and bands having nourishment ministered, and knit together, increases with the increase of God" (Col 2:19).

nm265 » Thus, we see that you are in Christ or in the Church, if God's Spirit is in you. And that you will keep the commandments if God is in you as opposed to those who <u>say</u> they are in Christ, but have not God's Spirit and do not keep the commandments.

Keep the Commandments?

nm266 » What does the Bible mean, keep the commandments? We know that only one person who ever lived on earth was sinless, and he was Christ (Heb 4:15; John 8:46; John 15:10; 1Pet 1:19). And we know that all others have transgressed or sinned (Rom 3:9; 1John 1:8, 10). What does God mean when through John, he says, "And hereby we do know that we know him, if we keep his commandments" (1John 2:3). Doesn't this verse, and other similar ones, mean to keep the law as Christ the man did while he was living? Doesn't this mean keep the law of love perfectly?

nm267 » When we keep God's law of love in this age we keep it Spiritually. That is, we keep it in our attitude or mind. But because we are in the age of the other-mind, the mind of confusion, the mind of Satan that misleads us, then the other thoughts from the other-mind will sometimes confuse us, yet our true desire is toward the way of love. Now the Bible does say that those born of God do not sin: "We know that whosoever is born of God sins not" (1John 5:18). This should be taken in the Spiritual sense. That is, those with the Spirit of God in their minds will desire the good. But sometimes, in physical weakness, they may do what is evil because of the other-mind and outside pressures. Yet in their Spiritual mind they will hate their act. They will never enjoy their wrong act like most of this age which do enjoy their evil. It is only when one is BORN of God that one won't sin at all (see "Begotten, Born Paper" [NM 5]). See the "Freedom and Law Paper" [NM 17] to understand what sin is.

Christians Do Not Sin Willfully

nm268 » Paul is speaking,

- "I do not know what I am doing. For what I want to do I do not do, but what I hate I do. And if I do what I do not want to do, I confirm [by my actions] that the law is good. As it is, it is no longer I myself who do it, but it is sin living in me. I know that nothing good lives in me, that is, in my sinful flesh. For I have the desire to do what is good, but I cannot carry it out. For what I do is not the good I want to do; no, the evil I do not want to do – this I keep on doing. Now if I do what I do not want to do, it is no longer I who do it, but it is sin living in me that does it. So I find this law at work: When I want to do good, evil is right there with me. For in my inner being I delight in God's law; but I see another law at work in the members of my body, waging war against the law of my mind and making me a prisoner of the law of sin at work within my members" (Rom 7:15-23).

Paul does not of his true self want to sin, it is the law of sin that dwells in him that wishes to sin. When Christians sin, it is because of this law of sin (the other-mind), that satanic spirit in their minds or that "spirit that dwells in us lusts to envy" (James 4:5). See the "Old Mind" paper [NM 21] for more details.

nm269 » Therefore Christians may sometimes physically sin, but not willfully or deliberately or intentionally. True Christians want to follow in the way of love. They do not willfully sin because it proves something:

- "For *if* we sin willfully after we received the knowledge of the truth, there remains no more sacrifice for sins, but a terrifying expectation of judgment and the fury of a fire which will consume the adversaries" (Heb 10:26).

If we sin willfully, we go to judgment. This judgment as we learn in NM24 will be with fire for the angels of sin, and death for mankind sent to the judgement. But notice that it says, "*if* we sin willfully . . ." It does not say after we have received the Spirit of God, but after we receive the knowledge of truth. And it did say IF. "If" is a hypothetical word. The hypothetical word "if" is used to begin a train of thought "based on, involving, or having the nature of a hypothesis" (Webster's Dictionary). A hypothesis is a supposition. Another word for "if" is suppose. So this train of thought beginning in Hebrews 10:26 is a hypothetical situation: IF Christians do this, then they can expect to go to the judgment. Notice verse 39: "but we [Christians] are not of them who draw back into perdition; but of them that believe to the saving of the soul." Now that is no hypothetical statement. It is a positive statement. Real Christians do not fall back. Those that sin willfully are those who follow their "other-mind" and sin willingly. When you sin willfully you are on the way to proving that you may not be a Christian.

nm270 » Notice the positive statement: "and grieve not the holy Spirit of God, whereby you are sealed unto the day of redemption" (Eph 4:30; see Isa 59:21). This isn't a statement of hope! If one was to say this was only positive thinking on Paul's part, then what about the statement about the Messiah's return? How would we distinguish between "positive thinking" statements and fact? Who would decide? No, Ephesians 4:30 and Hebrews 10:39 are to be taken as factual statements. Christians do not sin willfully. They will sin, but they will not be proud of their sins and will repent of them quickly. Real Christians are sealed with the Spirit to the day of redemption and their belief will save their souls.

Tests to Prove Yourself

Hypothetical Word Formations

nm271 » We'll explain why Paul used the hypothetical word formation in Hebrews 10:26ff. This is not the only place Paul uses this type of word formation. For example, Hebrews 6:6 is the beginning of another hypothetical train of thought, yet notice once again the "but" sentence which is somewhat like Hebrews 10:39, "but, beloved, we are persuaded better things of you, and things that accompany salvation, though we thus speak" (Heb 6:9).

nm272 » These word constructions are much like those in the First Letter of John. For example, "and hereby we do know that we know him, IF we keep his commandments ... IF any man love the world, the love of the Father is not in him" (1John 2:3, 15). These are tests of proof of one thing or another.

nm273 » In 1John 2:3 what are we testing for? If one passes this test in this verse, what does he prove? "If we keep his commandments," if we pass this test what do we prove? "And hereby we do know that we know him." If we keep his commandment we know God. If we pass the test we prove that we know him.

nm274 » In 1John 2:15, what are we testing for? If one passes this test what does he prove? "If any man love the world," If we pass this test (if we love the world's way), what do we prove? We prove that the love of the Father is not in us. If we love the world's way the Father's love is not in us.

nm275 » In Hebrews 10:26-39, what are we testing for? If we pass this test in these verses, what does it prove? "If we sin willfully after that we have received the knowledge of truth," if we pass this test (if we sin willfully), what does it prove? "There remains no more sacrifice for sins, but a certain fearful looking for judgment." If we sin willfully, then we must look fearfully for judgment which shall devour the adversaries of which we would be one. If we pass the test (by sinning willfully), we prove that we shall be devoured. But this word formation adds, after further amplification in verses 28-38, that "we [Christians] are *not* of them who draw back into perdition; but of them that believe to the saving of the soul" (Heb 10:39).

Lose The Spirit, Lose Salvation?

nm276 » Do you see the pattern? In Hebrews 10:26-39 it says that those who sin willfully will receive judgement of being devoured for such a sin. If any that are called Christian sin willfully, then they prove that they belong to those who are going to be devoured. But in verse 39 it qualifies the "we" in verse 26 by stating a positive fact that we, the real Christians, are to the salvation of the soul. And verse 39 is confirmed by Ephesians 4:30 where it says those sealed with the Spirit are sealed to redemption. And Ephesians 4:30 can be confirmed by the fact there is not a verse in the Bible that states as fact that one who receives the Spirit of God can lose it.

nm277 » Notice: "And grieve not the holy Spirit of God whereby you are sealed unto the day of redemption" (Eph 4:30). Christians are sealed with the Spirit to the day of redemption. This is so because in Christ's words, "My Father, who has given them [Christians] to me, is greater than all; no one can snatch them [Christians] out of my Father's hand" (John 10:29).

nm278 » Notice further proof that once the Spirit is given it is sealed to the day of God. "For whatsoever is begotten of God overcomes the world: and this is the victory that overcomes the world: our faith" (1John 5:4). Faith is the power that helps the Christian to overcome the world. Now Faith is the fruit of the Spirit (Gal 5:22). "For by grace are you saved through faith; and that [faith] not of yourselves: it is the gift of God" (Eph 2:8). Why does Faith help us to overcome and be saved? Or better yet, why does the Spirit, for Faith comes from the Spirit, help Christians to overcome and be saved? "You are of God, little children, and have overcome them: because greater is he [God] that is in you, than he [Satan] that is in the world" (1John 4:4).

With The Spirit You Are Saved

nm279 » Do you see? Once one has the Spirit of God he is sealed to the day of redemption. Once one becomes a Christian, he will be saved (Heb 10:39). There is no way that anyone once begotten of God's New Mind can lose out on salvation. But once begotten, can you do anything? No, "for we are his workmanship, created in Christ Jesus unto good works" (Eph 2:10). If one wants to do anything but good works, how can he be a Christian? Christians are created for good works (Eph 2:10). A Christian wants to do good works; he has a good attitude.

nm280 » "If any man love the world, the love of the Father is not in him" (1John 2:15). The "love of God" can only come from the Spirit of God, for the love of God is a fruit of God's Spirit (Gal 5:22). With this knowledge what is the test being given here to man by God through John? "If any man love the world, the Spirit of the Father is not in him." If you pass the test of loving the world, you prove that you have not the Spirit or Mind of God, thus, you are not a Christian. Remember to be a Christian one must have a changed attitude away from the world's way. If one is convinced that the world's way is wrong, why would he go back after he had received God's Spirit which is greater than the other-mind or other spirit. "Prove yourselves, whether you be in the Faith; prove your own selves. Know you not your own selves, how that Jesus Christ is in you, except you be reprobates" (2Cor 13:5). Prove yourselves to see if you have God's Spirit that does produce much fruit, and helps you to have a good attitude. If you do not find this proof, then you are worthless (a reprobate) with a worthless mind concerning the way to love, peace, and harmony (see Rom 1:28-31).

More Tests To Give Yourself

nm281 » What are some tests you can give yourself in order to prove to yourself that you are a true Christian? We have given you many tests already in this paper. Do you love God's law of love? Why not?, unless you are a reprobate. If you sin willfully, doesn't that mean you love sin? And if you love sin, how can you love God's law? For "love is the fulfilling of the law" (Rom 13:10). "But he that sins against me [God] wrongs his own soul: all they that hate me love death" (Prov 8:36). If one loves to watch violence, isn't he projecting the fact that he loves forms of death-producing activity? He loves death! (note Rom 1:32)

nm282 » Look at the test in Romans 1:28-31, if you pass that test you prove yourself a reprobate or one with a worthless mind. If you love the world's way, then you prove you do not have the Spirit (1John 2:15).

nm283 » Which of the following tests do you pass. "He that loves his life [in this world] shall lose it; and he that hates his life in this world shall keep it unto life of aeonian" (John 12:25). If the world is as bad as God tells us through his Bible, why, if you have God's New Mind would you like your life in this world or this old age?

nm284 » "They [the ones who call themselves Christians] went out from us, but they were not of us; for if they had been of us, they would have continued with us" (1John 2:19). Those who physically go out of the Church prove they were never a part of the Church. But this does not mean that those who were in the Church physically and then went out, can't at some future time come Spiritually into the Church.

nm285 » "In this the children of God are manifest, and the children of the devil: whosoever does not righteousness is not of God, neither he that loves not his brother" (1John 3:10). A person proves he is not a child of God by not doing righteousness, and by not loving his Spiritual brother.

nm286 » "Whosoever hates his brother is a murderer: and you know that no murderer has aeonian life abiding in him. Hereby perceive we the love of God, because he laid down his life for us: and we ought to lay down our lives for the brethren" (1John 3:15-16). If one hates his Spiritual brother he is as good as a murderer, and he has not the aeonian life in him, or he has not the Spirit that brings this aeonian life in him; he is not a true Christian (1John 3:10). Then verse 16 shows that those who have the love of God, prove they have God's Spirit if they do lay down their life for their Spiritual brother like Christ did. "He that finds his life shall lose it [in the seventh millennium]: and he that loses his life for my sake shall find it [in the seventh millennium]" (Mat 10:39). If one is willing to give his life for Jesus Christ's sake, this proves God's Spirit is in him. A Christian if called upon must give up his life, if not, he proves he is not a Christian. There are two senses of giving up one's life: (1) physical sense – the giving up of one's physical life; (2) the Spiritual sense – the giving up of one's former spiritual life of confusion.

nm287 » "My little children, let us not love in word, neither in tongue; but in deed and in truth. And hereby we know that we are of the truth, and shall assure our hearts before him" (1John 3:18, 19). If one is a hypocrite and only does God's law through words and not deeds, he is not of the truth. God's truth comes from his Spirit (John 14:17). One does not have the Spirit if he is a hypocrite.

nm288 » "And he that keeps His commandments dwells in Him, and He [Christ] in him. And hereby we know that he abides in us, by the Spirit [New Mind] which he has given us" (1John 3:24).

nm289 » "We are of God: he that knows God hears us; he that is not of God hears us not. Hereby know we the Spirit of truth, and the spirit of error" (1John 4:6). The one that hears has the Spirit of truth; the one that does not hear has the spirit of error. "God has given them the spirit of slumber, eyes that they should not see, and ears that they should not hear" (Rom 11:8). But those of the Spirit of truth (the New Mind) will hear Spiritually. "And when he puts forth his own sheep he goes before them, and the sheep follow him: for they know his voice" (John 10:4).

nm290 » "We glory in trial also; knowing that trial works patience; and patience proof [good works like patience are proof one has the New Mind]; and proof, hope [hope for a better resurrection, Heb 11:35]: and hope makes not ashamed [shame of aeonian contempt, Dan 12:2]; because the love of God is shed abroad in our hearts through the Holy Spirit which is given to us" (Rom 5:3-5).

Prove Yourself

nm291 » "Prove yourselves, whether you be in faith; prove your own selves, how that Jesus Christ is in you; if not you be reprobates?" (2Cor 13:5)

nm292 » Test yourselves to see if you have the Spirit or Mind of God, for he who does have it does produce much fruit. Those who do not have the Spirit are reprobates or worthless and are the ones of the "dead," "for as the body without the Spirit is dead" (James 2:26).

nm293 » **You will be resurrected, if the Spirit is in you.** "Now if man have not the Spirit of Christ, he is none of his ... But if the Spirit of him [God] that raised up Jesus from the dead dwell in you, he that raised up Christ from the dead shall also quicken your mortal bodies by his Spirit that dwells in you" (Rom 8:9, 11). That is a statement of *fact*, not hope, for as we have shown, once one has received the Spirit he can't lose it. It is the Spirit of God, or the New Mind which brings salvation.

nm294 » *To Review*, the Bible tells us those begotten of God are sealed with the Spirit to the day of redemption. Further, the Bible gives its readers many tests to take. If one passes one kind of test, then this proves he has the Spirit or New Mind and will be saved. If one passes the other kind of test he proves himself a reprobate, and manifests that he does not have God's Spirit, thus, is not a Christian. All the tests that prove one a Christian have one thing in common: you prove you have the Spirit of God when you keep the law of love (see "Freedom & Law Paper" [NM 17]). All the tests that prove one is a reprobate also have one thing in common: you prove you do not have the Spirit of God when you do not follow the law of love.

nm295 » A Christian's good works are his proof that he is a Christian. We do not prove anything to others when we do good works. We do not try to show-up others when we do good works. When a Christian does good works they come from his heart. A Christian has the New Mind with the new attitude. This New Mind gives real Christians the power to do good works. We keep God's law of love because it comes from the heart, not because we are trying to prove anything to others.

Why Paul Ran the Race

nm296 » When we do good works it is our proof that we do have the New Mind – the Spirit of God. That is why Paul ran the race, to prove to himself he was a Christian. If Paul let up on his good works, it would mean that he was a reprobate. But it was God's Spirit in Paul that gave Paul the power to overcome the world (see 1Cor 9:24-27; 1John 5:4 & 1Cor 15:10). Paul ran to prove to himself his salvation.

What about Doubts?

nm297 » You run the race to prove to yourself about your salvation. But what about doubts? Some admit that they have doubts about their Christianity. This is not unusual. Every Christian in the old age will have doubts about their own Christianity. This is because of the other-mind (NM 21). The other-mind puts doubts, fear, and other uncomfortable ideas into our minds. Look at Elijah. He doubted himself and felt he was no better than anyone else (1Kings 19:4), yet God chose him to do his will. But we are the overcomers; we will overcome to reach our salvation because we have the Spirit and our Spirit is greater than the one who rules the evil age (1John 4:4).

   "But let every man prove his own work, and then shall he have rejoicing in himself alone, and not in another."(Gal 6:4)

   Caution must be had here. Each Christian is given the Spirit by measure (Rom 12:3; Eph 4:7). There may be some very weak Christians. We not only need to be careful how we judge others (NM23), but also how we judge ourselves.

NM 11: "Reward" for Christians

Eternal Life: Our Reward?
Aeonian Life?
Immortality Promised to each Christian
Aeonian Life: What is it?
Aeonian Life: When does it Begin?
Aeonian Life: Where will this Age be?
Aeonian Life: How Long is this Age?
Aeonian Life: An Age within an Endless Age
Aeonian Punishment
Resurrection from Aeonian Punishment

NM11 Abstract

In this paper we will learn the very important distinction between aeonian life and immortality. We will again analyze and examine the words mistranslated into eternal and forever. Because these words were mistranslated in the Bible the difference between aeonian life and immortality has been hidden from almost everyone.

Eternal Life: Our Reward?

nm298 » What is the "reward" for being a Christian? That is, what is the result or effect of being a Christian besides having the New Mind of love, joy, and peace. "The gift of God is *eternal* life through Jesus Christ our Lord ... the righteous into life *eternal*" (Rom 6:23; Mat 25:46).

nm299 » Many believe that the reward for being a Christian is eternal life. (This is not to say that a Christian has *earned* the reward by himself. See the "Predestination Paper" [NM 8].). What they mean is that at the resurrection they will be made alive forever, because they can't mean eternal life, for life eternal means: life without beginning or end.

Key Word Means Aeonian, not Eternal

nm300 » The Bible was inspired mainly in two languages, Hebrew and Greek. In Romans 6:23 and Matthew 25:46 the Greek word that was translated into English as "eternal," is *aionios*. This Greek word at the time it was inspired to be used in the New Testament meant, agelasting, aeonian, or a period of time of significant character, or an indefinite period of time, or a indeterminate period of time, or simply an age. Thus *aionios* means an agelasting period of time of unknown length. This Greek word has been mistranslated into such English words in the New Testament as: eternal, everlasting, and forever. But the word does not mean forever. At the time it was written by the New Testament writers it meant – an agelasting period of unknown length. One can only ascertain the length of time by the context in which the word is used, or from other scriptures related to the subject. The inspired word means: *agelasting* or aeonian (see "Age Paper" [NM 7]).

nm301 » ***Meaning of Words***. Just because a word has evolved through misuse to mean something, are we to take its evolved meaning, or its original meaning? Words are only symbols of meaning. The important quality about a word is the meaning that was meant to be conveyed by the speaker or writer. When the New Testament writers were inspired to write, they were inspired to write down meanings through the medium of symbolic words. A word is only as good as the meaning it stands for. If we want God's inspired meaning, we should take the word for what it meant when it was written, and not the evolved meaning.

Agelasting or Aeonian Life?

nm302 » After we correct the Greek word we get, "the gift of God is *aeonian* life through Jesus Christ our Lord ... the righteous into life *aeonian*" (Rom 6:23; Mat 25:46). Now these verses are in context telling us about one result of being a Christian is aeonian life. What does that mean? It means what it says, life for an aeonian period of unknown time.

nm303 » But we have a problem here. Does this mean the result of being a Christian is an aeonian period of time? Yes. But does it mean, then, that Christians born of God will die after this aeonian life, for an aeonian period of time to be aeonian or agelasting indicates or implies the possibility of an end to the age at some time? (see below, *An Endless Age?*)

Immortality Promised to each Christian

nm304 » Will Christians die after this period of time? No, for those resurrected will be born of God (1John 5:18). God is a spiritual being. Those born of spirit are spirit (John 3:6). We know that spiritual beings do not die (Luke 20:36). In Christ's own words, those resurrected, "neither can they die any more ... and are the children of God, being the children of the resurrection" (Luke 20:36). This is confirmed in

1Corinthians 15:52, "for the trumpet shall sound [Rev 11:15], and the dead shall be raised incorruptible [immortal], and we shall be changed." Thus, those resurrected will have life forever.

Paradox

nm305 » After we correct the translation for Romans 6:23 and Matthew 25:46 we have a paradox: the gift, or the "reward," or the result of being a Christian is life aeonian not life forever. But because they will be resurrected or born into an immortal state as 1Cor 15:52 and other verses say, they, of course, will not die. But immortal life is not the promise made by such verses as Romans 6:23 or Matthew 25:46. These verses only promise aeonian life, or life for an age. We need to know what this *aeonian life* means and why it was used. There is a logical answer to this as you shall see shortly.

nm306 » We have shown that Christians when born of God in the resurrection will not die. We will now show you several more verses to confirm that one benefit for being a Christian is aeonian life. In other words, immortal life is but one result of being a Christian. But immortal life will also be given to those who will not become Christians in the age of Satan's spiritual rule (NM13). Therefore, Christians from the present age will receive *another gift* besides immortality, and that gift is called aeonian life by the Bible (Rom 6:23). What is this aeonian life?

Aeonian Life What is it?

nm307 » "There is no man that has left house, or parents, or brethren, or wife, or children, for the kingdom of God's sake, who shall not receive manifold more in this present time, and in the age ["world"] to come life *aeonian*" (Luke 18:29-30).

- ■ "Labor not for the meat which perishes, but for that meat which endures unto *aeonian* life" (John 6:27).

- ■ "That whosoever believes in him should not perish, but have *aeonian* life" (John 3:15).

- ■ "And he that reaps receives wages, and gathered fruit unto life *aeonian*" (John 4:36).

- ■ "Search the scriptures; for in them you think you have *aeonian* life" (John 5:39).

Thus, the effect of being a Christian, as projected by the above five verses and Romans 6:23 and Matthew 25:46, is *aeonian* life. But we still haven't any real knowledge about this aeonian life. What is it?

- "Whereas you have been forsaken and hated, so that no man went through you, I will make you an *aeonian* excellency, a joy of many generations" (Isa 60:15). Even in the Old Testament such words as eternal, everlasting, and forever are mistranslated. Over 400 places in the Old Testament the Hebrew word "olam" is mistranslated into eternal, everlasting, and forever, while it should have been translated, *aeonian*. Isaiah 60:15 is speaking about Zion. Zion in the Spiritual sense represents Christians. God says he will make them an aeonian excellency.

- "And every one that has forsaken houses, or brethren, or sisters, or father, or mother, or wife, or children, or lands, for my name's sake, shall receive a hundredfold, and shall inherit *aeonian* life" (Mat 19:29).

- "And if children, then heirs; heirs of God, and joint-heirs with Christ; if so be that we suffer with him, that we may be also glorified together" (Rom 8:17).

Those who will receive an aeonian excellency (Isa 60:15) and inherit aeonian life (Mat 19:29), will be glorified together (Rom 8:17). When? Where?

Aeonian Life: When Does it Begin?

nm308 » "Therefore I [Paul] endure, all things for the elect's sake, that they [the elect] may also obtain the salvation which is in Christ Jesus with *aeonian* glory" (2Tim 2:10). "He [Christ] became the author of *aeonian* salvation unto all them that obey him" (Heb 5:9). Here it is speaking of aeonian salvation (Heb 5:9), and that with this salvation will be aeonian glory (2Tim 2:10). When and where is this aeonian excellency, aeonian salvation, aeonian glory, and aeonian inheritance of life?

nm309 » "And this is the will of him that sent me, that everyone which sees [Spiritually] the Son, and believes [Spiritually] into him, may have *aeonian* life: [when?] and **I will raise him up at the last day**" (John 6:40). "This is that bread which came down from heaven: not as your fathers did eat manna, and are dead: he that eats of this bread shall live in the *age*" (John 6:58).

nm310 » Those Christians who will have aeonian life will be raised or resurrected up at the last day (the 1000 year Sabbath). As Revelation 20:4-6 indicates, this is the resurrection at the beginning of the millennium. And they shall live in the age. This aeonian life begins at the start of the 7th millennium when Christ physically returns (see

"Thousand Years and Beyond" and "Last Judgment" papers). At that same time Christians will be made immortal (1Cor 15:52-55).

nm311 » Thus, the aeonian excellency, glory, and salvation begins at Christ's physical return. And Christians will live in that age. What age? We know when this age begins (at Christ's return), but when does it end, and what happens in it, and where will this age period of glory be located at?

Aeonian Life: Where will this Age be?

nm312 » Romans 8:17 tells us Christians will be glorified *together* with Christ. Isaiah 60:15 speaks of an aeonian excellency, and 2Timothy 2:10 speaks of an aeonian glory. And all these begin at Christ's return ("Thousand Years and Beyond" paper [NM 15]). What else begins at Christ's return?

- "The *aeonian* kingdom of our Lord and Savior Jesus Christ" (2Pet 1:11). The word, "everlasting," in this verse in the KJV is translated from the Greek word *aionion* which means, aeonian. What does this mean? It means that the ruling kingdom of God under Christ will be an aeonian one.

- "The most High [Christ], whose kingdom is an *aeonian* kingdom" (Dan 7:27). "How great are his signs and how mighty are his wonders! his [Christ's] kingdom is an *aeonian* kingdom" (Dan 4:3).

- In Daniel 7:14 it is speaking about the return of Jesus, "and there was given him dominion, and glory, and a kingdom, that all people, nations, and languages, should serve him: his [Christ's] dominion is an *aeonian* dominion, which shall not pass away, and his kingdom that which shall not be destroyed."

- Even the promised land that was promised to Abraham and his seed, was promised for an aeonian period of time *not* forever as mistranslated in Genesis 13:15.

- Christians will be glorified with Christ in the kingdom of God as rulers (Rev 20:4) in this age-Kingdom that has been put under the authority of Christ the God, who will be King of kings. This Kingdom will be located *on* the earth (Rev 5:10). It is the government of God under the aeonian dominion of Christ the God (Dan 7:14; 1Cor 15:27-28, 24).

nm313 » **Therefore the effect for being Christians** (besides immortality, which all others will eventually obtain) is aeonian existence and rulership, in the aeonian glory of the kingdom of God under Christ the God, until the typical end of the Spiritual creation when all of the God family will typically take over the kingdom in equality. The Family of God will continue forever since they are immortal, but the government under Christ the God will be given over to the God, who at that time will be all in all (1Cor 15:28; *God Papers*).

Aeonian Life: How Long is this Age?

nm314 » The *aionios* time or aeonian time begins when Christ returns (Rev 11:15) and exists during the 1000 years (Rev 20:4-6). After this age there will be a short age before the creation of the New Heaven and Earth, wherein *every*one will be alive (Isa 65:20; John 7:37; see "Thousand Years and Beyond"). Thus, the only special "reward" of being a Christian is rulership for 1000 years, an aeonian time. After this aeonian kingdom of God under Christ, the kingdom of God will continue into the next age of unity until the God is all in all (see the *God Papers*).

Aeonian Life: An Age within an Endless Age

nm315 » There are ages within the great new age of the True god. The 1000 years is an age, as well as the short age after the 1000 years. These are ages within the greater age. As shown in the "Age Paper" [NM 7] there is an age of Satan and an age of God. Satan's age *ends* at Jesus Christ coming back to the earth. But God's age does not end: (1) "His dominion is an aeonian dominion *which shall not pass away*, and his kingdom that which shall not be destroyed" (Dan 7:14, see Hebrew text).; (2) "And he will reign over the house of Jacob into the ages, and of his kingdom there will be no end" (Luke 1:33, see Greek).

nm316 » To repeat. This aeonian kingdom has a beginning: it starts at Christ's return. (In a sense it started with Christ first appearance.) But this aeonian kingdom has no end, 'which shall not pass away, and his kingdom that which shall not be destroyed.' It is an aeonian system because it has a beginning, but it has no end. Contrariwise, Satan's system has a beginning, and it has an end.

nm317 » Thus, the Bible by definition tells us that God's age will not end. This does not mean *aionios* means forever. It still means age or eon, but this new age or eon of harmony will never end. God won't allow it to end like other ages. Christians are "rewarded" with life throughout the new age – from its very beginning at the start of the 1000 years. The others miss the full 1000 years.

Aeonian Punishment

nm318» Conversely, the effect for the others, besides the Christians who lived during the age of the other-mind (Satan), will be death (Rom 6:23) as punishment (Mat 25:46; Ezek 33:8; see Last Judgment paper [NM 24]). This punishment will be an "aeonian punishment" (Mat 25:46). These are those "who shall be punished with aeonian destruction [death, Rom 6:23] from the presence of the Lord, and from the glory of his power" (2Thes 1:9). How long will this aeonian punishment last? As a whole the non-Christians will be punished with death for 1000 years during the seventh millennium. Then after this 1000 year death the "dead" will be resurrected as humans in the resurrection of the dead (1Cor 15:21; Acts 24:15; Rev 20:5, 13). They will live after the 1000 year age in the atonement period (Great Last Day) as humans begotten of God's Spirit. Then after this atonement period they will be born of God at the antitypical or true end of creation (1Cor 15:24-28) much like those real Christians who are still alive at Christ's physical return (1Cor 15:52-55).

Resurrection from Aeonian Judgment

nm319» John 5:29 which reads, "the resurrection of judgment," is one and the same with the "resurrection of the dead." This is so because the people called the "dead" by the Bible will be dead during the 1000 year judgment or punishment. The resurrection of judgment is the resurrection of those of the judgment of the dead. Therefore the "dead" will be raised from their judgment in the "resurrection of the judgment" (See Last Judgment paper [NM 24]).

NM 12: According to Works

God Awards Every Man According to his Work
Negative Rewards for Negative Behavior
God Gives Good for Good
God Rewards According to Works
God Gives the Power
Grace Given According to Measure
Paul as an Example
Notes: Parable of Pounds and Talents
Usury

NM12 Abstract

What does the Bible mean when it talks about mankind being awarded "according to his works"? Does this mean we can actually earn our way into paradise by working at it, or is paradise a gift given by the grace of God? What is grace? We will examine scripture pertaining to Paul to learn more about these things.

God Shall Award Every Man According to his Work

nm320 » "For the Son of man shall come in the glory of his Father with his angels; and then [at that time] he shall reward every man according to his work" (Mat 16:27). God through his word tells us he rewards men according to their works. "I will judge you every one after his ways" (Ezek 33:20). What does he reward for men's work?

By Grace you are Saved

nm321 » Before we show you what is meant by according to works, we need to know the fact that "by grace you are saved ... for by grace are you saved through faith; and that [Faith] not of yourself: it is the gift of God: Not of works, lest any man should boast" (Eph 2:5, 8-9). People are saved (freed) by the free gift of God. People aren't freed or saved through something they do. It is a free gift. But what does God reward *according to works*?

Negative Reward for Negative Behavior

nm322 » "Alexander the coppersmith did me [Paul] much evil: the Lord reward him according to his works" (2Tim 4:14). "Therefore it is no great thing if his [Satan's] ministers also be transformed as the ministers of righteousness; whose end shall be according to their works" (2Cor 1:15). "And the dead were judged out of those things which were written in the books [Bible], according to their works" (Rev 20:12). Thus, those doing bad works are judged according to their works and given the reward suitable for their ways. What is the "reward" for wrong?

Wages of Sin is Death

nm323 » "For the wages of sin is death" (Rom 6:23). The reward or wages for bad works is death. And this death is for an age: "these shall go away into aeonian punishment" (Mat 25:46).

Punished by Aeonian Destruction

nm324 » And these, "shall be punished with aeonian destruction from the presence of the Lord, and from the glory of his power" (2Thes 1:9). As we show in the paper, "Reward for Christians" [NM 11], the punishment for those who do evil will be a 1000 year death away from the coming utopia. The words "forever" and "eternity" in the Bible are wrong translations of words that mean either *age* or *agelasting (aeonian)* (see "Age Paper" [NM 7]). Those rewarded for wrong behavior will be given their "reward" of death in the aeonian judgement that lasts for 1000 years. They are dead and in the ground ("hell") while the utopia goes on above them on earth. This "reward" begins at the Messiah's coming (Rev 22:12; Mat 16:27). But what is the reward for good works?

God Gives Good For The Good

nm325 » "I will give unto every one of you according to your works" (Rev 2:23). "And he that overcomes, and keeps my works unto the end, to him will I give power over the nations: and he shall rule them with a rod of iron" (Rev 2:26-27). "To him that overcomes will I grant to sit with me in my throne, even as I also overcame, and am set down with my Father in his throne" (Rev 3:21). Those doing good works to the end will become rulers in the New Age, the kingdom of God, beginning on the first day of the 1000 years (Rev 20:4c). "And has made us unto our God kings and priests: and we shall reign *on* the earth" (Rev 5:10). Those who do good works will become rulers on earth as the kings and priests of

God's Kingdom on earth beginning at his coming (Mat 16:27). But God says he will reward *according* to their works. What does that mean?

God Rewards *According* to Works

nm326 » "They thought that the kingdom of God should immediately appear. He said therefore, A certain nobleman [J.C.] went into a far country [heaven] to receive for himself a kingdom [of God], and to return. And he called his ten servants, and delivered them ten pounds, and said unto them, Occupy till I come" (John 14:2-3). "And it came to pass, that when he had returned, having received the kingdom [of God], then he commanded these servants to be called unto him to whom he had given the money, that he might know how much every man had gained by trading. Then came the first, saying, Lord, your pound has gained ten pounds, and he said unto him, Well, you good servant: because you have been faithful in a very little, have you authority over ten cities." This servant gained ten times what he was given. According to this work he was given rulership over ten cities. "And the second came, saying, Lord, your pound has gained five pounds. And he said likewise to him, Be you also over five cities" (Luke 19:11-19). The second servant who had increased what was given to him five fold, according to his work, he received rulership over five cities. When God rewards good works *according* to them, he is rewarding according to the amount of good works. The more good works in this age, the more service one will do in the new age (note Mat 20:25-28).

Not for Reward

nm327 » From this we know what the Bible means by "reward according to works." Or do we? Just whose works are these that are performed? Did the person who will receive rulership over ten cities earn these rewards through his own will and power? Is the degree of good works achieved through a person's *own* will and power? Is the degree of good works from, and of, the person who performs them? Or, do they come from another source? Could it be that one is *given* the power to perform these good works? Notice the following: "I have raised him up in righteousness, and I will direct all his ways: he shall build my city, and he shall let go my captives, not for price nor reward, says the LORD [YHWH] of hosts" (Isa 45:13).

God Gives the Power to do Good Works

nm328 » "Are you so foolish? having begun in the Spirit, are you now made complete by the flesh?" (Gal 3:3) Are those who have the New Mind (Spirit of God) made complete through the flesh? Notice Paul is speaking to those who are supposed to be Christians. He asks now after you have the Spirit are you made complete through the flesh or by the flesh?

nm329 » Paul reveals something when he says: "But when it pleased God, who separated me from my mother's womb, and called me by his grace, to reveal his Son in me" (Gal 1:15-16). Paul was called by grace to reveal Jesus in himself. What does this mean? How does Paul reveal Christ in himself?

nm330 » "But by the grace of God I am what I am" (1Cor 15:10). Paul is what he is through God's grace. "And his grace which was bestowed upon me was not in vain; but I labored more abundantly than they all: Yet not I" (1Cor 15:10). It was Paul who labored more than the other apostle's (1Cor 15:9), yet he says it wasn't him who worked. "But the grace of God which was with me" (1Cor 15:10). It wasn't Paul who worked (the fleshly Paul – Gal 3:3), but it was the grace *given* to Paul. Isn't that what is being said here? Or was Paul being falsely modest? For if what Paul said is not true, then Paul is being falsely modest! This verse, 1Cor 15:10, is to be taken literally. Paul does not lie in these inspired scriptures! What is this grace Paul is speaking of that allows him to work so abundantly?

Grace Given According to Measure

nm331 » "But unto everyone of us is given grace according to the measure of the gift of Christ" (Eph 4:7). "Now, concerning spiritual gifts, brethren, I would not have you ignorant ... But the manifestation of the Spirit is given to every man to profit everybody. For to one is given by the Spirit the word of wisdom; to another the word of knowledge by the same Spirit; to another faith by the same Spirit; to another the gifts of healing by the same Spirit ... But all these works that one and the selfsame Spirit, dividing to every man separately as He desires" (1Cor 12:1, 7-9, 11). These free gifts of Spiritual power that work the works described in this chapter of First Corinthians, are *given* by God's will. "And there are diversities of operations, but it is the same God which works all in all" (1Cor 12:6).

nm332 » When Paul told us that it wasn't him that worked or labored but the grace within him (1Cor 15:10), he meant, by grace, the free

Spiritual gifts and the power of these gifts (1Cor 12:11, 6 & all of 1Cor 12). Is this confirmed elsewhere in the Bible?

nm333 » "Whereunto I also labor, striving according to his workings, which works in me mightily" (Col 1:29). Paul works or strives according to God's workings inside him through the power of God's Spirit or New Mind.

nm334 » "According to the grace of God which is given unto me, as a wise master builder, I have laid the foundation, and another builds thereon" (1Cor 3:10). According to Paul's grace, he works.

nm335 » "I speak not of myself: but the Father that dwells in me, he does the works" (John 14:10). Even Christ didn't do his great works; God's Spirit in him did the works!

nm336 » "Now the God of hope fill you with all joy and peace in believing, that you may abound in hope, through the power of the Holy Spirit" (Rom 15:13). Even hope comes through the power of the Holy Spirit.

nm337 » Again Paul reiterates God's message that it's the power of God's Spirit that works: "Whereof I was made a minister, according to the gift of the grace of God given unto me by the effectual working of his power" (Eph 3:7).

Paul As An Example

nm338 » Paul epitomizes what God is doing on earth. It is through Paul that we can understand how God is working his wonder on earth! (1Tim 1:16, 12-16) Paul had been the antithesis of a Christian, for he had persecuted the Church of God before his conversion (1Cor 15:9 & Acts 8:3). How was Paul converted to a Christian? Read yourself about it in Acts 9:1-18. Paul was not seeking to be a Christian. It was Christ through the power of God's Spirit that changed Paul's attitude towards Jesus Christ. Even a changed mind (repentance) is *given* to people by God (2Tim 2:25; Acts 11:18). Paul was given repentance (a changed mind) by God.

nm339 » Paul was "appointed a preacher, and an apostle, and a teacher of the Gentiles" (2Tim 1:11) in spite of what Paul was up to the time God brought him to repentance. Paul received his Spiritual gifts of being a preacher, apostle, and teacher through the will of God (1Cor 12:28, 11). Hear Paul's inspired words: "Who has saved us, and called us with a holy calling, not according to our works, but according to his own purpose and grace, which was given us in Christ Jesus before the world began" (2Tim 1:9).

nm340 » Good works come through the power of God's Spirit (grace), and God's Spirit is given to man because of God's purpose. It does not matter what a man was before God gives him his Spirit. As in the case of Paul, God gives it to one in spite of what that one has done before; he gives his Spirit of power to those who were set aside before the world began. See the paper on Predestination [NM 8] to understand this last point.

God Gives The Power for Good

nm341 » God gives us Spiritual power to do good works; He makes us good through his Spiritual power. God is the source of energy for good works:

- "But when he sees his children, the work of mine [God's] hand" (Isa 29:23).

- Speaking about Zion (God's church): "I will make you an aeonian excellency" (Isa 60:15).

- "But now, O Lord, you art our Father; we are the clay, and you our potter; and we are the work of your hand" (Isa 64:8). "We will not boast of things apart from our measure, but according to the measure of the rule which God has distributed to us, a measure to reach even unto you" (2Cor 10:13). What is this measure spoken of here? "But unto every one of us is given grace according to the measure of the gift of Christ" (Eph 4:7).

- Faith, a grace of God, for example, is given according to measure (Rom 12:3). Thus, Christians are given a measure of grace "according to the measure of the rule which God has distributed." "Not boasting of things apart from our measure, that is, of other's labors: but having hope [Hope comes from the Spirit, Rom 15:13] when your faith [Faith is a gift of God, Eph 2:8; Rom 12:3] is increased [God gives the increase, 1Cor 3:6; Col 2:19], that we shall be enlarged by you according to our rule [measure of rule is from God, 2Cor 10:13] abundantly" (2Cor 10:15). Are you beginning to see?

nm342 » Paul adds, "but he that glories, let him glory in the Lord" (2Cor 10:17). "And whatsoever you do in word or deed, do all in the name of the Lord Jesus, giving thanks to God and the Father by him" (Col 3:17). Why?: for God does all through his Spiritual power! It's God's Spirit that does the good works (Isa 26:12). All men are clay in God's molding Spirit. But how does God create through his Spirit?

nm343 » Paul again gives us the answer, Paul had a thorn in his flesh – the angel (KJV "messenger") of Satan that troubled him (2Cor 12:7). This angel of Satan (the other-mind) was the other spirit in Paul's mind that was warring against God's Spirit (Eph 6:12; Rom 7:22-23, see "Old Mind Paper" [NM 21]). Paul had prayed to God that God would take this spirit from him (2Cor 12:8). God had answered, "My grace [Spiritual power] is sufficient for thee." Paul concludes, "for my strength is made perfect in weakness." What does Paul mean that weakness makes for strength?

From Trials to Strength

nm344 » "No trial has taken you except what is common to man. But God is faithful, who will not permit you to be tested above what you are able. But with the trial, he will make a way of escape, so that you may be able to bear it" (1Cor 10:13). Thus so far we see God's grace to Christians is sufficient, and that God will not permit any Christian to be tested in a Spiritual trial above what he is able to endure. God further tells us that for Christians "all things work together for good" (Rom 8:28). This includes trials.

nm345 » "And not only so, but we glory in trial also: knowing that trial works patience; and patience, proof; and proof, hope" (Rom 5:3-4). "My brethren, count it all joy when you fall into divers trials; knowing this, that the trying of your faith works patience. But let patience have her complete work, that you may be perfect and entire, lacking nothing" (James 1:2-4). It is through trials that God works good fruit in Christians.

nm346 » "Now no chastening for the present seems to be joyous, but grievous: nevertheless afterward it yields that peaceable fruit of righteousness unto them which are exercised thereby" (Heb 12:11). Those exercised by these trials produce good fruit, if they have the grace that allows them endurance and overcoming of these trials (2Cor 12:9 & 1Cor 10:13). The whole world is now in a trial because of the "other-mind." See *New Mind* 20.

nm347 » Of course some fruits of the Spirit are not produced through trials such as those described in Mark 13:11, "but when they shall lead you, and deliver you up, take no thought beforehand what you shall speak, neither do you premeditate: but whatsoever shall be given you in that hour, that speak you: for it is not you that speak, but the Holy Spirit."

nm348 » *Review*. It is God's Spirit that produces good works, and God calls and chooses people to fulfill positions in the Church according to his will (2Cor 10:13; 2Tim 1:9). God gives to Christians

Spiritual power by measure (Eph 4:7). God gives roles in the aeonian Kingdom of God under Christ, by the fact that God through his Spirit and by the measure of power given, does the good works. Why?

No Reason To Boast: God Gives The Power

nm349 » "Not of works, lest any man should boast" (Eph 2:9). Although in this verse it is referring in context to being saved through Faith, and is not speaking about reward according to works, the same conclusion is still valid. The scriptures quoted in this paper clearly indicate it is God who does the good works, not man. Even Christ the man said it was his Father that did his works (John 14:10). Shall we take Christ's word as true? Further Christ the man did his works according to the power given him: "And declared to be the Son of God with power, according to the Spirit of holiness" (Rom 1:4). But unlike regular Christians, Christ the man was given the Spirit without measure (John 3:34). He was a man given enough power to be the only sinless human in this age (see *God Papers*).

But We Work

nm350 » Let's clarify something here through an allegory. We are like the branches of a tree (Rom 11:17), and God is like the root and trunk. God as the root and trunk supports us, the branches (Rom 11:18). God provides the sap (Spirit), for us, the branches, to produce the good fruit (John 15:5). Without the sap and support from the root and trunk, we would produce nothing. God does the works by providing the support and sap for us to produce the fruit. Yet we, the branches, do perform works, but only because of the support of the sap from the trunk and root. We, the branches, produce fruit according to the amount and quality of sap from the roots reaching us.

nm351 » Hear what Paul says, "I have in a figure transferred to myself and to Apollos for your sakes; that you might learn in us not to think of men above that which is written [God gives the increase, 1Cor 3:7], that no one of you be puffed up for one against another. For who makes you to differ from another? and what have you that you didn't receive? now if you did receive it, why do you glory, as if you hadn't received it?" (1Cor 4:6-7) "And base things of the world, and things which are despised, has God chosen, yes, and things which are not, to bring to nought things that are: that no flesh should glory in his presence ... That, according as it is written, he that glories, let him glory in the Lord" (1Cor 1:28, 29, 31).

nm352 » It is God who does the good works; it is God who creates Spiritual men according to the measure of Spiritual power given them

(Deut 8:17-18). God gives his Spiritual power; one cannot earn Spiritual power; one cannot qualify for Spiritual power, it is given to those it is given to (see "Predestination Paper" [NM 8]). Spiritual power is given as a non-earned gift, so people won't become puffed up and have glory in their own selves.

nm353 » Let's summarize this topic through a few scriptures. Note the following verse in a Spiritual way:

- "Surely your turning of things upside down shall be esteemed as the potter's clay: for shall the work say of him that made it, He made me not? or shall the thing framed say of him that framed it, He had no understanding?" (Isa 29:16)

nm354 » God is the potter; we are the clay (Isa 45:9-10; 64:8). Notice the rhetorical question in Isaiah 29:16. Shall real Christians, the clay, the Spiritual work of God's hand, say God made them not? The answer, "we all are the work of your [God's] hand" (Isa 64:8).

Notes for NM 12

Parables of Pounds And Talents

nm355 » We have just seen in the paper, "According to Works" [NM 12], that God gives Spiritual power by measure. As explained, God gave Paul just enough Spiritual power to do the task he was commissioned to do, "my grace is sufficient for you" (2Cor 12:9).

nm356 » We saw in that paper that the parable of pounds shows us that Spiritual Christians are given rulership (serviceship) over cities according to how much they produce from the one "pound" that was given to each at the start. One gained ten times as much as what he was originally given, and he received rulership over ten cities. Another gained five times as much, and he was given rulership over five cities in the kingdom of God. Remember rulership in the kingdom of God will be different from how it is now done in this age (see Mark 10:42-44). But the one who gained nothing, his only pound was taken away from him because he gained nothing.

nm357 » Now the "pounds" of this parable can be looked at as being good Spiritual fruit. The more good fruit (pounds) one produces, the more responsibility that person will have in the kingdom of God. Look up the following verses and see how those who will rule in the kingdom of God are those who produce much good Spiritual fruit: Mat 13:23; Luke 8:8, 15; John 15:5, 8, 16; Rev 2:26. Thus, those who produce much Spiritual good fruit receive rulership (serviceship) according to their production of good fruit (pounds).

nm358 » Notice that all the servants in the parable of pounds received just one pound to begin with. This should be looked upon as what any one person has in good fruit without God's Spirit. Someone without God's Spirit is like one who has one pound. But with God's Spirit, one produces much good Spiritual fruit (pounds).

Now let's examine the parable of talents:

- "Again, it will be like a man going on a journey, who called his servants and entrusted his property to them. To one he gave five talents [a talent was worth about a thousand dollars] of money, to another two talents, and to another one talent, each according to his ability. Then he went on his journey. The man who had received the five talents went at once and put his money to work and gained five more. So also, the one with the two talents gained two more. But the man who had received the one talent went off, dug a hole in the ground and hid his master's money. After a long time the master of those servants returned and settled accounts with them. The man who had received the five talents brought the other five. 'Master,' he said, 'you entrusted me with five talents. See, I have gained five more.'

- His master replied, 'Well done, good and faithful servant! You have been faithful with a few things; I will put you in charge of many things. Come and share your master's happiness!'

- The man with two talents also came. 'Master,' he said, 'you entrusted me with two talents; see, I have gained two more.'

- His master replied, 'Well done, good and faithful servant! You have been faithful with a few things; I will put you in charge of many things. Come and share your master's happiness!'

- Then the man who had received the one talent came. 'Master,' he said, 'I knew that you are a hard man, harvesting where you have not sown and gathering where you have not scattered seed. So I was afraid and went out

and hid your talent in the ground. See, here is what
belongs to you.'

- His master replied, 'You wicked, lazy servant! So you knew
that I harvest where I have not sown and gather where I
have not scattered seed? Well then, you should have put
my money on deposit with the bankers, so that when I
returned I would have received it back with interest [KJV,
"usury"].

- 'Take the talent from him and give it to the one who has
the ten talents. For everyone who has will be given more,
and he will have an abundance. Whoever does not have,
even what he has will be taken from him. And throw that
worthless servant outside, into the darkness, where there
will be weeping and grinding of teeth.'" (Mat 25:14-30, NIV)

nm359 » Notice the servants in this parable were apparently given
talents according to their ability. Since we are to perceive Spiritual
lessons out of the Bible (John 4:24), then the "ability" spoken about is
Spiritual ability. These servants were given "talents" according to their
Spiritual ability. And we showed in the paper, "According to Works"
[NM 12] that Spiritual ability is a gift. Thus, the "talents" given
correspond exactly to the given Spiritual ability. Hence, these "talents"
can be looked upon as being one and the same as the degree of
Spiritual ability that is given to each Christian. The person receiving
five talents can be looked upon as one who is given five times the
Spiritual ability as the person with one talent; he thus will grow five
times, so to speak, in Spiritual ability.

nm360 » You can see in this parable that as each was given, so did
they gain, except the person given one talent. The person who was
given five talents brought back to Christ an increase in good Spiritual
works according to what was given to him in Spiritual ability. And the
one given two talents brought back two more talents. But the one
given one talent brought back just one talent – the one talent given to
him. Each (except the one) brought back an increase according to what
was given to him. And each was given talents according to their ability,
Spiritually speaking. Therefore, each produced according to what was
given to him, except the person given the one talent: he produced no
increase.

Both Parables Together

nm361 » The servant in the parable of pounds who gained ten pounds is merely a servant who was given ten talents of Spiritual ability (cf. Mat 25:28 with Luke 19:24 in context noting in Mat 25:15 that the parable didn't mention someone receiving ten talents). Not only do these parables need to be looked upon as going together, they have to be looked upon that way in order to understand them. The servant who gained five "pounds" is merely the one who was given five "talents" of Spiritual ability. The servant who gained two "pounds" is the servant who was given two "talents" of Spiritual ability.

nm362 » Now the one who gained nothing, who just kept the one "pound" was the one given the one "talent" of ability. Yet since we know that those who are real Christians do produce much fruit (John 15:5, 8, 16; and paper called "Prove Paper" [NM 10]), then we know that the one who produced no pounds above and beyond the original one given him, is a non-Christian. A non-Christian is one without the New Mind, he is one with the old mind. The one "talent" can be looked upon as the normal Spiritual ability of anyone without God's Spirit. And the one "pound" can be looked upon as the degree of good fruits one has without God's Spirit.

Usury

nm363 » For another way to prove that the person who had but one talent and one pound was a non-Christian please note Luke 19:23 and Mat 25:27. Here it says God was requiring usury (interest) from this person. But notice it is against the law of God in the Old Testament to take interest from a member of Israel, yet it is alright to take interest from a stranger or Gentile (Deut 23:20). Now Spiritual Christians are Spiritual Israelites (Gal 6:16). Therefore those without God's Spirit are spiritual strangers or spiritual Gentiles. Since God is a brethren of the Israelites, he is their Father, he cannot require interest from them, but he can require interest from strangers. Since God does not break his own laws in an antitypical way, the person from whom God requires usury or interest is a spiritual stranger, a non-Christian. The persons with one talent and one pound God required usury from. Thus, they are spiritual strangers, or non-Christians.

NM 13: All Saved

Scriptural Proof
God's Will
As One Goes All Must Go
Lazarus and the Rich Man
Unpardonable Sin?
Sin to Death?

NM13 Abstract

Why are we calling this paper, "all saved"? Can all be saved when in our translations of the Bible it says some will be damned or judged forever? Again, in this paper, we are dealing with the mistranslation of words that mean aeonian or age but have been mistranslated into the words forever or eternal. We will examine some scripture that says that God will save all and we will thus begin to see that God will save all by three orders or ranks or at three different times. We will also look at the parable pertaining to Lazarus and the rich man and the scripture about the unpardonable sin.

nm364 » Why do we call this paper, "all saved" when so many believe that some will be damned forever? There is a good reason for many believing in an *ever*lasting punishment for when you read most of today's translations of the Bible you see scripture that says some will be damned forever. But these scriptures have been mistranslated. In the Bible words that mean aeonian or age in the original languages were mistranslated into everlasting: resulting in the confusion and wrong doctrine of the majority who call themselves Christians.

nm365 » There are many verses in the Bible that indicate that *all* will be saved. Because of the mistranslation of words that mean aeonian into words like "forever," many are blinded to the fact that all will be saved. In this paper we will show you some of the scripture, and amplify on the scripture.

God: Good to All & Mercy on All.

nm366 » Notice the following scripture: "The LORD is good to *all*, and His mercies are over *all* His works. *All* Thy works shall give thanks to Thee, O LORD" (Psalm 145:9-10, NASB). This scripture is speaking about ALL. God's mercies are over *all* His works. In the truest sense, all means all (see, "Does All Mean All Paper" [NM 14]). In the higher meaning, or Spiritual meaning of the Bible we take this for what it means. All will receive mercy (note Romans 11:32). As Romans 9:23-24 indicates, Christians (the ones with the New Mind) are given mercy. As with the Christians, so too with the rest of mankind. All will obtain mercy. All will receive the Spirit (New Mind) that brings with it true freedom and true salvation because God is not partial. Each receives salvation in his own order or appointed time (1Cor 15:23-24).

All Saved: Scriptural Proof

nm367 » *Everyone into the Kingdom*. Let's look at other scriptural proof that all will be saved, eventually. "The law and the prophets were until John: since that time the kingdom of God is preached, and *everyone* presses into it" (Luke 16:16). This says that EVERYONE presses into the kingdom of God. It does not say some, or most, but it does say everyone presses into it. This scripture means what it says.

nm368 » *All Israel Saved*. "And so *all* Israel shall be saved" (Rom 11:26). Now either this statement is true or it is wrong. It says that ALL Israel will be saved. It does say *all* Israel, therefore it means all who ever lived in Israel. But what about the Gentiles? The Bible uses the word "Gentile" to mean all who are not part of Israel. Now God's word says that God is not a respecter of persons (Deut 10:17; Job 34:19; Acts 10:34; Eph 6:9; Rom 2:11). God is not biased. God has no partiality. Now if it is true that God is not partial, why would He save *all* of Israel and not save all of the Gentiles? Thus, since God is not partial, then all of Israel *and* all of the Gentiles will be saved. We just showed you (Luke 16:16) that God says all will be pressed into the Kingdom. Now through a logical construction, we have shown you the same thing. God meant what He said when He said: "in him [Christ] shall the Gentiles trust" (Rom 15:12).

nm369 » *All to Worship God*. "All people whom You have made shall come and worship before You, O Lord; and shall glorify Your name" (Psalm 86:9). If *all* will, in the truest sense of the word, worship God and glorify Him, then doesn't that mean all will turn to God and be saved thereby?

nm370 » **Mercy on All**. "For God has concluded them all in unbelief, that He might have mercy upon *all*" (Rom 11:32). Now in the 11th chapter of Romans, Paul is speaking to true Christians. Paul tells them that they have obtained mercy (v. 30). God gave mercy on all of them and made them part of the vessels of mercy (Rom 9:23). Now since we have proved in this book that all true Christians will be saved, and since in Romans 11:30 it shows Christians being allowed to be Christians through mercy, then when God shows mercy on the rest of mankind, the rest of mankind will be saved. Did it or did it not say, "mercy upon *all*" (Rom 11:32).

nm371 » **Lost Saved**. "But if our gospel be hid, it is hid to them that are lost" (2Cor 4:3). God, through Paul, says the gospel has been *hidden* from some who are called the "lost." Other scripture clearly indicates that God has hidden from many the good news of God for a purpose (Rom 9:18; 11:8-10; Mat 13:10-17; etc.). That purpose is for man to have a time, or an age with wrong so he will be able to know good (see "Reason Why" paper [NM 19] and the *God Paper* [GP 7]). "For the Son of man is come to seek and to save that which was lost" (Luke 19:10). Jesus is not only the savior of the Christians, but to those the gospel has been hidden from – the lost. "And we have seen and do testify that the Father sent the Son to be the Savior of the world" (1John 4:14). Now the word "world" is used to mean those of the worldly ways (1John 2:15-16). Jesus Christ was sent to save the "lost." He was sent to save the whole world, not just Christians.

nm372 » **Those that Erred will Understand**. "They also that erred in spirit shall come to understanding, and they that murmured shall learn doctrine" (Isa 29:24). Who are those who erred in spirit? In 1John 4:1-6 it gives a test so as to ascertain who are real Christians, and who are not. Those who do not pass the test are in the spirit of error (1John 4:6). Those who erred in spirit, are those who are being led by a satanic spirit of error (the other-mind), and are not being led by the Spirit of God (the New Mind). Thus, according to Isaiah 29:24, those who were led by the spirit of error shall understand, they will learn doctrine. Other scripture shows that they will learn after they are resurrected in the resurrection of the dead, which occurs after the 1000 years (Rev 20:5; 1Cor 15:21; NM24).

nm373 » **All to Bow to and Agree with God**. "I have sworn by myself, the word is gone out of my mouth in righteousness, and shall not return, that unto Me *every* knee shall bow, *every* tongue shall swear" (Isa 45:23). What does the Bible mean "every knee shall bow"? What does it mean to bow?

nm374 » Now when a person bows before an important person, he is in essence saying he respects the person he bows down to. Today many bow to a god, and think they bow to the God. Yet these people bow falsely to *their* god. If they were true in their bowing, they would show their respect by obeying their gods. To bow before something or someone is to show respect, or to humble one's self.

nm375 » When God says that *all* will bow before God, He means to bow truly to God. The world already bows hypocritically to their gods, while thinking these gods are the true God. Why would God say *all* would bow to God, or to Christ (He is in the God), when most do already, but hypocritically? God is not talking about hypocritical bowing to God. There is enough of that now. That kind of bowing is wrong. God desires truth.

nm376 » But notice further, "every tongue shall swear" (Isa 45:23). This does not mean swear against God. No, all will swear with God. All will pledge or bow with God, by God, and for God.

nm377 » Let's look at another very similar verse to Isaiah 45:23: "As I live, says the Lord, every knee shall bow to me, and every tongue shall confess to God" (Rom 14:11). Let's look at the phrase, "every tongue shall confess to God." What does the word "confess" mean? The word translated "confess" here comes from a Greek word that means, to acknowledge; to agree fully. Thus a better translation would read: "and every tongue shall agree with God." *All will acknowledge God, and agree with God.* "That at the name of Jesus *every* knee should bow, of things in heaven, and things in the earth, and things under the earth; and that *every* tongue should confess that Jesus Christ is Lord, to the glory of God the Father" (Phil 2:10-11).

nm378 » **Jesus Died for All**. "For there is one God, and one mediator between God and man, the man Christ Jesus; Who gave himself a ransom for *ALL*, to be testified in due time" (1Tim 2:5-6). "And He Himself is the forgiveness [propitiation] for our sins; and not for ours only, but also for *those of* the whole world" (1John 2:2). Now it is due time that everyone knows that Christ died for *all*, not just Christians. Jesus came to save *all* those of this age (1John 4:14).

God's Will: All To Be Saved

nm379 » Let's look at God's will. What does God wish or will for mankind? Can God do what He wishes? Can anyone prevent God from doing His will? Let's see what God has to say about this subject. "For this is good and acceptable in the sight of God our Savior; Who wishes *all* to be saved, and to come unto the knowledge of the truth" (1Tim 2:3-4). That is His wish or will. What else is His will? The Lord is "not willing that any should perish, but that ALL should come to repentance" (2Peter 3:9). Now the Lord does his Father's will (Heb 10:7; John 6:38). Thus, God the Father's will is for all to come to repentance, and for all to be saved and come to the knowledge of the Truth (2Pet 3:9; 1Tim 2:4)..

nm380 » *All to Repent*. How does one come to repentance? How does one come to turn away from the confusion of the world's ways? As 2Timothy 2:25 and Acts 11:18 show, it is God who *gives* or grants repentance (see "Repentance Paper" [NM 3]). Thus, this clearly shows that God can have His wish that all will come to repentance. All God has to do is give mankind the power to repent. Why hasn't God done this? God is allowing most people in this age to do wrong for a purpose (see "Reason Why" paper [NM 19]).

nm381 » *Christ Does God's Will*. Now Christ had come to do just one overall thing. He came to do the will of his Father (Heb 10:7; John 6:38). "My food is to do the will of Him [the Father] that sent me, and to FINISH HIS WORK" (John 4:34). Christ is the savior of the world (1John 4:14). Jesus prayed not too long before his death "that the world may believe that You have sent me" (John 17:21). How does one pray? "If we ask any thing according to His will, He hears us" (1John 5:14). Jesus was asking according to his Father's will when he prayed asking that the world believe. It is through Faith that one overcomes (1John 5:4-5). And those who overcome shall be saved (Rev 2:7). Jesus said he came to do his Father's will. Will Jesus do his Father's will? Or will Christ fail? Christ will do his Father's will, and the whole world will believe. They will come to believe when they are raised-up to life in the Great Last Day after the Thousand Years (see "Thousand Years and Beyond Paper" [NM 15]).

God's Will Shall Be Done

nm382 » "So shall my word be that goes forth out of my mouth: it shall not return unto me void, but it shall accomplish that which I please [will or wish], and it shall prosper in the thing whereto I sent it" (Isa 55:11). "Declaring the end from the beginning, and from the ancient times the things that are not yet done, saying, My counsel shall stand, and I will do all my pleasure [will] ... I have spoken it, I will also bring it to pass; I have purposed it, I will also do it" (Isa 46:10-11). God said He would do *all* his pleasure (his will), and that He will bring it to pass. God's will is to have all to be saved (1Tim 2:4). **God does his will, God is God, who can stop God**?

As One Goes All Must Go

nm383 » **Everything that a person is, has been given to him either by his parents, his environment, or his spiritual father**. All the great minds of the world are what they are from what they received physically or mentally from their parents and environment. All the great Spiritual people are what they are through the gifts of the Spirit (1Cor 12:1-31). Thus, if what we are, is because we have received it from outside of us, then as some go (saved at Christ's return, 1Cor 15:23), then *all* must go, or God is being partial to some in the creation. Since God says He is not partial (Rom 2:11), then what He *gives* to one (Christ the man), or to some (the Christians), He must give to ALL. Doesn't God's word say you are what you are because of what you have received? (Prov 22:6; 1Cor 4:7; etc.) Does not common sense tell us this also? Did not God's word say God wasn't partial? So as one goes, ALL must go. Is this confirmed elsewhere in God's word?

nm384 » Compare the following verses. "Therefore as by the offense of one [Adam's] judgment came upon all men to condemnation; even so by the righteousness of one [Christ] the free gift came upon *all* into justification of life" (Rom 5:18). And, "for as in Adam all die, even so in Christ shall *all* be made alive" (1Cor 15:22). In verses 45-47 of 1Corinthians, chapter 15, it tells us that Adam is the first man and Christ is the second man (the antitypical man). By comparing Romans 5:18 (first part) and 1Corinthians 15:22 (first part) we see that Adam died for his offense – the first man died for his sins. But by comparing the last parts of these two verses we see that through the medium of Christ, "ALL men into justification of life," and "in Christ shall ALL be made alive." Thus, as Adam died, all died. And as Christ went, all will go eventually (see, "Does All Mean All Paper" [NM 14]).

nm385 » ***Potter and the Clay***. To prove the point we are making, "has not the potter power over the clay, of the same lump to make one vessel unto honor, and another unto dishonor?" (Rom 9:21) Yet Romans 11:16 shows us that as the first fruit (Jesus) goes, so will the whole lump. And Romans 9:21 says from the same lump God has made two groups of people – the vessels of wrath, and the vessels of mercy. In the "Predestination Paper" [NM 8] we proved that the vessels of mercy were the real Christians, while the vessels of wrath were the rest who have only the "other-mind." In the "Predestination Paper" [NM 8] we proved that *all* the vessels of mercy will be saved. Since we know that God is not partial (Rom 2:11), then if the first fruit (Christ) is saved, and the vessels of mercy (real Christians) are saved, then *all* of the lump of mankind will be saved.

Three Divisions/Orders/Groups

nm386 » There are three groups or divisions being saved. One, Jesus Christ the man, was saved from death at his resurrection from the dead. The next to be saved is at Christ's (the Messiah's) coming (1Cor 15:23). This group is the called and chosen *few* (Mat 22:14) who are allowed to see the way "which leads unto life" (Mat 7:14). As Matthew 7:14 says, "*few* there be that find it." This group is also called the "vessels of mercy" (Rom 9:23).

nm387 » The last group or division is called the "vessels of wrath," the "dead," the "children of Satan," and so forth. The first book of Corinthians 15:24 shows us **when** this last group will be saved – at "the end." This "end" is the end of the Spiritual creation. It is at this "end" of creation, which is also the beginning of the totally NEW cosmos, that all will be in God, for at that time all will be "the God, all in all" (1Cor 15:28). As we have shown in the *God Papers*, all went out of God in the beginning of creation, but all will go back into God so that may be "the God, all in all" (1Cor 15:28; see *God Papers*, GP 6). This is the great cycle. All went out of God, but all will go back into God. God tells us through scripture that all will be in God (see Greek text: John 17:23; 2Cor 5:17-21; Eph 1:9-10; John 12:32; Col 1:20; 1Cor 15:28; etc.). Thus, all will be saved.

nm388 » ***Three Measures***. "Another parable spake he unto them; the kingdom of heaven is like unto leaven, which a woman took and hid in THREE measures of meal, till the WHOLE was leavened" (Mat 13:33). These three measures of meal are shown in 1Corinthians 15:23-24. The FIRST measure is Christ (the first fruit). The SECOND measure is the Christians (the first fruits). The THIRD measure is the rest of mankind (the vessels of wrath). There are three measures or groups from the same lump (mankind). They will all be saved, but at different times (see "God's Appointed Times Paper" [16]). Here Christ uses "leaven" to teach us a truth even though leaven is used in a negative way in other scripture. This is good leaven (not sin) because the parable teaches us about the "kingdom of heaven," and how the *whole* lump of bread is saved – in three measures.

Lazarus and the Rich Man

nm389 » Many "prove" their "hell" and "lake of fire" theories from the parable of Lazarus and the Rich Man. Let's look at this parable. Turn to Luke 16:19-31 and read verses 19-21. "And it came to pass, that the beggar [Lazarus] died, and was carried by the angels into Abraham's bosom." Now this parable has no time element. Jesus does not say *when* this will take place or if it already happened. Of course, remember this is a *parable*. Notice that the beggar died. The Bible tells us that those who die have no consciousness after death (Eccl 9:5; Psalm 146:4). Those who die are dead. Man is not immortal. Man is mortal, he has no immortal soul, but he will have an immortal Spirit (see "Body, Soul Paper" [PR1]).

nm390 » Next it says that Lazarus was carried to Abraham's bosom by the angels. Now scripture tells us that Abraham is also dead now, but he still is "waiting" dead in his grave for the promise (read Acts 7:1-5; Heb 11:8-13). The promise given to Abraham was a kingdom in the land of Palestine (Gen 12:5-7; 13:15,18). This land was to Abraham and his seed for an aeonian period of time. As other scriptures show this land for an aeonian time is the same Kingdom of God that is promised to Christians (see "Seed Paper" [PR1]). Jesus said that Abraham would be in the kingdom of God (Luke 13:28). Notice that Lazarus was carried by angels into the bosom of Abraham. Now, we know the beggar will be carried into "Abraham's" bosom by angels at Christ's return (Mat 16:27; 24:31; 25:31). And that they will meet Christ in the air at cloud level (after being resurrected) to bring Jesus down to earth (1Thes 4:17; Rom 10:6) to rule *on* earth (Rev 5:10).

nm391 » We see that Lazarus will be carried to Abraham's bosom. Turn to Isaiah 40:11. Here God will care for His people as a shepherd does for his sheep, which He will carry "in His bosom." Jesus was "in the bosom" of his Father (John 1:18), enjoying the Father's Spiritual power. Moses carried the children of Israel in his bosom. To be in one's bosom is to have that one's love and protection, and share in his inheritance. Therefore at the resurrection to the kingdom of God at Christ's coming, Lazarus will be carried into the care of "Abraham" and his seed.

- ■ ***Rich Man in Hell***. In the last part of verse 22 of the parable we see that the rich man dies and is buried. "And in hell [the grave] he lifts up his eyes, being in torments, and sees Abraham afar off, and Lazarus in his bosom" (v. 23). The word "hell" comes from the inspired word "hades" in the Greek language. It simply means "grave." But look, the rich man lifts up his eyes. He is in the grave, and he lifts up his eyes. Now it did say he died, that he was in the grave, and that he lifted up his eyes. But this isn't all. After the rich man cried to Abraham to have Lazarus come and cool his tongue with a few drops of water, the rich man said: "I am tormented *in* this flame" (v. 24). He said he was tormented IN a flame. It didn't say he was beside the flame, it said he was *in* the flame. In the inspired Greek it says he was *in* the

flame. Does this mean there is a hell as the world knows it?
No, but it does mean this "rich man" was in the flame, and
that he was being tormented in the flame. It also says he
was in the grave ("hell"), that he lifted up his eyes in this
grave, and that he was *in* a fire. Thus, his grave must have a
fire in it. The Bible clearly describes a grave with fire in it –
the lake of fire (Rev 20:10).

nm392 » How can a man be dead, and in a grave with fire, while
being tormented in it, when the Bible clearly tells us a dead man is
dead and unconscious? The Bible does say the rich man was in a flame,
not near it, or about to go into it, but in a flame which is also called the
rich man's grave. Have we disproved the reliability of the Bible? No, for
is the rich man, in reality a human being?

Satan and the Rich Man

nm393 » Turn to Ezekiel chapter 28. "Son of man, say unto the prince
of Tyrus, Thus says the Lord GOD; Because your heart is lifted up, and
you have said, I am a God, I sit in the seat of God, in the midst of the
seas, yet you art a man, and not God" (v. 2). Now continue to read on
until verse 13, "You have been in Eden the garden of God; every
precious stone was your covering, the sardius, topaz, and the
diamond..." (v. 13). Now this physical prince of Tyrus was not in the
Garden of Eden. Further these precious stones mentioned in verse 13
are used throughout the Bible to describe spiritual beings (see Mal 3:17;
Isa 54:11-12; Rev 4:3). Man is not a spiritual being. Now look at verse 14.
"You art the anointed cherub that covers . . ." By noting what we have
shown so far and by examining the whole chapter we can see it is dual.
The typical version speaks about the prince of Tyrus as a man. The
antitypical version speaks about the prince of Tyrus as Satan, for it was
Satan who was in the Garden of Eden, who is a spiritual being, and who
is an anointed cherub. In fact, not only is chapter 28 of Ezekiel dual,
but all the Bible (see the "Duality Paper"). **The parable of Lazarus and the
rich man is only a parable, but it is a parable with a higher
meaning**.

nm394 » Notice verse 5, "By your great wisdom and by your traffic
have you increased your *riches*, and your heart is lifted up because of
your *riches*." Verse 16, "By the *multitude of your merchandise* they have
filled the midst of you with violence" (see also Rev 18:11-16). Thus, both
the prince of Tyrus and the spirit of Tyrus (Satan) are called RICH. "I
will cast you to the ground ... by the iniquity of your traffic; therefore
will I bring forth a fire from the midst of you, it shall devour you..." (v.
17, 18).

nm395 » God is describing the coming fate of Satan, he is to be cast into a pit of fire. The prince of Tyrus in Ezekiel 28 is used metonymically to represent Satan as is the Pharaoh and the tree in Ezekiel 31. Note the same fate for Satan in Ezekiel 31:18, 14 – cast into a pit.

nm396 » In Isaiah 14 it also describes Satan in the antitypical, and Babylon in the typical meaning of this chapter. What does God, through the medium of Isaiah, say about Satan?: "Yet you shall be brought down to hell [the grave], to the sides of the pit" (v. 15). Therefore, from the above verses we see that Satan is rich, has a multitude of merchandise, and will go down to hell (a pit in the ground with fire in it).

nm397 » We are beginning to see that the rich man in the *parable* is much like the prince of Tyrus. This prince in Ezekiel 28 is called a man, but some of the things attributed to him could only be attributed to Satan. Ezekiel 28 is dual, as the parable of Lazarus and the Rich Man is dual. The rich man of this parable not only represents a rich *man*, but also the spiritual Satan. In Ezekiel 28 the man prince could not have been in the garden of Eden, thus we know it was talking only of Satan at that point in the chapter. The same with the parable of the rich man – it was Satan who lifted up his eyes in the flame, not a man. For a man cannot live in a burning flame, but a spiritual being can. Satan is a spiritual being. **Transpose "Satan" for the rich man in the parable and the parable comes alive**.

nm398 » "And the devil that deceived them was cast into the lake of fire and brimstone, where the Beast and the false prophet are [the Beast and the false prophet are physical, thus, they are burned up and their ashes are left in the pit, but the spiritual Beast (Satan) and the spiritual false prophet (Satan) are in the pit of fire], and shall be tormented day and night into the ages of ages" (Rev 20:10). Revelation 20:1-3 describes the place of Satan's "*death*" (he is as good as dead since he can't come up out of the pit of death, Rev 20:1-3), and Satan's *trying* (the Greek word translated "tormented" means – trying as by fire).

nm399 » **How is Satan being tormented?** (Luke 16:23-25) A few verses in the Bible, project that Satan and his spiritual demons *need* to dwell inside animal beings, if not, they are tormented thereby (see Luke 11:24; Acts 8:7; Mark 5:12). Thus, since Satan will be sealed in a burning pit where there can be no animal (mortal) life because of the flame, Satan will be tormented because he cannot dwell inside animals.

nm400 » For 1000 years Satan and his demons (the "other-mind") must live in a state of torment (Rev 20:3, 7). But the torment of not dwelling in another physical being is not the only factor that will torment Satan. "You believe that there is one God? You do well, the demons also believe, and tremble" (James 2:19). Satan and his demons will be "in perpetual chains sealed under darkness into the judgment of the great day" (Jude 6). Satan is in the dark Spiritually, will be in a sealed bottomless pit that burns with fire, and will be tormented mentally thereby.

Great Gulf

nm401 » The "great gulf" that is fixed between Abraham and Lazarus, and the Rich Man (Satan) is: (1) the seal that will be set upon Satan (Rev 20:1-3) for the 1000 years (Rev 20:7).; (2) in the case of the typical rendition of the parable (a rich man belonging to the vessels of wrath), it speaks of the great gulf between the two appointed parts of mankind, that is, between the vessels of mercy and the vessels of wrath. After the vessels of mercy are saved, it will be 1000 years before the vessels of wrath are saved.

nm402 » The "problem" of the parable of Lazarus is solved when one sees the higher meaning of the parable. Remember this parable is just that – a parable. Parables are meant to teach us something; they are aids to understanding God and his plan.

Unpardonable Sin?

nm403 » Is there an unpardonable sin? Is there a sin that God will not pardon?:

- "'Assuredly, I say to you, all sins will be forgiven the sons of men, and whatever blasphemies they may utter; but he who blasphemes against the holy Spirit never has forgiveness, but is subject to eternal condemnation' – because they said, 'He has an unclean spirit.'" (Mark 3:28-30, NKJV)

- "Therefore I say to you, every sin and blasphemy will be forgiven men, but the blasphemy against the Spirit will not be forgiven men. Anyone who speaks a word against the Son of Man, it will be forgiven him; but whoever speaks against the Holy Spirit; it will not be forgiven him, either in this age or in the (age) to come" (Mat 12:31-32, NKJV).

nm404 » IF there is an unpardonable sin – a sin that can *never* be forgiven, then God cannot keep his word. There are many scriptures that speak of ALL being saved (see *Does All Mean All*, GP 6 of *God Papers*, etc). God tells us through the Bible to forgive and not to repay evil for evil (Rom 12:17); overcome evil with good (Rom 12:21); do not render evil with evil or insult with insult but with blessing (1Pet 3:9); to forgive your brother time after time (Mat 18:21-35).

nm405 » From Mark 3:28-30 and Matthew 12:31-32, some think they prove that there is a forever judgement or damnation for sinners. BUT they are using a mistranslation of the words *aion* and *aionios*. There are many scriptures that speak about ALL being saved (see "All Saved" and "Does All Mean All" papers, and *God Papers*, GP 6). *If* there is an unpardonable sin, then God will not keep his Word – all will not be saved. But God keeps all his words, thus, all will be saved and all will go into the God (see *God Papers*). Notice what the correct translation does to the so-called unpardonable sin:

- "Verily I say to you, that all the sins shall be forgiven to the sons of men, and evil speakings with which they might speak evil, but whoever may speak evil in regard to the Holy Spirit hath not forgiveness – to the *age*, but is in danger of *age-during* judgment; because they said, 'he hath an unclean spirit.'" (Mark 3:28-29, Young's *Literal Translation of the Holy Bible*)

- "And whoever may speak a word against the Son of Man it shall be forgiven to him, but whoever may speak against the Holy Spirit, it shall not be forgiven him, neither in this *age*, nor in that [age] which is coming" (Mat 12:32, Young's *Literal Translation of the Holy Bible*).

nm406 » Because they were speaking against Jesus Christ's Holy Spirit ("He said this because they were saying, 'He has an evil spirit.' " – Mark 3:30, NIV), Christ said their sin is not forgiven "neither in this age [age of Satan] nor in that (age) which is coming" (Mat 12:32). That age that is coming is the age of the true God. Further their sin would not be forgiven "into the age but is in danger of agelasting [*aionios*] judgment" (Mark 3:28-29, Young's translation and see Greek text – the Greek word for "judgment," Strong's #2920, is in the older Greek texts instead of the word for "sin," Strong's #265; see Greek text, George Ricker Berry, Zondervan, 1969 printing).

nm407 » Those who speak against Jesus, also speak against His Holy Spirit, and they are in danger of the aeonian judgment *because* they do not have the Spirit that enables them to see the truth. "Therefore I tell you that no one who is speaking by the Spirit of God says, 'Jesus be cursed.'" If you have the Spirit of God you cannot speak against the real Jesus Christ. It is impossible because you have the Spirit of Truth that knows the truth when it sees it. That is why Christ said their sin is not forgiven, 'neither in this age [Satan's] nor in that (age) which is coming'– because they did not have the Spirit to see the Truth of Christ. And those without the Spirit of Truth will not be forgiven in this age of evil or in the coming 1000 years. But after the 1000 years they will be forgiven (see "Thousand Years and Beyond" paper [NM 15]). These scriptures about the so-called unpardonable sin are tests that one can take to prove to one's self if he is or is not a Christian. If one blasphemes the Spirit, or those with the Spirit, he is in danger of the aeonian punishment if he does not repent, because he is proving he does not have the Spirit that sees the Truth and brings life during the 1000 years instead of the judgment during the 1000 years.

Sin to Death?

nm408 » Now we can understand the sin to death (1John 5:16). Those who sin to death (aeonian death as judgment for their sins) are those not in the Spirit. Those who sin not to death (aeonian death) are those begotten of the Spirit. Remember there are sins among real Christians (1John 1:8-10), but not willful or intentional sinning. If they do sin, it is because of weakness, not because they wish to sin or want to sin. Those in the Spirit sin in this age of Satan, but not to the aeonian death and judgment.

Let us look at 1John 5:16:

- **"If any man see his brother sin a sin which is not unto death** [he has the Spirit, he is not sinning willfully], **he shall ask, and he shall give him life** [aeonian life] **for them that sin not unto death. There is a sin unto death** [those without the Spirit]: **I do not say that he shall pray for it.**"

nm409 » How should we pray? "If we ask anything according to his will, he hears us" (1John 5:14). Now the will of God is to have two groups of people on earth (the vessels of mercy and the vessels of wrath – Rom 9:22-23). The vessels of mercy are for aeonian life and rulership (but they are to suffer like Christ in order to rule – Rom 8:17), and the vessels of wrath are for aeonian punishment away from the glory of the 1000 years (2Thes 1:9). The vessels of mercy were predestinated to be what they are to be. They were set out before the world began for their job. The person predestinated as a vessel of mercy cannot become a vessel of wrath, and contrariwise. Thus, when we pray, we cannot ask God to save a person for aeonian rule, if God had not predestinated that person to be a vessel of mercy. Hence, we should pray thusly: "If you have chosen him to be a vessel of mercy, please give him aeonian life." If he is a vessel of mercy God will give him that life and forgive him his sins. If that person is not a vessel of mercy, then God will not answer and give him mercy in this age.

All Saved: Review

nm410 » We see in this paper that all will be saved. That is, *all* will be freed from the confusion and tears of the old age, and all will be made NEW in the New Age. The tears and confusion of the old age are for a purpose (see *Reason Why* NM 19). Eventually ALL will be made into immortal beings, and all will live in freedom and harmony forever. Many will be punished, for there is a time when people will be punished, but it does not last forever. As we have shown in this book, this age of punishment is for 1000 years. Those who do not receive the New Mind (Spirit of God) in the old age will be dead during the 1000 year age. Their death is their punishment. They will miss 1000 years of life. And as we have shown in the paper called, the "Thousand Years and Beyond Paper" [NM 15], the evil spirits (the invisible evil powers of the old age) will be punished during the 1000 year age: this is the evil minds' (spirits') aeonian punishment for misleading mankind during the old age. Even the evil spirits know that they will be punished at a certain time. About 2000 years ago demons who possessed two individuals said the following to Jesus:

- "And they [demons] cried out, saying, What business do we have with each other, Son of God? Have You come here to torment us before the appointed time?" (Mat 8:29)

nm411 » See "Predestination," "Proof," and "According to Works" papers to better understand the vessels of mercy and wrath; see the "Prayer" [NM 18] to understand praying.

NM 14: Does All Mean All?

NM14 Abstract

This is a follow-up paper to NM13 ("All Saved") in which we examine more scripture about all being saved. We will, in so doing, consider whether or not the Bible really meant to say "all." Does all mean all?

"All" in Context

nm412 » This paper is concerned with the word "all" as it appears in scripture. When God, through the writers of the Bible, uses the word "all," does He mean *all*, or does he exaggerate? Does God stretch the truth like humans? This is very important. There are scriptures in which, if we take the word "all" to mean *all*, we see a different view of scripture than those who think God makes overstatements or exaggerates. There are psychological and spiritual reasons for some not understanding "all" as meaning *all* in scripture.

nm413 » Let us first examine some of the "all" scriptures. Then we will discuss some of the alleged impossibilities about taking "all" as truly meaning ALL.

From Paul's resurrection chapter we read:

> For as in Adam ALL die, even so in Christ shall ALL be made alive (1Cor 15:22; see Rom 5:14-18; Psa 82:7-8).

nm414 » In this one sentence we have "all" repeated twice. Most believe the first "all," that is, because of Adam's sin *all* die. Most do *not* believe the second "all," that is, because of Christ *all* will be made alive. Does God, through Paul's writing, use "all" in two different ways in the same sentence? Is the second "all" ("all be made alive") a hyperbole or just a positive hope? Is the *all* powerful God just exaggerating here?

All Made Alive in Christ

nm415 » What is meant in 1Corinthians 15:22 by "be made alive"? Does it mean be made alive (resurrected) and thereafter be killed in some kind of hell fire? In context what does it mean to "be made alive"?

- "For since by a man came death, by a man also came the resurrection out of the dead. For as in Adam all die, so also in Christ *all* shall be made alive. But each in his own order" (1Cor 15:21-23, NASB).

Christ is the First

nm416 » Here it speaks of the resurrection of the dead. All shall be made *alive*, but not at the same time. There is an *order* to the "all shall be made alive." In context this resurrection has something to do with "the resurrection of the dead.":

- "But each in his own order: Christ the first fruit, after that those who are Christ's at His coming" (1Cor 15:23, NASB).

nm417 » Who was the first one in this "order" of being made alive or thus being resurrected? Christ was the first one resurrected from the dead to life (1Cor 15:12, 19; Rom 1:4; Rev 1:18; etc.). This resurrection of Christ was not a resurrection like Lazarus or like other resurrections reported in the Bible (John 11:23-44; Mat 27:52-53). Lazarus was merely resurrected back to physical and mortal life. But Christ the first of the "order" of the "all shall be made alive," was resurrected to permanent life – to immortal life. Paul in this very important chapter of 1Corinthians chapter 15, explains what kind of resurrection he had in mind:

- "So also is the resurrection of the dead. It is sown a perishable body, it is raised an imperishable body ... for this perishable must put on the imperishable, and this mortal must put on immortality" (1Cor 15:42, 53).

nm418 » So in context of this chapter in Paul's writings, Christ the first of the *order* was resurrected to immortal life.

- "For as in Adam *all* die, so also in Christ *all* shall be made alive. But each in his own order: Christ the first fruit, after that those who are Christ's at His coming."

nm419 » After Christ, the first of the order, comes "those who are Christ's at his coming." After Christ's resurrection to immortal life there is another resurrection at Christ's coming.

Two More Resurrections

nm420 » Scripture speaks of two more great resurrections. Acts 24:15 speaks of the resurrection of the JUST and UNJUST. John 5:29 speaks about the good having a "resurrection of life" and those who have done evil having a "resurrection of judgment." Those doing good, those that come to Christ and eat of the Spiritual manna will be resurrected "at the last day" and live "into the age" (John 6:39-44, 58, Greek text). These are those who are "worthy to obtain that age" – and who "are the children of God, being children of the resurrection" (Luke 20:35, 36).

nm421 » This "last day," this "age" can be ascertained by other scripture and Biblical patterns. This last day is the 1000 year day (2Pet 3:8; Rev 20:2; see "Thousand Years and Beyond Paper" [NM 15]). Thus, "they lived and reigned with Christ a thousand years. (But the rest of the dead lived not until the thousand years were finished.) This is the first resurrection" (Rev 20:4, 5). There are two resurrections pictured here. The first one being those who will reign with Christ for 1000 years (Christians); the others are not resurrected until *after* the 1000 years.

nm422 » This first resurrection of Revelation 20:4-5 is also the "resurrection of the just," or "the resurrection of life" (Acts 24:15; John 5:29). These are resurrected to "that age," the "last day," or that is, the 1000 year antitypical Sabbath day – the last day. The next resurrection after the one at Christ's coming or at the beginning of the "last day," is the resurrection *after* the 1000 year day (Rev 20:5a). This is the "resurrection of the unjust," or the "resurrection of judgment," that is, the resurrection of the evil bunch who are to be judged-down for the 1000 years.

> "For as in Adam all die, so also *in Christ all shall be made alive.* But each in his own order: Christ the first fruit, after that those who are Christ's at his coming." (1Cor 15:22-23)

nm423 » The first in the "order" to the new life was Christ who was the first to be resurrected from death to immortality. The second order in the resurrections mentioned in 1Cor 15:22-24 is also the "first resurrection" of Revelation 20:4-5, and is the resurrection of the real Christians who will be resurrected to immortality at Christ's coming and will rule with Christ for the 1000 years.

nm424 » Scripture says "in Christ ALL shall be made alive. But each in his own order." If ALL are to be made alive, then most will be resurrected in the third of the "order." Christ was one person. Christians are few in number compared to the billions who died without Christ's Spirit. Thus, the resurrection with the greatest number of persons is the third order of resurrections, which is the resurrection after the 1000 years (Rev 20:4-5).

nm425 » *Pattern*. As we have seen, these resurrections are resurrections to immortality. There is a pattern here. Christ, the first in the order, was the first to be resurrected to immortality. Christians, the second in the order, will be resurrected to immortality. The third in the order must *also* be resurrected to immortality. Thus, "in Christ ALL shall be made alive" (1Cor 15:22). They will truly be made alive; they will be given immortality. By taking these scriptures in context, by taking "all" to mean ALL, then "as in Adam all die, so also in Christ *all* shall be made alive." Thus, "so then as through one transgression there resulted condemnation to ALL men, even so through one act of righteousness there resulted justification of life to ALL men" (Rom 5:18) Or, "for since by man came death, by man came also the resurrection of the dead" (1Cor 15:21).

Three orders to immortality

nm426 »

- "And again he said, Whereunto shall I liken the kingdom of God? It is like leaven, which a woman took and hid in THREE measure of meal, till the whole was leavened" (Luke 13:20-21).

- "For the earth brings forth fruit of herself; first the blade [Christ], then the ear [Christians], after that the full corn in the ear" (Mark 4:28).

- "Three times in a year shall your males appear before the LORD your God in the place which he shall choose; in the feast of unleavened bread, and in the feast of weeks, and in the feast of tabernacles" (Deut 16:16).

nm427 » Christ's resurrection was represented by the waving of the sheaf of the first fruits of Israel's first harvest of the year. Christians' resurrection was represented by Israel's spring harvest and its feast of weeks. The resurrection of the final harvest is represented by the final harvest of Israel in its feast of tabernacles (see "God's Appointed Times or Seasons Paper" [NM 16]). Another antitypical pattern is the Biblical Joseph (Christ), Manasseh (Christians), and Ephraim (the resurrection of the multitude of nations) (see "Seed Paper" [PR1]).

Notice:

- "For as in Adam ALL die, so also in Christ ALL shall be made alive. But each in his own order: Christ the first fruit, after that those who are Christ's at his coming, *then comes the end*" (1Cor 15:22-24).

nm428 » The third order is resurrected at the *end*. The "end" Paul is speaking about here is amplified on in verses 24 to 28. The end comes when:

- Christ has abolished all rule and all authority and power of his enemies (v. 24b & 25).

- The last enemy abolished is death.

- At that time ALL things have been put under Christ's feet (The exception to "all" is indicated in verse 27b).

- At that time God will be ALL in ALL.

nm429 » At the *end* there will be no death. This chapter in 1Corinthians chapter 15 is speaking about resurrections to life, about immortality. Thus, after the third resurrection to immortality, then death is abolished, then the God is ALL in ALL. Satan and his evil influence will be abolished. Death, Satan's greatest power (Heb 2:14), is abolished at the END. Since God is ALL in ALL at the "end," and since God is love (1John 4:8), then Biblical love will be in ALL at the "end." There will be NO evil. In Christ all shall be made alive. This is, *alive* in the Spiritual sense of alive – being immortal and being inside the true life, being inside of God and His true Biblical love.

nm430 » After death is abolished, then comes true the saying, "death is swallowed up in victory. O death, where is thy sting? O grave where is thy victory?" (1Cor 15:54, 55; see Hosea 13:14)

More Scriptural Proof that All Will Be Saved

nm431 » Here is some further proof that *all* will be saved:

- **(1)** "For God has concluded them ALL in unbelief, that he might have mercy upon ALL" (Rom 11:32).

- **(2)** "For out of Him, and through him, and to Him, are ALL things" (Rom 11:36, see Greek text).

- **(3)** "The LORD is good to ALL, and His mercies are over ALL his works. ALL thy works shall give thanks to thee, O LORD" (Psa 145:9-10, NASB).

- **(4)** "And so ALL Israel shall be saved" (Rom 11:26).

- **(5)** "In the LORD shall ALL the seed of Israel be justified, and shall glory" (Isa 45:25).

- **(6)** "ALL the ends of the world shall remember and turn unto the LORD: and ALL the kindreds of the nations shall worship before thee" (Psa 22:27). [Here, in the antitype, it speaks of *real* worship; the only way you can really worship God is with the Spirit of God (Rom 8:8-9; John 4:24).]

- **(7)** "Behold, I am the LORD, the God of ALL flesh: is there any word too hard for me?" (Jer 32:27)

  God is the God of ALL flesh. But now in this age Satan is the god of the flesh belonging to this present evil age (2Cor 4:4). Thus at some future time God will truly be God of all flesh.

  After Abraham, Isaac, and Jacob were dead, God spoke to Moses, "I am the God of thy fathers, the God of Abraham, the God of Isaac, and the God of Jacob" (Exo 3:6). To give proof for the resurrection of the dead Christ said, "now that the dead are raised, even Moses showed at the bush, when he called the Lord the God of Abraham, and the God of Isaac, and the God of Jacob. For he is not a God of the dead, but of the living: for ALL live unto him" (Luke 20:37-38).

  By God calling Himself the God of Abraham, Isaac, and Jacob *when* they were dead, He was projecting their future resurrection to life. **By God saying He is "God of ALL flesh," He is projecting the resurrection of *all* flesh to life in the future**.

- **(8)** "Praise ye the LORD: praise ye the LORD from heavens: praise him in the heights. Praise ye him, ALL HIS ANGELS ... Praise the LORD from the earth ... kings of the earth, and ALL people, princes, and ALL judges of the earth: both young men, and maidens; old men, children ... Let EVERYTHING that has breath praise the LORD" (Psa 148:1, 2, 7, 11-12; 150:6).

  These Psalms were not placed in the Bible for mere words of hope; they are words of prophecy like Psalms 22, 110, and all others. All will praise God in the truest sense (note Phil 2:10-11; Rom 14:11; Isa 45:23).

In order for ALL to praise God, then ALL must be resurrected to life. Thus,

- **(9)** "For the grave cannot praise thee, death cannot celebrate thee: they that go down into the pit cannot hope for thy truth. The living, the living, he shall praise thee" (Isa 38:18, 19).

As this scripture shows, for number (8) to come true, then all must be resurrected to life - Spiritual life.

- **(10)** "The Father loves the Son, and has given ALL things into his hand. He that believes on the Son has aeonian life: and he that believes not the Son shall not see life [in the aeonian life – 1000 years]; but the wrath of God abides on him" (John 3:35-36).

  In order to understand the wrath of God, when it is, and what it is; and in order to understand the aeonian life, you must read the "God's Wrath Paper" [PR4], the "Thousand Years and Beyond Paper" [NM 15], and the "Reward for Christians Paper" [NM 11]. Those that do not believe the Son are those resurrected with the unjust after the 1000 years (see above).

- **(11)** "For the love of Christ controls us, having concluded this, that one died for ALL, therefore ALL died; and he died for ALL, that they who live should no longer live for themselves, but for Him who died and rose again on their behalf" (2Cor 5:14-15).

  He died for ALL (1John 2:2); we live for Him and to Him.

- **(12)** "The man Christ Jesus; Who gave himself a ransom for ALL to be testified in due time" (1Tim 2:5, 6).

  Now is that time.

- **(13)** "And the bread that I will give is my flesh, which I will give for the life of the world [kosmos]" (John 6:51).

- **(14)** "And he [Christ] is the propitiation [mercy seat] for our sins: *and not for ours only*, but *also* for the sins of the whole world [kosmos]" (1John 2:2)

- **(15)** "And we have seen and do testify that the Father sent the Son to be *savior of the world* [kosmos]" (1John 4:14).

- **(16)** "And I, if I be lifted up from the earth, will draw ALL unto me" (John 12:32).

- **(17)** "And the nations shall bless themselves in him [God], and in him shall they glory" (Jer 4:2).

- **(18)** "And ALL the nations shall be gathered unto it, to the NAME of the LORD" (Jer 3:17).

- **(19)** "And teach ALL nations, baptizing them [all nations] into the NAME of the Father..." (Mat 28:19).

- **(20)** "For the Son of man is not come to destroy men's lives, but to save" (Luke 9:56).

- **(21)** "For I came not to judge the world [kosmos], but to save the world [kosmos]" (John 12:47).

- **(22)** "I bring you good tidings of great joy, which shall be to ALL people" (Luke 2:10).

- **(23)** "And ALL flesh shall see the salvation of God" (Luke 3:6).

- **(24)** "With a view to an administration suitable to the *fullness of the times*, that is, the summing up of ALL things in Christ, things in the heavens [angels] and things upon the earth [mankind]" (Eph 1:10).

- **(25)** "For it was the Father's good pleasure for ALL the fullness to dwell in Him, and through Him to reconcile ALL things to Himself ... whether things on earth or things in heaven" (Col 1:19-20).

- **(26)** "And has put ALL things under his feet, and gave him to be the head over ALL things to the church, which is his body [the Church is his Body], the fullness of him [his Body, his Church] that fills ALL in ALL" (Eph 1:23).

- **(27)** "He who ascended far above all the heavens, that he might fill ALL things" (Eph 4:10).

- **(28)** "Who will transform the body of our humble state into conformity with the body of his glory, by the exertion of the power that he has even to subject ALL things to himself" (Phil 3:21).

Remember the True God is ALL powerful; He can "even subject ALL things to himself."

- **(29)** "Therefore if any man is in Christ, he is a new creation; the old things passed away; behold, new things have come. Now ALL things are out of God, who reconciled us to Himself through Christ, *and gave us the ministry of reconciliation, namely, that God was in Christ reconciling the world [kosmos] to Himself, not counting their trespasses against them*, and He has committed to us the word of reconciliation. Therefore, we are ambassadors for Christ" (2Cor 5:17-20).

We are ambassadors for Christ, and our word, our message, is the message of reconciliation, that is, the reconciliation of the whole cosmos to Christ. All are to go into the Church of Christ, that is the body of Christ (Eph 1:23; and other above scripture).

What Is Meant By *all*?

nm432 » "Therefore also God highly exalted him, and bestowed on him the name which is above every name, that at the name of Jesus EVERY knee should bow, of those who are in heaven [angels], and on earth [mankind], and *under* the earth [the dead]" (Phil 2:9-10).

nm433 » By putting the above scriptures together, how can anyone with the Spirit of God say anything else but that Christ is the Savior of the whole cosmos – all the angels and all the flesh. The ALL powerful God has the Spirit of Biblical love. This love, this Spirit is one of MERCY:

- "For God has concluded them ALL in unbelief, that he might have mercy upon ALL" (Rom 11:32).

God's Spirit is one of forgiveness:

- "If your enemy be hungry, give him bread to eat; and if he be thirsty, give him water to drink" (Prov 25:21, 22).

nm434 » The higher meaning here is giving your enemy *Spiritual* bread to eat, and *Spiritual* water to drink. The truest enemy of God is Satan. Since Satan is a spiritual angel, and since angels cannot die (Luke 20:36), then the only way God can be ALL in ALL at the "end," is for Satan to be given repentance and then given the Spiritual bread and Spiritual water. Remember God is ALL powerful, and it is God who *gives* repentance (Acts 5:31; 11:18; 2Tim 2:25; Rom 11:29; 2:4; 2Peter 3:9).

nm435 » If you look up these scriptures just listed you will see God does *give* repentance. If you read other papers we have like, "Predestination Paper" [NM 8], the "Proof Paper" [NM 10], the "Reward for Christians Paper" [NM 11], the "According to Works Paper" [NM 12], the "All Saved Paper" [NM 13], and other papers, then you will begin to understand that the ALL powerful God is in total control of the cosmos and is leading it to the final state where God will be in the truest sense – ALL in ALL.

How Much Does The Spirit of Love Forgive?

nm436 »

- "Then came Peter to him, and said, Lord, how often shall my brother sin against me, and I forgive him? till seven times? Jesus said unto him, I say not unto you, until seven times: but seventy times seven" (Mat 18:21-22).

- But love covers ALL sins (Prov 10:12).

- "It [love] covers ALL, it believes ALL, it hopes ALL, it endures ALL" (1Cor 13:7, Greek text).

- Christ came to save ALL (John 4:42; 1John 4:14). Christ saves ALL, by forgiving ALL sin or by covering ALL sin by his sacrifice.

- "And the bread that I will give is my flesh, which I will give for the life of the world" (John 6:51).

- "But this one [Christ] after he had offered one sacrifice for sins for all time..." (Heb 10:12).

- "And he is the propitiation for our sins: and not for ours only, but also for the sins of the whole world" (1John 2:2).

nm437 » The ALL powerful God will be ALL in ALL (1Cor 15:28) because God's Spirit of love will fill the whole universe at the true END or at the true fullness of the ages (Jer 23:24 – truest sense of this scripture, see *God Papers*).

What About *forever* Punishment?

nm438 » If we are to believe that the ALL powerful God is in full control, and will be the Savior of the whole cosmos through his Son, and will fill ALL in ALL with his Spirit, then what about the scriptures that apparently say that those who do evil will be punished with *forever* punishment?

nm439 » First it is true that God through his built-in laws (cause and effect) does punish (Exo 34:7; etc). Satan – the main cause of evil (see "Old Mind Paper" [NM 21]) – will be punished for 1000 years (Rev 20:2).

God's Wrath and Punishment

nm440 » But how does God judge? How does God's wrath work? How does God make war against his enemies?

- **(1)** "And if any man hear my words, and believe not, I judge him not: for I came not to judge the world, but to save the world. He that rejects me, and receives not my words, has one that judges him: the **word** that I have spoken, the same shall judge him in the **last day**" (John 12:47-48; see Hosea 6:5; Rev 20:12-13).

Notice they will be judged in the last day – that 1000 year day (see above, see "Thousand Years and Beyond Paper" [NM 15]).

- **(2)** "In RIGHTEOUSNESS he does judge and make war" (Rev 19:11).

- **(3)** "The LORD: for he comes, for he comes to judge the earth: he shall judge the world with RIGHTEOUSNESS" (Psa 96:13; 98:9; 1Chron 16:33).

- **(4)** "The LORD is known by the judgment which he executes. The wicked is snared in the work of his own hands" (Psa 9:16).

nm441 » God's wrath is not like man's wrath, "but the wrath of man works *not* the righteousness of God" (James 1:20). God's wrath is to let evil destroy evil (Psa 9:15; 10:2; Prov 11:6; 12:13; Isa 3:11; 59:18; Joel 3:4; Obad 1:15; Jer 25:32; Isa 19:2; Mat 24:7; Ezek 38:21; 32:12; Hag 2:22; Zech 14:13; Rev 17:16; see "God's Wrath Paper" [PR4]).

- Psa 10:2 (NKJV): The wicked in his pride persecutes the poor; Let them be caught in the plots which they have devised.

- Pro 11:6 (NKJV): The righteousness of the upright will deliver them, but the unfaithful will be taken by their own lust.

- Pro 12:13 (NKJV): The wicked is ensnared by the transgression of his lips, but the righteous will come through trouble.

- Isa 3:11 (NKJV): Woe to the wicked! It shall be ill with him, for the reward of his hands shall be given him.

- Isa 59:18 (NKJV): According to their deeds, accordingly He will repay, fury to His adversaries, recompense to His enemies; the coastlands He will fully repay.

- Joe 3:4 (NKJV): Indeed, what have you to do with Me, O Tyre and Sidon, and all the coasts of Philistia? Will you retaliate against Me? But if you retaliate against Me, swiftly and speedily I will return your retaliation upon your own head;

- Oba 1:15 (NKJV): For the day of the Lord upon all the nations is near; as you have done, it shall be done to you; your reprisal shall return upon your own head.

- Jer 25:32 (NKJV): Thus says the Lord of hosts: Behold, disaster shall go forth from nation to nation, and a great whirlwind shall be raised up from the farthest parts of the earth.

- Isa 19:2 (NKJV): I will set Egyptians against Egyptians; everyone will fight against his brother, and everyone against his neighbor, city against city, kingdom against kingdom.

- Mat 24:7 (NKJV): For nation will rise against nation, and kingdom against kingdom. And there will be famines, pestilences, and earthquakes in various places.

- Eze 38:21 (NKJV): I will call for a sword against Gog throughout all My mountains, says the Lord God. Every man's sword will be against his brother.

- Eze 32:12 (NKJV): 'By the swords of the mighty warriors, all of them the most terrible of the nations, I will cause your multitude to fall.' They shall plunder the pomp of Egypt, and all its multitude shall be destroyed.

- Hag 2:22 (NKJV): I will overthrow the throne of kingdoms; I will destroy the strength of the Gentile kingdoms. I will overthrow the chariots and those who ride in them; the horses and their riders shall come down, every one by the sword of his brother.

- Zec 14:13 (NKJV): It shall come to pass in that day that a great panic from the Lord will be among them. Everyone will seize the hand of his neighbor, and raise his hand against his neighbor's hand;

- Rev 17:16 (NKJV): And the ten horns which you saw on the beast, these will hate the harlot, make her desolate and naked, eat her flesh and burn her with fire.

nm442 » There is nothing righteous about man's wrath, but God's wrath is fair – mankind punishes themselves. Satan also punishes himself. He will start the Last War, through his evil influences. This Last War's bombs will be flying everywhere at once. The earth will actually begin to burn up (2Pet 3:10; Isa 64:1-3; Psa 97:1-5; Rev 18:8; Mal 4:1; etc.). But Christ is the Savior, thus he will cut this day of wrath short (Mat 24:22). But Satan and his angels will dwell in the fire they made for 1000 years (Rev 20:2; Mat 25:41).

nm443 » But what about the *forever* punishment? There are scriptures in many English translations that speak of "forever" or "everlasting" punishment. How can God be ALL in ALL at the "end," if at the same time there are those being punished with forever punishment? How can God have mercy on ALL if some are being punished forever? How can God be the Savior of the whole cosmos, if some are being punished forever? How can ALL praise and worship God, even those *under* the earth (in graves - Phil 2:9-10), if some are being punished forever? Isn't this a great contradiction? You bet it is!

The Contradiction

nm444 » We know that all the words that go out of God will happen (Isa 55:11; 46:10-11; etc.). We also have intuitive knowledge about the Law of Contradiction: One thing or event cannot *at the same time* be and not be (see *God Papers*). We know that God, who created wisdom and logic, cannot be illogical. God does not think against the very basic Law of Contradiction. It would be pure foolishness to reason against the Law of Contradiction as Aristotle once showed (*GP1; and Metaphysics*). We have in this paper gone over in some detail the scriptures on ALL being saved. It would be very difficult for someone with God's Spirit to deny these scriptures and their ordinary meaning. Thus, we come to the word translated "forever" in many (but not all) translations of the Bible. The apparent contradiction has to do with a gross mistranslation.

nm445 » The mistranslation of "forever" appalled me when I first found it out. The mistranslation projects the length some will go to feed *fear*, *hate*, and *unforgiveness* to their sheep. This mistranslation also forces some not to take God's word for what it says – all will be saved – God is in control. Satan is foolish and does not know the mercy and kindness of God. Satan was allowed his evil power for a purpose much like the Pharaoh (a type of Satan):

- "For scripture said unto Pharaoh, even for this same purpose have I raised thee up, that I might show my power in thee, and that my NAME might be declared throughout all the earth" (Rom 9:17; see the "Predestination Paper" [NM 8]).

nm446 » But because Satan does not understand God's mercy, he is *very* dangerous. So dangerous is he, that he will influence mankind to begin to destroy themselves in the Last War (see "God's Wrath Paper" [PR4]).

nm447 » The mistranslation of "forever" has helped to cause many to ignore the predestination scriptures. But what is "free" choice? Did Israel have *free* choice? They did not have God's Spirit, thus could not "please God" (Rom 8:7-9). Because of this, physical Israel did not have the power to choose good (note Deut 30:15-20). Adam and Eve also did not have any "free" choice (see "Free Will Versus Predestination" paper [NM 9]).

nm448 » Not all English translations have mistranslated "forever." These translations correctly translate this word(s):

- **(1)** *The Emphasized Bible*,

  by Joseph Bryant Rotherham

- **(2)** *Young's Literal Translation of the Holy Bible*,

  by Robert Young

  Author of the *Analytical Concordance to the Bible*

- **(3)** *The Holy Scriptures: A New Translation from the Original Languages*, by J. N. Darby [not in all verses]

nm449 » Many Interlinear Bibles in Greek also translate these words correctly (the Zondervan Parallel New Testament in Greek and English). Some English translations from time to time correctly translate these words. (Note "for ever" in the KJV versus "lasting" in NIV, Exo 28:43; in Gen 17:13 note "everlasting covenant" in the KJV versus "a covenant to time indefinite" in the New World Translation; etc.)

The Correct Translation

Aeonian Punishment not Forever Punishment

nm450 » In many English translations "forever," "everlasting," and "eternal" have been mistranslated from words from Hebrew (*olam*) and words from Greek (*aion, aionios*) that mean age, ages, agelong or aeonian, hidden time, life-long, life-age. We have covered this subject in our "Age Paper" [NM 7]. We constantly use the correct translation throughout our study of the Bible. Thus, those of evil go to *agelong* punishment, not "forever" punishment. That age is the 1000 year age (Rev 20:2). Thus, an agelong or aeonian plan of God is projected in scripture once the correct and proper translation is used. Therefore, it is not only possible for God to save ALL, but it will be. God will be ALL in ALL. God will prove his ALL powerfulness. God is God. Who can stop Him?

NM 15: Thousand Years and Beyond

Sabbath Patterns
Baptism Patterns
Great Last Day Patterns
Atonement Patterns
Eighth Day of Festivals & Rituals
1000 Year Judgment of God
Seven Times of Nubuchadnezzar
Notes: More info on when Spirit given

NM15 Abstract

In the Bible there is a reoccurring cycle of seven units of time or activity followed by an eighth one in which atonement is given. In many of these seven unit patterns there is a rest period during the seventh unit. In this paper we are going to learn the higher meaning of these patterns and in so doing we will understand more about the meaning of the millennium rest period and the time period after it when atonement will be given. This paper should be read in conjunction with NM16, which adds to the meaning of this paper.

Patterns and the Thousand Years

nm451 » There are patterns in the Bible. There is a physical meaning and there is a spiritual meaning to scripture throughout the Bible. We learned something about these patterns in the Premises of this book (see also NM16) and in the previous parts of this book. Moses was told to make a tabernacle according to the pattern (Ex 25:8-9; NM16). Paul wrote about scripture foreshadowing the Spiritual things in his letters.

nm452 » The Bible shows us something about a millennium period of time in the book of Revelation. An utopian society will be set up at that time and continue for 1000 years (Rev 20:4 ff). Concerning these 1000 years we need some more information. Also after these 1000 years we need to know what will happen. We will find some not so obvious things about the millennium by examining various patterns in the Bible. For example, we have learned in earlier parts of this book that before the millennium Christians receive the good Spirit that enables them to eventually be resurrected and live in the millennium, but will people born during the 1000 years receive the good Spirit or is there some reason for them not to receive it then? By looking at the various patterns in the Bible we will find the answer to this question.

Sabbath Patterns

nm453 » There is a great pattern in the Bible. This pattern is a cycle of seven units of time, or seven units of action. But in many of these cycles, *the seventh unit of time or action is different from the other six units.* For example, six days were for working and the seventh day was for resting. Six years were for sowing the fields and the seventh was for resting the land. These and other cycles of seven were not mentioned in the Bible for no reason. Rituals and ceremonies in the Bible have a higher meaning. The pattern of the cycles of seven units also has a higher meaning.

Sabbath of Rest

nm454 » "For if Jesus had given them rest [physical or Spiritual Israel], then would he not afterward have spoken of another day [7th millennium]. There remains therefore a rest to the people of God. For he that is entered into his rest [7th millennium] he also has ceased from his own works; as God did from his" (Heb 4:8-10; see, Heb 4:4-5).

nm455 » The seven day week with its Sabbath prefigured the true week or the seven millenniums with its millennial Sabbath. As there is a rest day at the end of the week, on the seventh day, so too with the antitypical week, there is a rest period in the seventh millennium.

nm456 » "And God blessed the seventh day, and sanctified it [set it apart]: because that in it he had rested from all his work which God created and made" (Gen 2:3).

nm457 » "Six days may work be done; but in the seventh is the Sabbath of rest, holy to the LORD: whosoever does any work in the Sabbath day, he shall surely be put to death" (Ex 31:15).

nm458 » The Bible is dual, the prefigure and the true figure (type and antitype) or physical and spiritual. There are seven physical days and seven spiritual days or seven millennia (2Pet 3:8). Satan, the spiritual enemy, has been busy sowing his spirit and word in the world for six spiritual millenniums; while God has sowed his Spiritual seed only in a few called/chosen by God the Father, who were chosen at the foundations of the world (see Mat 13:38-39). The seventh millennium day of rest is closing in upon us, when Satan will have to be bound and chained from any spiritual work during the seventh millennium (Rev 20:1-3).

nm459 » During the seventh millennium Satan will be prevented from spiritually sowing souls with his spiritual seed (note Mat 13:38-39; NM16), *and* God during this seventh millennium will not sow souls with His Spiritual seed. The cycles of seven in the Bible indicate in their higher meaning that the seventh millennium, the Spiritual Sabbath, will be different from the previous six millenniums. There will be spiritual rest for mankind.

nm460 » *Weekly Sabbath*. "Six days you shall work, but on the seventh day you shall rest; in plowing time and in harvest you shall rest" (Ex 34:21). As there is no harvest on a physical Sabbath so too will it be on the Spiritual Sabbath. God says the physical is a type or shadow of the real in God's plan (Rom 1:20; Heb 8:5; 9:23-24; 10:1). God tells us to look at the higher meaning (Phil 3:19; Col 3:2; John 6:63; 4:24; see "Duality Paper").

nm461 » *Land's Sabbath*. "Six years you shall sow your field and six years you shall prune your vineyard, and gather the fruit thereof; but in the seventh year shall be a Sabbath of rest unto the land, a Sabbath for the LORD: you shall neither sow your field nor prune your vineyard. That which grows of its own accord of your harvest you shall not reap, neither gather the grapes of your vine undressed; for it is a year of rest unto the land" (Lev 25:3-5). There will not be a Spiritual harvest during the Spiritual Sabbath, for none will be sowed with the Spirit during this period.

nm462 » *Manna*. Concerning the manna given to the children of Israel in the wilderness, Moses relayed the law of the LORD to the people: "six days you shall gather it; but on the seventh day, which is the Sabbath, in it there shall be none" (Ex 16:26). As there was no manna given on the typical seventh day, so too on the antitypical seventh day, the Spirit will not be given to man (note John 6:32, 35, 63).

nm463 » *Dual Meaning*. When one understands that the Old Testament laws apply to both the physical and Spiritual units of time, then he will understand what is wrong with saying God will sow his Spirit in the seventh millennium. The land is dealt with in a seven-unit cycle. In Matthew 13:38-39, we see the land or field being compared with the world, and the good seed that is planted is God's Spirit as opposed to the evil seed of the devil.

nm464 » "And six years [or millennia] you shall sow your land [sowing of the good and evil spirits], and shall gather in the fruits thereof [the evil seed produced the tares in Matthew 13:40 which 'are gathered and burned in the fire' at the end of this age as opposed to the good seed which are the first fruits in Revelation 14:4 and in Matthew 13:30]: But the seventh year you shall let it rest and lie still; that the poor of your people may eat" (Ex 23:10-11). The "poor" are those that are to inherit the kingdom of God (Mat 5:3). Thus the Spiritual poor must be those with the New Mind or the Spirit of God.

Sabbath of Purifying

nm465 » Not only is the seventh unit of time for resting from work, and resting the land, and so forth; but also the seventh unit of time or activity is for purifying and cleansing:

- "And you shall wash your clothes on the seventh day, and you shall be clean, and afterward you shall come into the camp" (Num 31:24).

- "And he shall look on the plague on the seventh day ... then the priest shall command that they wash the thing wherein the plague is, and he shall shut it up seven days more" (Lev 13:51, 54). On the seventh day the priest came, and if they were still not clean of the plague, then on that seventh day he ordered them to wash.

- "This shall be the law of the leper in the day of his cleansing: He shall be brought unto the priest ... But it shall be on the seventh day, that he shall shave all his hair off his head and his beard and his eye-brows, even all his hair he shall shave off: and he shall wash his clothes, also he shall wash his flesh in water, and he shall be clean" (Lev 14:2, 9).

- "Then he shall shave his head in the day of his cleansing, on the seventh day shall he shave it" (Num 6:9). Note: It is true that there was cleansing on a daily basis (Lev 15:16, 18), but what we are speaking about herein are ceremonies with a cycle of seven units of time or activity.

Baptism Patterns

nm466 » These physical cleansing ceremonies were foreshadows of the Christians Spiritual baptism (Eph 5:26-27; Titus 3:5; 1John 1:7, 9) which makes possible the Spiritual washing away of sin instead of filth in the typical ceremonies. These old ceremonies happened on the seventh unit of time. Therefore baptism can be said to be a seventh unit ceremony.

nm467 » But as we know baptism is representative of a death (Rom 6:4; Col 2:12; 3:3). And as with the old ceremonies so too with their higher meaning. The seventh 1000 year period will be for purifying or cleansing: the fire baptism for the enemy angels (see later in this paper); and the death for mankind who lived in the first six millenniums without the Spirit. This is man's aeonian death. Thus, this 1000 year period is a baptism in a sense, for the earth will be cleansed of sin because the transgressors will be dead, or as good as dead in the case of the enemy angels. The Spiritual Sabbath or the seventh Spiritual day does both the things that baptism does: (1) it cleanses away sin; and (2) it destroys sin because sin and the sinner are dead. Hence, we can call the seventh millennium a baptismal period.

nm468 » During this time period while the transgressors are being purified either by death or fire, the kingdom of God will be renewing the face of the earth (Psa 104:29-30). The earth itself will be cleansed after 6,000 years of misuse by man and Satan.

nm469 » With the exception of the set-apart people, everyone during the seventh millennium period will be made ready for the atonement or unity with God. Ever since the garden of Eden when it was said, "man is become as one out of us, to know good and evil" (Gen 3:22), man has been away from the way of love, that is, away from the good God's way.

Sin And Satan Put Away

nm470 » During the seventh millennium all human beings[1] living will be without either God's Spirit or Satan's spiritual influence. Satan's spiritual influence will be locked up or sent away (Zech 13:2; Rev 20:1-3). This is the Spiritual Sabbath, a time of spiritual rest. No working of spirit or spirits will be allowed to form man's mind during the Spiritual Sabbath. The proof of this is the physical Sabbath which is a type or shadow of the Spiritual and real Sabbath – the seventh millennium. Since it can be proven that the other-mind's influence (satanic influence) is the cause of sin, then when this influence is sent away to the pit we know there will be no willful sin.

nm471 » Now when one is baptized it is "for the remission of sins" (Acts 2:38). This word translated "remission" in the KJV comes from a Greek word that means: *sending away*. When one is baptized, sin is sent away. This same Greek word is translated in the KJV as "remission" (Acts 2:38); "forgiven" (Col 1:14; Acts 13:38; etc). The same is true during the world's baptism – the seventh millennium. Since sin and Satan are metonymical terms in that Satan is the cause ("father," John

---

[1] Of course we are not talking about the resurrected saints here, for they will be new creations with the new mind infused into their new nature.

8:44) of sin, and in that a satanic spirit in man causes sin (see, the "Old Mind Paper" [NM 21]); then in the Spiritual baptism Satan and sin are also *sent away* into the bottomless pit (Zech 13:2; Rev 20:1-3, 10), for their fire baptism.

Fire Baptism

nm472 » At Christ's return to the physical dimension there will be the Last War. And because of this war many people alive at that time will die (see "Last War and God's Wrath" paper [PR5]). At the same time one-third of the angels will also "die" (note Rev 12:4). This death will be their fire baptism of 1000 years in the lake of fire. This fire baptism will help to purify the evil spirits. This is the fire baptism mentioned in the Bible (Mat 3:9-12; Luke 3:16, 17). Notice carefully "every tree which brings not forth good fruit is hewn down, and cast into the fire" (Mat 3:10). And again "he will burn up the chaff with unquenchable fire" (v. 12). Study the context carefully. Now compare it with Malachi 4:1 and Matthew 13:30, 39-43 which proves this fire baptism begins at Christ's return. This is an aeonian fire "prepared for the devil and his angels" (Mat 25:41). ("Everlasting" should be "aeonian" in this verse since "everlasting" is translated from a Greek word that means aeonian.) The fire lasts for 1000 years, or the time period that the angels will be in this pit of fire. While the peace goes on above, in this pit Satan and his demons will be kept in a fire for 1000 years. This is the fire baptism Christ spoke about.

nm473 » Now baptism is a Biblical type which indicates washing away of the dirt of sin from the person (Eph 5:26-27; Titus 3:5). In other words, baptism represents the washing away of sins or of purifying one's self. What baptism does for humans, so does fire baptism do for spirits like Satan.

nm474 » Notice: "Only the gold, and the silver, the brass, the iron, the tin, and the lead, Every thing that may abide the fire, you shall make it go through the fire, and it shall be clean: nevertheless it shall be purified with the water of separation: and all that abides not the fire you shall make go through the water" (Num 31:22-23). Notice that these two verses were an "ordinance of the law which the LORD commanded Moses" (Num 31:21). As you are seeing all the apparently non-important ceremonies are representative of higher meanings. The basic patterns of these ceremonies are of a great significance in finding out God's plan.

nm475 » Notice that anything that can abide in fire shall be made to go through this fire to be cleansed. Now flesh and blood can't abide in fire, for it burns up. But spirit can abide in fire, for spirit can't die (Luke

20:36). Further, the Bible makes comparisons between spiritual things and the metals described in Numbers 31:22. For example, see the symbolic image of Satan's spiritual kingdoms in Daniel 2:31-40. The metals described in Numbers 31:22 are used to describe the make-up of the image in Daniel 2:31-40. During the 1000 years this fire baptism will purify the satanic spirits of their spiritual impurity. This is their judgement.

nm476 » The satanic spirits are in the dark Spiritually about God's plan (Jude 6). These spirit beings do not know their fate. They think God will come to permanently destroy them (Mark 1:23-24; Luke 4:33-34). Jude 6, 2Peter 2:4, and 1Corinthians 2:7-8 prove they do not know their true and final end. They too will be freed from their evil ways like all of mankind (see "All Saved Paper" [NM 13]). They do not know that this trial of fire is a fire baptism that will purify them. They do not understand God gives repentance or the changed mind (2Tim 2:25). They do not understand that they are tools of the spiritual creation. They are helping to build knowledge in man (Rom 9:17, the Pharaoh as a shadow of Satan, cf Isa 14:12, 17-18; Ezek 28:17-18; 31:18). Thus, during the 1000 year utopia Satan and his angels will be refined in the lake of fire, in their fire baptism.

Great Last Day Patterns

nm477 » What happens after one goes through baptism? As shown in the "Baptism Paper" [NM 4] after one is baptized, one receives the Spirit of God, which is the New Mind. The same is true after the seventh millennium baptism. After the seventh millennium the world as a whole will receive the Spirit (John 7:37-39). And that age after the 1000 years is called the Great Last Day.

nm478 » God has set aside a great day of Spiritual atonement for mankind which we call The Great Last Day. This is a Spiritual day when all will be in Spiritual unity with God. This great last day is the first day *after* seven units of time, or *after* the seven millenniums. This Spiritual Great Last Day has been pictured in the Bible as the eighth day of the Feast of Tabernacles (Lev 23:34-42; John 7:37-39). The first seven days of this festival represents the first seven millenniums (see God's Appointed Times). The eighth day of the festival represents the eighth Spiritual day of the Spiritual creation.

nm479 » At the beginning of this eighth spiritual day, which is after the 1000 years, all the dead will be resurrected to human life (Rev 20:4-5, 13; Ezek 37:1-13). This will fulfill the verse "through man came also the resurrection of the dead" (1Cor 15:21). After mankind is resurrected, then they will receive the Spirit (Ezek 37:14). After mankind has gone

through a cycle of seven 1000 years, then they are atoned to God by
the medium of God's Spirit. At the beginning of the eighth spiritual day
man is atoned to God by the Spirit of God. When mankind receives the
Spirit in the Great Last Day, it will fulfill the typical day of atonement
which always came on the eighth day. In the Old Testament,
atonement was always after seven units of time or activity. This
atonement represents or typifies the true atonement of man to God in
the Great Last Day.

nm480 » Hereafter, in an outline form, we will show you that
atonement comes on the eighth unit of time or after seven units of time
or activity. We will show you this, for we want to reconcile what the
Bible calls atonement with the Great Last Day and the giving of the
Spirit of God to ALL of mankind on that day.

Atonement Patterns

Atonement Is on The 8th Day or After 7 Units of Time:

nm481 »

- cleansing on the 7th day [Num 6:9]
- 8th day is for offering [Num 6:10] and 8th day for atonement Num 6:11]
- 7th day is to prepare offerings [Ezek 43:25]
- 7 days for purifying the altar [Ezek 43:26]
- after these days (on the 8th) God will accept, God will atone [Ezek 43:27]
- 7th day is to cleanse [Lev 15:28]
- 8th day offering is made [Lev 15:29] for atonement [Lev 15:30]
- 7 days for cleansing [Lev 15:13]
- 8th day is for offering to [Lev 15:14] make atonement [Lev 15:15]
- 7th day is for cleansing [Lev 14:9]
- 8th day is for offering for [Lev 14:10-17] atonement [Lev 14:18]
- 7 days for consecration of priests [Lev 8:33]
- 8th day is for offering for [Lev 9:1-6] atonement [Lev 9:7]
- 7 days the sheep are with their mother [Ex 22:30]
- 8th day they are given to God [Ex 22:30; see Lev 22:27]

- at the *end* of 7 years a release [Deut 15:1 (31:10)] is called the LORD's release [Deut 15:2] a release from debt [Deut 15:2]

["Debt" indicates sin, compare Matthew 6:12 with Luke 11:4 and with Matthew 18:21-35. Thus, this is a release from sin or the cause of sin, which is Satan.]

The set-apart people are released from Satan after six units of time, at the beginning of the seventh millennium (Deut 15:12, 18).

Atonement Is After 7 Units of Activity

nm482 »
- 7 units of activity (sprinkling blood 7 times) [Lev 4:17]
- *after* this comes atonement [Lev 4:20]
- 7 times sprinkling blood [Lev 8:11] for reconciliation (atonement) [Lev 8:15]
- 7 times sprinkling blood [Lev 14:16]
- *after* this comes atonement [Lev 14:18]
- 7 times sprinkling blood [Lev 14:27]
- *after* this comes atonement [Lev 14:29]
- 7 times sprinkling of blood [Lev 14:51]
- *after* this comes atonement [Lev 14:53]
- 7 times sprinkling of blood [Lev 16:14]
- *after* this comes atonement [Lev 16:16]
- 7 times sprinkling of blood [Lev 16:19]
- *after* this comes reconciliation (atonement) [Lev 16:20]

nm483 » All these atonement rituals in their higher meaning represent or prefigure the future when all mankind is to be atoned to God on the Great Last Spiritual Day of Creation.

Eighth Day of Festivals or Rituals

nm484 » ***Eighth Day of Festival***. Another proof that the Spirit will be given on the eighth day to the rest of mankind is John 7:37-39. Christ is pictured on the great last day of the feast of tabernacles. The great last day of this Biblical festival was the *eighth* and last day of the festival. On that day, Christ said, "if any man thirst, let him come unto me, and drink. He that believes on me, as the scripture has said, out of his belly shall flow rivers of living water. But this he spoke of the *Spirit*" (John 7:37-39). By the living waters, Christ meant his Spirit would be given. What day will he give his Spirit? The Great Last Day. This is the day *after* seven days of the Biblical feast of tabernacles (Lev 23:34-42). This feast is symbolic of the whole creation. The first seven days represents the first seven Spiritual days of creation. The last day represents the unity of man to God through the medium of God's Spirit – the living water of Christ (John 7:38-39; Rev 21:6).

Pentecost

nm485 » **Pentecost**. Still another proof that God's Spirit will be given out in the period after the seventh millennium is the feast of Pentecost. The Pentecost is a Biblical feast or appointed time after seven units of time (seven weeks of weeks, Deut 16:9; Lev 23:15-16). The day after these seven units of time is the Pentecost. The Pentecost is at the beginning of the eighth cycle of weeks. It was on the Pentecost that the New Testament Church first received its Spirit (Acts 2:1-41). The pattern of the Pentecost proves further that the Spirit will be given on the eighth Spiritual day or time period of creation.

Circumcision

nm486 » **Circumcision**. Also circumcision points to the 8th Spiritual day of creation. Circumcision was done always on the 8th day after birth (Gen 21:4; Lev 12:3; Luke 2:21). A circumcised person represents the Spiritual person (Col 2:11-13; Phil 3:3). A Spiritual person is a person with a circumcised heart as opposed to an uncircumcised heart which one can have even if he is physically circumcised (Jer 4:4; 9:26; Rom 2:28-29). Since the physical circumcision happens on the 8th physical day, then the Spiritual circumcision will happen on the 8th Spiritual day.

nm487 » Therefore the 8th Spiritual day of creation will be a period where man will be with God in Spirit. It will come after a 1000 year death of sin, a fire baptism. It is the great last day of the Spiritual creation, just before the creation of the new heaven and earth.

Jubilee

nm488 » **Jubilee**. The year of the jubilee is a type of this 8th Spiritual day of creation. The jubilee year was every fiftieth year after seven weeks of years (Lev 25:8, 10), or thus after seven seven of years (49 years). Notice the jubilee came at the beginning of the 8th cycle of seven years, or after seven units of time (7 units of 7 years).

nm489 » "That fiftieth year shall be a jubilee year for you ... and in the year of jubilee each man of you shall go back to his own property" (Lev 25:11, 13 – *Moffatt*). The year of jubilee for Israel was a year when everyone was released from slavery, debts, and so forth, and "when every man of you" (Israel) goes back to his own property and family (Lev 25:10 – *Moffatt*). Chapter 25 of Leviticus explains the year of jubilee.

nm490 » The jubilee thus represents the Great Last Day, wherein everyone will be released from Satan's misrule, and released from the 1000 year baptismal death. The Great Last Day is the age when everyone will return to life and to his own property: "O my people, I will open your graves, and cause you to come up out of your graves, and bring you into the land of Israel" (Ezek 37:12). Ezekiel 16:53-55 also indicates that at this same time when Israel will be resurrected and brought back to their land of Israel, so too will the other nations be returned to their property: "I will restore their fortunes, the fortunes of Sodom and her daughters, and your fortunes along with theirs ... When Sodom and Samaria, your sisters, and their daughters, regain their former state [at the resurrection of the dead, after the millennium, in the beginning of the atonement age], you and your daughters also shall regain your former state" (Ezek 16:53-55 – *Moffatt*).

nm491 » If God's Spirit, which is the New Mind, is one of joy, happiness, and so forth, then the Great Last Day will prove this absolutely. The Great Last Day will be even more joyous than the millennium, for during the millennium no one except those born of God at, or by the time of, the physical return of Christ, will have God's Spirit. The millennium will be great because of the lack of Satan's ways. Man during the millennium will be led physically by the resurrected who will rule this age period. But the Great Last Day will be an exceptionally beautiful age of joy much better than the great last day in the feast of tabernacles. Now let's show the references of Satan coming into the atonement period. Satan will be atoned to God in the Great Last Day. But first we must know something else about the 7th millennium.

1000 Year Judgment of God

nm492 » Not only is the 7th millennium like a baptismal, a cleansing, and/or a death period for mankind and/or the satanic spirits who lived during the first six thousand years; but, also, it is the judgment period. "And as it is appointed unto men once to die, and with [#3326] this the judgment" (Heb 9:27).

nm493 » The judgment for sin is death (Ezek 18:11-13; Gen 2:17; Rom 6:23). This judgment is an aeonian punishment or death (Mat 25:46). It is a death judgment of an "aeonian destruction from the presence of the Lord, and from the glory of his power [in the seventh millennium]" (2Thes 1:9).

nm494 » This 1000 year judgment begins at Christ's return (see Mat 25:31-33, 41, 46; Rom 2:5; Joel 3:12, 14; 2Pet 3:7; Rev 11:18; Dan 7:10, 26). At that time the saints are resurrected to judge-down the way of man/Satan (Rev 11:18; 1Cor 6:2-3).

nm495 » Satan and his angels are now in Spiritual darkness because of their rebellion, and are being reserved for the day of judgment (2Pet 2:4; Jude 6). The day of judgment is the day of wrath when Christ returns (Acts 17:31). Also the day of judgment is the antitypical 1000 year day of judgment, the aeonian judgment, or the aeonian death of the way of man/Satan.

nm496 » This judgment is the sending away of sin. The sentence for this judgment is given at Christ's return. The judicial sentence is for the 1000 years during the millennium. This is pictured in Revelation 20:1-3 where Satan's power is put in chains (prison) for 1000 years.

nm497 » This is also pictured typically by baptism which is the Christians' judicial sentence (note 2Cor 1:9). And because of this "death," sin is sent away (Acts 2:38).

Azazel – Removal of Sin And Satan

nm498 » That the real judgment of God is the sending away or destruction of sin is further proven by the once-a-year ritual on the Day of Atonement mentioned in Leviticus 16. Here the second goat was brought before Aaron (v. 21) who confesses the sins of Israel over the goat's head. In other words, he put the sins of the people on the head of the goat, and then sends it away "by the hand of a fit man" (v. 21). This pictures the sending away of sin, or the remission of sin by Aaron (a type of Christ). This goat is let go "for the entire removal" (Lev 16:26). The Hebrew word "Azazel" translated "scapegoat" in the KJV means according to *Brown Driver Briggs Gesenius Hebrew Lexicon* (p. 736) – "entire removal." And in the Greek text it means – "for the dismissal." Thus, the sending away of the goat pictures the entire removal of sin because the goat had all the sins on its head.

nm499 » There were two "twin"[1] goats in this ritual, so they cast lots to find out which goat was for the LORD and which goat was for Azazel (Lev 16:8). The first goat was killed or offered and had its blood sprinkled on the mercy seat for a sin offering for the people and the Holy Place without the priest laying his hands on its head (Lev 16:9,15-16,20). After the first goat was killed and its blood sprinkled on the mercy seat, the second goat had the sins of Israel confessed over his head and was let go or sent away for Azazel or for an "entire removal"

---

[1] "The two goats, however, must be altogether alike in look, size, and value." (*The Temple*, by Alfred Edersheim, p. 312)

into the wilderness (Lev 16:21). The first goat and the offering of that goat signified Christ's sacrifice (Isa 53:10; Heb 9:11-14,23-25). The second goat (sent away *after* the first goat was killed) signifies Satan being sent away with his sins into the 1000 years of separation (Rev 20:1-4; 2Thes 1:9). As the second goat was sent away *after* the first one died, other scriptures show that Satan will be sent away two millenniums *after* Christ died (see NM16 & *Prophecy Papers*). Even though Christ died for sin (Rom 5:6; 6:10; 8:3,34; 1Cor 15:3; 1Pet 3:18), and even though he was accounted with the transgressors and bore their sins (Isa 53:11-12), he had no sin (2Cor 5:21; 1Pet 2:21-22), thus sin in the truest sense could not be placed on his head, but had to be placed on the head of the second goat. It is the true or antitypical scapegoat (Azazel) that bears the real blame for sin, because it is Satan and his "other-mind" that put sin in the world (see NM20). In order to understand more on this subject, you must read and understand the scriptures on the right and left side of God. In the *God Papers* we discuss this.

Satan Let Loose

nm500 » Satan and his angels are judged for 1000 years (Rev 20:1-3; Isa 24:22). And after this 1000 year period they will be let loose out of their prison (Rev 20:7; Isa 24:22). They will be let loose for atonement to God's way, not to wage war again as Revelation 20:8 *seems* to indicate.

nm501 » First Revelation is in parts generally sequential, but it has insert or qualifier verses and chapters throughout the book. Second, Revelation reiterates in many cases the same events in sightly different words (see "Last War and God's Wrath" paper [PR5]). And third, always remember that there is no authority as to where the punctuation ought to be in the Bible. The original text had no punctuation. Translators have added punctuation where they felt the punctuation should be placed in the sentence structure. After Revelation 20:7 should be a period; and verses 8 to 10 should be in parentheses for they indicate what Satan did *before* he was cast into the pit. Verses 8 to 10 are simply telling the reader that this one that is to be let loose, will go out at some time and gather the nations together. But it does not say *when*. It does not say that after he is let loose out of the prison that he will gather the nations. It merely tells us he is the one who will gather the nations, but it does not say *when*. We find out when he gathers the nations from other verses in Revelation and other books in the Bible.

nm502 » Let's prove that Satan will not gather the nations again once the kingdom of God is set up on earth. Remember if Satan does gather the nations to make war after he is let loose from the pit, he would be doing wrong in God's kingdom. But once God's kingdom is set up there will be no evil.

nm503 » If we can prove that there will be no more war or wrong behavior after the kingdom of God is set up, then we prove that verses 8 to 10 are not speaking about Satan misleading the nations *after* God's kingdom is set up, but *before* it is set up. Verses 8 to 10 do *not* say that after he is released he will go out to gather the nations, for these verses are vague in their original language as to *when* he will gather the nations to fight.

nm504 » Revelation 20:8-10 is at the time of Christ's physical return, not after Satan is released. The proof is in Isaiah 2:4. The verses around this one describe Christ at his return. Note in verse 4 it speaks of nations *not* learning war again. Micah 4:3 says the same thing! And in speaking about God's return to earth: "He makes wars to cease unto the end of the earth" (Psa 46:9). And again speaking about his return: "but with an overrunning flood he will make an utter end of the place thereof, and darkness shall pursue his enemies. What do you imagine against the LORD? he will make an utter end: AFFLICTION SHALL NOT RISE UP THE SECOND TIME" (Nah 1:8-9).

nm505 » So Satan can *not* bring Gog and Ma Gog against the saints camp a second time. By comparing scriptures we can see that Revelation 20:8-10 is speaking about the gathering against the Saint's camp at Christ's return. Compare Revelation 20:8, 9 with Revelation 16:16; Isaiah 54:15; Ezekiel 38:8, 16; Joel 3:11-12, 14. Now for Revelation 20:10 compare it with Ezekiel 28:12-19 (especially Ezek28:17, 19); Isaiah 27:1, 4; Isaiah 14:11-12, 18-20; Ezekiel 31:18, 14 (Pharaoh as a type of Satan; the "tree of Eden" as a type of Satan's kingdom). You can now see that verse 10 is an amplification of Revelation 19:20-21. And these latter verses can be compared with Ezekiel 38:22; 39:11; 32:26; etc, which are all amplification of Revelation 16:21 (see "God's Wrath, An Outline" PR6).

nm506 » Thus, Satan is set loose on the Great Last Day of atonement and will not make war. The Great Last Day of creation will prove once and for all that God's way of Love is the best and only way. Everyone will be resurrected to human life into this Great Last Day except of course those who are already born of God. Those resurrected in the Great Last Day are those of the "resurrection of the dead" (Acts 24:15; 1Cor 15:21). Those resurrected into the Great Last Day as humans will then be begotten of God's Spirit and will live as Spiritually begotten children of God. But then comes the true end (1Cor 15:24) of creation after the atonement period and then all will be *born* of God (see "Begotten, Born Paper" [NM 5]; see "God's Appointed Times Paper" [NM 16]).

Seven Times of Nebuchadnezzar

nm507 » In Daniel, chapter 4, Nebuchadnezzar, the king of Babylon had a dream, "thus were the visions of mine head in my bed; I saw, and behold a *tree* in the midst of the earth, and the height thereof was great. The tree grew, and was strong, and the height thereof reached unto heaven, and the sight thereof to the end of earth" (Dan 4:10-11).

nm508 » But then a watcher and a holy one came down from heaven; He cried aloud, and said:

- cut the tree down and destroy it (V. 23), scatter the fruit, and cut down the branches of the tree (Dan 4:14).

- but leave the stump of the roots with a band of iron and brass (Dan 4:15)

    - change the tree's heart from a man's to a beast's heart, (Dan 4:16)

    - and let SEVEN TIMES pass over him.. Why?

    - to show who rules in the kingdom of men (Dan 4:17) God gave Daniel power through the spirit in him (Dan 4:9) to interpret dreams (Dan 1:17). Daniel interprets the dream (Dan 4:19)

- the TREE represents the KING (Dan 4:20-22)

- and SEVEN TIMES will pass over the KING until he knows that the most High rules in the kingdom of men (Dan 4:25).

- the king's kingdom will be sure to the king after he learns who rules in the kingdom of men. Thus, it would be sure to him after the SEVEN TIMES (Verse 25) (Dan 4:26).

    - a warning is given to the king (Dan 4:27-28)

    - But after 12 months the king lifted up his heart and spoke proud words about himself alone building the great kingdom which he controlled (Dan 4:28-30).

    - While these words were in his heart, a voice out of heaven spoke: "The kingdom is departed from you" (Dan 4:31).

Seven Times as a Mad Man

nm509 » The kingdom departed from the king, and the king was to dwell with the beasts of the field until SEVEN TIMES should pass over the king so that the king would learn who really rules in the kingdom of men (Dan 4:32).

nm510 » Nebuchadnezzar "was driven from men, and did eat grass as oxen, and his body was wet with the dew of heaven, *till his hairs were grown like EAGLES' feathers*, and his nails like birds' claws" (Dan 4:33). But at the end of the seven times, the king's understanding or reasoning was returned to him (Dan 4:34, 36).

nm511 » Now for SEVEN TIMES the king was given the mind or reasoning of a beast, "let his heart be changed from man's, and let a beast's heart be given unto him" (Dan 4:16). The king for SEVEN TIMES or seven years was given a beast's mind, he acted like a beast, like an animal. But after the *seven times* a man's mind was again given to him.

Now what is the meaning of these seven times?

Duality

nm512 » The Bible is dual. this is the consistent pattern of the Bible. Duality: *type* and *antitype*. God works in twos. He created male and female throughout His creation. He created the spiritual and physical dimensions. But further He created the Bible through inspiration to be dual in meaning (note Heb, chaps. 8, 9, 10). The old and new covenant, and the physical Passover and the Spiritual Passover are examples. If you read the "Duality Paper" you may see duality throughout God's plan, and the duality throughout the Bible. Prophecy is also dual. Genesis has a dual or antitypical meaning. Revelation has a dual meaning. Matthew, Mark, Luke, and John have a dual meaning. Not every word has a dual meaning, but every complete thought in the Bible, or every event pictured has a dual meaning. Everything prophesied about will be fulfilled in duality. The antitypical fulfillment is its truest sense.

nm513 » The duality of the Bible can't be overemphasized. It is because the Jews did not comprehend the duality of the Bible that they did not accept Christ. They did not understand that the Messiah was to come twice: once physically to die and be ridiculed, and the second time to rule the earth for 1000 years.

nm514 » Moses was warned to make the earthly tabernacle according to the pattern shown him in mount Sinai (Heb 8:5). Hebrews, chapters 8, 9, and 10 project that this pattern is one where the physical or type is a shadow of the heavenly or Spiritual or antitype.

nm515 » With this understanding of duality, is the only way one can comprehend the seven times. If one does not understand the duality of the Bible we suggest he read our "Duality Paper" or other papers we have written to begin to see the duality of the Bible. In fact if you do not understand the duality, or believe in the duality of the Bible, then you can't possibly believe the content of this paper. For the premise of this paper is the fact of duality. From now on we will take it for granted that the content of Daniel 4 has a dual significance.

Seven Times Higher Meaning

nm516 » Now the king was punished for SEVEN TIMES (years) for his false pride (Dan 4:30-31; 5:18-21). Why?, "a high look, and a proud heart ... is sin" (Prov 21:4). It is sin because everything a man has, or is, was given to him (1Cor 4:7). To say that one has glory because of himself, like Nebuchadnezzar did (Dan 4:30), is a lie, for it is the LORD who grants everything (Dan 5:18-19). And to lie, is to sin, for to lie is to transgress the law of Truth.

nm517 » So because of the king's sin, he was punished SEVEN TIMES or years. During these seven years he was given a mind of a beast (Dan 4:16). And after these seven years he was given back the mind or reasoning of a man (Dan 4:34, 36). But since the Bible is dual, and the king also represents an antitypical or Spiritual truth.

nm518 » Note Nebuchadnezzar during the seven years was given a beast's mind, and "his hairs were grown like EAGLES' feathers" (Dan 4:33). Now notice Daniel 7:4, the first beast. This first beast represents Babylon, Nebuchadnezzar's kingdom (see "Beast-Man Paper" [PR2]). Notice what Daniel 7:4 says about the king's KINGDOM, "the first was like a lion, and had EAGLE's wings [eagle wings are made of feathers]: I beheld till the wings thereof were plucked, and it [the kingdom] was lifted up from the earth, and made to stand upon the feet as a man, and a man's heart was given to it."

nm519 » Notice the parallel between the KING Nebuchadnezzar and his KINGDOM (1). Both had eagle wings or feathers (Dan 4:33; 7:4). (2). Both had their reasoning returned to them so that they could think like a man instead of a beast (Dan 4:34, 36; 7:4). Further we know in Daniel he uses "king" and "kingdom" interchangeably (Dan 7:17, 23). Because the king was punished SEVEN TIMES, the kingdom also would be punished seven times.

nm520 » Also in speaking about the tree, which signified the king and the kingdom, the scripture said that the kingdom would be cut down, and seven times would pass over it before the kingdom would know who ruled in the kingdom of men (Dan 4:23-25). Now the king was cut down and made to dwell among the beasts (Dan 4:32-33), and after seven times (years) he knew who ruled on earth (Dan 4:34-35). The seven times that affected the physical king and kingdom of Babylon was seven *years*. **The seven times that affect the spiritual king (Satan) and kingdom (Satan's kingdom) is seven spiritual days, or *seven thousand years*.** The book of Genesis showed the start of the kingdom of Satan. Ever since the beginning of this kingdom, its leaders have acted beast-like. After 7000 years a clear mind will be given to Satan and his kingdom, they will be resurrected and given the New Mind in the Great Last Day, the short period after the 1000 year period.

Notes

More on when the Spirit will be Given by God

nm521 » Now we have shown that the millennium will be a rest from spiritual work. Let's note other verses about the Spirit not being given out in the seventh millennium but in the period after it. In Isaiah 55:1, 3, 6 we read:

nm522 » "Every one that thirsts, come you to the waters ... incline your ear, and come to me: hear, and your soul shall live; and I will make an aeonian covenant with you ... Seek you the LORD while he may be found, call upon him while he is near."

nm523 » Compare the above with John 4:13: "whosoever drinks of the water that I shall give shall never thirst; but the water that I shall give him shall be in him a well of water springing up into aeonian life."

nm524 » Notice the similarities in these verses. By studying the context of these verses from Isaiah and John we see it is talking about a future salvation, in an aeonian covenant or life, through the waters that are now being poured out through the Church. These running waters represents God's Spirit being poured out (John 7:37-39).

nm525 » Also Revelation 21:6 denotes the physical waters that will pour out of Jerusalem at Christ's coming (Zech 13:1; Ezek 47:2, 8-9), as well as denoting the *Spiritual* water being poured out in the Great Last Spiritual Day.

nm526 » Note that Isaiah 32:15 has no time element. We ask the question *when* will the Spirit be poured down? This verse does not say, but we've shown you when it will be poured down.

nm527 » We ask the same question about Isaiah 44:3. *When* will it be poured down? Now Zechariah 12:10 is dual. It speaks about people looking on Jesus "whom they *have* pierced." This happened while Jesus was on the cross. It will also happen when Christ returns (Rev 1:7). The world will look upon Christ who *was* pierced by the old age. (This is not to say that Christ at His return will have pierced marks on Him, for Christ was resurrected with a new perfect body.) This verse also says God will pour down his Spirit on the house of David and the inhabitants of Jerusalem. This happened typically on the Pentecost (Acts 2:1-41). Antitypically this will happen at God's return, when he sends his Spirit (his angels) to resurrect New Jerusalem, the true Christians. See the paper on New Jerusalem [NM 18] where it equates real Christians, when born of God, with the New Jerusalem described in Revelation. Thus, God sends his Spirit, his angels, to the inhabitants of the antitypical Jerusalem, which is the New Jerusalem.

nm528 » Now turn to Joel 2:27-28: "and my people shall not aeonian be ashamed" (v. 27). Notice the correct translation is: "not aeonian" as against "never." The translation of "never" is incorrect. From the Hebrew it should read, "not aeonian." In the Greek translation (Septuagint) it should read, "not into the age" instead of "never." This aeonian period is proven to be the seventh millennium (see the "Reward Paper" [NM 11]). Thus Joel 2:27 speaks about God's people ("my people") not being ashamed during the seventh millennium. Notice Joel 2:28: "and it shall come to pass *afterward* [after the millennium, v. 27], that I will pour out my Spirit upon all flesh; and your sons and daughters shall prophesy" (Joel 2:28). This is one more proof that the Spirit will be given after the millennium.

NM 16: God's Appointed Times: Tabernacle, Festivals, and Sacrifices Foreshadowed Christ

Patterns Foreshadowed Future
Sabbath
Three Harvests
First Harvest: Passover
Sheaf of First Fruit: Time of First Harvest
Second Harvest: Pentecost
Trumpets
Feast of Trumpets
Day of Atonement
Third & Final Harvest: Feast of Tabernacles
Jubilee Harvest
Review: Three Orders of Creation
Sacrifices and Jesus Christ
Tabernacle Table
Tabernacle's Measurement: Higher Meaning
Spiritual Bread & Other Higher Meanings
What is the Lord's Body?
Passover Scriptures
Washing of Feet

NM16 Abstract

Appointed times were festivals and holy days such as the Sabbath, Passover, and Pentecost. During these appointed times there were various rituals and sacrifices that were performed. Moses constructed a Tabernacle in which to perform these rituals. What we show in this paper is that all these things foreshadowed the appointed times of God's plan and the Coming Christ and his Spiritual Body (Church). This paper again manifests the type and antitype of the Bible.

Patterns in the Bible Foreshadow the Future

nm529 » When attempting to understand the higher or Spiritual meaning in the Bible, the patterns of the Bible *must be* observed, marked and understood. If our beliefs go against the patterns in scripture we are in error. Moses wrote the first five books of the Bible. When you read these books you see patterns occurring again and again. For example, again and again, you see the pattern of six periods of work, one of rest, and one of atonement (see NM15). What we do in the *BeComingOne Papers* is to point out these patterns, and the type and antitype aspect of these patterns. Not only in the books of Moses do you see these patterns, but in all the books of the Bible. But why did Moses and others write down these patterns? It is because God directed this to be done. In Moses' case, Moses was directed to make the tabernacle and all its furniture by the pattern shown to him on the mountain:

- Let them construct a sanctuary for Me, that I may dwell among them... According to all that I am going to show you, *as* the **pattern [type or image] of the tabernacle** and the **pattern [type or image] of all its furniture**, just so you shall construct *it.* (Ex 25:8-9)

- See that you make *them* **after the pattern** [type or image] for them, which was shown to you on the mountain. (Exodus 25:40)

- Then you shall erect the tabernacle **according to its plan** which you have been shown in the mountain. (Exodus 26:30)

- Now this was the workmanship of the lampstand [candlestick], hammered work of gold; from its base to its flowers it was hammered work; **according to the pattern** [type or image] which the LORD had showed Moses, so he made the lampstand. (Numbers 8:4)

- Our fathers had the tabernacle of testimony in the wilderness, just as He who spoke to Moses directed *him* to make it **according to the pattern** which he had seen. (Acts 7:44)

- [Priests] who serve a **copy and shadow of the heavenly things**, just as Moses was warned *by God* when he was about to erect the tabernacle; for, see, He says, that you make all things **according to the pattern** which was shown you on the mountain. (Hebrews 8:5)

- For the Law, since it has *only* a **shadow of the good things to come** *and* not the very form of things, can never, by the same sacrifices which they offer continually year by year, make perfect those who draw near. (Hebrews 10:1)

- Now **these things** [in O.T.] **happened as examples** for us, so that we would not crave evil things as they also craved. (1 Corinthians 10:6)

nm530 » Even the way the sacrifices were performed was done by the direction of God. The book of Leviticus was primarily devoted to the ministry and ceremonies of the priests. In this book, over fifty-times Moses wrote that God spoke, or, that is, God told Moses what to write pertaining to the sacrifices and ceremonies. In this book there was

- the **law of** the grain offering (Lev 6:14)
- the **law of** the sin offering (Lev 6:25)
- the **law of** the guilt offering (Lev 7:1)
- the **law of** the sacrifice **of** peace offerings (Lev 7:11)

In fact there was a "law of the burnt offering, the grain offering and the sin offering and the guilt offering and the ordination offering and the sacrifice of peace offerings, which the LORD commanded Moses at Mount Sinai in the day that He commanded the sons of Israel to present their offerings to the LORD in the wilderness of Sinai." (Lev 7:37-38) These laws were a shadow of things to come (Heb 10:1).

nm531 » Not only were there patterns to the tabernacle and the rituals of the Old Testament, but as Paul indicated also other laws, even laws that dealt with animals were a shadow of future things that pertain to Christians:

- The elders who rule well are to be considered worthy of double honor, especially those who work hard at preaching and teaching. For the Scripture says, "you shall not muzzle the ox while he is threshing," and "The laborer is worthy of his wages." (1Timothy 5:17-18)

Notice how Paul used a scriptural law meant for an ox to teach Christians about how to best treat their Spiritual elders.

Appointed Times

nm532 » In Leviticus, chapter 23, it describes the appointed times ("feasts") of God: "And the LORD spoke to Moses, saying, Speak unto the children of Israel, and say to them, Concerning **the appointed times of the LORD**, which you shall proclaim to be holy convocations, even these are my appointed times" (Lev 23:2).

Festivals Foreshadowed the Future

nm533 » Most of the so-called Christians say these appointed times or seasons were done away with. But we will show that these appointed times or seasons have a higher and Spiritual meaning. The New Testament Church, unlike the physical Israelites, perceived these appointed times in a Spiritual way because of Christ's own Spirit and these words: "But the hour comes, and now is, when the true worshipers shall worship the Father in Spirit and in truth: for the Father seeks such to worship him. *God is Spirit: and they that worship him must worship him in Spirit and in truth*" (John 4:23-24). "Therefore no one is to act as your judge in regard to food or drink or in respect to a festival or a new moon or a Sabbath day – things which are a *mere* shadow of what is to come; but the substance belongs to Christ" (Col 2:16-17). These Old Testament festivals were a shadow of things to come.

nm534 » Throughout Paul's scripture, he manifests Spiritual worship, or Spiritual thoughts toward God. Paul's writings show the type and antitype of the Bible. Paul, speaking about the Old Testament scripture, says:

- "These things were our **types** . . .. Now all these things happened **typically** unto them: and they are written for our admonition, upon whom the ends of the ages have come" (1Cor 10:6, 11).

- The things described in the Old Testament were typical events just as Moses' tabernacle was a shadow of the heavenly things to come" (Heb 8:5).

- The tabernacle "which *is* a type for the present time. Accordingly both gifts and sacrifices are offered which cannot make the worshiper perfect in conscience." (Hebrews 9:9)

- "For the Law, since it has *only* a shadow of the good things to come *and* not the very form of things, can never, by the same sacrifices which they offer continually year by year, make perfect those who draw near." (Hebrews 10:1)

nm535 » The Old Testament festivals and Sabbaths were typical representations of things to come afterward. We will explain these appointed times and show their higher meanings. In short, we will see that the appointed times or seasons pictured the appointed times of God's plan and Jesus Christ and his Spiritual Body (Church).

Sabbath

Six Days of Work; One Day of Rest

nm536 » The Sabbath is one of God's appointed times. Notice in Leviticus 23:2, "these are my appointed times." Then in the next verse, "Six days shall work be done: but the seventh day is the Sabbath of rest, a holy convocation; you shall do no work therein: it is the Sabbath of the LORD in all your dwellings."

nm537 » The Sabbath is the seventh day of the week. The Jews of today celebrate the Sabbath. The Sabbath is what we call Saturday. Most so-called Christians keep Sunday, but there is no scripture that says we should keep Sunday. God instituted the Sabbath as the seventh day, the day of rest:

- "Thus the heavens and the earth were being [imperfect verb] finished, and all the host of them. And on the seventh day God will end [imp. verb] his work which he had made; and he will rest [imp. verb] on the seventh day from all his work which he had made. And God blessed the seventh day, and set it apart: because that in it he had rested from all his work which God created and made" (Gen 2:1-3).

So God blessed and set the seventh day apart from the rest of the days.

nm538 » Before Moses was given the precepts of Jehovah, the Sabbath was pointed out to the children of Israel (Ex 16:23, 26, 29-30, 1-31). In the words of the ten commandments:

- "Remember the Sabbath day, to keep it set apart. Six says shall you labor, and do all your work: but the seventh day is the Sabbath of the LORD your God: in it you shall not do any work, you, nor your servant, nor your maidservant, nor your cattle, nor your stranger that is within your gates: for in six days the LORD made heaven and earth, the sea, and all that is in them, and rested [imp. verb] the seventh day: wherefore the LORD blessed the Sabbath day, and set it apart" (Ex 20:8-10).

nm539 » The Sabbath is a memorial. The Sabbath has us remember the six days of creation when God created the universe. On the seventh day of this creation God rested from his work. But further, the Sabbath is a memorial to the Israelite people coming out of Egypt:

- "And remember that you were a servant in the land of Egypt, and that the LORD your God brought you out of there through a mighty hand and by a stretched out arm: therefore the LORD your God directed you to keep the Sabbath day" (Deut 5:15).

nm540 » Now as Paul projected to us in his letters, the Old Testament was the type of the antitype, or the Shadow of the true or real. The Sabbath has an antitypical meaning. It foreshadows something (Col 2:16-17).

If God had given them Rest

nm541 » In the fourth chapter of Hebrews Paul shows us the antitypical meaning of the seventh day rest, the Sabbath:

- "For he spoke in a certain place of the seventh day this way, 'and God did rest [aorist verb] the seventh day from all his works.' And in this place again, 'If they shall enter into my rest [Sabbath].' Seeing therefore it remains that some must enter therein, and they to whom it was first preached entered not in because of unbelief . . .. For if Jesus had given them rest [aorist verb], then would he not afterward have spoken of another day. There remains therefore a rest [Sabbath] to the people of God. For he that is entered into his rest, he also has ceased from his own works, as God did from his. Let us labor therefore to enter into that rest [Sabbath] lest any man fall after the same example of unbelief" (Heb 4:4-11).

Now this other rest that God's people shall enter is the 1000 year rest (Rev 20:4-5), the millennium Sabbath of peace. This is the 1000 year Sabbath when the Spiritual "Israel of God" (Gal 6:16) shall have fled out of spiritual Egypt and entered God's promised land. "The Son of man [Christ] is Lord also of the Sabbath" (Mark 2:28). It is Christ who shall rule as King of kings in the 1000 year Sabbath wherein the Israel of God will cease from its own works.

Physical Sabbath	Spiritual Sabbath
Sabbath Begins When?	*Spiritual Meaning*
nm542 » *Physical Sabbath* The Sabbath begins on Friday at the setting of the sun as it begins to darken, for the days of the Bible begin at evening, the very last part of sunlight. The physical Sabbath lasts the whole day, from sunset on Friday to sunset on Saturday (Neh 13:19; Lev 23:32).	The Spiritual Sabbath begins at the return and physical manifestation of the Messiah, Jesus Christ, and will last for 1000 years because a day to God is like 1000 years (2Peter 3:8).

Physical Sabbath	Spiritual Sabbath
Sabbath Preparation nm543 » *Physical Sabbath* The Sabbath must be prepared for on the sixth day of the week by: preparing & cooking the food for the Sabbath (Ex 16:5, 22-23, 29), for there should be no cooking on the Sabbath. Further one was to prepare in any other way so there wouldn't have to be any unnecessary work on the Sabbath (Ex 35:2-3).	*Spiritual Meaning* The Spiritual meaning of this is that all the preparing of the Spiritual food for the 1000 year Sabbath will happen in the sixth millennium and before.
Sabbath a Delight nm544 » *Physical Sabbath* The Sabbath is to be a delight (Isa 58:13; Ex 20:8-10; Neh 13:15-21; 10:31).	*Spiritual Meaning* The higher meaning here is that the New Mind, will delight in the new ways of the New Age. Those of the New Mind and those of mankind will cease from their old way during the Spiritual Sabbath.
Sabbath: an Assembly nm545 » *Physical Sabbath* The Sabbath is kept by assembling with others (Lev 23:3; Luke 4:16).	*Spiritual Meaning* This pictures the higher meaning of those of the Spirit of God who will be gathered by God at the end of the old age to live in the New Age, the 1000 year Sabbath, together with the others who are gathered. The gathering of physical Israel in their physical Sabbath pictures the gathering of Spiritual Israel (the Church) in the Spiritual Sabbath which will last for 1000 years.
Sabbath for Good Works nm546 » *Physical Sabbath* Christ taught that it was right to do good works on the Sabbath (Luke 13:14-16; 14:3-5; Mark 3:1-6; John 5:8-16; Mat 12:11-12).	*Spiritual Meaning* This pictures the good works that will be done on the Spiritual Sabbath by Spiritual Israel.

Physical Sabbath	Spiritual Sabbath
Sabbath Fulfillment: A Rest Period from Satan nm547 » *Physical Sabbath* The physical Sabbath was a day of rest.	*Spiritual Meaning* The Spiritual Sabbath will be a day of rest also, that is, rest from the evil spiritual work of the spiritual enemy of mankind. Only the good works of the true and good God will be performed during the 1000 year Sabbath. It will be an utopia for those in the Spirit because the enemy, that spiritual enemy of mankind, will be put away during the 1000 year rest (Rev 20:2-3).

Three Harvests of the Land

Agricultural Metaphor

nm548 » In the past, and until recent times, most people in the world were involved intimately in agriculture. The Bible appropriately uses agriculture metaphorically to manifest God's plan of salvation. Notice the metaphor of sowing seed and harvesting the crop from the seed:

- Jesus presented another parable to them, saying, The kingdom of heaven may be compared to a man who **sowed good seed** in his field. 25 "But while his men were sleeping, his enemy came and **sowed tares** among the wheat, and went away. (Matthew 13:24-25)

- and the field is the world; and *as for* the **good seed, these are the sons of the kingdom**; and the **tares are the sons of the evil one**; (Matthew 13:38)

- And another angel came out of the temple, crying out with a loud voice to Him who sat on the cloud, "Put in your sickle and reap, for the hour to reap has come, because the **harvest of the earth is ripe**." (Revelation 14:15)

There were three harvest festivals in the year. One was at the beginning of the grain harvest at the Passover feast, one at the end of the grain harvest at the Pentecost, and one at the end of the last and final harvest at the Feast of Tabernacles or Booths.

Barley, Wheat, Fruit Harvests

nm549 » To many of us, harvest time is of little concern, because in our complex life we are far removed from the actual production of our food supplies, but for the Hebrew people, as for those in any agricultural district today, the harvest was a most important season (Gen 8:22; 45:6). Events were reckoned from harvests (Gen 30:14; Josh 3:15; Jdg 15:1; Ruth 1:22; 2:23; 1Sam 6:13; 2Sam 21:9; 23:13). The three principal feasts of the Jews corresponded to the three harvest seasons (Ex 23:16; 34:21,22):

- **(1)** the feast of the Passover in April at the time of the barley harvest (compare Ruth 1:22);

- **(2)** the feast of Pentecost (7 weeks later) at the wheat harvest (Ex 34:22),

- and **(3)** the feast of Tabernacles at the end of the year (October) during the fruit harvest.

The seasons have not changed since that time. Between the reaping of the barley in April and the wheat in June, most of the other cereals are reaped. The grapes begin to ripen in August, but the gathering of crops for making wine and molasses (*dibs*), and the storing of the dried figs and raisins, is at the end of September. [Paragraph taken from *ISBE* (1915), under "Harvest"]

Three Harvests Correspond to the Three Times Before YHWH

nm550 » Corresponding to the three harvests, the males of Israel were to stand before God three times in a year:

> **Three times in a year all your males shall appear before the LORD** your God in the place which He chooses, at the **Feast of Unleavened Bread** [Passover] and at the **Feast of Weeks** [Pentecost] and at the **Feast of Booths** [Tabernacles], and they shall not appear before the LORD empty-handed. (Deuteronomy 16:16)

> **Three times a year you shall celebrate a feast to Me.** 15 "You shall observe the **Feast of Unleavened Bread**; for seven days you are to eat unleavened bread, as I commanded you, at the appointed time in the month Abib, for in it you came out of Egypt. And none shall appear before Me empty-handed. 16 "Also *you shall observe* the **Feast of the Harvest** *of* **the first fruits** of your labors *from* what you sow in the field; also the **Feast of the Ingathering** in the produce of the year when you gather in *the fruit of* your labors from

the field. 17 Three times a year all your males shall appear before the Lord GOD. (Exodus 23:14-17)

nm551 » Notice that all three times the males were to appear before God was at the time of the three harvests. The second main festival which was the feast of the harvest of the first fruits is also known as the feast of the wheat harvest, and the last of the three main festival was also known as the Feast of Ingathering:

> You shall celebrate the **Feast of Weeks**, *that is*, **the first fruits of the wheat harvest**, and the **Feast of Ingathering** at the turn of the year. (Exodus 34:22)

There are many patterns in the Bible, but the pattern of the three harvests corresponded to the three times males were to stand before God and as we will see this in turn pointed to the harvest of souls at the appointed times.

Three Pilgrim-Feasts for Males & Angels

nm552 » The three main feasts were pilgrim-feasts, which the males were required to attend. "In Hebrew two terms are employed – the one, *Moed*, or appointed meeting, applied to all festive seasons, including Sabbaths and New Moons; the other *Chag*, from a root which means 'to dance,' or 'to be joyous,' applying exclusively to the three festivals of Easter [Passover], Pentecost, and Tabernacles, in which all males were to appear before the Lord in His sanctuary" (*The Temple*, by Alfred Edersheim, p. 196) This word [*Chag*] is closely related to an Arabic word that means pilgrimage (BDBG Lexicon, p. 290). These three main feasts were *pilgrim-feasts*, a time of great joy. When you understand the type and antitype of the Bible you understand that males represent the angels, while females represent mankind (*God Papers*). Notice that Job wrote about how Satan also came before God when the sons of man came to present themselves:

- Now there was a day when the sons of God came to present themselves before the LORD, and Satan also came among them. (Job 1:6)
- Again there was a day when the sons of God came to present themselves before the LORD, and Satan also came among them to present himself before the LORD. (Job 2:1)

The higher meaning of "all males of Israel standing and presenting themselves before God" (Deut 16:16) points to the fact that all angels ("sons of God") will and must stand before God and present themselves to God, and "all" means all.

Not Empty Handed

nm553 » The males were to stand before God <u>not</u> empty handed (Deut 16:16; 23:15). They were to bring the fruits of their labor with them.

- "Three times in a year all your males shall appear before the LORD your God in the place which He chooses, at the Feast of Unleavened Bread and at the Feast of Weeks and at the Feast of Booths, and they shall not appear before the LORD empty-handed. 17 "Every man shall give as he is able, according to the blessing of the LORD your God which He has given you. (Deut 16:16-17)

Angels are the antitypical meaning of "males" in the Bible. Therefore in the higher meaning, all angels were to appear before God three times with the blessings that God had given to them. These three times were at harvests, and at these harvests the males or angels were to bring their blessings. These blessings were usually from the harvest. So if it was the Pentecost or the harvest of the wheat, then the males brought their first fruits or blessings from that harvest. Notice that at the end of the age it is the angels who are the ones to do the harvesting:

- And the field is the world; and *as for* the good seed, these are the sons of the kingdom; and the tares are the sons of the evil *one*; and the enemy who sowed them [tares or weeds] is the devil, and the harvest is the end of the age; and **the reapers are angels**. (Mat 13:38-39)

This "the end of the age harvest" is the harvest of the bodies of Christians who died in the old age, therefore the blessings that the angels bring to God are the physical bodies of Christians who are united with their own angels and become one with God thereby.

nm554 » From the *God Papers 6*, we take the following which shows that Christians do have their own angel:

Our Own Angel

Now everyone that becomes a "son of God" must be begotten of the Spirit (Rom 8:9-10, 16). What is this Spirit? What does it mean to be begotten of God's Spirit? Notice that those begotten of the Spirit are led by it (Rom 8:14). The Spirit in them, leads them.

Notice that "these little ones" have in heaven "their angels" (Mat 18:10). Now the Greek word translated "their" means "of one's self." These "little ones" are Spiritual children of God (1 John 2:12-13). And these little ones have angels of their own self. Or, thus, since angels are spirits (Heb 1:7), Christians have their own angels or Spirits.

What do these angels or Spirits do? "For he shall give his angels charge over you, *to keep you in all your ways*" (Psa 91:11). In other words, angels lead them, as the Spirit leads the little ones or sons of God (Rom 8:14). Now Psalms 91:11 was used in a physical sense concerning Christ (Mat 4:6). But the Bible is dual and speaks in a dual sense, the physical sense and the Spiritual sense. We are to look to the higher sense — the Spiritual (Col 3:1-2). Not only do angels help out physically, but they help out Spiritually. And since Christ is our example, and the forerunner, then what applies to him applies to all others (cf Col 1:18; Rom 8:17; John 14:6).

Each son of God has his own angel (Mat 18:10). And these angels lead them in the way (Psa 91:11), as the angel of the BeComingOne led Christ (John 14:10, GP 3 & 4), who is our example. Thus, the Spirit of God that leads Christians (Rom 8:14) is an angel of God that is in them. One of God's own Spirits leads each one of them. These Spirits or angels are for the elect humans who are the sons of God (1Pet 1:1-2). These angels or Spirits serve the elect, they are ministers or servants "for them who shall be heirs of salvation" (Heb 1:14). These angels are the "elect angels" (1Tim 5:21).

nm555 » It is the angels (Mat 13:38-39) who will be sent by God to resurrect the dead in Christ (Christians):

> "For this we say to you by the word of the Lord, that we who are alive and remain until the coming of the Lord, will not precede those who have fallen asleep. 16 For the Lord Himself will descend from heaven with a shout, with the voice of *the* archangel and with the trumpet of God, and the dead in Christ will rise first". (1Thes 4:15-16)

> "Behold, I tell you a mystery; we will not all sleep, but we will all be changed, 52 in a moment, in the twinkling of an eye, at the last trumpet; for the trumpet will sound, and the dead will be raised imperishable, and we will be changed." (1Cor 15:51-52)

Remember it is the angels (who are spirits of God) who will resurrect (Mat 13:39; Rev 14:15; Mat 24:31; Mark 13:27; Mat 16:27; 2Thes 1:7)

Three Harvests Point to Three Orders of Resurrection to Immortality

nm556 » God directed that all males must stand before the LORD during three of the annual harvest-festivals: "Three times in a year shall your males appear before the LORD your God in the place which he shall choose; in the feast of unleavened bread, and in the feast of weeks (Pentecost), and in the feast of tabernacles" (Deut 16:16). And they were supposed to offer gifts from the harvest, "not empty handed." We project in this book that the words in the Bible are shadows or types of the real and true. There is a duality of meaning in the Bible: a physical meaning and a spiritual meaning. Thus, the three harvests and three main festivals have a higher meaning. Through comparison of scripture we can see the connection between the three harvests in Israel and the three resurrections mentioned by Paul.

nm557 » Paul wrote about three resurrections in 1Corinthians, chapter fifteen:

"In Christ shall *all* be made alive. But every man in his own order:

> [1] Christ the first fruit;

> [2] afterward they that are Christ's at his coming [Rev 14:1-4].

> [3] Then the end...." (1Corinthians 15:22-24)

Paul called these three resurrections, orders, "each man in his own order." This word translated "order" is *tagma* in the Greek text, which means rank or division or proper order. Paul manifested the three orders or ranks of resurrections. Christ fulfilled the first festival ceremony (sheaf of 1st fruit) by being resurrected and then going to his Father on the exact day that the sheaf of first fruits was waved (see below). Christians will fulfill the second festival by becoming the first fruits of the creation (1Cor 15:23; Rev 14:4).

nm558 » Other allusions to these three resurrections are found in the Bible:

- **(1)** Mark 4:28: "For the earth brings forth fruit of herself; first the **blade** [Christ], then the **head** [first-products], after that the **full gain** in the head."

- **(2)** Luke 13:20-21: "And again he said, Whereunto shall I liken the kingdom of God? It is like leaven, which a woman took and hid in **three measures** of meal, till the whole [*all* of mankind] was leavened." [Leavened here is used in a different way than when it is used to signify sin or the way of sin in the Feast of Unleavened Bread.]

- **(3) Noah's ark with three stories** was also a foreshadow of the three orders of salvation of mortal mankind to immortality. All life forms were saved in the ark that was built with <u>three</u> stories: "You shall make a window for the **ark**, and finish it to a cubit from the top; and set the door of the **ark** in the side of it; **you shall make it with lower, second, and third decks**. (Genesis 6:16)

- **(4)** Three sections of the tabernacle of Israel indicated and pointed to the three orders of resurrection. The **Holy of Holies** definitely points to the first resurrection to immortality – Jesus Christ. The **Holy Place** points to the Church and represents the second resurrection to immortality. Both of these were called the inner court or the upper court. The **outer court** was for the gentiles and pointed to the last resurrection to immortality. The inner court, with its Holy of Holies and Holy Place, was holy and set apart from the outer court. In the Bible the inner court was counted or measured, but the outer court was not (Rev 11:1-2). We know the count of the inner court (Holy of Holies & Holy Place) represents Jesus Christ and the first fruits of 144,000 (Rev 14:3-4), but we do not know the count or number of the outer court (Rev 11:1-2; Rev 7:9).

> Then there was given me a measuring rod like a staff; and someone said, "Get up and measure the temple of God and the altar, and those who worship in it. 2 **"Leave out the court which is outside the temple and do not measure it**, for it has been given to the nations; and they will tread under foot the holy city for forty-two months. (Rev 11:1-2)

> After these things I looked, and behold, **a great multitude which no one could count**, from every nation and *all* tribes and peoples and tongues, standing before the throne and before the Lamb, clothed in white robes, and palm branches *were* in their hands; (Revelation 7:9; Notice the palm branches, see below under Feast of Tabernacles)

- **(5)** The *three orders* or divisions of mankind can be seen typically in Joseph and his two sons, Manasseh and Ephraim: [1] *Joseph*, the one set apart from his brethren (Deut 33:16), represents Jesus Christ, who was the first to be born of God (1Cor 15:22-28). [2] *Manasseh*, the one that was to become a great nation, represents the second group of first fruits to be presented to God, which are the Christians who lived in the old age. [3] *Ephraim*, the one that was to become a multitude of nations, represents the third group to be presented to God, which are the multitudes of peoples who will be born of God at the end of creation. (See PR1)

- Also see NM24 for more details on these three resurrections or harvest of souls.

Harvest of Souls

nm559 » The Bible speaks about the saving of souls (1Pet 1:9; Heb 10:39; James 1:21; 5:20; Luke 21:19). In a sense, souls are sown with a seed, either a good seed or a bad one.

- **"I will sow her for Myself in the land**. I will also have compassion on her who had not obtained compassion, And I will say to those who were not My people, 'You are My people!' And they will say, '*You are* my God!'" (Hosea 2:23)

- "Behold, days are coming," declares the LORD, "when **I will sow the house of Israel and the house of Judah** with the seed of man and with the seed of beast. (Jeremiah 31:27)

- Jesus presented another parable to them, saying, "The kingdom of heaven may be compared to **a man who sowed good seed in his field**. 25 "But while his men were sleeping, **his enemy came and sowed tares among the wheat**, and went away. (Matthew 13:24)

- Then He left the crowds and went into the house. And His disciples came to Him and said, "Explain to us the parable of the tares of the field." 37 And He said, **"The one who sows the good seed is the Son of Man, 38 and the field is the world; and** *as for* **the good seed, these are the sons of the kingdom; and the tares are the sons of the evil** *one*. (Matthew 13:36-38)

nm560 » This harvest of the antitypical wheat occurs at the coming of Christ (1Cor 15:23) when the first fruits (the "wheat") are redeemed from among men (Rev 14:4).

- "His winnowing fork is in His hand, and He will thoroughly clear His threshing floor; and **He will gather His wheat** into the barn, but He will burn up the chaff with unquenchable fire." (Mat 3:12)

- Allow both to grow together until the harvest; and in the time of the harvest I will say to the reapers, First gather up the tares and bind them in bundles to burn them up; but **gather the wheat into my barn**. (Mat 13:30)

- Then He left the crowds and went into the house. And His disciples came to Him and said, "Explain to us the parable of the tares of the field." 37 And He said, "The one who sows the good seed is the Son of Man, 38 and the field is the world; and *as for* the good seed, these are the sons of the kingdom; and the tares are the sons of the evil *one*; 39 and the enemy who sowed them is the devil, and the harvest is the end of the age; and the reapers are angels. 40 "So just as the tares are gathered up and burned with fire, so shall it be at the end of the age. 41 "The Son of Man will send forth His angels, and they will gather out of His kingdom all stumbling blocks, and those who commit lawlessness, 42 and will throw them into the furnace of fire; in that place there will be weeping and gnashing of teeth. (Mat 13:36-42)

nm561 » Therefore at the end of the evil age the evil ones are taken out of the world and burned, while God through his angels gathers the wheat into the barn (Mat 13:30).

When was the harvest of wheat in Israel? It occurred typically just before the Pentecost, which was the festival that celebrated the harvest of wheat and other first grain products (fruits). Is this telling us something about *when* the coming of Christ is and when the harvest of Spiritual first fruit happens?

We will now study the Feast of the Passover. From this study we will see that what the Passover typified was fulfilled perfectly by Christ, our Spiritual Passover.

Feast of the Passover							
Represents first Harvest (Barley)							
Beginning of the Harvest (Rev 3:14; Col 1:15, 18)							
First in Rank (1Cor 15:23)							
Preparation	1st day	2nd day	3rd day	4th day	5th day	6th day	7th day
Passover 14th Nisan Death & burial	Sabbath 15th [1st day in grave]	Friday 16th [2nd day in grave]	Weekly Sabbath 17th [3rd day in grave] Resurrection>	Sunday 18th Sheaf-wave offering			Sabbath 21st Nisan
Signifies predestination of Christ's suffering	< Signifies First seven millenniums of creation > < Seven Days of unleavened bread: signifying purity of Jesus Christ >						

First Harvest: <u>Passover</u>

Passover Foreshadowed Christ

nm562 » As we will see in this section, the Passover Feast foreshadowed Christ's death and resurrection. The Passover was one of God's appointed times:

- "These are the appointed times of the LORD, even holy convocations; which you shall proclaim in their seasons. In the fourteenth day of the first month between the two evenings is the LORD's Passover" (Lev 23:4-5).

Sacred Months

nm563 » First of all what does the Bible mean by, "in the fourteenth day of the first month"? The Old Testament uses the Hebrew's Sacred Calendar, which some call the Jewish Sacred Calendar. The first month is also called Nisan or Abib, and occurs in March to April on today's calendar. Hence on the fourteenth day of Nisan is the Passover. But the Passover occurs "between the two evenings" on the 14th day as correctly translated in the following verses: Lev 23:5 (Hebrew and Greek); Num 9:3,5; Ex 12:6. In the King James Version "between the two evenings" is translated wrongly as "even" or "evening."

Between the Two Evenings

nm564 » There is error concerning the meaning of "between the two evenings." First of all note that the Passover is in the fourteenth day of the first month between the two evenings. The Passover is between the two evenings. This merely means that the Passover happens on the 14th between the evening of the 13th and the evening of the 14th.

Morning and Evening Time

nm565 » The proof of this is shown in the appointed time for Atonement: "Also on the tenth day of this seventh month there shall be a day of atonement . . .. It shall be unto you a Sabbath of rest, and you shall afflict your souls: in the ninth day of the month at even, from even until even, shall you celebrate your Sabbath" (Lev 23:27, 32). The day of Atonement is on the tenth of the seventh month, but it is celebrated from the evening of the ninth to the evening of the tenth, thus between these two evenings. And the word "evening" is defined by the Bible: "at even, at the going down of the sun" (Deut 16:6; note Neh 13:19; Lev 22:6). Evening is the latter part of the 24 hour day. In the Bible "evening" is used in two ways: (1), the later hour(s) before sunset; (2) the time or moments just before sunset, or at sunset.

Hence, the Passover is on the fourteenth of the first month in the Hebrew Sacred Calendar, between the two evenings, or thus from the evening of the 13th to the evening of the 14th.

Festival of Unleavened Bread

nm566 » Now with this day of the Passover there are seven other days that are called the festival of unleavened bread or the appointed time for unleavened bread:

- "And they killed the Passover on the fourteenth day of the first month . . . .. And the children of Israel that were present kept the Passover at that time, and the feast of unleavened bread" (2Chron 35:1, 17).

- "In the fourteenth of the first month is the Passover of the LORD. And in the fifteenth of this month is the festival [appointed time]: seven days shall unleavened bread be eaten. In the first day [15th] shall be a holy convocation; you shall do no manner of servile work therein . . . .. And on the seventh day [the 21st, the 7th day of the festival] you shall have a holy convocation; you shall do no servile work" (Num 28:16-18,25).

- "In the first month, on the fourteenth day of the month at even [sunset], you shall eat unleavened bread, until the one and twentieth [21st] day of the month at even [sunset]. Seven days shall there be no leaven found in your houses . . .. Seven days shall you eat unleavened bread; even the first day you shall put away leaven out of your houses: for whoever eats leavened bread from the first day until the seventh day, that soul shall be cut off from Israel" (Ex 12:18-19, 15).

nm567 » By putting together the above, we see that the fourteenth is the Passover, from the evening of the 13th to the evening of the 14th. After this begins the festival of unleavened bread from the evening of the 14th until the evening of the 21st, which is exactly seven days of eating unleavened bread.

Passover's Various Names

nm568 » The killing of the Passover occurred on the 14th (Lev 23:5; Num 28:16; 2Chron 35:1; Ezra 6:19); the festival of unleavened bread began on the 15th and ended on the 21st at sunset (Lev 23:6-7; Num 28:17-18, 25; Ex 12:18-19; Note: Referring to Ex 12:18, remember the 15th day begins at evening, sunset, of the 14th). Yet sometimes the "Passover" refers to the whole event from the 14th to the 21st, or thus both the Passover day and the festival of unleavened bread: "Now the feast [appointed time] of unleavened bread drew near, which is called the Passover" (Luke 22:1). "Then were the days of unleavened bread ... intending after the Passover to bring him forth to the people" (Acts 12:3-4). Therefore technically, the Passover is *on* the 14th (evening of the 13th to the evening of the 14th), and the festival of unleavened bread is from the 15th (at the end of the evening of the 14th) to the 21st at evening. Yet the words "Passover" or "feast," or "days of unleavened bread" are used interchangeably in the Bible. Thus, we should be careful when we read about this event, so that we do not misunderstand the descriptions of it.

Sabbaths: 15th and 21st of Nisan

nm569 » Now the scripture indicates that the 15th is a day of "holy convocation" or assembly, and the 21st is another assembly or holy convocation (Num 28:17-18, 25; Deut 16:8; Ex 1:18). A holy convocation or assembly is a coming together of set-apart people or holy people. Actually these appointed days of assembly are called Sabbaths (Lev 23:24, 27, 32, 39). Therefore the 15th is an annual Sabbath, and the 21st of the first month is an annual Sabbath.

Passover's Meaning

nm570 » Now we know *when* the Passover and the Festival of Unleavened Bread occur. But we must find out what is the meaning of this event. We will explain the event as described by the Bible, and at the same time explain the higher or Spiritual meaning. Because of the way we will present this subject, we suggest that the reader go over this paper at least twice before forming an opinion. Many of the things presented are different, therefore they may seem strange, yet they are strange only because they are different or new to you.

Physical Passover	Spiritual Passover
Tenth of Nisan (Abib)	*Higher Meaning*
nm571 » *Physical Passover* A lamb was picked out on the 10th of the first month, "a lamb for a house" (Ex 12:3).	Jesus Christ is the lamb of God (John 1:29, 36). Jesus Christ was betrayed by Judas to the chief priests on the 10th of the first month: "And he promised, and sought opportunity to betray him unto them in absence of the multitude" (Luke 22:3-6; see notes in back of this paper).
Passover Without Blemish	*Higher Meaning*
nm572 » *Physical Passover* This lamb was to be without blemish.(Ex 12:5) The lamb without blemish is called the Passover (Ex 12:21).	Christ is the lamb without blemish, or spot (1Pet 1:19; Heb 9:14). This means Christ is sinless (1Pet 2:21-22). Jesus is the Passover lamb (1Cor 5:7). He is the true Passover lamb that was set forth or predestinated to be the Passover lamb before the world began (1Pet 1:19-20; Rev 13:8).

Physical Passover	Spiritual Passover
Fourteenth: Preparation Day nm573 » *Physical Passover* The 14th day was the day of preparation for the Passover lamb, for other ceremonies of the day, and for the Passover meal (2Chron 35:1-6, 10-13, 16).	*Higher Meaning* The 14th was the day Christ the true Passover was taken and prepared before his slaughter: it was the day of preparing Christ for his death, just before the high Sabbath, or the 15th day of Nisan which is a Sabbath day for the Feast of Unleavened Bread (John 19:14, 31, 42).
Passover Killed on 14th of Nisan nm574 » *Physical Passover* The lamb was killed on the 14th of the first month, between the evening of the 13th and 14th towards the evening of the 14th (Ex 12:6; 2Chron 35:1; Deut 16:6).	*Higher Meaning* Christ the true Passover was killed on the 14th of Nisan (John 18:28; and the rest of the scripture on the death of Christ, see notes).
Passover Killed Outside Gates nm575 » *Physical Passover* The lamb was killed outside the gates of the city (2Chron 35:11; Ex 12:6, 21; Deut 16:5).	*Higher Meaning* The lamb of God died also outside the camp, or city of Jerusalem (Heb 13:11-12). Christ had not yet ascended into the New Jerusalem; He died outside or before the kingdom of God (New Jerusalem) was set-up on earth.
Passover's Blood on House nm576 » *Physical Passover* The blood of the lamb was sprinkled on the door posts of the house wherein the people had gathered to eat one Passover lamb, for only *one* lamb per gathering house was allowed (Ex 12:6-7, 3-4, 46; Exo 12:21-22; 2Chron 35:11).	*Higher Meaning* Christians are of the house of God (1Pet 2:5; 4:17; etc); they have the blood of Christ (the Passover) sprinkled on them (1 John 1:7; Heb 10:22; 12:24; 13:12, 20). Christ is the *one* lamb of God for all the house of God (John 1:36; 1Pet 1:19; 1Pet 2:3-5; Heb 10:4; Heb 3:6).

Physical Passover	Spiritual Passover
Passover Roasted As One nm577 » *Physical Passover* Thereafter, since one could not eat the flesh raw, they roasted it as a unit (head, body, legs together), which takes some time (Ex 12:9; Deut 16:7; 2Chron 35:13).	*Higher Meaning* Christ the Passover was "roasted" out in the sun light for hours (Mark 15:25, 33-34).
All Passover's Blood Spilled Out nm578 » *Physical Passover* No blood could be eaten with the sacrificed lamb; his blood had to be spilled completely out (Lev 7:27; 17:12-14).	*Higher Meaning* All of Christ's blood was poured out, until water came out instead of blood (John 19:34).
Passover Had No Bone Broken nm579 » *Physical Passover* No bone could be broken on the Passover lamb (Ex 12:46; Num 9:12).	*Higher Meaning* No bone of Christ was broken (John 19:33, 36).
Passover Eaten in One House nm580 » *Physical Meaning* The Passover was eaten in one house; no flesh was to be carried outside the gathering place (Ex 12:46), or outside the house on which the blood was sprinkled.	*Higher Meaning* Only those Spiritually in the house of God (those with the "blood" of Christ sprinkled on them) can eat the Passover, if we attempt to eat it without being in the Church, we are guilty (1 Cor 11:26-27).
No Stranger May Eat the Passover nm581 » *Physical Passover* No stranger (non-Israelite) could eat the Passover unless he was circumcised, for no uncircumcised person could eat the Passover lamb (Ex 12:43-44, 48).	*Higher Meaning* No stranger outside of the Spiritual Israel of God, can eat the Passover Christ (Eph 2:12, 19; 1Cor 11:28-29). That is, eat his Spiritual bread (see John 6:56-63; see "Spiritual Bread" below).

Physical Passover	Spiritual Passover
Unleavened Bread nm582 » *Physical Passover* No leavened bread was to be eaten with the Passover (Deut 16:3; Ex 23:18; 12:8).	*Higher Meaning* No "old leaven" or "the leaven of the Pharisees," or the doctrines of man can be eaten with the Spiritual Passover (Christ). When you have Christ (the Spiritual Passover) you have his Spirit or the New Mind with the doctrine of the good God, not the doctrines and ideas of mankind belonging to this age (Mat 16:6, 11-12; 1Cor 5:7-8; Mark 8:15; Luke 12:1).
Passover Eaten in the Night nm583 » *Physical Passover* The lamb was eaten in the night of the 15th; the flesh had to be roasted, and eaten with unleavened bread (Ex 12:8, see *Septuagint*).	*Higher Meaning* In a physical sense, the Passover Christ was consumed by the tomb in the late evening of the 14th as it became night (Mark 15:42-47). But, in real sense, since Paul called Christians "unleavened" (1Cor 5:7), and since unleavened bread is that of truth (1Cor 5:8); then Christ and his truth are the unleavened bread consumed by Spiritual Israelites during the spiritual night – the darkness of Satan's kingdom.
Passover Eaten in Haste in the Night nm584 » *Physical Passover* The Passover lamb was eaten in *haste* in the *night* with shoes on their feet, fully clothed, and ready to leave Egypt in a moment's notice (Ex 12:11, 33, 39; 2Chron 35:13).	*Higher Meaning* Spiritually, the Passover Christ is eaten in the night of Satan in trepidation or tribulation as we are fleeing spiritual Egypt.

Physical Passover	Spiritual Passover
Passover Saves Us from the Destroyer nm585 » *Physical Passover* The houses wherein the Passover was eaten in the night, and where the blood of the Passover was put on, therein the destroyer would not smite the first born of the house as the destroyer struck down the first born of the Egyptians (Ex 12:7, 13, 22-23; Heb 11:28; Ex 12:29; 13:15: 11:5).	*Higher Meaning* Because Christians so to speak have Christ's blood sprinkled on them, they will become the first born of mankind to immortality (Heb 12:23; Rev 14:4; James 1:18). The destroyer (Satan) does not spiritually destroy them in the "night." But the first born of the Pharaoh is destroyed in the "night." The "night" is the darkness of Satan's kingdom. The "destroyer" was and is Satan (Psa 78:49; Isa 14:17, 12-17).

Physical Passover	Spiritual Passover
Passover and the Seven Days	*Higher Meaning*
nm586 » *Physical Passover* Now after Israel went out of Egypt, or as they were going out, they ate unleavened bread for seven days from the 15th to the 21st day, from the evening of the 14th to the evening of the 21st day. The main reason they baked unleavened bread seven days was "because they were thrust out of Egypt, and could not tarry, neither had they prepared for themselves any victual" (Ex 12:39). The eating of unleavened bread for the seven days was for a memorial or remembrance of Israel's delivery from the bondage of Egypt (Deut 16:3; Ex 13:3-16; Exo 12:14-19).	Now the True unleavened bread, is Truth (1Cor 5:8). And God's word or Bible is the Truth (John 17:17; James 1:18). And since Christ spoke the word of God, which is the Truth (John 12:49), which comes from the Spirit of Truth (John 14:17; 15:26; 16:13), then the real unleavened bread is Christ's Spiritual Word, his Truth, his Living Bread (see "Spiritual Bread" below). Moreover, since the True seven days are the seven 1000 year days (2Pet 3:8), then the True picture of the Passover Festival is that Christ the Passover Lamb of God was predestinated before the world began to die for all mankind's sin, and because he was slain, it makes it possible for Spiritual Israel (Christians) to come out of spiritual Egypt (Satan's kingdom). Now in the typical Passover festival the unleavened bread was eaten as a remembrance of Israel's deliverance out of Egypt. We eat the Spiritual unleavened bread (The Spiritual Christ is the bread of life) in remembrance of Christ's sacrifice (1Cor 11:24-26) which makes it possible for us to come out of spiritual Egypt.

Sacrifices Fulfilled in Christ's One Sacrifice

nm587 » As Paul showed in Hebrews and as Daniel 9:27 indicated all ritual sacrifices for sin have been fulfilled in Christ's great sacrifice for sin, with the one important qualification, that where the remission of sin is, there is no more offering for sin (Heb 10:18). But this remission or forgiveness of sin only occurs when one has the laws of God in their heart (Heb 10:16-17). And you only have the laws in your heart or mind when you have the Spirit of God inside you leading you (2Cor 3:3-6). Therefore, although Christ died as the Passover for all sin (1John 2:2), all have not been forgiven yet for "we see not yet all things put under him" (Heb 2:8b). But when the true end comes:

- 1Cor 15:24: then *comes* the end, when He hands over the kingdom to the God and Father, when He has abolished all rule and all authority and power. 25 For He must reign until He has put all His enemies under His feet. 26 The last enemy that will be abolished is death. 27 For he has put all things in subjection under his feet. But when He says, "All things are put in subjection," it is evident that He is excepted who put all things in subjection to Him. 28 When all things are subjected to Him, then the Son Himself also will be subjected to the One who subjected all things to Him, **so that God may be all in all.** (1Cor 15:24-28)

When our God is all in all, then all will be atoned to God because when one receives atonement or reconciliation, his sins are covered, and he is brought back to God (Rom 5:9-11).

nm588 » Paul wrote to us about Christ's sacrifice as the real Passover (1 Cor 5:7) who takes away the sins of the world in due time:

- And not through the blood of goats and calves, but through His own blood, He entered the holy place once for all, having obtained eternal redemption. 13 For if the blood of goats and bulls and the ashes of a heifer sprinkling those who have been defiled sanctify for the cleansing of the flesh, 14 how much more will the blood of Christ, who through the eternal Spirit offered Himself without blemish to God, cleanse your conscience from dead works to serve the living God? (Heb 9:12-14)

- 22 And according to the Law, *one may* almost *say*, all things are cleansed with blood, and without shedding of blood there is no forgiveness. 23 Therefore it was necessary for the copies of the things in the heavens to be cleansed with these, but the heavenly things themselves with better sacrifices than these. 24 For Christ did not enter a holy place made with hands, a *mere* copy of the true one, but into heaven itself, now to appear in the presence of God for us; 25 nor was it that He would offer Himself often, as the high priest enters the holy place year by year with blood that is not his own. 26 Otherwise, He would have needed to suffer often since the foundation of the world; but now once at the consummation of the ages He has been manifested to put away sin by the sacrifice of Himself. 27 And inasmuch as it is appointed for men to die once and after this *comes* judgment, 28 so Christ also, having been offered once to bear the sins of many, will appear a second time for salvation without *reference to* sin, to those who eagerly await Him. (Heb 9:22-28)

- For the Law, since it has *only* a shadow of the good things to come *and* not the very form of things, can never, by the same sacrifices which they offer continually year by year, make perfect those who draw near. 2 Otherwise, would they not have ceased to be offered, because the worshipers, having once been cleansed, would no longer have had consciousness of sins? 3 But in those *sacrifices* there is a reminder of sins year by year. 4 For it is impossible for the blood of bulls and goats to take away sins. (Heb 10:1-4)

- 9 then He said, "behold, I have come to do your will." He takes away the first in order to establish the second. 10 By this will we have been sanctified through the offering of the body of Jesus Christ once for all. 11 Every priest stands daily ministering and offering time after time the same sacrifices, which can never take away sins; 12 but He, having offered one sacrifice for sins for all time, **Sat down at the right hand of God**, waiting from that time onward **until his enemies be made a footstool for his feet**. (Heb 10:9-13)

- Now where there is forgiveness of these things, there is no longer *any* offering for sin. (Heb 10:18)

- "And he will make a firm covenant with the many for one week, but in the middle of the week **he will put a stop to sacrifice and offering**; and on the wing of abominations *will come* one who makes desolate, even until a complete destruction, one that is decreed, is poured out on the one who makes desolate." (Dan 9:27; there are two different interpretations here and both may be partly correct)

What these scriptures are saying is that Christ's great Passover sacrifice of himself perfectly fulfilled all ritual sacrifices for sin. Thus, in the middle of the week (Christ died on a Wednesday in the middle of the seven year period: he fulfilled 3 ½ years of it) Christ's death cut off the need of sacrifice for the forgiveness of sin. But men will continue to suffer because of sin until they stop sinning, for sin is wrong behavior that causes suffering.

Spiritual Unleavened Bread as Memorial

nm589 » Now in the typical Passover festival the unleavened bread was eaten as a remembrance of Israel's deliverance out of Egypt. We eat the Spiritual unleavened bread (The Spiritual Christ is the bread of life) in remembrance of Christ's sacrifice which makes it possible for us to come out of spiritual Egypt.

See Spiritual keeping of the Passover in the last part of this paper for more information on other Spiritual aspects of the Passover rituals.

Sheaf of the First Fruits: <u>Time of First Harvest</u>

Foreshadowed First Resurrection

Christ is the Sheaf of First Fruits

nm590 » Now within the festival of the Passover there was another ritual performed, and that was the waving of a sheaf of the first fruits of the first harvest:

- "And the LORD spoke to Moses, saying, Speak unto the children of Israel, and say unto them, When you come into the land which I give unto you, and shall reap the harvest thereof, then you shall bring a sheaf of the first fruits of your harvest unto the priest: And he **shall wave the sheaf before the** [faces or presence of the] **LORD**, to be accepted for you: on the day *after* the Sabbath the priest shall wave it ... And you shall eat neither bread, nor parched corn, nor green ears, until the selfsame day until you have brought an offering [Sheaf] unto your God: a statute aeonian throughout your generations in all your dwellings" (Lev 23:9-11, 14).

Higher Meaning

nm591 » This festival of the Passover and the ritual of the sheaf of first fruits had an important higher meaning. The man Jesus Christ died on the Passover (14th of Nisan), was buried at the very end of the 14th of Nisan, was resurrected three days later, and went back into his Father on the very day the Jews used to wave the sheaf of barley "before the LORD." Paul shows us that Christ was that sheaf of first fruits:

- 21 For since by a man *came* death, by a man also *came* the resurrection of the dead. 22 For as in Adam all die, so also in Christ all will be made alive. 23 But each in his own order: **Christ the first fruits**, after that those who are Christ's at His coming (1Corinthians 15:21)

nm592 » Jesus and Paul explained how even nature projects to us a reason for Christ's death:

- Truly, truly, I say to you, unless a grain falls into the earth and dies, it remains alone; but if it dies, it bears much fruit [produce]. (John 12:24)
- You fool! That which you sow does not come to life unless it dies; and that which you sow, you do not sow the body which is to be, but a bare grain, perhaps of wheat or of something else. (1Cor 15:36-37)

So from this very first fruit (Jesus Christ) will come "much fruit."

nm593 » Notice Leviticus 23:9-11 that the sheaf was waved "before the LORD." Compare this to the order for all males to stand before the LORD three times a year in the three main harvest festivals (Deut 16:16):

- He shall **wave the sheaf before the LORD** for you to be accepted; on the day after the Sabbath the priest shall wave it. (Lev 23:11)
- Three times in a year all your males shall appear **before the LORD** your God in the place which He chooses, at the Feast of Unleavened Bread and at the Feast of Weeks and at the Feast of Booths, and they shall not appear **before the LORD** empty-handed. Every man shall give as he is able, according to the blessing of the LORD your God which He has given you. (Deut 16:16-17)

Jesus Christ was the first of the first fruits (Rev 3:14; 1Cor 15:23; Col 1:15,18) who fulfilled the sheaf of first fruits ritual, perfectly. Only through Christ can anyone be acceptable to God, because you must have the Spirit of God to be acceptable to God as this book prove through Biblical scripture. It is Christ who gives this Spirit (Acts 2:33). So it was by the death of Christ, the Seed [PR1], that "much fruit" will come (John 12:24).

Sheaf of First Fruits Perfectly Fulfilled

nm594 » This ceremony of waving the sheaf of first fruits towards heaven was perfectly fulfilled by Jesus Christ when he ascended to his Father at the beginning of the new 24 hour day *after* the Sabbath, after sunset (see the *Chronology Papers*, CP4). The sheaf of barley, the first of the first fruits, was cut down at the very end of *the Sabbath*, "just as the sun went down" and was waved on the day after the Sabbath (*Unger's Bible Dict.*, p. 355). This Sabbath being the regular weekly Sabbath as the Sadducees and others interpreted Lev 23:9-11 (*Unger's Bible Dict.*, p. 356). As we see when we study the scripture (CP4) Jesus Christ was resurrected just before or at sunset on Saturday (the Sabbath) exactly three days after he was buried. After sunset in the beginning of the first day of the week, he was made into one with his Spirit, and at that time became the first-fruit of the new creation (1Cor 15:23a; Rev 3:14). Christ was foreshadowed by the "sheaf of the first fruits" in this ceremony; He is the first of the first fruits. Christ is the first product, or the first born of the new creation (note Rev 3:14; 1 Cor 15:23; Rom 8:29; Col 1:15, 18; Rev 1:5; see "All Saved Paper" [NM 13]).

Fulfillment on Exact day

nm595 » This ceremony happened typically on the day *after* the weekly Sabbath, a Sunday, within the seven days of unleavened bread (Lev 23:15-16,9-11, 14). Christ fulfilled this perfectly by going back to his Father on that Sunday (cf John 20:17; Mat 28:9; see the *God Papers*). As of now Jesus is the only born of God, or only born God as John 1:18 says in certain Greek texts ("only born God").

Also see *Prophecy Papers 7* [PR7] under "Sheaf of the First Fruits," and *Chronology Papers 4* [CP4] under "Ascension."

Feast of Pentecost Represents second Harvest (Wheat) Harvest of First Fruits 144,000 (Rev 14:3-4; Rev 7:4) Second Order or Rank (1Cor 15:23)							
< Grain Harvest Period >							**Pentecost**
1st Sabbath after sheaf waved	2nd Sabbath after sheaf waved	3rd Sabbath after sheaf waved	4th Sabbath after sheaf waved	5th Sabbath after sheaf waved	6st Sabbath after sheaf waved	7st Sabbath after sheaf waved	Sunday Celebrated after grain harvest
< **Signifies** the seven millenniums of creation >							Two leavened loaves waved
							Atonement

Second Harvest: <u>Pentecost</u>

Foreshadowed Second Resurrection

Feast of First Fruits; Feast of Weeks

nm596 » This festival or appointed time is sometimes called in the
Bible, the Feast of Weeks, or the Feast of First Fruits (Exo 34:22).

- "And you shall count unto you from the day after the Sabbath
  [thus the 1st day of the week, the day Christ went back to his
  Father], from the day that you brought the sheaf of the wave
  offering; seven Sabbaths shall be complete: Even unto the day
  after the seventh Sabbath shall you number fifty days ... And
  you shall proclaim on the selfsame day that it may be a holy
  convocation unto you: You shall do no servile work therein: it
  shall be a statute aeonian in all your dwellings throughout your
  generations" (Lev 23:15-16, 21).

Counting <u>weeks</u> from the Sheaf of First Fruits

nm597 » "Seven weeks shall you number unto you: begin to number
the seven weeks **from such time as you begin to put the sickle to
the grain [barley]**. And you shall keep the feast of weeks unto the
LORD your God with a tribute of freewill offering of your hand, which

you shall give unto the LORD your God, according as the LORD your God has blessed you" (Deut 16:9-10).

nm598 » One counts seven weeks "from such a time as you begin to put the sickle to the crop." Or as it said in Leviticus 23:15-16: "you shall count unto you from the day after the Sabbath, from the day that you brought the **sheaf of the wave offering**; seven Sabbaths shall be complete: Even unto the day after the seventh Sabbath **shall you number fifty days**."

Counting of the 50 Days

nm599 » Now since Christ is the antitypical or Spiritual sheaf, and since Christ the man went to his or ascended to his Father (see John 20:17) after sunset on a Sunday (the day *after* the weekly Sabbath), and since this was the beginning of the time the sickle was put to the harvest, and since seven weeks or seven Sabbaths from the beginning of the Sunday is complete at the end of the Sabbath seven weeks later; then the 50th full day is the Sunday after the seventh Sabbath. The word *from* means: "used to specify a starting point in spatial movement: a train running west from New York City." Or "used to specify a starting point in an expression of limits." Or "used to indicate source or origin" (from the Random House Dictionary). Since we count from a point, the origin point, and since the Pentecost is *the* 50th full day of a limited period; then we count seven weeks from the starting point or origin day to the end of a Sabbath seven weeks thereafter. The 50th full day is the Sunday, the day after the seventh Sabbath (Lev 23:15-16).

Pentecost of the Church not Perfect Fulfillment

nm600 » Exactly 50 days (seven Sabbaths [49 days] plus one day) from when the sheaf of barley was waved by the Jews at the Festival of the Passover (which was 50 days after Christ went to the Father), the apostles gathered together to celebrate the Pentecost (Acts 2). On that day the Spirit was first given to the Church. Some therefore think (as I once mistakenly believed) that this is the antitypical or higher meaning of the Pentecost – the giving of the Spirit to the Church. But this is mistaken. We see in this paper that Christ **fulfilled** the Passover festival, perfectly (see also Luke 22:15-16). So what the Pentecost represented typically, the antitypical Pentecost must fulfill it perfectly, not partially. If the physical Pentecost was the day Israel celebrated the harvest of the first fruits of the land, then the antitypical Pentecost must perfectly fulfill the *harvest* of the first fruits of the new creation (1Cor 15:23, 2nd part; James 1:18; Rev 14:4; See "All Saved Paper" [NM 13]). The Spirit on the first Church Pentecost was given to only a few of the total "first fruits" – only about 3,000 (Acts 2:41), not all of them.

nm601 » **Thus, not all of the first fruits mentioned in Rev 14:3-4 received the Spirit on this first Pentecost of the Church. But in order to fulfill the Pentecost perfectly, all things pertaining to the physical Pentecost must be fulfilled Spiritually and perfectly, as Christ fulfilled the physical Passover.**

Trumpets Blown on the Pentecost

nm602 » We need to know something about the blowing of trumpets, as in all other holy days, trumpets were blown on the Pentecost:

- "Also in the day of your gladness **and in your appointed feasts**, and on the first *days* of your months, **you shall blow the trumpets** over your burnt offerings, and over the sacrifices of your peace offerings; and they shall be as a reminder of you before your God. I am the LORD your God." (Numbers 10:10)

Blowing of Trumpet versus Blowing an Alarm

Trumpet for Assembly

nm603 » There were two different types of trumpet blowing. One way was for assembly and one was for an alarm of war. The trumpet for assembly, "the calling of the assembly"(Num 10:2-3, 7; Judges 3:27), was blown in "the day gladness, and your solemn days you shall blow with trumpets" (Num 10:10).

Trumpet for War

nm604 » There was a difference between blowing the trumpets for the assembly or gathering of Israel, and the blowing of trumpets to sound an alarm for war: "If you go to war in your land against the enemy that oppresses you, then you shall blow an alarm with the trumpets; and you shall be remembered before the LORD your God, and you shall be saved from your enemies" (Num 10:9; Neh 4:20), "the sound of the **trumpet**, the alarm of war" (Jer 4:19). "Declares the LORD, That I will cause a **trumpet** blast of war" (Jer 49:2). Therefore when Israel "is to be gathered together, you shall blow, but you shall not sound an alarm" (Num 10:9); one kind of trumpet blowing was for gathering Israel for a holy assembly, and one was for a gathering for war.

Trumpets at end of World

nm605 » There are also the blowing of trumpets associated with the end of the old age and the beginning of the Kingdom of God.

- **Blow a trumpet in Zion**, And sound an alarm on My holy mountain! Let all the inhabitants of the land tremble, For the day of the LORD is coming; Surely it is near, A day of darkness and gloom, A day of clouds and thick darkness. As the dawn is spread over the mountains, *So* there is a great and mighty people; There has never been *anything* like it, Nor will there be again after it To the years of many generations. (Joel 2:1-2)

- 'They have blown the **trumpet** and made everything ready, but no one is going to the battle, for My wrath is against all their multitude. (Ezekiel 7:14)

- "And He will send forth His angels with a great **trumpet** and they will gather together His elect from the four winds, from one end of the sky to the other. (Matthew 24:31)

- In a moment, in the twinkling of an eye, at the last **trumpet**; for the **trumpet** will sound, and the dead will be raised imperishable, and we will be changed. (1Corinthians 15:52)

- For the Lord Himself will descend from heaven with a shout, with the voice of *the* archangel and with the **trumpet** of God, and the dead in Christ will rise first. (1Thessalonians 4:16)

- I was in the Spirit on the Lord's day, and I heard behind me a loud voice like *the sound* of a **trumpet**, (Revelation 1:10)

- "And the seventh angel sounded [his *trumpet*, cf Rev 8:6, 7, 8, 10, 12; 9:1, 14]; and there were great voices in heaven, saying, the kingdoms of this world are become the kingdoms of our Lord, and of his Christ" (Rev 11:15).

Trumpets at the Presence of the King

The blowing of trumpets also represented other things such as to introduce a new king (1Kings 1:34-41), and were used in the Bible to indicate the presence of God (Ex 19:16, 19; 2Kings 9:13). This is fulfilled on the antitypical Pentecost when Christ comes with his saints.

Perfect Fulfillment of Pentecost

Pentecost is the Second Order of Persons to Immortality

nm606 » The Pentecost was a day of assembly for the Israelites, but it foreshadowed the first harvest of the earth's people to become immortal beings, the first fruits or products of God (Rev 14:4). The typical or physical Pentecost occurred after the grain harvest in Palestine. The higher meaning of this indicates the harvest of the first fruits of mankind to God (Rev 14:14-20, 4; Mat 13:38-43; James 1:18).

Because at the harvest of first fruit there will be the Last War (see PR 4-6), then the blowing of trumpets on the Feast of Pentecost will perfectly fulfill this, and any other blowing of trumpets at future feasts will not represent war. The blowing of trumpets on the antitypical Pentecost represents the (1) gathering; (2) Last War; (3) presence of the King of Kings.

Two Loaves of Leavened Bread Waved Before Yehowah

nm607 » Leviticus 23:17 You shall bring in from your assembly places **two loaves of bread for a wave offering**, made of two-tenths *of an ephah*; they shall be of a fine flour, **baked with leaven** as first fruits to the LORD ...19 'You shall also offer **one male goat for a sin offering** and two male lambs one year old for a sacrifice of peace offerings. 20 The priest shall then **wave them with the bread of the first fruits for a wave offering with two lambs** [peace offering] **before the LORD**; they are to be holy to the LORD [and] to the priest. (Lev 23:17-20)

Notice a few things here:

- The two *baked* leavened loaves of bread were waved before the LORD.

- Two *baked* leavened loaves were taken out of Israel's assembly.

- The two *baked* leavened loaves of bread were made of *leaven*.

- The two *baked* leavened loaves of the first fruits were waved with two lambs for the peace offering (Lev 23:19-20).

- Leavened bread could be used for peace offerings (Lev 7:13).

- Leaven was not to be used in any offering made by fire (Lev 2:11).

- The offerings of first fruits were not to be burnt on the altar (Lev 2:12).

- Therefore the two leavened loaves were not placed in the fire because they were *baked* with leaven (Lev 23:17).

- All offerings *baked* in an oven are for the Priest (Lev 7:9, 13-14) and therefore, of course, not burnt on the altar.

- The two leavened loaves were waved with one male goat being offered for a sin offering (Lev 23:19), while the waving of the sheaf of first fruits (barley) did not require a sin offering since it was without leaven (cf. Lev 23:12-14)

- The two leavened loaves were holy in reference to the LORD and to the priest (Lev 23:20).

What does this all mean?

Leavened Bread

nm608 » Israel was forbidden from eating leavened bread during seven days of the Passover Festival beginning on the 15th of Nisan and ending on the 21st of Nisan (Ex 12:18-19; 13:6-7; Lev 23:6-7; Num 28:16-8,25; Deut 16:3). This rule was a memorial of Israel coming out of Egypt because they were driven out before their bread was leavened (Ex 12:39). Spiritually, the leavened during these seven days represent the doctrines and hypocrisy of the Pharisees, Sadducees, and those like Herod (Mat 16:12; Mark 8:15; Luke 12:1; 1Cor 5:8). This festival foreshadowed Christ's unleavened sacrifice. And thus, blood could not be sacrificed with leavened bread (Ex 23:18; 34:25) because this blood foreshadowed Christ's blood, which was sacrificed without sin (leaven). As we see from the evidence above leaven could be used in a few offerings as long as it wasn't burnt on the altar (Lev 7:13; 23:17-20; 2:11). Although generally, leaven indicated sin or the doctrines of sin, in at least two places leaven and leavening of bread is used allegorically to represent a positive activity:

- The **kingdom of heaven is like leaven**, which a woman took and hid in three pecks of flour until it was all leavened (Mat 13:33; Luke 13:21)

The meaning here has nothing to do with sin (leaven), but with the three separate pecks of flour that were hidden (unknown to most) until the bread was ready to eat (when it had fully risen).

Leavened Bread & Sin Offering

nm609 » Since there was a sin offering (Lev 23:19) associated with the waving of the two loaves, then sin is somehow connected with the two baked loaves. Remember, there was no sin offering associated with the waving of the sheaf of first fruits (Lev 23:10-14). Yet does this mean that the two leavened loaves themselves represented sin? No, because they were waved before God to be accepted by God. And they were for the Priest to eat after being waved or heaved (Lev 7:9, 13-14). Since the Priest could not touch or eat anything defiled (Lev 7:21; 10:10), then these two *baked* loaves are not defiled, for they were "holy to the LORD" (Lev 23:20). The sin offering made it possible for the loafs to be accepted. Considering the relevant scriptures, whatever the loaves represented, we know that the leaven in the bread somehow was associated with sin, but the sin offering made it possible for them to be waved and accepted by God.

Time of Wave Offering at a Harvest

nm610 » We must consider in our analysis the time of the loaves being waved. It was done at the time of the harvest of wheat. In the case of the waving of the sheaf of first fruits, which was the beginning of the *harvest* of barley grain, it was waved before the LORD. As we saw previously this represented Jesus Christ the man going back into his Father and becoming one with his Father. Thus, to follow the metaphor, the two loaves must also become one with God as Christ prayed in John 17:21-23 that Christians would become one with God. The two loaves represented the grain harvest since they were taken from the grain of the harvest belonging to the assemblies or households of Israel (Lev 23:17).

Two Loaves Baked with Leaven

nm611 » The two loaves of bread were baked with leaven. Since this was not the Feast of the Passover, but an offering of *baked* bread (Lev 23:17) which was for the priest (Lev 7:9) and thus could be baked with leaven (Lev 7:13-14), then leavened-baked bread was perfectly correct for this ritual. Baked leavened bread is edible bread, edible in the way most people eat bread. It is a finished product while the sheaf of first fruits was not baked, but was an unbaked sheaf of grain.[1] This wave offering of two loaves of baked bread at the Pentecost was a finished product, so to speak. It was baked; it was baked with leaven. It was a finished product that used leaven (or sin, since leaven represents sin) to make it. If we take the leaven in these two loaves as somehow

---

[1] We learn more about Jesus Christ in the *God Papers*, so we will not mention the significance of the sheaf wave offering in the Passover festival. But there is meaning to this. As there is meaning to the fact that the unleavened bread was eaten for seven days and not eight days.

representing sin or the effects of sin, then sin played a part in the making (baking) of the two loaves. As leaven was used to make the finished product (bread), so must sin be used in some way to produce the finished or harvested man. To understand how sin could play any part, you must understand the law of knowledge and the reason for good and evil (see NM 19 and GP7). Remember, we learn from John that Christians are forgiven through Christ, for Christ's sacrifice (blood) made us acceptable to God, yet we are not without sin (leaven):

- but if we walk in the Light as He Himself is in the Light, we have fellowship with one another, and the blood of Jesus His Son cleanses us from all sin. 8 If we say that we have no sin, we are deceiving ourselves and the truth is not in us. 9 If we confess our sins, He is faithful and righteous to forgive us our sins and to cleanse us from all unrighteousness. 10 If we say that we have not sinned, we make Him a liar and His word is not in us. (1John 1:7-10)

So Christians, even though Christ cleansed them from all sin (forgave all their sins), still are sinners and have sin and the results of sin in them: they still have leaven in them; none are perfect like Jesus Christ. The leaven in the two loaves represented the sin or age of sin that gives us the knowledge of evil, which in turn allows us to understand and appreciate good (study NM19).

Two Loaves Represent ...

nm612 » So what do the two loaves of baked leavened bread mean in the Feast of Pentecost?

- Knowing, first that this festival represents the second order to salvation as explained by Paul (1Cor 15:20-28);

- knowing, second that it occurs at the time of the coming of Christ and the setting up of his kingdom on earth (1Cor 15:23);

- knowing, third that there will be two witnesses representing Christ 3 ½ years before Christ returns (PR8; Rev 11);

- knowing, that two churches are associated with the two witnesses ("two candlesticks," Rev 11:4 cf. Rev 1:20);

- then we know that the two loaves represent, all in the second order to salvation and also the two witnesses with their associated two churches at the end of the world.

nm613 » But also since we know there is only ONE church of Christ (which includes both the living and the dead in Christ [1Cor 15:52-56]), then these two loaves or churches also represent metaphorically the

ONE church. The <u>two</u> loaves only add another point of information as do the <u>seven</u> churches in Revelation add to our information of the state of the Church at the end of the age. It is the 144,000 that will be infused into God at Christ's coming and it is one Church with one Spirit.

- But each in his own order: Christ the first of the first fruits, **after that those who are Christ's at His coming,** (1Cor 15:23)

- Then I looked, and behold, the Lamb *was* standing on Mount Zion, and **with Him one hundred and forty-four thousand,** having His name and the name of His Father written on their foreheads.... 14:4 These are the ones who have not been defiled with women, for they have kept themselves chaste. These *are* the ones who follow the Lamb wherever He goes. These have been purchased from among men **as first fruits to God and to the Lamb.** (Rev 14:1,4)

- For even as the body is **one and *yet* has many members,** and all the members of the body, though they are many, are **one** body, so also is Christ. For **by one Spirit** we were all baptized **into one body,** whether Jews or Greeks, whether slaves or free, and we were **all made to drink of one Spirit.** (1Cor 12:12-13)

Feast of Trumpets: Great Assembly

Trumpets for Resurrection

nm614 » On the first day of the seventh month of Israel's Sacred Calendar (Sept-Oct) Israel had a festival of trumpets, which we call the Feast of Trumpets and others call the "Day of the Awakening Blast," which started a repentance period ("days of repentance") of nine days before the Day of Atonement (*The Temple*, by Alfred Edersheim, p. 291). Moses in the Bible writes about the Feast of Trumpets as follows:

- "Speak unto the children of Israel, saying, In the seventh month, in the first day of the month, shall you have a Sabbath [that is, an annual Sabbath], a memorial of blowing of trumpets, a holy convocation [an assembly]. You shall do no servile work therein: but you shall offer an offering made by fire unto the LORD" (Lev 23:24-25). "And in the seventh month, on the first day of the month you shall have a holy convocation; you shall do no servile work; it is a day of blowing the trumpets unto you" (Num 29:1). Therefore the feast of trumpets was another annual Sabbath for the Hebrews. It wasn't a festival where all males had to appear before God in Jerusalem, nor was it a harvest, but it was a holy convocation, a Sabbath. It happened on the first day of the seventh month. The main aspect of this holy day was that trumpets were blown on it, some accounts tell us that trumpets were sounded all day long:

- Speak to the sons of Israel, saying, 'In the seventh month on the first of the month you shall have a rest, **a memorial by blowing *of trumpets***, a holy convocation. (Leviticus 23:24)

- Now in the seventh month, on the first day of the month, you shall also have a holy convocation; you shall do no laborious work. It will be to you **a day for blowing trumpets**. (Numbers 29:1)

Feast of Trumpets not for War

The time when the Kingdom of God is set up on earth is after Jesus Christ comes, *after* the great tribulation (Mat 24:29-30), on the antitypical *Pentecost*. And since after the kingdom of God is set up there will never be war again (PR6, Sec [13]), then the fulfillment of the Feast of Trumpets has to do with something else besides war.

Trumpet blowing also represented other things such as to introduce a new king (1Kings 1:34-41), and was used in the Bible to indicate the presence of God (Ex 19:16, 19; 2Kings 9:13). But these two aspects of trumpet blowing were fulfilled by the trumpet blowing on the antitypical Feast of Pentecost.

There will be trumpets blown at the end of the world, but just because the trumpets are blown at the end of the world and just because the feast of trumpets is a day of blowing of trumpets, does not necessarily mean that the feast represents the end of the world. Originally, the trumpet blowing on the Feast of Trumpets was not for war, but to assemble Israel for a holy day where no work was to be done (Num 29:1; Lev 23:24-25). Remember that *every* festival had horns blown on them (Num 10:10).

Perfect Fulfillment always occurs on Same Day

nm615 » The various meanings of blowing the trumpets are telling us something. As we have seen by our study of the Passover, events were fulfilled anti-typically on the exact day on which they happened in the Old Testament feast. The typical Passover was killed on the 14th of the first month; the antitypical Passover (Christ) was killed on the 14th also. The taking of the sheaf of the first fruits typically was performed at the beginning of the day after the Sabbath; antitypically this was fulfilled when Christ ascended to his Father on the beginning of the day, after sunset, after the weekly Sabbath. The Pentecost typically happened after the harvest of first fruits; antitypically the Pentecost indicates the first harvest of the world's people to immortality and this harvest will happen on the antitypical Pentecost. The first giving of the Spirit that makes this harvest of people to immortality possible also happened on the exact day of the Pentecost (Acts 2).

Feast of Trumpets Fulfillment

nm616 » The Feast of Trumpets will be the resurrection of the <u>third order</u> or rank of all that died in the first seven 1000-year periods. Trumpets were used to gather Israel together. As we see in the "Seed Paper" [PR1], physical Israel represents allegorically all of mankind. The Feast of Trumpets was the grand day of trumpet blowing for trumpets were blown all day long. The Pentecost foreshadowed the resurrection at the beginning of the 1000 year-day of rest (Rev 20:4-5), while the Feast of Trumpets foreshadows the far greater (in number) resurrection of all the rest of the dead from their graves after the 1000 year-day (Rev 20:4-5). This is the resurrection of judgment, or those from the 1000 year judgment (John 5:29; see NM24). All the dead will be resurrected and taught from the Bible the meaning of life and the plan of God as foreshadowed by such verses as Nehemiah 7:73; 8:1-10. Remember all resurrected in this great resurrection did not understand who or what God was or the purpose of life while they lived on earth previously. So at the time of their resurrection from the dead and from their judgment they will learn the truth and they will weep and repent when they start to understand how grand God was/is/will be, and how evil they had been in their past behavior.

- "For the people wept when they heard the words of the law" (Neh 8:9)

The people wept on the first day of Israel's seventh month (Neh 7:73).

But their weeping will turn to joy as they learn of the great good news of God's great plan of creation. As in the book of Nehemiah, the people on the first day of the seventh month (Neh 7:73) and on the second day of that month gathered "to understand the words of the law" (Neh 8:13). From the first day when they will be resurrected on the Feast of Trumpets until the Day of Atonement, they will study and learn from the Bible all that they overlooked while on earth. The Feast of Trumpets gathers the people of the earth from their judgment and starts to teach them the truth until the Day of Atonement when something even greater happens.

Day of Atonement

Atonement for All

Physical and Spiritual Join

nm617 » "And the LORD spoke unto Moses, saying, also on the tenth day of the seventh month there shall be **a day of atonement**: it shall be a holy convocation unto you; and you shall afflict your souls and offer an offering made by fire unto the LORD. And you shall do no work in that same day: for it is a day of atonement, to make an atonement for you, before the LORD your God. For whatsoever soul it be that shall not be afflicted in that same day, he shall be cut off from among his people. And whatsoever soul it be that does any work in that same day, the same soul will I destroy from among his people. You shall do no manner of work: a statute aeonian throughout your generations in all your dwellings. It shall be unto you a Sabbath of rest, and you shall afflict your souls: in the ninth day of the month at evening, from evening unto evening, shall you celebrate your Sabbath" (Lev 23:27-32).

nm618 » "*This* shall be a permanent statute for you: in the seventh month, on the tenth day of the month, you shall humble your souls and not do any work, whether the native, or the alien who sojourns among you; 30 for it is **on this day that atonement shall be made for you to cleanse you; you will be clean from all your sins before the LORD**. 31 "It is to be a sabbath of solemn rest for you, that you may humble your souls; it is a permanent statute. 32 "So the priest who is anointed and ordained to serve as priest in his father's place shall make atonement: he shall thus put on the linen garments, the holy garments, 33 and **make atonement for the holy sanctuary**, and he shall make **atonement for the tent of meeting and for the altar**. He shall also make **atonement for the priests and for all the people of the assembly**. 34 "Now you shall have this as a permanent statute, to make **atonement for the sons of Israel for all their sins** once every year." And just as the LORD had commanded Moses, *so* he did. (Lev 16:29-34)

The key word here is soul as we will see below after we see what is the antitypical meaning of "fast."

Physical Fast and Soul

nm619 » Therefore the day of Atonement was a day of rest, and a day to "afflict your souls." The day of Atonement was an annual Sabbath for the Hebrews wherein they came together; it was a day of rest from labor. Now what does it mean to afflict their souls? First of all, "soul" here is translated from a Hebrew word that means, *breathing animal* (NM6). To afflict one's soul is to afflict one's living body.

Real Fast is Behavior without Evil

nm620 » The word "afflict" is translated from a Hebrew word that means, to humble, or to lower. Therefore on the day of Atonement we humble or lower our bodies. Now this means to the physical Jews to *fast* on that day, and thus to humble their bodies. Isaiah 58:3 seems to use afflicting one's soul and fasting interchangeably. Therefore to afflict one's souls is to fast. But we are to worship God Spiritually (John 4:23-24). What is the Spiritual or higher meaning for fasting?:

- ▪ "Is not this what I require of you as a fast: to loose the fetters of injustice, to untie the knots of the yoke, to snap every yoke and set free those who have been crushed? Is it not sharing your food with the hungry, taking the homeless poor into your house, clothing the naked when you meet them, and never evading a duty to your kinfolk?" (Isa 58:6-7, NEB)

nm621 » In other words, Spiritual lowering of our bodies, or fasting, is the way or system of love. When Christian's fast, they fast from "fat" as used negatively in the Bible. On Israel's festivals "fat" was burned up. Spiritually speaking, all fat (evil) is burnt up by God's Spirit and God's way. Therefore since we are to worship God Spiritually, then to Spiritually fast is to follow in the way of love. Since Christians are supposed to have the Spirit, which brings them atonement to God, then Spiritual Christians always Spiritually fast – they always follow in the way of love, at least in their inner minds, according to the power given them.

New Soul

Also notice that the fast on the Day of Atonement is a fast of the soul. As we learned in the *Body, Soul, and Spirit Paper* [NM6], there are two meanings to soul. The physical meaning is that a soul is a physical body with breath in it; while the higher meaning of soul is a physical body with God's Spirit in it. At the antitypical Feast of Atonement, the Spiritual meaning of "fast" will apply and the Spiritual meaning of soul will apply. At the antitypical Atonement all will be in their soul: a physical body with a good Spirit of God in them (Rom 5:11).

Atonement to God

nm622 » The Hebrew's Day of Atonement Spiritually represents to us the atonement of man to God. In the paper "Thousand Years and Beyond" we explained that the time of Atonement for mankind to God through the medium of the Spirit of God is in the eighth Spiritual time period, the Great Day of Atonement. This Spiritual day of Atonement lasts for 100 years, and occurs after the seventh millennium as shown in the paper just mentioned. The day of Atonement pictures the snapping of all the yokes of bondage from mankind and angelkind, and the practicing of the way of love for ALL. We receive atonement through Christ (Romans 5:11). And we receive this atonement when we have the Spirit of God in us.

Trumpets on the Day of Atonement on the Jubilee

nm623 » In Leviticus, chapter 25, it explains the year of jubilee. This was a year when all returned to their homeland and families. This jubilee pictures the Great Day of Atonement to God when everyone ever born of mankind has been resurrected and will return to their families and live in that age. It is significant that on the day of atonement, just at the beginning of the jubilee that there was to sound "the trumpet of jubilee" throughout the land (Lev 25:9). This trumpet does not antitypically represent a resurrection (1Cor 15:52; 1Thes 4:16), since that happened earlier on the Feast of Trumpets. The trumpet here does not signify war because at the beginning of the 7th millennium, all war will be stopped and will never happen again (see "Last War and God's Wrath" paper [PR5]). On the Great Day of Atonement after the thousand years, all will have been resurrected back to life (Ezek 37:1-13; 16:55). Thereafter on the Day of Atonement the Spirit of God will be given them (Ezek 37:13-14). The trumpets on the Day of Atonement signify the gathering of the physical and Spiritual coming together into atonement.

Day of Atonement Fulfillment: Release From Sin

nm624 » At the end of seven units of time ("years"), which represents the Spiritual seven units of time (millenniums), is the release from debt (Deut 15:1-2). Debt and sin are used interchangeably in the Bible (Luke 11:4). Therefore, according to the pattern, after the seven millenniums, all will have been released from sin. The Spiritual law will be imputed to all and thereafter they shall follow all the ways of love perfectly because on the eighth Spiritual day they will receive the Spirit or New Mind in the full measure of power as Christ had when he was on earth.

nm625 » The festival of Atonement pictures the atonement of all mankind in the eighth Spiritual day and receiving the Spirit in the eighth unit of Spiritual time. This is pictured in John 7:37-39:

- Now on the last day, the great *day* of the feast, Jesus stood and cried out, saying, "If anyone is thirsty, let him come to Me and drink. 38 "He who believes in Me, as the Scripture said, 'From his innermost being will flow rivers of living water.'" 39 But this He spoke of the Spirit, whom those who believed in Him were to receive; for the Spirit was not yet *given*, because Jesus was not yet glorified. (John 7:37-39)

nm626 » The Jubilee also started on the day of Atonement and the Jubilee represented atonement of all the people to God.

- You shall then sound a ram's horn abroad on the tenth day of the seventh month; on the day of atonement you shall sound a horn all through your land. (Lev 25:9)

Everyone was to return to his family and possessions, and the poor and servants were able to redeem themselves and their property. It was a year of liberty and freedom: You shall "proclaim liberty throughout the land and unto all the inhabitants." (Lev 25:10) But the only true way to get true freedom is through the Spirit of God (2Cor 3:17; Gal 5:1). "And not only *so*, but we also joy in God through our Lord Jesus Christ, by whom we have now received the **atonement**" (Rom 5:11). The real atonement is through Christ and his Spirit of God. When the last group or order receives the Spirit, at that time, *all* will be atoned to God through the New Mind or new Spirit of God. But all will not yet be immortal as we see by studying how the seed was sown in the Jubilee. **See Below.** Spiritual atonement must happen on the <u>eighth</u> period of time after the seven millenniums as shown in NM15.

Ritual of the "twin" goats fulfilled on the antitypical Day of Atonement

The ritual of "twin" goats on the Day of Atonement was partially fulfilled when Christ died for our sins. Christ fulfilled the ritual of the first goat mentioned in Leviticus 16:7-9,15-19. But the fulfillment of the second goat's ritual will not be fulfilled until the antitypical Day of Atonement, when all sin is sent away for ever. The antitypical Day of Atonement will fulfill perfectly atonement to God because all mankind on that day will receive the Spirit, and because of this, **sin will on that day be sent away** in the perfect sense. This will fulfill the **Azazel** ritual perfectly, and thus complete perfectly the typical Day of Atonement (see NM15, under "Azazel").

Feast of Tabernacles Represents third and Final Harvest Great Multitude with white robes and palms (Rev 7:9) Third Order or Rank fulfills God all in all (1Cor 15:23-28)								Time after
Sabbath 15th of 7th mo.							Sabbath 22nd of 7th mo.	23rd day [1Ch 7:10]
1st day Living in temp. palm booths	2nd day Living in temp. palm booths	3rd day Living in temp. palm booths	4th day Living in temp. palm booths	5th day Living in temp. palm booths	6th day Living in temp. palm booths	7th day Living in temp. palm booths	8th day Great Last Day Atonement with God	9th "day" Forever Time >
< **Signifies** eight periods of the creation (seven millenniums & one shorter period) >								Forever>

Third Harvest: <u>Feast of Tabernacles</u>

Third and Final Resurrection to Immortal Life

nm627 » The typical Feast of Tabernacles, also called the Feast of Booths, occurred <u>after</u> the last harvest of the year:

- Leviticus 23:34 "Speak to the sons of Israel, saying, 'On the fifteenth of this seventh month is the Feast of Booths for seven days to the LORD. 35 'On the first day is a holy convocation; you shall do no laborious work of any kind. 36 'For seven days you shall present an offering by fire to the LORD. On the eighth day you shall have a holy convocation and present an offering by fire to the LORD; it is an assembly. You shall do no laborious work. 37 'These are the appointed times of the LORD which you shall proclaim as holy convocations, to present offerings by fire to the LORD-- burnt offerings and grain offerings, sacrifices and drink offerings, *each* day's matter on its own day-- 38 besides *those of* the sabbaths of the LORD, and besides your gifts and besides all your votive and freewill offerings, which you give to the LORD. 39 'On exactly the fifteenth day of the seventh month, when you have gathered in the crops of the land, you shall celebrate the feast of the LORD for seven days, with a rest on the first day and a rest on the eighth day. 40 'Now on the first day you shall take for yourselves the foliage of beautiful trees, palm branches and boughs of leafy trees and willows of the brook, and you shall rejoice before the LORD your God for seven days. 41 'You shall thus celebrate it *as* a feast to the LORD for seven days in the year. It *shall be* a perpetual statute throughout your generations; you shall celebrate it in the seventh month. 42 'You shall live in booths for seven days; all the native-born in Israel shall live in booths, 43 so that your generations may know that I had the sons of Israel live in booths when I brought them out from the land of Egypt. I am the LORD your God.'" 44 So Moses declared to the sons of Israel the appointed times of the LORD. (Lev 23:34-44)

Temporary Booths

nm628 » This festival lasted eight days. The first day was an assembly, and the eighth day was an assembly. But during the first seven days, physical Israel was to live in temporary booths made up of branches of trees (Lev 23:40; Neh 8:15).

- Now on the first day you shall take for yourselves the foliage of beautiful trees, palm branches and boughs of leafy trees and willows of the brook, and you shall rejoice before the LORD your God for seven days. (Leviticus 23:40)

- So they proclaimed and circulated a proclamation in all their cities and in Jerusalem, saying, "Go out to the hills, and bring olive branches and wild olive branches, myrtle branches, palm branches and branches of other leafy trees, to make booths, as it is written." (Nehemiah 8:15)

- You shall live in booths for seven days; all those born in Israel shall live in booths (Lev 23:42)

All born in Israel were to live in booths for seven days. This Spiritually signifies the seven Spiritual days, the seven millenniums, and all of mankind born in the seven millenniums. Why? Because everyone will eventually become a Spiritual Israelite (see, "Seed Paper" [PR1]), this thus signifies that all ever to be born of God will be born of man during the first seven millenniums. During the seven millenniums all of mankind will have lived in their temporary bodies. After the seven millenniums, mankind as a whole will be typically complete, or joined with their Spirit. Two (the Spirit and the physical body) will be typically complete in the eighth Spiritual day. Therefore they will <u>not</u> be dwelling in their temporary tabernacles (old temporary bodies) after the seven millenniums, but they will be dwelling in their new bodies as a New Soul. But in the short eighth Spiritual day, they will be in their New Soul as a *begotten* son of God. Later they will be *born* of God (see "Begotten, Born Paper" [NM 5]).

100 Years

nm629 » The eighth day of the Feast of Tabernacles indicated the eighth Spiritual period of the Spiritual creation. This eighth Spiritual day will be shorter than the first seven Spiritual days as indicated by the eighth period of time in the Jubilee and Pentecost festival:

(1) The Jubilee is the eighth year <u>after</u> seven periods of seven years;

(2) The Pentecost is the eighth day <u>after</u> seven periods of seven days.

This shorter eighth period of time will last 100 years. The proof for the length is indicated by Isaiah 65:20 and other scripture (Ex 26:3, 7; 36:10, 14; 26:12; see Sacrifice Table below). Here it shows all people living to the age of 100 years. People will live that long once the typical new heaven and earth is created (Isa 65:17-19). This begins at Christ's return and lasts until the creation of the true new heaven and earth. Since there is to be an eighth Spiritual day of creation, as indicated by the pattern of various festivals and rituals of the Bible (see NM15), and since the life spans will be 100 years in the typical new heaven and earth, and since those resurrected after the seven millenniums will still be human beings, but with the Spirit joined to them, and since in the Biblical patterns the eighth unit in the cycle is pictured as being smaller than the previous seven units; then the eighth day of creation will be smaller than the previous ones, and it will last for 100 years, which is the length of human life in the typical new heaven and earth. Note: To understand the patterns and cycles of eight, see the paper, "Thousand Years and Beyond" [NM 15].

nm630 » When Jesus kept the feast of tabernacles, he on the eighth day ("the last day") stood up and said, "if any man thirst, let him come unto me, and drink" (John 7:37). By this he meant the water of the Spirit (John 7:39). Therefore this indicates the giving of the Spirit in the eighth Spiritual day of creation.

Feast of Tabernacles Fulfillment

nm631 » Notice that the Festival of Tabernacles was celebrated *after* the gathering of the harvest (Lev 23:39; Deut 16:13; Ex 23:16). This indicates in the higher sense the time after the gathering of all the harvest of mankind. Mankind is totally gathered together in the eighth Spiritual day, wherein all will be resurrected to life with the new Spirit given them. The festival is thus fulfilled perfectly after all have been harvested. Harvest, in the first two harvests, always meant being harvested to immortality and with that being placed back into the God.

After The Eighth Day

nm632 » Now notice: "and in the eighth day they made a solemn assembly: for they kept the dedication of the altar seven days, and the feast [of tabernacles] seven days [that is, the 7 days before this 8th day]. And **on the three and twentieth day** [23rd] of the seventh month he sent the people away into their tents, glad and merry in heart for the goodness that the LORD had showed unto David, and to Solomon, and to Israel his people. **Thus Solomon FINISHED the house of the LORD**, and the kings's house" (2Chron 7:9-11). Now the eighth day of the feast happens on the 22nd day of the seventh month. Solomon sent them back to their tents on the 23rd day (the 9th day after the feast began) when the house of God was finished.

House of God Finished

Since Christians are the antitypical temple and house of God (1Cor 3:16; 1Pet 2:5), and since all will eventually go into God (NM13), then when the house of God is finished (all in God), so too will be the creation, in its truest sense. Also we show in PR1 that the antitypical Solomon is Jesus Christ. Jesus Christ will build and finish the house of God for all things are built through Christ (1Pet 2:5; Col 1:16-19).

nm633 » Therefore the higher meaning of 2Chron 7:9-11 indicates that after the eighth Spiritual days of creation, then the family (house) of God will be finished. The house of God is the Spiritual house that Jesus Christ is to build. That is, the creation of God will be finished – all will be born of God – right after the eighth Spiritual day of creation. The next instant after the eighth Spiritual day would be the ninth Spiritual day. But since right after the eighth Spiritual day is when the true creation of the new heaven and earth will happen (Rev 21:5), then it is at that point that Jesus Christ (the Spiritual Solomon) will have finished the creation. At the end of the 100 year Great Last Spiritual Day of Creation (at the end of the eighth day of the feast of tabernacles) those who are still human will be born of God as in the description of 1Corinthians 15:52-55. At that time the new universe will be created and the immortal state of happiness will begin for everyone.

So when does this happen? This happens at the very end of the eighth day of the Feast of Tabernacles, on the very last moments of the last day of the Great Last Day (8th Spiritual day of creation), then the last group and all the universe will be created new, so that God will be all in all.

Jubilee Harvest Sowing the Seed			
6th Yr	7th Yr **Land Rest**	8th Yr = **Jubilee**	9th Yr
Seed sown	No seed sown people eat from 6th year's harvest	Seed sown, but not harvested this year; people eat from 6th year's harvest	People eat harvest sown in the 8th year
< Seed sown in 6th year produces enough for these three years (Lev 25:21) >			
Lev 25:3, 20-22	Lev 25:4-5, 20-21	Lev 25:11, 22	Lev 25:22

Jubilee Harvest: Sowing of the Seed

nm634 » The year of jubilee is the year *after* seven Sabbatical years. A Sabbatical year occurs every seventh year wherein there is not to be sown any crop (Lev 25:3-5). Now the jubilee year is the eighth year, the year after the seventh Sabbatical year. In the seventh year is the year people were not to sow at all, while in the jubilee year the people were supposed to sow, but not to reap the fruit thereof *in* the jubilee year (Lev 25:11,22). And "the jubilee; it shall be holy unto you: you shall eat the increase thereof out of the field" (Lev 25:12). But you were not to eat the sown fruit, that you sowed in the eighth year, the jubilee year (Lev 25:22, 11). One was to eat of the fruit sown in the sixth year until the ninth year, until the fruit sown in the eighth year came in (Lev 25:20-22). Therefore in the sixth year, God would give a blessing that would last for three years (Lev 25:21). Since one was not to sow in the eighth jubilee year to reap or harvest that same year (Lev 25:11), yet one was to sow in that year (Lev 25:22, 1st part), then they did sow the land in the eighth jubilee year. But thereafter when this crop came forth in the *ninth* year they were eating the increase of the eighth jubilee year, but not in the jubilee year as the laws required (cf Lev 25:12, 11, 22).

Higher Meaning of the Sowing and Harvest

nm635 » The higher meaning of this indicates that during the sixth millennium enough of the good Spiritual crop of the earth (Christians, Mat 13:38-41) will be harvested to provide for the sixth, seventh, and eighth Spiritual days of creation. And on the seventh Spiritual day, the seventh millennium, there will be no souls sown with the good Spiritual seed (see "Thousand Years Paper" [NM 15]). But in the eighth Spiritual day (the 100 year Great Last Day of Creation) souls will be sown with the good Spiritual seed, but they will not be reaped in the eighth Spiritual day. They will be reaped on the ninth or thus at the very end of the eighth Spiritual day, when the antitypical new heaven and earth will be created. At that time the others will be Spiritually harvested. They will then be born of God like those who were born after the first harvest of the world (Rev 14:4, 14-20; Mat 13:38-41).

nm636 » The Feast of Tabernacles thus represents the full creation; it pictures the eight Spiritual days of Creation, and the GREAT Spiritual harvest of them.

Review: Three Orders of Creation

nm637 » God directed that all males must stand before the LORD during three of the annual festivals: "Three times in a year shall your males appear before the LORD your God in the place which he shall choose; in the feast of unleavened bread, and in the feast of weeks [Pentecost], and in the feast of tabernacles" (Deut 16:16). These three appearances indicate the three times when those of the creation will be born of God, or go back to God, or be resurrected immortal, or be infused to God and be one with God:

- **(1)** During the Feast of Unleavened Bread the sheaf being waved indicated Christ ascending to his Spiritual Father, and thus being born of God. He was the first-born of God – the first fruit of creation (John 1:18; 1Cor 15:23).

- **(2)** The Feast of Pentecost (50 weeks) indicates those of the first-fruits or *first-products* of God. That is, the first-ones after Christ returning to God (Rev 14:4; 1Cor 15:23).

- **(3)** The Feast of Tabernacles indicates the gathering of the rest of mankind to God (1Cor 15:24-28; Rev 7:9, note the "palms in their hands").

Do Christians keep the above mentioned feasts or appointed times?

nm638 » Christians keep these feasts in a Spiritual manner and in the place where God has placed his NAME (note Deut 12:5, 18; etc.). A place where God has placed his NAME is inside true Christians. The NAME of God is in anyone who has the Spirit of God or the New Mind, for anyone with the Spirit of God is a child of God (Rom 8:16). Christ was the first to keep a festival in a Spiritual manner. Christ kept the Passover in a Spiritual manner. The New Testament Christians on the antitypical Day of Pentecost will be the first to keep the Pentecost in a Spiritual manner. All the rest will keep the Feast of Tabernacles in a Spiritual manner.

Sacrifices and Jesus Christ

nm639 » Sacrifices were an almost universal way for mankind to worship God up until the time of Christ. Then things began to change until today when most religions no longer practice sacrifices. The reason for this former universal practice of ritualistic sacrifice is hidden in history, but it has to do with the other-mind (NM20).

Quick Review of Sacrifices in the Bible

Cain and Abel

nm640 » The book of Genesis first mentions sacrifices in the story about Cain and Abel:

- Now the man had relations with his wife Eve, and she conceived and gave birth to Cain, and she said, "I have gotten a manchild with *the help of* the LORD." 2 Again, she gave birth to his brother Abel. And Abel was a keeper of flocks, but Cain was a tiller of the ground. 3 So it came about in the course of time that Cain brought an offering to the LORD of the fruit of the ground. 4 Abel, on his part also brought of the firstlings of his flock and of their fat portions. And the LORD had regard for Abel and for his offering; 5 but for Cain and for his offering He had no regard. So Cain became very angry and his countenance fell. (Gen 4:1-5)

The account of the offerings of Cain and Abel shows that ritualistic sacrificing dated from almost the beginning. The custom of offering the firstlings and first-fruits had already begun. Cain's offering was grain and is called *minchah*, "a gift" or "presentation." The same term is applied to Abel's. There is no hint that the bloody sacrifice was in itself better than the unbloody one, but it is shown that sacrifice without a right attitude is not acceptable to God.

Noah

nm641 » The sacrifices of Noah followed and celebrated leaving the ark after the flood. He offered burnt offerings of the clean animals (Gen 8:20 ff). Remember he brought seven sets (male & female) of the clean animals onto the ark (Gen 7:2).

Abraham

nm642 » Abraham on his arrival at Shechem erected an altar (Gen 12:6-7). At Beth-el he also built an altar (12:8), and on his return from Egypt he worshiped there (Gen 13:4). At Hebron he built an altar (Gen 13:18). In Gen 15:1-18 he offers a "covenant" sacrifice, when the animals were slain, divided, the parts set opposite each other, and prepared for the appearance of the other party to the covenant. In Genesis 22 Abraham attempts to offer up Isaac his son as a burnt offering, but instead offered up a lamb for a burnt offering because of what the angel of God said to him (Gen 22:8, 11-13). What God really wanted was an obedient heart (Gen 22:12). Abraham continued his worship at Beer-sheba (Gen 21:33).

Isaac

nm643 » Isaac built an altar at Beer-sheba apparently to have regularly offered sacrifices (Gen 26:25).

Jacob

nm644 » Jacob poured oil upon the stone at Beth-el (Gen 28:18-22). After his covenant with Laban he offered sacrifices (*zebhachim*) and ate bread with his brethren (Gen 31:54). At Shechem, Jacob erected an altar (Gen 33:20). At Beth-el (Gen 35:7) and at Beer-sheba he offered sacrifices to Isaac's God (Gen 46:1).

Israelites in Egypt

nm645 » Sacrifices were not something new to the fathers of Israel. Therefore because Egyptians had a sacrificial system this meant that the Israelites were also accustomed to spring sacrifices, spring feasts, and fall feasts. Such sacrifices also had been found among the Arabs, Syrians and others. Such festivals were handed down even to the Romans. For example, according to Pliny Romans never ate their new corn or wine, till the priests had offered the first-fruits to the gods (*Clarke's Commentary*, vol 1, p. 417) which is similar to the fact that Israel could not eat of the first fruits until the sheaf of first fruits was waved by the priest (Lev 23:14, 10-14). According to Plutarch, the false god Bacchus had a festival like the feast of tabernacles, "they celebrated [the festival] in the time of vintage, bringing tables out into the open air furnished with all kinds of fruit, and sitting under tents made of vine branches and ivy" (*Clarke's Commentary*, vol 1, p. 587[1]; cf. Lev 23:35-41). As in most nations, in Egypt at these festivals sacrifices and food were offered to their gods. Apparently it was to some such feast Moses said Israel as a people wished to go in the wilderness (Ex 3:18; 5:3 ff; 7:16) to sacrifice to Yehowah. Pharaoh understood and asked who was to go (Ex 10:8). Moses demanded flocks and herds for the feast (Ex 10:9). Pharaoh wanted to keep the flocks (Ex 10:24), but Moses said they must offer sacrifices and burnt offerings (Ex 10:25 ff). The sacrifice of the Passover soon occurred thereafter, but according to the pattern that God manifested to Moses, not according to Egyptian traditions (Ex 12:1-17). [Some of the above material taken from *ISBE* (1915)]

Moses

Not Sacrifice, but Obedience

nm646 » One main difference between the sacrificial system initiated by Moses and the other systems was that the foundational principle was obedience (Ex 19:4-8). The main aspect in Israel's religion was obedience and loyalty to Jehovah, not sacrifices. God spoke about obedience, not sacrifices:

- Thus says the LORD of hosts, the God of Israel, "Add your burnt offerings to your sacrifices and eat flesh. 22 "For **I did not speak to your fathers, or command them in the day that I brought them out of the land of Egypt, concerning burnt offerings and sacrifices**. 23 "But this is what I commanded them, saying, **'Obey My voice, and I will be your God, and you will be My people**; and you will walk in all the way which I command you, that it may be well with you.' (Jer 7:21-23)

---

[1] "In imitation of this feast among the people of God, the Gentiles had their feasts of tents. Plutarch speaks particularly of feasts of this kind in honour of Bacchus, and thinks from the custom of the Jews in celebrating the feast of tabernacles, that they worshipped the god Bacchus, "because he had a feast exactly of the same kind called the feast of tabernacles, *skhnh*, which they celebrated in the time of vintage, bringing tables out into the open air furnished with all kinds of fruit, and sitting under tents made of vine branches and ivy."-PLUT. Symp., lib. iv., Q. 6. According to Ovid the feast of Anna Perenna was celebrated much in the same way. Some remained in the open air, others formed to themselves tents and booths made of branches of trees, over which they spread garments, and kept the festival with great rejoicings."

- Sacrifice and meal offering You have not desired; My ears You have opened; Burnt offering and sin offering You have not required. (Psa 40:6)

- For You do not delight in sacrifice, otherwise I would give it; You are not pleased with burnt offering. (Psa 51:16)

- To do righteousness and justice Is desired by the LORD more than sacrifice. (Prov 21:3)

- "What are your multiplied sacrifices to Me?" Says the LORD. "I have had enough of burnt offerings of rams, And the fat of fed cattle; And I take no pleasure in the blood of bulls, lambs or goats. (Isa 1:11)

nm647 » At Mount Sinai on the day that God asked Israel to obey his law, he didn't ask for sacrifices, he asked for obedience

- 'If you walk in My statutes and **keep My commandments** so as to carry them out, 4 then I shall give you rains in their season, so that the land will yield its produce and the trees of the field will bear their fruit. (Lev 26:3-4)

- **These are the statutes and ordinances and laws** which the LORD established between Himself and the sons of Israel through Moses at Mount Sinai. (Lev 26:46)

- "Then the LORD spoke to you from the midst of the fire; you heard the sound of words, but you saw no form-- only a voice. 13 "So He declared to you **His covenant which He commanded you to perform**, *that is*, the Ten Commandments; and He wrote them on two tablets of stone. 14 "The LORD commanded me at that time to teach you statutes and judgments, that you might perform them in the land where you are going over to possess it. (Deut 4:12-14)

- Then Moses summoned all Israel and said to them: "Hear, O Israel, **the statutes and the ordinances** which I am speaking today in your hearing, that you may learn them and **observe them carefully**. 2 "The LORD our God made a covenant with us at Horeb. 3 "The LORD did not make this covenant with our fathers, but with us, *with* all those of us alive here today. 4 "The LORD spoke to you face to face at the mountain from the midst of the fire, 5 *while* I was standing between the LORD and you at that time, to declare to you the word of the LORD; for you were afraid because of the fire and did not go up the mountain. He said. (Deut 5:1-5)

- Then you shall say to your son, 'We were slaves to Pharaoh in Egypt, and the LORD brought us from Egypt with a mighty hand. 22 'Moreover, the LORD showed great and distressing signs and wonders before our eyes against Egypt, Pharaoh and all his household; 23 He brought us out from there in order to bring us in, to give us the land which He had sworn to our fathers.' 24 "So **the LORD commanded us to observe all these statutes**, to fear the LORD our God for our good always and for our survival, as *it is* today. 25 "It will be righteousness for us if we are careful to observe all this commandment before the LORD our God, just as He commanded us. (Deut 6:21-25)

If Israel Brings an Offering

Paradoxes of Sacrifices

nm648 » Although God did not wish or require sacrifices, if Israel brought them He wanted them offered in the way or pattern he commanded: "If any man of you bring an offering unto the LORD, you shall bring your offering ...." (Lev 1:2; 2:1; 22:18; Ex 25:2) But on the other hand, God apparently used mankind's inclination towards sacrifices as a form of worship in order to reveal Jesus Christ. When one studies the Old Testament scriptures on sacrifices, one finds the paradoxical situation of God not wanting sacrifices, yet commanding certain ways of performing these unwanted sacrifices. This may have something to do with the left and right side of God as mentioned in the *God Papers*. We cannot speak about this subject here.

Even Physical Circumcision...

nm649 » Also God was really looking for a circumcision of Israel's heart or mind, not their foreskins:

- "So circumcise your heart, and stiffen your neck no longer. (Deut 10;16)

- "Moreover the LORD your God will circumcise your heart and the heart of your descendants, to love the LORD your God with all your heart and with all your soul, so that you may live. (Deut 30:6)

- "Circumcise yourselves to the LORD And remove the foreskins of your heart, Men of Judah and inhabitants of Jerusalem, Or else My wrath will go forth like fire And burn with none to quench it, Because of the evil of your deeds." (Jer 4:4)

Sinai's Covenant

nm650 » The covenant was made and the terms and conditions are then laid down by Moses and accepted by the people (Ex 24:3). After the ten commandments and covenant code were given, an altar is built, burnt offerings and peace offerings of oxen are slain by young men servants of Moses, not by priests, and blood is sprinkled on the altar (Ex 19:25-24:8). The Law was read, the pledge given, and Moses sprinkled the representatives of the people, consecrating them.

First Forty Days, Moses Shown the Patterns of Tabernacle

nm651 » After Moses, Aaron, Nadab, Abihu, and seventy of the elders of Israel saw a vision of God, Moses went up onto Mt Sinai for forty days (Ex 24:9-18). At that time God gave Moses the "pattern of the tabernacle, and the pattern of all the instruments thereof" (Ex 25:9,40; Heb 8:5).This pattern given to Moses was a pattern of the heavenly or spiritual things to come:

- "And almost all things by the law are cleansed with blood; and without shedding of blood there is no remission [sending away of sin]. Therefore it was necessary for the copy [Moses' Tabernacle] of the things in the heavens to be cleansed with these [physical] sacrifices, but the heavenly things themselves [are cleansed] with better sacrifices than these [physical sacrifices]. For Christ [the better sacrifice] did not enter a holy place made with hands, a *mere* copy of the true one, but into heaven itself, now to appear in the presence of God for us." (Heb 9:22-24)

- "For the Law, since it has *only* **a shadow of the good things to come** *and* not the very form of things, can never, by the same sacrifices which they offer continually year by year, make perfect those who draw near." (Heb 10:1)

A better or Spiritual sacrifice was needed to fulfill the physical things in the Tabernacle that foreshadowed things to come. In table form let us look at some of the patterns of Moses' Tabernacle, its furniture, and its sacrifices and manifest to you the things that have come and are coming:

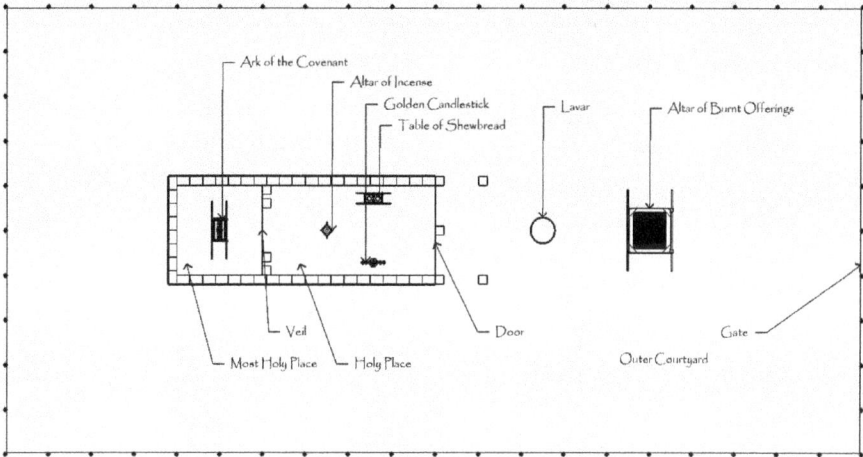

Drawing through Wikimedia Commons by Gabriel Fink

Tabernacle, Sacrifices and Jesus Christ	
Physical Aspect	**Spiritual Aspect**
Tabernacle or Temple	**Tabernacle or Temple = Spiritual Body of Christ**
Holy of Holies 1. **Golden Ark of the Testimony**: Cherubs and Mercy Seat [west side of tabernacle] (Ex 25:10-22; 26:34)	**Ark = Christ Fulfilled (Now is Right Side)** Jesus Christ went into the Holy of Holies as the Right side of God (Heb 9:24; Acts 2:33-35; Heb 10:10-12; *God Papers*).
2. **Veil Between Most Holy and Holy Place** of Blue, Purple, and Scarlet (Ex 26:33)	**First Veil = Christ's Flesh** Luke 23:45: because the sun was obscured; and the **veil** of the temple was torn in two. Hebrews 10:20: by a new and living way which He inaugurated for us through the **veil**, that is, His flesh,

Tabernacle, Sacrifices and Jesus Christ	
Physical Aspect	**Spiritual Aspect**
nm653 » Holy Place 3. **Golden Altar of Incense** placed before the Holy of holies atoned with the blood of the sin offering once a year (Ex 30:1-10) [located west side of Holy Place]	**Incense = Prayer** Revelation 8:3: Another angel came and stood at the altar, holding a golden censer; and much **incense** was given to him, so that he might add it to the **prayers** of all the saints on the golden altar which was before the throne. 4 And the smoke of the **incense**, with the **prayers of the saints**, went up before God out of the angel's hand.
4. **Golden Table of Showbread**, (Ex 25:23-30); 26:35) [located north side of tabernacle]	**Bread = Christ's Spiritual Bread** The showbread was unleavened bread continually present in the Most Holy place of the tabernacle. Also see NM16 under "Spiritual Bread"
5. **Golden Candlestick** [south side of tabernacle], Lit Always by Aaron & Sons with Beaten Olive Oil (Ex 25:31-39; 26:35; 27:20-21) Oil was from beaten olives (Ex 27:2; Lev 24:2)	**Candlestick = Christ's Body (Church)** Revelation 1:20: The mystery of the seven stars which you saw in my right hand, and the seven golden **candlesticks**. The seven stars are the angels of the seven churches: and the seven **candlesticks** which you saw are the seven churches. For antitypical beaten oil see Isa 53:4-5; 1Pet 2:24.

Tabernacle, Sacrifices and Jesus Christ	
Physical Aspect	**Spiritual Aspect**
6. **Tabernacle Covering** of Blue, Purple, and Scarlet *Ten Curtains* with Needlework of Cherubs (Ex 26:1)	**Ten Curtains = Ten Life-Span Era of the Kingdom** Ten curtains over the tabernacle indicate the ten 100 year life-spans or ten generations (1000 years) of the seventh period of time. See Deut 23:2-3 (non-Spiritual Israelites will not enter the kingdom for ten generations or ten 100 year life spans); Isaiah 65:20 (life spans in the kingdom will be for 100 years);
7. **Additional Tabernacle Covering** of Eleven Curtains of Goat [skin or hair] (Ex 26:7); More Tabernacle Coverings (above the Goat's hair) of Ram Skins Dyed Red and Badgers' Skins covered and hid the eleven curtains (Ex 26:14).	**Eleventh Curtain = 11th Life-Span Era** As these additional coverings hid and protected the tabernacle, the Spiritual tabernacle and truth have been hidden from the world. See PR15 for scripture that points to the hidden atonement period, the eighth period of time.
8. **Veil outside of the Holy Place** at the entrance of the Tabernacle of Blue, Purple, and Scarlet (Ex 26:36)	**Second Veil = Flesh of Christians** As the veil to the holy of holies was torn to manifest Christ's death (see # 2 above) in order for him to enter into it, so too those who enter into the holy place die (through Spiritual baptism) in order to go into it.

Tabernacle, Sacrifices and Jesus Christ

Physical Aspect	Spiritual Aspect
nm654 » Tabernacle Outer Court 9. Court Surrounds Tabernacle (Ex 27:9-1538:9-20) [There can be reasonable disagreement with what the outer court in Ezekiel and Revelation represented. Did it represent Moses' Tabernacle or not. We think it did, because the scripture on the "outer court" outside of scripture in Exodus (Ex 27:9-18; 38:9-20) is extremely vague as to the nature size, and location of it. When we understand that the first Tabernacle is a pattern for our time (see below), we understand this matter better.]	The outer court represented the non-Christians, who are not counted because God's holiness (Spirit) was not transmitted to them. "When they go out into the outer **court**, into the outer **court** to the people, they shall put off their garments in which they have been ministering and lay them in the holy chambers; then they shall put on other garments so that **they will not transmit holiness to the people** with their garments. (Ezek 44:19) "Then there was given me a measuring rod like a staff; and someone said, "Get up and measure the temple of God and the altar, and those who worship in it. 2"Leave out the court which is outside the temple and do not measure it, for **it has been given to the nations**; and they will tread under foot the holy city for forty-two months."(Rev 11:1-2)
10. **Brass Water Basin** (laver) for Aaron and his sons to wash hands and feet (Ex 30:17-21)	**Water = Spiritual Water or Spirit** Christ, was anointed and washed by the Spirit of God; his sons are washed and anointed by God's Spirit also. (John 7:37-39; 1 Cor 6:11; Heb 10:22)

Tabernacle, Sacrifices and Jesus Christ	
Physical Aspect	**Spiritual Aspect**
11. **Brass Four Horned Altar** outside the entrance of the Tabernacle (Ex 27:1-8)	**Antitypical Horned Altar** The four horns symbolize the four beasts of Daniel and Revelation, which in turn represent Satan's kingdoms (PR2) in the four corners of the world. The sacrifices and death on this altar represent the death and sacrifices of all mankind under Satan's chaos: Revelation 12:9: ... **Satan, who deceives the whole world.... Romans 8:22: ...the whole creation groans and suffers the pains of childbirth together until now.** Christ releases the creation from Satan at his second coming by sending sin away at his coming (Rev 20:1-3; & see **Azazel**).
12. **Veil** of Blue, Purple, and Scarlet at Court Entrance	**Third Veil = Flesh of the Third Order** Entrance into the court outside the holy tabernacle also must be through the blue, purple, and scarlet veil (death). See # 2 and # 8 above.
nm655 » Priests' Garments	
13. **Garments**, Robe, Coats, and Breeches for the Priests (Aaron & Sons) made of White Linen of Gold, Blue, Purple, and Scarlet trim and designs (Ex 28:1-8; 28:31-35)	**Garments = Spiritual Garments** Since Christ is the chief priest (Heb 7:21-22), The white represents holiness and the gold represents the Spiritual aspect of Christ and his body (See Rev 7:13-14) while the blue, purple, and scarlet represent the death of Christ.

| Tabernacle, Sacrifices and Jesus Christ ||
Physical Aspect	Spiritual Aspect
14. **Two Onyx Stones** engraved with the Names of the son of Israel (Ex 28:9-10)	**Engraved Stones = Reveals that Christ Represents Spiritual Israel** Christ and his Church are the antitypical Priest and priests (Heb 7:21-22; Rev 1:6; 5:9-10). Christ (his Spiritual Body) is Spiritual Israel. (PR1; Rev 7:4-8)
15. **Breastplate** of Twelve Precious Stones representing the tribes of Israel (Ex 28:15-21)	**Breastplate = Reveals that Christ Represents Spiritual Israel** Christ and his Church are the antitypical Priest and priest (Heb 7:21-22; Rev 1:6; 5:9-10). Christ (his Spiritual Body) is Spiritual Israel. (PR1; Rev 7:4-8)
16. **Golden Plate** on Forehead of Priest engraved with "Holiness to the YHWH" (Ex 28:36-38)	**Engraved Insignia = Indicates God's Name is on Christ and His Body** Christ came in his Father's Name, and all in Christ's Spiritual Body are baptized into God's Name (John 17:11; Mat 28:19; John 20:31)
nm656 » Priests	
17. **Aaron and Sons** are the priests. See Exodus 28:1.	**Jesus and Sons = Body of Christ** Christ and his Church are the antitypical Priest and priests (Heb 7:21-22; Rev 1:6; 5:9-10).
nm657 » Sacrifices and Offerings for Priests' Consecration	

Tabernacle, Sacrifices and Jesus Christ	
Physical Aspect	**Spiritual Aspect**
18. Sacrifice of Bull and Two Rams without Blemish (Ex 29:1)	**Unblemished Sacrifice = Christ** Christ is the real unblemished sacrifice: "but with precious blood, as of a lamb **unblemished** and spotless, *the blood* of Christ." (1Peter 1:19)
19. **Basket of Unleavened Bread**, Cakes, and Wafers with Oil and made of Wheat (Ex 29:2)	**Christ's Spiritual bread** See # 4 above.
20. **Priests washed with Water** (Ex 29:4)	**Spiritual Baptism washes** (NM4)
21. **Anointed with Oil** (Ex 29:7) Oil was from beaten olives (Ex 27:2; Lev 24:2)	**Spiritual Oil of Christ** (Heb 1:9; 1John 2:20; 2:27). Christ was beaten for our sins
22. **Blood** of Bull put on Horn of Altar and **poured out** at bottom of altar (Ex 29:12)	**Christ's Blood Poured Out** Not blood of bulls and goats, but Christ's blood being poured out is forgiveness of sins for all including the four beasts and to all the creation (Heb 9:12-14, 28; NM13)

Tabernacle, Sacrifices and Jesus Christ	
Physical Aspect	**Spiritual Aspect**
23. **Fat** of Bull, liver, two kidneys burned on the Altar (Ex 29:13)	**Fat = Evil Burned up on the Altar** Leviticus 7:25: For whoever eats the fat of the animal from which an offering by fire is offered to the LORD, even the person who eats shall be cut off from his people. In a sense, God's food is the fat and blood (Ezek 44:7; see *God Papers*). To destroy sin, God eats up the blood or life of the sinners and the "fat," which is the evil in mankind: Ezekiel 34:16 "I will seek the lost, bring back the scattered, bind up the broken and strengthen the sick; but **the fat and the strong I will destroy. I will feed them with judgment**. 17 "As for you, My flock, thus says the Lord GOD, 'Behold, I will judge between one sheep and another, between the rams and the male goats.... 20 Therefore, thus says the Lord GOD to them, "Behold, **I, even I, will judge between the fat sheep and the lean sheep**. Their heart is covered with **fat**, *But* I delight in Your law.(Ps 119:70) And their [wicked] body is **fat**. (Ps 73:4) But Jeshurun grew **fat** and kicked-- You are grown **fat**, thick, and sleek-- Then he forsook God who made him, And scorned the Rock of his salvation. (Deut 32:15)

Tabernacle, Sacrifices and Jesus Christ	
Physical Aspect	**Spiritual Aspect**
24. Flesh, skin, dung of the sacrifices for sin were **burned outside of camp**: a sin offering (Lev 16:17; Ex 29:14)	**Christ Suffered Outside the Gate** Christ was the antitypical sacrifice and therefore Christ had to die outside of the gate of Jerusalem and outside (before) the kingdom on earth: Hebrews 13:11 For the bodies of those animals whose blood is brought into the holy place by the high priest *as an offering* for sin, are burned outside the **camp**. 12 Therefore Jesus also, that He might sanctify the people through His own blood, suffered outside the gate.
Laying on of Hands 25. First Ram killed after Priest placed his hands on head of Ram (Ex 29:18)	**Laying on of Hands** In the Old Testament, the placing of the hands on the animal represented placing the sins on the animal (Lev 16:21); the animal's death made atonement for sin by destroying sin with the animal. But in the New Testament Jesus laid hands on the little children (Mt 19:13,15; Mk 10:16) and on the sick (Mt 9:18; Mk 6:5, etc.), and the apostles laid hands on those whom they baptized that they might receive the Holy Spirit (Acts 8:17,19; 19:6), and in healing (Acts 12:17). Christians received the Spirit and sin was thus sent away when hands were laid on them (1Tim 4:14; 2Tim 1:6).
26. First Ram's blood poured out and is therefore burnt on altar: a burnt offering (Ex 29:18)	See # 22 above

Tabernacle, Sacrifices and Jesus Christ	
Physical Aspect	**Spiritual Aspect**
27. Second Ram killed, blood placed on right side of Priest (Ex 29:19-20)	By blood being placed on the **right** side it foreshadowed Christ death and his going to the right side of God.
28. Second Ram's Blood and anointing oil sprinkled on Aaron and his sons (Ex 29:21)	It is the antitypical Aaron (Christ) and his sons (Body of Christ) that have forgiveness because of Christ's blood and sacrifice.
29. Second Ram's fat, oiled and unleavened bread waved before LORD (Ex 29:22-24)	These are types of the real sacrifice of Christ, who is the real unleavened bread and oil who was an offering offered (waved) to God (Heb 10:10-12).
30. Waved items are then burned on the Altar as a burnt offering (Ex 29:25)	As the waved items were burnt or destroyed so was Christ. Christ is the antitype of the burnt offering of Abraham (Gen 22:2-8; Heb 11:17-19).
Eating the Sacrifice 31. Aaron and sons shall eat the flesh (Ex 29:27) of the ram and the bread in the basket (which atonement was made for) by the door of the tabernacle to consecrate them and make them holy (Ex 29:32-33; Lev 10:14-15,17)	**Communion: Christians eat the Sacrifice** Christians who are the sons of Christ Spiritually eat the sacrificed body of Christ in this age before they go into the golden Holy Place. See NM16 under "Spiritual Bread" through "Communion" section.
Day of Atonement Sacrifices 32. A special "twin" goat ritual was performed on the day of Atonement (Lev 16)	**One died for sin; the other was sent away** never to appear as sin again. See NM15, under "Azazel" for more detail.

Tabernacle, Sacrifices and Jesus Christ

Physical Aspect	Spiritual Aspect
nm658 » Continual Daily Offering 33. **Daily offering** on the altar before the door (veil) of two lambs, one in the evening and one in the morning, continual burnt offering, throughout Israel's generations (Ex 29:38-42) The daily offering was offered on the altar before the door of the tabernacle, where God and his glory would meet the children of Israel and sanctify them along with the priests (Ex 29:42-44).	**Daily Sacrifices** These daily offerings of two lambs represent Christ's sacrifice for all the sins of mankind for all time, and also represent the sacrifices and suffering of mankind because of sin. It is a continuous suffering for mankind, until God sanctifies mankind. The sacrifices for mankind end at the coming of Christ when the door of the tabernacle (temple) is opened and the Saints are brought into the temple of God (Rev 15:5; 11:19; PR6; PR2 under "Daily Sacrifice").
nm659 » Sin offering only for sin through ignorance 34. See Lev 4:13; 5:2-4, 13	**All sin through ignorance** But even the killing of Christ was through ignorance (Luke 23:34; Acts 3:17; John 16:3; 1Cor 2:7-10; see NM13)
nm660 » God Meets Israel in His Glory 35. **God will meet Israel by the door** of the tabernacle at the altar and will sanctify Aaron, the priest, and Israel there with his glory (Ex 29:43-44)	**The door of the antitypical tabernacle opens** and God's great glory is revealed for all when he returns (Rev 15:5-8; 11:19) At the time the tabernacle or temple is opened is at the time of the wrath (Rev 11:18; see PR4-6) The tabernacle and temple are metonymical names for the same thing: The coming glorified Body of Christ.

Look and Dimensions of Tabernacle

Does it have any meaning?

nm661 » We figure the size of Moses' Tabernacle in the following way:

- We know some things like the size of the tent coverings and the length of the boards (ten cubits) used to construct it (Ex 26:1-12). So the measurement may have been ten cubits wide, ten cubits high, and thirty cubits long or **10 x 10 x 30 cubits** in size with the Holy of Holies being 10 x 10 x 10 cubits and the Holy Place being 10 x 10 x 20 cubits. This can be checked by examining David and Solomon's temple which kept the same relative shape of Moses' Tabernacle, but the measurement was increased to twice the width, length, and height of Moses' Tabernacle (1Kings 6:16-20). The Holy of Holies (Oracle) was 20 x 20 x 20 cubits in size, while the Holy Place (house in front of the Oracle) was 20 x 20 x 40 cubits; thus, the all over size was **20 x 20 x 60 cubits** which was twice the size of Moses' Tabernacle.

Without the tent covering, looking down from the top it looked something like this:

Picture through Wikimedia Commons of "Degem Mischan made by Michaael Osnis"

With the tent coverings, Moses' Tabernacle and outer court area looked something like this:

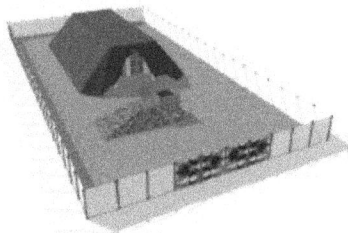

Drawing through Wikimedia Commons by Gabriel L. Fink

Tabernacle's Measurement: Higher Meaning

Holy Of Holies' Cubic Measurement and Time

nm662 » One interpretation of the measurement of Moses' Tabernacle is that the cubic size of the Holy of Holies represented the length of Jesus Christ's kingdom on earth, since the Holy of Holies represents Christ since Christ went Spiritually into it after his death (Heb 9:8-11, 23-24). The cubic volume is 10 x 10 x 10 cubits or 1000 cubits, or if cubits here indicate years (one cubit for each year), then Christ's kingdom will last for 1000 years.

Holy Place' Cubic Measurement and Time

nm663 » One interpretation of the measurement of Moses' Tabernacle is that the cubic size of the Holy Place represented the length of time of the Church's age, since the Holy Place represents the Church with its candlesticks and incense of the prayers of the Church or saints (Rev 1:20; 8:3). The cubic volume is 10 x 10 x 20 cubits or 2000 cubits, or if cubits here indicate years (one cubit for each year), then the Church's age will last for 2000 years. The Holy Place was located just before the Holy of Holies, as the age of the Church is located in time just before the presence of God or the Holy of Holies.

Distance or Time between Israel and the Ark of the Covenant

nm664 » The ark of the Covenant held God's presence and glory (1Sam 4:21-22). As physical Israel was going into the promised land, they were commanded to follow at a distance of 2000 cubits behind the Ark (and the priests carrying it):

- And they commanded the people, saying, "When you see the ark of the covenant of the LORD your God with the Levitical priests carrying it, then you shall set out from your place and go after it. "However, there shall be between you and it a **distance of about 2,000 cubits** by measure. Do not come near it, that you may know the way by which you shall go, for you have not passed this way before." (Joshua 3:3-4)

Using the same logic as the two previous items, if cubits here indicate years, we see here that in the higher meaning, the people of *Spiritual* Israel are 2000 years (cubits) behind Christ who first went in and sat down on the Ark on the right side of God's presence about 2000 years ago (Heb 9:8-11, 23-24). Spiritual Israel or the Church is 2000 years behind Christ (the first-one) on the way to a place they have not passed before

(Joshua 3:4b). The place they were going was into the presence of God (1Thes 2:19; Judah 1:24) unlike the others who are punished away from the presence of God (2Thes 1:9; Rev 6:16). At the end of the age, after the wrath and great tribulation, the temple or tabernacle of God will be opened (Rev 11:19; 15:8) and the Spiritual Israel (Church) will be in the presence and glory of God, "Behold, the tabernacle of God is with men, and he will dwell with them ... and God himself shall be with them" (Rev 15:8; 21:3). "For we are the temple of the living God. As God has said: I will live with them and walk among them, and I will be their God, and they will be my people" (2Cor 6:16).

Do the Tabernacle Dimensions Mean Anything?

nm665 » Do the dimensions really mean anything? Wasn't the dimension of Solomon's temple different than Moses' Tabernacle? Wasn't the second temple at Christ's time also different in dimensions? Why should we think there is something important about Moses' Tabernacle?

- First, Moses Tabernacle was made just as God commanded on Mt Sinai: "Make the tabernacle and all its furnishings exactly like the pattern I will show you" (Ex 25:9).

- Second, look at what Paul said, "while the first tabernacle was yet standing, which was a type for the present time" (Heb 9:8-9). What this means is that Moses' Tabernacle was an example or type for the present era, the era of God's Spiritual Israel, the Church, his Body.

nm666 » Even though Solomon's temple was built by the pattern given by David with the help of "the Spirit" (1Chron 28:11-12), the direction for Moses' tabernacle was given by God with great emphasis so that Moses would be very careful how he constructed the Tabernacle and its furniture (Ex 25:9, 40; Num 8:4; Heb 8:5). Because Paul said that Moses' Tabernacle was a type for our time, we must give much more weight to the dimensions of Moses' Tabernacle versus Solomon's temple. In Solomon's temple the dimensions of the Holy of Holies and Holy Place were twice that of Moses' Tabernacle (see above).

Other Tabernacle or Temple Measurement Scripture

nm667 » Other scripture also projects that the dimensions of certain key objects also are to give us hints. For example, the wall in Revelation 21:17 was 144,000 cubits according "to the measurement of man, that is, angel." The number 144,000 happens to equal the number of the saints who are harvested at the end of the age (Rev 14:3-4; 7:4). And we know by other scripture, each man has an angel, his own angel (see, "Our Own Angel" above), so this verse points to the 144,000 with their own angel.

nm668 » Another scripture to look at is Revelation 11:1-2, where John was told to measure the temple of God "and them that worship therein," but to leave the outer court out of his measurement. When we study the Bible we see we can count or measure the number of the harvest, that is the 144,000 (Rev 14:3-4), but not the others outside of the symbolic "outer court" (see "Outer Court" above).

Spiritually Keeping The Passover

More Details

nm669 » How then is Spiritual Israel to keep the feast or appointed time of the Passover? "Therefore let us keep the feast, not with old leaven [the doctrines of man], neither with the leaven of malice and wickedness; but with the unleavened bread of sincerity and truth" (1Cor 5:8).

nm670 » When do we keep this feast or this appointed time? Spiritually we keep it always, since we are out of spiritual Egypt and are in one of the seven Spiritual days.

Sacrifice?

nm671 » What about sacrifice? Christ's death was for the new covenant with His Spirit that puts the law of God (love) in the minds of Christians, and their sins are no more remembered, they are forgiven. Therefore there is no more offering for sins by animals, for Christ's sacrifice takes away animal offerings (Heb 10:1-18), which were not pleasant to God anyway (Heb 10:5-6). Christians are living sacrifices (Rom 12:1) who sacrifice "the sacrifice of praise to God continually, that is, the fruit of lips confessing to his name" (Heb 13:15).

Spiritual Bread

nm672 » Do Christians eat unleavened bread for some religious reason? No! Christians do not do this because they Spiritually worship God as God asks us to worship (John 4:23-24). Since the higher or Spiritual meaning of unleavened bread is Truth (1Cor 5:8), and since God's Word is Truth (John 17:17; James 1:18); then Christ's Word is the unleavened bread which we eat. Therefore Christians eat Christ's Spiritual Word for the rest of the Spiritual seven days, they eat

Spiritual food (1Cor 10:3) with the Spirit of Truth that comes from the Father through Christ (John 16:13; 15:26; 17:17, 22 etc.).

nm673 » Let's amplify on the eating of Spiritual unleavened bread. "I am the living bread which came down from heaven: if any man eat of this bread, he shall live into the age" (John 6:51). Let's see what context this statement was made in.

nm674 » The day after Jesus performed the miracle of feeding five thousand with a few loaves of bread, when it was near the time of the Passover festival (John 6:4-13), some people came to him (John 6:25-26). At that time Christ said to those who came to him:

- "You seek me, not because you saw the miracles, but because you did eat of the loaves, and were filled. Labor not for the food which perishes, but for the food which endures unto aeonian life, which the Son of man shall give unto you: for him has God the Father sealed" (John 6:26-27).

This was said around the Passover (v. 4), and Christ said to seek the bread that endures into aeonian life – the millennium and beyond.

Bread from Heaven

nm675 » Then he went on and said, "Moses gave you not that bread from heaven; but my Father gives you the true bread from heaven . . .. I am the bread of life: he that comes to me shall absolutely not hunger; and he that believes on me shall absolutely not thirst" (John 6:32, 35). Here Jesus speaks of Spiritual bread, and Spiritual drink.

Water from Heaven

nm676 » There is Spiritual food and drink as the following verses indicate: "And did all eat of the same Spiritual food, and did all drink the same Spiritual drink" (1Cor 10:3, 4). "Jesus answered and said unto her, whosoever drinks of this water that I shall give him shall not into the ages thirst; but the water [Spiritual] that I shall give him shall be in him a well of water springing up into aeonian life" (John 4:13-14). "Jesus stood and cried, saying, If any man thirst let him come unto me, and drink. He that believes on me, as the scripture has said, out of his belly shall flow rivers of living water (But this spoke he of the Spirit, which they that believe on him should receive.)" (John 7:37-39).

Living Bread

nm677 » Christ continued: "I am the living bread which came down from heaven: if any man eat of this bread, he shall live into the age: and the bread that I will give is my flesh, which I will give for the life of the world ... Whoso eats my flesh, and drinks my blood, has aeonian life;

and I will raise him up at the last day ... He that eats my flesh, and drinks my blood, dwells in me, and I in him ... It is the Spirit that makes alive; the flesh profits nothing: the words that I have spoken unto you, they are Spirit, and they are life" (John 6:51, 54, 56, 63).

Eating His Flesh

nm678 » Notice that after Christ finished speaking about eating his flesh and drinking his blood, he said the words he had just spoken were Spiritual, and that they were life. He said we must eat his flesh, or his bread, since he said they were the same (v. 51), in order to live into the age of peace. And when we do eat his bread, or flesh, and drink his blood we would be in him and he in us. Since these words were Spiritual, Christ meant that if we "ate" his Spiritual bread, or if we were nourished by his Spiritual body; then we would dwell in him, and he in us (cf Eph 5:30, 29; 1Cor 12:27, 12-13; Rom 8:9-17; John 1:5; see "Proof of Being a Christian"). When we are in Christ's Spiritual body (the Church) we are nourished by his Spiritual flesh, which is his Spiritual bread, and by his Spiritual blood.

nm679 » "Whoso eats my flesh [bread, v. 51], and drinks my [Spiritual] blood, has aeonian life . . .. I live through the Father [his Father is Spirit, John 4:24]: so he that eats me [his Spiritual bread, or Spiritual body, or Spiritual blood], even he shall live through me" (John 6:54, 57). The only way one can get aeonian life, and to live through Christ, is to be in the Body of Christ, which is the Church. And the only way one can be in the Church is to have the Spirit of God the Father (1Cor 12:12-13). It was by this Spirit that Christ lived; it is by this Spirit that we live. We can only eat his bread, flesh, and blood when we have the Spirit. When we have his Spirit we are "eating" his flesh.

Eat, This is my Body

nm680 » "Then it came [aorist – a verb of action, not time] towards the day of unleavened bread, when the Passover must be killed" (Luke 22:7). Or, "And towards the first day of unleavened bread, when they killed the Passover..." (Mark 14:12). It was the day just before the Passover – the 13th – that he sent his apostles to make ready for the Passover (Luke 22:8-13, see Notes). "And when the hour was come, he sat down, and the twelve apostles with him. And he said unto them, With desire I have desired to eat this Passover with you before I suffer: for I say unto you, I will not eat it, until it be fulfilled in the kingdom of God" (Luke 22:14-16; see the Greek). It was the evening of the 13th when he was eating, and he said he would not eat it, until it was fulfilled in the kingdom of God. Of course he did not eat the Passover that evening because:

- **(1)** it was one day *before* it was to be eaten according to scripture (John 18:28);

- **(2)** he said he would *not* eat it until it was fulfilled in the kingdom of God;

- **(3)** it was fulfilled perfectly only after he died as the antitypical Passover;

- **(4)** the meal of the 13th was not eaten in haste as the Passover was commanded to be eaten (Ex 12:11), for in this evening during this meal Christ stopped and washed all the apostles feet (John 13:1-12; see notes).

nm681 » But right after the evening of the 13th, in the night of the 14th right near or at sunset, Christ "took bread: and when he had given thanks, he broke it, and said, 'take, eat: this is my body, which is broken for you: this do in remembrance of me.' After the same manner also he took the cup, when he had the supper, saying, 'this cup is the new covenant in my blood: this do you, as often as you drink it in remembrance of me.' For as often as you eat this bread, and drink this cup, you do proclaim the Lord's death till he come ... For he that eats and drinks unworthily, eats and drinks judgement to himself, not recognizing the Lord's body" (1Cor 11:23-29).

What Is The Lord's Body?

nm682 » "For as the body is one, and has many members, and all members of that one body, being many, are one body: so also is Christ. For by one Spirit are we all baptized into one body . . .. Now you are the body of Christ, and members in particular . . .. For we are members of his body, of his flesh, and of his bones . . .. for his [Christ's] body's sake, which is the Church" (1Cor 12:12-13, 27, Eph 5:30; Col 1:24). Christ's body is the Church. Christians are members of Christ's body, we are of his flesh, blood, and bones. We are nourished by his body (Eph 5:29). His body, or Church, is Spiritual. We eat and drink his flesh, bread, or blood when we are nourished by it, if we are of his body. And we are only of his body when we are in the Church and have the Spirit of God in us. And if we have the Spirit, then we are of Christ's body – his flesh and blood – and are nourished by it Spiritually.

Communion and Breaking of Bread

nm683 » Therefore "the cup of blessing which we bless, is it not the common sharing of the blood of Christ? The bread which we break, is it not the common sharing of the body of Christ? For we being many are one bread, and one body: for we are all partakers of that one bread" (1Cor 10:16-17). That one bread is Christ – the bread of life (John 6:35, 48, 51). And that bread is Spiritual. We are in communion, or in sharing with Christ's body when we share the Holy Spirit (2Cor 13:14; 1Cor 12:12-13). Hence, we drink his blood and eat his flesh when we are Spiritually in the Church; and we are in remembrance of Christ, and we do proclaim the death of Christ until he comes because we are Spiritually in his Church; and his Spirit and those in his Spirit project Christ's Spirit and proclaim Christ's death and gospel *always* until he comes (Mat 24:14). Christ was the real sacrificial lamb of God, the real sacrifice for sin (John 1:29; 1Pet 1:18-19). By Spiritually eating his Spiritual Body or Bread, we fulfill the Old Testament scripture where the priests ate parts of the sacrificed animals for a peace offering (Ex 29:32-33; Lev 10:14-15,17).

Unleavened v. Leavened Bread

nm684 » The unleavened bread Christians eat are the doctrines of Christ since the leaven are the doctrines of the Pharisees and of the Sadducees, which are merely the doctrines of mankind, which are hypocrisy (Mat 16:12; Mark 7:5-9; Luke 12:1). The unleavened bread that Christians eat is that truth (1 Cor 5:8). The bread we break is the bread of Christ – the doctrines of Christ with the sharing of his Spirit and the sharing of the Spirit's understanding of Christ's doctrines. The apostles continued after Christ's death "in breaking of bread" (Acts 2:42; 20:11). The Christians "come together to eat" (1Cor 11:33) the doctrines of Christ and share in the Spirit.

When Eating Wait for Each Other

nm685 » Paul in 1Corinthians 11:17-34, was telling them when they came together to eat Christ's bread to tarry "one for another," "for in eating every one takes before the others his own supper: one is hungry, and another is drunken." In other words, when Christians come together they should not go over some of the congregation's heads in the teaching of doctrine. If some are hungry for deeper doctrines on Christ, let them do it at home, and let the Church assembly be for the not so deep doctrines, or not so complex doctrines of Christ. Some doctrines may make some "weak" Christians "drunk." Yet to others the same teaching of these doctrines will not satisfy them because the teachers may not go into even more difficult aspects of the doctrines. Read 1Corinthians 11:17-34 in a Spiritual way, remembering that the bread eaten is the doctrines of Christ.

Break Bread

nm686 » Notice how Christ broke the bread: "And he commanded the multitude to sit down on the grass, and took the five loaves, and two fishes, and looking up to heaven, he blessed, and broke, and gave the loaves to his disciples, and the disciples to the multitude" (Mat 14:19; 15:36; Mark 8:6; etc). This antitypically signifies the Spiritual words originating from Christ who gave, and gives, it to his disciples then, and now, through his physical word and Spiritual word. His disciples gave, and now give, the bread of Christ's doctrines to the people.

Showbread and Candlesticks

nm687 » The bread is typically represented as the "showbread" or as translated – "loaves of the setting before" (see Luke 6:4-5). These loaves of bread were set before the candlesticks of the physical tabernacle (Lev 24:5-6; Ex 40:22-24). The candlesticks represent the Church (Rev 1:20). The olive oil used with these lamps represents the Spirit in the Church (1Sam 16:13; 1John 3:27). Thus, the "showbread" typified the bread of Christ and his doctrines put before the Church.

Olive Oil

nm688 » The oil in the candlesticks was "pure olive oil beaten for light" (Ex 27:20). This typified the oil (Spirit) that was given to the Church because Christ, the True Olive Tree (Rom 11:17-24) was beaten for us. The loaves of bread before the candlesticks were unleavened bread made with olive oil (Ex 29:2-3; Lev 2:4). This oil signifies the only way Christ's unleavened bread (doctrines) can be eaten; they must be eaten with oil of the Spirit, that is, with God's Spirit.

Sacrifices

nm689 » Christians are set apart by Christ's sacrifice (Heb 10:10). The "ram of consecration" is only one of the sacrificed animals that were representative of Christ's sacrifice (Lev 8:22-24; Ex 29:19-22). The eating of this ram of consecration, and the unleavened bread with it, typified the eating of Christ's body and bread (Ex 29:31-33, 2), for we are the Spiritual sons of Aaron because Christ is the antitypical high priest who has Spiritually taken over Aaron's office (Heb chaps. 8, 9, 10).

Law

nm690 » Christ's sacrificed blood is the blood of the new covenant (Luke 22:20). His blood makes it possible for us to receive God's laws into our hearts and minds (Heb 10:12-17). This is the antitypical event corresponding to Moses sprinkling blood on physical Israel when they received the laws of God (Ex 24:5-8). But physical Israel didn't receive the laws of God inside their minds and hearts at that time (Deut 29:4; 30:6

Jer 9:26). It is the Spiritual Israel of God which receives the law of God into their minds through the medium of God's Spirit. The Israel of God is the Church (Gal 6:16). This new law is what Paul called the "law of God" (Rom 7:22; see "Old Mind Paper" [NM 21]). The old law that was done away with because of Christ's death, was the law of Moses that was only written on stone and not in the minds of man (Eph 2:15). Paul called this old law the "law of sin" (Rom 7:23, 25). The law given by Moses was a law of sin because Israel was without God's Spirit, and thus unable to keep the commandments in Truth (Rom 8:7). Physical Israel only had the other-mind or enemy spirit, which misleads people to the way of sin. This adverse spirit uses the written ten commandments to mislead people into the way or law of sin (Rom 7:8). The other-mind enjoys doing the opposite to the laws of love, and since it is inside the minds of mankind, this law of sin, this other-mind, transmits its desire to the world's people. But since to break the laws of love, or the system of love (see the "Freedom & Law Paper" [NM 17]), brings unhappiness, the person who breaks the laws is harmed thereby, yet feels inside his confused mind a twisted delight in breaking the laws of harmony. This delight comes from the other-mind or other spirit inside of him.

Sacrifice for All

nm691 » As the sacrifices of atonement were made for the Israelites and the stranger (Num 15:28-29), so too was Christ's sacrifice for ALL (1Tim 2:5-6).

Eat Leavened Bread: Be Cut Off

nm692 » As those who ate leavened bread in the typical festival of the Passover were cut off, so too are those in this age who eat leavened bread, or the doctrines of man with only the other-mind to guide them, they are cut off from Christ's sacrifice in this age (Ex 12:19).

Notes

Passover Scriptures

nm693 » The chief priests of the Jews had a meeting wherein they took counsel to kill Christ (John 11:47-53; Luke 22:2).

Because of those out to kill him, Christ no more could walk openly (John 11:54).

The Passover wherein Christ was killed was near, and many had come to Jerusalem for the festival and were wondering among themselves whether Christ would show up at the festival or not. The chief priests had given directions that if any knew where Christ was that they should point him out to them so the priests could take Jesus (John 11:55-57).

9th of NISAN, a Friday

nm694 » Then six days before the Passover (the 9th of Nisan), Christ came to Bethany which is only a few miles from Jerusalem (John 12:1; 11:17).

At that time they had a supper wherein Mary anointed the feet of Jesus, and wiped his feet with her hair (John 12:2-3; Mark 14:3; Mat 26:6-7).

Some of the disciples had indignation inside their minds at this act, and one named Judas Iscariot, said: "Why was not this ointment sold for three hundred pence, and given to the poor?" (Mark 14:4-5; Mat 26:8-9; John 12:4-6)

Then when Jesus understood what was being said, he spoke saying, "let her alone: that of the day of my burial may she keep it" (John 12:7). The Mary that anointed Christ was Mary Magdalene, who later brought this ointment to Christ's tomb on the day of his resurrection along with some spices she and others had bought and prepared the day before Christ's resurrection (Luke 23:56-24:1; Mark 16:1; Mat 28:1) (John 12:7-8; Mark 14:6-9; Mat 26:10-13).

10th of NISAN, a Saturday

nm695 » Now right after this supper, right after sunset, thus on the 10th of Nisan, Judas the betrayer of Christ went to the chief priests and said he would help them take Jesus in the absence of a great crowd. Because of this the priests were glad that Judas would betray Christ, and gave him 30 pieces of silver. Further, they consulted if they shouldn't also put Lazarus to death since many of the Jews believed in Jesus because Christ had previously resurrected Lazarus from the dead (Mark 14:10-11; Mat 26:14-16; Luke 22:3-6; John 12:9-11).

On the next day after Christ came to Bethany, which was the daylight hours of the same 24 hour day that Judas had betrayed Christ to the priests, Christ came into Jerusalem – 10th day of Nisan (John 12:12).

Christ rode on an ass into Jerusalem, and the people cried, "Hosanna; Blessed is he that comes in the name of the Lord [YHWH]." This was the 10th day of the Jews 1st month – Nisan (Mark 11:1-10; Mat 21:1-11; Luke 19:28-40).

In the 10th day of Nisan after he entered into Jerusalem, Jesus went into the temple (Mark 11:11).

Then in the evening just before sunset, Christ went into Bethany, a town a few miles from Jerusalem (Mark 11:11).

11th of NISAN, a Sunday

nm696 » Now in the morrow (the next day, that is the 11th of Nisan), Christ came from Bethany back into Jerusalem (Mark 11:12-15).

It was the 11th, and again Christ goes into the temple in Jerusalem (Mark 11:15; Luke 19:45; Mat 21:12).

At this time Christ put the money changers out of the temple (Mat 21:12-16; Mark 11:15-18; Luke 19:45-46).

During this time period just before the Passover, Christ was teaching daily in the temple (Luke 19:47).

Then in the evening of the 11th he went out of Jerusalem again and went into Bethany (Mark 11:19; Mat 21:17).

12th of NISAN, a Monday

nm697 » After he stayed in Bethany, he came back into Jerusalem on the next day, the 12th (Mark 11:20; Mat 21:18).

When they returned into Jerusalem, the disciples with Christ noticed the tree Christ cursed the previous day (Mark 11:13-14), and how it already had dried up (Mark 11:21; Mat 21:19-20).

At this time on the 12th Christ entered again into the temple (Mat 21:23; Mark 11:27; Luke 20:1).

At this time on the 12th, Christ taught various parables (Mat 21:23-23:39; Mark 11:27-12:44; Luke 20:1-21:4).

Then Christ went out of the temple, and taught his disciples on the mount of Olives about the time of the end of the age (Mark 13:1-33; Luke 21:5-36: Mat 24:1-25:46).

At that time on the 12th of Nisan, Christ noted that after two days would be the feast of unleavened bread, which some call the Passover festival (Luke 22:1) (Mat 26:1-2; Mark 14:1).

At this time Christ mentioned that he is betrayed (for on the 10th remember Judas went to the chief priests to betray Jesus) (Mat 26:2).

The chief priests had decided at that time that Christ shouldn't be taken on the feast day (the 15th, Num 28:17), because there might be an uproar among the people (Mat 26:3-5; Mark 14:1-2).

But remember on the 10th Judas had come to the chief priests, and said he would betray Jesus (John 12:1-11; Luke 22:3-6; Mark 14:3-11; Mat 26:6-16).

After Christ had returned from the temple on the 12th, after he taught many parables (see above), and after he on Mount Olives had spoken of the end of the age that late evening of the 12th (or early on the 13th after sunset), he then stayed on Mount Olives in Bethany (note Luke 24:50 with Acts 1:12) (Luke 21:37).

13th of NISAN, a Tuesday

nm698 » The next day on the 13th, Jesus taught in the temple again after he abode in Bethany the night of the 13th, for at this time Jesus was teaching daily in the temple (Luke 19:47; Luke 21:38).

Before the feast of the Passover, on the evening of the 13th, after Christ had taught during the daylight of the 13th in the temple, he was again in Bethany, and was eating his supper, as he had been doing each evening since he had began teaching in the temple on the 10th (John 13:1).

The home he was staying in was that of Mary Magdalene, Martha, and Lazarus (John 12:1).

Jesus on the 13th had instructed the apostles to get a room and make it ready for the Passover meal, which was to occur on the 14th (Mat 26:17-19; Mark 14:12-16; Luke 22:7-13).

[[Let's correct a few verses that were mistranslated in many English translations of the Bible. These corrections were made using a Greek text. Mat 26:17 should read: "now *towards* the first [day] of unleavened [bread] approaches the disciples to Jesus ... " And Mark 14:12 should read: "and *towards* the first day of the unleavened [bread], when they kill the Passover, his disciples say to him . . .." And Luke 22:7 should read: "now it came *towards* the day of unleavened [bread], in which was needful to be killed the Passover." Therefore what these verses are saying is that *towards* or near the 14th day when the Passover was to be killed, the disciples had asked Christ where they would eat the Passover the next day. Now in Matthew 26:19, Mark 14:16, and Luke 22:13 the Greek verbal word translated "they made ready" is an aorist word that indicates a verbal action without indicating the time of the action. Thus, it can mean action in the past, present, or future. According to the context of this verse this Greek word should have been rendered in the following manner: "were to make ready" the Passover in the certain house where Christ said to prepare it. Christ had ordered them to prepare for the Passover, but the events surrounding Christ's betrayal made it impossible to go and eat the Passover.]]

The evening of the 13th came and Christ was in Bethany at supper with his disciples. "And supper taking place..." (John 13:2; Mat 26: 20-21; Mark 14:17-18; Luke 22:14).

"Washing Feet" and Principle of Serving

nm699 » Now at this supper taking place on the evening of the 13th just before sunset, "the devil already having put into the heart of Judas" to deliver Christ up, Jesus "rises from supper, and laid aside his garments; and took a towel, and wrapped himself" (John 13:2-4). It was on the 10th of Nisan that Judas had gone to the chief priests, and now Judas was at this meal on the 13th. Christ thus rose from the meal and began to wash the disciples feet, and did wash their feet (John 13:4-11).

nm700 » Then Jesus sat down again to supper (John 13:12). After he sat down Christ told the disciples what he had just done, "you call me teacher and the Lord: and you say well; for so I am. If then, your Lord and teacher have washed your feet; you also ought to wash one another's feet. For I have given you an example, that you should do as I have done to you. Truly, truly, I say unto you, the servant is not greater than his Lord; neither he that is sent greater than he that sent him. If you know these things, happy are you if you do them" (John 13:12-17).

nm701 » Some who only look to the physical meaning of Christ's words have gotten the meaning from this that we should perform some kind of ritual on the Passover that has to do with washing others' feet. Somehow they think that evening that Christ instructed them in a ritual to be performed by Christians. But we are to worship God Spiritually (John 4:23-24), not with rituals.

nm702 » Christ was speaking of a principle of serving one another. He was saying if the Lord serves, then his disciples should also serve others, for the disciple is not above the Lord. While they were eating that evening some had a strife among themselves as to who was the greatest (Luke 22:24). Christ's answer to this strife was, "and he said unto them, The kings of the Gentiles exercise lordship over them; and they that exercise authority upon them are called benefactors. But you shall not be so: but he that is greatest among you, let him be as the younger; and he that is chief, as he that does serve. For whether is greater, he that sits at meat, or he that serves? Is not he that sits at meat? *But* I am among you as he that serves" (Luke 22:25-27).

nm703 » Jesus was saying that the kind of lordship exercised by man is not the kind of lordship he himself was performing. Christ who is to be King of kings *serves*, and so are the apostles to do so. The leaders of the world should serve the peoples' needs, but they do not, they oppress. Christ showed the way to lead and lord over people – He served them.

- "And whosoever will be chief among you, let him be your servant: Even as the Son of man came not to be ministered unto, but to minister, and to give his life a ransom for many" (Mat 20:27-28).

- "But he that is greatest among you shall be your servant. And whosoever shall exalt himself shall be abased; and he that shall humble himself shall be exalted" (Mat 23:11-12).

- "If any man desire to be first, the same shall be last of all, and servant of all" (Mark 9:35).

nm704 » Christ time after time taught the disciples that the greatest thing was to serve others (Luke 9:46-48; Mark 10:42-44). And again on the evening of the 13th he again by using the example of washing their feet, said that the greatest thing was to serve, not to lord over others. "It is more blessed to give then to receive" (Acts 20:35). The washing of the feet was a reiteration of the principle of giving and serving. We must try our best to follow this principle always, not just on one day of the year.

nm705 » During this meal Jesus broke the bread, and passed it around, and said he could "not eat it," the Passover, with them until it was fulfilled in the kingdom of God (Luke 22:15-20; Mark 14:22-24; Mat 26:26-29).

nm706 » And during this meal, Christ revealed who would deliver him up that night (14th, after sunset; after the supper they were eating on the 13th before sunset) (Mat 26:21-25; Mark 14:18-21; Luke 22:21-23; John 13:21-29).

14th of NISAN, a Wednesday

nm707 » **(1)** It was Judas Iscariot, and right after he took the piece of bread, which pointed him out as the betrayer (yet the apostles didn't understand), Judas immediately went out, "and it was night." That is, right after sunset Judas went out to bring the chief priests to take Jesus (John 13:30). They were in Bethany, which is on the side of Mount Olives, when they were eating this meal (see above).

(2) After they sang a hymn, they went onto Mount Olives, and brought two swords with them so scripture could be fulfilled (Mark 14:26; Mat 26:30; Luke 22:35-39).

(3) On Mount Olives Christ speaks of various matters to the apostles. (The scripture is vague as to whether these things were spoke still in the house in Bethany, or near the house, or somewhere on the mount of Olives.) (Mark 14:26-31; Mat 26:31-35; John 13:31-17:36)

(4) At Gethsemane (probably on the mount of Olives) he enters into a garden to pray (Mat 26:36-46; Mark 14:32-42; Luke 22:40-46; John 18:1).

(5) Judas knew where this garden was, for Jesus came often to it to pray (John 18:2).

(6) It was in this garden that Judas came with the chief priests and Pharisees, who came with lanterns and torches because it was at night on the 14th after sunset in the night (John 18:3; Luke 22:47; Mark 14:43; Mat 26:47).

(7) At this time Judas revealed Christ by greeting him with a kiss. Peter cut off an ear of a guard, but Christ healed the ear. Then *all* the disciples "forsook him, and fled" (Mat 26:47-56; Mark 14:43-52; Luke 22:47-53; John 18:4-11).

(8) Then the band of men with the chief priests bound Christ and brought him, and led him away to Annas *first*, for he was the father-in-law to Caiaphas, who was the high priest that same year (John 18:12-13).

(9) Then they took Christ to Caiaphas the high priest (John 18:24).

(10) During that time Peter denied Christ three times as Jesus foretold (John 18:15-27; Luke 22:54-65; Mark 14:66-72; Mat 26:69-75).

(11) At dawn of the new day light (Mat 27:1; Mark 15:1; Luke 22:66; John 18:28), the chief priests and the elders came to take Christ, and right after they had him before the high priest, they brought him to the judgement hall to Pilate (John 18:28-29; Luke 22:66-71; 23:1; Mark 15:1; Mat 27:1-2). Pilate sent Jesus to Herod Antipas because "he knew that he was of Herod's jurisdiction" (Luke 23:6-7). But Herod after mocking Jesus sent him back to Pilate (Luke 23:8-12).

(12) Then Jesus was tried and sent to be crucified (John 18:29-19:16; Luke 23:2-25; Mark 15:2-20; Mat 27:2-31).

(13) During that 24 hour day Judas the Betrayer killed himself (Mat 27:3-10; Acts 1:16-20).

(14) Then they crucified Christ (Mat 27:32-56; Mark 15:21-41; Luke 23:26-49; John 19:16-37).

(15) The Passover was prepared and killed on the 14th of Nisan, and also the 14th was a day to prepare for the 15th, which was an annual Sabbath wherein no work was to be done. Thus, because of a law that a body could not hang or remain on a tree (stake or wood cross) during the night, but must be taken down the very same day (Lev 21:23; cf Josh 8:29; 10:26-27). "The Jews therefore ... besought Pilate ... that he might be taken away" (John 19:31).

(16) Therefore Christ was quickly buried just before sunset, just before the annual Sabbath of the 15th (John 19:40-42; Luke 23:53-55; Mark 15:42; Mat 27:57-61).

(17) Right after the burial "they returned" to their houses (Luke 23:56, 1st part of verse).

15th of NISAN, a Thursday

nm708» This was day of the annual Sabbath, a "high day" or festival Sabbath for Jews (John 19:31; Mark 15:42; Luke 23:54; see text under "Passover").

16th of NISAN, a Friday

nm709 » After this one annual Sabbath (the 15th) some women bought spices, and they prepared these spices and the ointments that Mary Magdalene had saved (John 12:7). (Mark 16:1; Luke 23:56, middle part of verse).

17th of NISAN, a Saturday

nm710 » Jesus was then resurrected on the last of the evening, just before or at sunset, on the 7th day Sabbath. He laid in the tomb from late Wednesday evening to late Saturday evening, three days and three nights as he said he would in Matthew (Matt 28:2-4; 12:38-40; Matthew 27:63; and Mark 9:31)

Note: The resurrection of the dead saints and the dividing of the door [veil] to the holy of holies occurred with the resurrection of Christ at the end of the 7th day Sabbath when the earth-quake happened. (Matt 27:51-54) There was only one earthquake.

NOTE: See the *Chronology Papers*, CP4, for more information on Christ's death and resurrection.

NM 17: Freedom And Law

NM17 Abstract

In this paper we are going to learn what the Bible says about law and freedom. Are Christians under the law or are they under freedom? What happened at the council of Jerusalem concerning this matter? What is the new commandment? And what kind of love did Christ teach?

Freedom and Law: Definition of

The definition of Freedom is

nm711 » Freedom is the lack of restriction. Freedom to do anything, including evil, is bad because the harm connected with such freedom can destroy life. Forms of freedom that do not destroy or diminish life are good. Therefore freedom can either be good or bad. The system of love that we will explain later in this paper is a form of freedom that does no ill towards others (Rom 13:10).

The definition of Law is

nm712 » Law is restriction of activity and movement; law is regulated order. Law restricts random or chaotic movement and dictates movement that is orderly. Law can either be good or bad. Law made by men must be in harmony with the true nature of mankind or it is bad law. Good law is not self-contradictory. Too much law makes life less spontaneous and less individualistic. If the abundance of law is against the nature of mankind, it makes life less enjoyable. There is a law of love or system of love that brings harmony which we will explain later in this paper.

No Total Freedom; Life has Structure

nm713 » Total freedom in the cosmos would mean there would be no structure in the cosmos: therefore there is no total freedom in the cosmos because the cosmos has order. All life has structure; life is the order of elements. Our bodies have structure. Our bodies are forms of life. Our bodies have law. Certain parts of our body must work in certain ways. A heart must beat (pump blood); it cannot breathe or fly. Our heart functions in a certain way. It has order. It has structure. It has law. A heart by itself would be meaningless. But a heart with a body has meaning. It has purpose. It's purpose is to keep the blood moving through the body and thus nurturing the body and keeping it alive.

nm714 » Not only is there a law of our body, there is also a law for the interaction within our society. Human beings can die. We can be harmed by each other either on purpose or by accident. We can harm each other in degrees, from hurting someone's feelings, to breaking someone's arm, to killing someone. Because some human actions can harm ourselves and others, there is law against them. Governments make law to order the behavior of people. Good law is law that keeps people functioning together towards harmony and life. Bad law is law that causes disharmony and death. Since God created the universe and everything in it, then God knows the law of the universe and consequently also knows freedom. This is why we look at Biblical freedom and Biblical law.

Law in the Bible

nm715 » As indicated in the "Old Mind Paper"[NM 21], the first law uttered to man was, "but of the tree of the knowledge of good and evil, you shall not eat of it" (Gen 2:17). God didn't give man a bookcase of law books. He gave man one law. But mankind broke that law when Eve took and ate and gave it to Adam who also ate from the tree. From this one act of law-breaking, sin entered the world. Sin is lawlessness (1John 3:4). Sin is action or behavior *against* law. The law in the garden of Eden was that man shall not eat from the tree of knowledge of good and evil; mankind broke that law; sin entered the world.

nm716 » Now, just because God orally only gave this one law, does not mean that God was saying that killing others was okay, or that lying was okay. God articulated that one law to them. It was a very simple law. Mankind could eat from all the trees in the garden except the tree of knowledge of good and evil. But it was from this one simple law that the evil in man's mind was manifested. As shown in the "Old Mind Paper" [NM 21], this evil is the enemy mind or spirit that dwells and works inside the mind of mankind in this, the old age. This old mind is an evil mind that actually enjoys evil and law-breaking. From the first sin, the "law of sin" was shown to be in the world. The "law of sin" is an order or system of law-breaking. It is a system of going against the way or order that God created. God created everything to work in a certain way. When you do things the right way, you are doing it the way God intended it to be done. Doing things God's way is doing it the right way. When one buys a car he follows the manufacture's instructions on how to operate it and keep it running in good shape. If the car was made to operate through the use of the fuel we call gasoline, we use gasoline, because if we do not we would harm our car engine. But the "law of sin" is illogical and confused. The "law of sin" acts like a person who puts a different fuel in the car's tank, just for the thrill of destroying the car or of breaking the law of the car.

nm717 » An example of the law of sin at work is homosexuality. It is confusion for males to perform sexual-like acts with males; it is confusion for females to perform sexual-like acts with females. Males were created to fit and complement females; Females were created to fit and complement males. But the law of sin in some people actually makes them desire their own sex. This is not only confusion, it is against the natural order that was created by God and a form of spiritual foolishness and rebellion. "He that created them, in the beginning made them male and female" (Mat 19:4).

nm718 » Man by breaking the one simple law shown in Genesis 2:17 manifested the law of sin in its thinking. But the only law that is True law is the law that is in harmony with God's laws. Today at least some, if not much more than some, of the law in the law books of governments is corrupt and unlawful, mostly because the law makers do not understand or know God the creator.

Use of "Law" in the Bible

nm719 » The word "law" is used in different ways in the Bible. "Law" in the Bible may refer to all Old Testament scripture as a whole (John 10:34) , or to the five books of Moses (Gal 3:17-21), or sometimes only to the tables of stone written by the finger of God (Deut 24:12). The New

Testament also talks about the "law of sin" (Rom 7:23), the law of the Gentile nations, etc. Therefore when studying "law" in the Bible one must be sure to know what law the scripture is speaking about. Careful attention must be given to context.

Law of Mount Sinai and the Promises

nm720 » Now, the main body of law that was given in the Bible was the body of law given to the nation of Israel from mount Sinai (Exodus chap. 19 ff; Deut 5 ff). This law not only had the ten commandments (Ex chap. 20; Deut 5:7-21) in them but also other laws and judgments (Ex chap. 21, 22, 23; Deut 12ff), and religious ordinances concerning offerings, the ark of testimony, the golden candlestick, the tabernacle, garments for the priests, sacrifices, the altars, atonement, the Sabbath as a sign, the holy feasts, etc (Ex 25-31 ff; Book of Leviticus; and the book of Deuteronomy). Before and after these laws were given, the people of Israel promised to follow them all: "*All* the words that the LORD has said we will do" (Ex 19:8; Deut 5:27). Israel gave its promise that they would do all these commandments of God (Exo 24:3, 7-8). God had promised Israel certain things (Ex 19:5-6; Deut chap 28) if they obeyed his voice. If Israel didn't follow all these laws they were cursed (Deut 11:26ff; 12:1; 26:16-18; 27:1, 10, 26; 27:26; 28:1, 15; 28:15ff; 30:15-20). But if they followed *all* these laws they would be blessed (Deut chap. 28).

Only Jesus Obeyed All the Laws and Received the Promises

nm721 » There has only been one Israelite who has followed all these laws of God. It is through this one, Jesus Christ, that all of mankind will be blessed by the promises of God (Rom 5:18-21). Jesus Christ is the one "to whom the promise was made" (Gal 3:19). This "promise" not only was the promise to Abraham, but the promises promised if Israel obeyed all of the law (Deut 28:1ff). The only way the people of Israel could be saved or could receive the True promises of God was for them to follow *all* the laws of God perfectly. This proved impossible for the people of Israel, and the curses for disobedience came on the head of the Israelites. It was impossible for them because they had the other-mind misleading them to destruction (see "Old Mind Paper" [NM 21]; Rom 8:7). It is only through Christ and his Spirit or mind of God that people can be saved or receive the promises of God (see Acts 4:12; John 14:6 & read all of this book). Before Christ, the only way people could be saved and receive the True promise of God was for them to belong to physical Israel and to follow *all* the laws of God (Gal 3:10; James 2:10). Those outside of Israel, the Gentiles, could not receive the promises of God (Eph 2:11-12). But now this condition has been abolished. Now even non-Israelites (Eph 2:11-12; Gal 3:13-14; Acts 4:12; Heb 11:39, 13; Rom 2:12-16; 3:9; 5:12, 18; 9:4-5) can receive all the promises first given to physical Israel (Eph 2:11-13).

We are free from the <u>letter</u> of the law to follow the <u>Spirit</u> of the law.

nm722 » What some believe about keeping the Old Testament law and about Grace depends on how they have been taught by their physical teachers. These teachings have become a part of their brain cells (See "Mindset Paper" in the Preface). Once you have these teachings imprinted on your brains it is difficult and sometimes painful to correct them. Although there are plenty of scriptures that say we are no longer under the letter of the Old Testament law, in order to be saved, nevertheless, some of us have been taught, at least in part, that the Old Testament law has *not* been abolished since Christ said he did not come to abolish it. With this in mind, lets review some of these scriptures to see what Paul meant when he said we are not under the law. Remember Paul was taught Spiritually and by the authority of Christ (Eph 3:1-11; 1Tim 1:11; Titus 1:3; 1Thes 4:15; 1Cor 15:3; Gal 1:11, 12). Christ called and changed Paul, a legalistic Jew, to start to teach to the Spiritual Church about the new Spiritual law of grace and love (Acts chap 9). The night of Christ's death, when he was speaking about the future (John 13:1-3; 15:26; etc.), he gave his Jewish followers his new commandment; he also called the law of Moses, "their law" (John 15:25), not the apostles' law. Here he was making the distinction between the physical Jew and the Spiritual Jew – the Jew led by the letter of the law versus the Jew led by the Spirit of the law

- **(1)** "Do not think I have come to abolish the Law or the Prophets; I have not come to abolish them but to **fulfill** [Strong's # 4137] them" (Mat 5:17). Christ did fulfill the law, he kept all of it, for he was sinless (John 8:46; 1Pet 1:19); since Christ was also a Spiritual Jew, he **fulfilled** [# 4138 from 4137] the law Spiritually through the Spiritual law of love (Rom 13:10); the law was for the physical-Israelite nation (Ex 19:1, 8; 20:1 ff), not the Gentiles (Rom 2:14). "What then, was the purpose of the law? It was added because of transgressions until the Seed to whom the promises referred had come" (Gal 3:19). "For we maintain that a man is justified by faith apart from observing the law. Is God the God of Jews only? Is he not the God of Gentiles too? Yes, of Gentiles too, since there is only one God, who will justify the circumcised by faith and the uncircumcised through the same faith. Do we, then, void the law, no we establish the law" (Rom 3:28-31).

- **(2)** "Before the Faith came, we were held prisoners by the law, locked up until Faith should be revealed. So the law was put in charge to lead us to Christ that we might be justified by Faith. Now that Faith has come, we are no longer under the supervision of the law" (Gal 3:23-25). This "Faith" is faith of the Spirit of God: the "Spirit of faith" (2Cor 4:13); "Faith by the same Spirit"(1Cor 12:9) "But if you are led by the Spirit, you are not under law" (Gal 5:18).

- **(3)** "What I am saying is that as long as the heir is a child, he is no different from a slave [he must follow the father's rules], although he owns the whole estate [through inheritance]. He is subject to guardians and trustees [of the inheritance law] until the time set by his father. So also, when we were children [of the evil world], we were in slavery under the basic principles of the world. But when the time had fully come, God sent his Son, born of a woman, born under law, to redeem those under law, that we might receive the full rights of sons. Because you are sons, God sent the Spirit of his Son into our hearts, the Spirit who calls out, 'Abba, Father.' So you are no longer a slave, but a son; and since you are a son, God has made you also an heir" (Gal 4:1-7).

- **(4)** "For through the law I died to the law so that I might live for God" (Gal 2:19).

- **(5)** "By abolishing in His flesh the law with its commandments and regulations" (Eph 2:15).

- **(6)** "Having canceled the written code, with its regulations, that was against us and that stood opposed to us; He took it away, nailing it to the cross" (Col 2:14).

- **(7)** "Now if the ministry that brought death, which was engraved in letters on stone, came with glory, so that the Israelites could not look steadily at the face of Moses because of its glory, fading though it was, will not the ministry of the Spirit be even more glorious? If the ministry that condemns men is glorious, how much more glorious is the ministry that brings righteousness! For what was glorious has no glory now in comparison with the surpassing glory. And if what was fading away came with glory, how much greater is the glory of that which lasts!

Therefore, since we have such a hope, we are very bold. We are not like Moses, who would put a veil over his face to keep the

Israelites from gazing at it while the radiance was fading away. But their minds were made dull, for to this day the same veil remains when the old covenant is read. It has not been removed, because only in Christ is it taken away. Even to this day when Moses is read, a veil covers their hearts. But whenever anyone turns to the Lord, the veil is taken away. Now the Lord is the Spirit, and **where the Spirit of the Lord is, there is freedom**. And we, who with unveiled faces all reflect the Lord's glory, are being transformed into his likeness with ever-increasing glory, which comes from the Lord, who is the Spirit" (2Cor 3:7-18).

- **(8)** "But thanks be to God that, though you used to be slaves to sin, you wholeheartedly obeyed the form of teaching to which you were entrusted. You have been set free from sin and have become slaves to righteousness" (Rom 6:17-18).

- **(9)** "For example, by law a married woman is bound to her husband as long as he is alive, but if her husband dies, she is released from the law of marriage. So then, if she marries another man while her husband is still alive, she is called an adulteress. But if her husband dies, she is released from that law and is not an adulteress, even though she marries another man.

  So, my brothers, **you also died to the law through the body of Christ**, that you might belong to another, to him who was raised from the dead, in order that we might bear fruit to God. For when we were controlled by the sinful nature, the sinful passions aroused by the law were at work in our bodies, so that we bore fruit for death. **But now, by dying to what once bound us, we have been released from the law so that we serve in the new way of the spirit, and not in the old way of the written code**" (Rom 7:2-6).

- **(10)** "Christ is the end of the law so that there may be righteousness for everyone who believes" (Rom 10:4).

- **(11)** "For I through the law am dead to the law, that I might live until God" (Gal 2:19).

- **(12)** "For you are not under the law, but under grace" (Rom 6:14).

- **(13)** "The law and the Prophets were proclaimed *until* John. Since that time, the good news of the kingdom of God is being preached, and everyone is forcing his way into it" (Luke 16:16; note Gal 3:19; 4:4-5).

- **(14)** Now you, if you call yourself a Jew; if you rely on the law and brag about your relationship to God... A man is not a Jew if he is only one outwardly, nor is circumcision merely outward and physical. No, a man is a Jew if he is one inwardly; and circumcision is circumcision of the heart, by the Spirit, not by the written code" (Rom 2:17, 28-29; Note: there is a physical Jew and there is a Spiritual Jew [Rom 2:29; Rev 2:9; 3:9; Deut 30:6]; Christ was a physical and Spiritual Jew [Gal 4:4; Luke 2:40; Isa 42:1; 11:2]).

- **(15)** "So I say, live by the Spirit, and you will not gratify the desires of the sinful nature.... But if you are led by the Spirit, you are not under law (Gal 5:16, 18).

- **(17)** "He has made us competent as ministers of a new covenant – not of the letter but of the Spirit; for the letter kills, but the Spirit gives life" (2Cor 3:6).

- **(18)** "In order that the righteous requirements of the law might be fully met in us, who do not live according to the sinful nature but according to the Spirit" (Rom 8:4).

- **(19)** "The time is coming, declares the LORD, when I will make a new covenant with the house of Israel and with the house of Judah.... This covenant I will make with the house of Israel after that time, declares the LORD. I will put my law in their minds and write it on their hearts. I will be their God, and they will be my people" (Jer 31:31).

- **(20)** "But now, we are delivered from the law, that being dead in which we were held, so that we may serve in newness of spirit, and not in oldness of letter" (Rom 7:6).

Council at Jerusalem

nm723 » In the fifteenth chapter of Acts we see more proof that the old testament law was done away with:

Some men came down from Judea to Antioch and were teaching the brothers: "Unless you are circumcised according to the custom taught by Moses, you cannot be saved." This brought Paul and Barnabas into sharp dispute and debate with them. So Paul and Barnabas were appointed, along with some other believers, to go up to Jerusalem to see the apostles and elders about this question. The church sent them on their way, and as they traveled through Phoenicia and Samaria, they told how the Gentiles had been converted. This news made all the brothers very glad. When they came to Jerusalem, they were welcomed by the church and the apostles and elders, to whom they reported everything God had done through them.

Then some of the believers who belonged to the party of the Pharisees stood up and said, "*The Gentiles must be circumcised and required to obey the law of Moses*."

The apostles and elders met to consider this question. After much discussion, Peter got up and addressed them:

"Brothers, you know that some time ago God made a choice among you that the Gentiles might hear from my lips the message of the gospel and believe. God, who knows the heart, showed that he accepted them by giving the Holy Spirit to them, just as he did to us. He made no distinction between us and them, for he purified their hearts by faith. Now then, why do you try to test God by putting on the necks of the disciples a yoke that neither we nor our fathers have been able to bear? No! **We believe it is through the grace of our Lord Jesus that we are saved, just as they are**."

The whole assembly became silent as they listened to Barnabas and Paul telling about the miraculous signs and wonders God had done among the Gentiles through them. When they finished, James spoke up:

"Brothers, listen to me. Simon [Peter] has described to us how God at first showed his concern by taking from the Gentiles a people for himself. The words of the prophets are in agreement with this, as it is written:

After this I will return and rebuild David's fallen tent. Its ruins I will rebuild, and I will restore it, that the remnant of men may seek the Lord, and all the Gentiles who bear my name, says the Lord, who does these things that have been known for ages.

It is my judgment, therefore, that we should not make it difficult for the Gentiles who are turning to God. Instead we should write to them, telling them to abstain from the pollution of idols, from fornication, from things strangled, and from blood. For Moses has been preached in every city from the earliest times and is read in the synagogues on every Sabbath." [That is, Moses' law has been taught for generations, but no one truly followed it – except Christ who died because of it.]

Then the apostles and elders, with the whole church, decided to choose some of their own men and send them to Antioch with Paul and Barnabas. They chose Judas (called Barnabas) and Silas, two men who were leaders among the brothers. With them they sent the following letter:

The apostles and elders, your brothers, To the Gentile believers in Antioch, Syria and Cilicia: Greetings. We have heard that some went out from us without our authorization and disturbed you, troubling your minds by what they said. So we all agreed to choose some men and send them to you with our dear friends Barnabas and Paul – men who have risked their lives for the name of our Lord Jesus Christ. Therefore we are sending Judas and Silas to confirm by word of mouth what we are writing. It seemed good to the Holy Spirit and to us not to burden you with anything beyond the following requirements: You are to abstain from things sacrificed to idols, from blood, from things strangled, and from fornication. You will do well to avoid these things. Farewell.

The men were sent off and went down to Antioch, where they gathered the church together and delivered the letter. The people read it and were glad for its encouraging message. Judas and Silas, who themselves were prophets, said much to encourage and strengthen the brothers. After spending some time there, they were sent off by the brothers with the blessing of peace to return to those who had sent them. But Paul and Barnabas remained in Antioch, where they and many others taught and preached the word of the Lord (Act 15:1-35).

nm724 » Notice that not only was the contention here concerning physical circumcision, but the contention of some that the Gentiles are "**required to obey the law of Moses**" (Acts 15:5). The answer to the argument was that the Gentiles did not have to follow circumcision and other aspects of the law (circumcision was part of the Old Testament law [Lev 12:3]), but "you are to abstain from things sacrificed to idols, from blood, and from things strangled, and from fornication."

What Does It Mean That Christians Are Not Under The Law?

nm725 » "What then, shall we sin, because we are not under the law, but under grace?" (Rom 6:15) Paul asked this question, but he also answered it – no ("God forbid" – KJV). Christians were not taken out from under the requirements of the law so they could sin. Christians were given liberty from a law that could not by itself bring salvation or justification: "Through Him [Christ] everyone who believes is justified from everything you could not be justified from by the law of Moses" (Acts 13:39). With the law of Moses, one had to follow perfectly *all* the commandments and orders (James 2:10; Gal 3:10). This law of Moses was prescribed through angels (Acts 7:38, 53; Gal 3:19; Heb 2:2). But we are no longer in subjection to angels, but to Christ (Heb 2:5ff). For with Christ and His Faith – the *Spirit* of Faith – you are free from the law of Moses. Be careful here. We are not free to sin. Do read on to see what is meant.

Liberty

nm726 » There is liberty in Christ: "our liberty which we have in Christ Jesus" (Gal 2:4). We are in liberty because "Christ has made us free" (Gal 5:1). "Where the Spirit of the Lord is, there is liberty" (2Cor 3:17). This *liberty* from the Spirit of Christ is actually a "law of liberty" (James 1:25; 2:12) or a system of liberty.

nm727 » This liberty is not the liberty to sin. "For brethren, you have been called unto liberty; only use not the liberty for an occasion to the flesh, but by love serve one another" (Gal 5:13). This law of liberty has nothing to do with the freedom to sin. Sure when you have the Spirit of God you do not have to follow the letter of all the Old Testament laws in order to be saved. (You are given the Spirit and you now follow the Spirit of the law.) But this does not make it right for you to kill, or for you to lie. Just because a Christian was released from the requirements of the Old Testament laws, does not mean the Old Testament laws were bad. As mentioned above the Old Testament laws had a curse for those who did not follow them *all*. In the truest sense, if the Jews didn't follow *all* the law, they were under a curse: "All who rely on observing the law are under a curse, for it is written: 'Cursed is everyone who does not continue to do everything written in the book of the law."' (Gal 3:10)

nm728 » And one of the curses was death: "But it shall come to pass, if you will not listen unto the voice of the LORD thy God, to observe to do *all* his commandments and his statutes which I command you this day; that all these curses shall come upon you, and overtake you … The LORD shall send upon you cursing, vexation, and rebuke, in all that you set your hand to do, until you be destroyed, and until you perish quickly" (Deut 28:15, 20).

nm729 » So the Old Testament commandments which were to be for life and happiness if Israel followed them all (Deut 28:1ff), were instead to death because Israel did not keep its word – they transgressed the written laws. Thus Paul said of this factor, "And the commandment, which was for life, I found for death [the curse of not following the law]. For sin, taking occasion by the commandment, deceived me, and by it killed me. So that the law is holy, and the commandment holy, and just, and good" (Rom 7:10-12).

nm730 » The commandments of the Old Testament are good, but the evil or the sin in man (the other-mind) took the good laws and used them to deceive mankind. The other-mind is an evil power that gets thrills from breaking laws (see the "Old Mind Paper" [NM 21]). The evil power took something that was good, the law, and used it to kill mankind by deceiving mankind into thinking that breaking these laws was fun. So the liberty of Christ is not the liberty to sin, "you have been called unto liberty; only use not liberty for an occasion to the flesh, *but by love serve one another*. For all the law is fulfilled in one word, even in this: You shall love your neighbor as yourself" (Gal 5:13-14). The freedom of Christians is the freedom from the written requirements of the old Testament. But these written requirements have been replaced with a Spirit – the very Spirit of love with the New Commandment of love.

New Law and Spirit Prophesied

nm731 » "And I scattered them among the heathen, and they were dispersed through the countries: according to their way and according to their doings I judged them" (Ezek 36:19). BUT, "I will take you from among the heathen, and gather you out of all countries, and will bring you into your own land … . *A new heart also will I give you, and a new spirit will I put within you: and I will take away the stony heart out of your flesh, and I will give you a heart of flesh. And I will put my spirit within you, and cause you to walk in my statutes, and you shall keep my judgments, and do them*" (Ezek 36:24, 26-27; see Ezek 11:19-20).

nm732 » These scriptures show the promise of God's Spirit. It was through Jesus Christ that this promise came (see Acts 1:4; 2:33; Eph 1:13). And it is this Spirit of promise that frees us from the old law written on stone, and replaces the old law with a New Law written on the heart. Therefore Paul could write, "You [Christians] are our letter, written in our hearts, known and read by all men; being manifested that you are a letter of Christ, cared for by us, written not with ink, but with the Spirit of the living God, not on tablets of stone, but on tablets of fleshly hearts" (2Cor 3:2-3).

New Commandment

nm733 » God in the Old Testament said he would send a Spirit, and through that Spirit man would follow his laws, not by letter, but by Spirit: "I will put my Spirit within you and cause you to walk in my statutes" (Ezek 36:27). This Spirit is God's Spirit. This Spirit is Christ's Spirit. All of this book manifests that we are saved only if we have this Spirit or New Mind, which is the Spirit or Mind of God. And with this New Mind comes a New Law, a New Commandment. That New Commandment was, and is, Love. Not any kind of love, but Love with the power of the Spirit of God. "For, brethren, you have been called unto liberty; only use not liberty for an occasion to the flesh, but by **love** serve one another" (Gal 5:13). True liberty, true law keeping has something to do with love. As we will see, "Love" is the New Commandment.

nm734 » In the 24 hours or so before Christ was killed he gave his commandment: "A new commandment I give unto you, That you love one another; as I have loved you, that you also love one another" (John 13:34). This new commandment was love. Paul shows us what love is: "Owe no man any thing, but to love one another: for he that loves another has fulfilled the law" (Rom 13:8). As Paul shows, the true fulfilling of the law is love. And this love can be stated simply, "You shall love your neighbor as yourself. Love works no ill to his neighbor: therefore love is the fulfilling of the law" (Rom 13:9-10). Christ said basically the same thing, "Jesus said unto him, you shall love the Lord your God with all your heart, and with all your soul, and with all your mind. This is the first and great commandment. And the second is like it, you shall love your neighbor as yourself. On these two commandments hang all the law and the prophets" (Mat 22:37-40). All the law of the Old Testament hung on love – first the love of God, second the love of our fellow man.

nm735 » Christ gave a new law. But this law was not really new for all the old commandments hung on love (Gal 5:14). Christ emphasized this great law of love. And as we have seen it was because of Christ and the Spirit that He gives, that real Christians are freed from the old law (which was good, but had no power because the people had no Spiritual power to truly follow that law). The old law was replaced by the New Law, the New Commandment of Christ, the New Law of Christ, which is love.

nm736 » John has something to say about the new commandment: "Again, a new commandment I write unto you, which thing is true in him and in you: because the darkness is past, and the true light now shines ... He that loves his brother abides in the light" (1John 2:8, 10). John speaks of love: "Beloved, let us love one another: for love is of God; and every one that loves is born of God, and knows God. He that loves not, knows not God; *for God is love*" (1John 4:7-8). God is love. That is, God is Spirit (John 4:24). Thus, God's Spirit is love. Christians are Christians only if they have the Spirit of God. With this Spirit comes the love.

nm737 » What is this love? Is it sexual desire? Can you hate something and still love it? What kind of love was Christ speaking about? What is Biblical love?

System of Love

nm738 » The love Christ spoke of is a system of behavior, or a law of behavior. Paul helped to define it:

- Love is patient, love is kind, and is not jealous; love does not brag and is not arrogant, does not act unbecomingly; it does not seek its own, is not provoked, does not take into account a wrong suffered, does not rejoice in unrighteousness, but rejoices with the truth; bears all things, believes all things, hopes all things, endures all things. Love never fails (1Cor 13:4-8, NASB).

nm739 » From the 1978 New International Version:

- Love is patient, love is kind. It does not envy, it does not boast, it is not proud. It is not rude, it is not self-seeking, it is not easily angered, it keeps no record of wrongs. Love does not delight in evil but rejoices with the truth. It always protects [covers], always trusts, always hopes, always perseveres. Love never fails (1Cor 13:4-8, NIV).

nm740 » From the BeComingOne Bible:

■   <1Cor 13:4> Love is enduring, is kind; the Love is not envious {jealous, spiteful}; love is not boastful, is not conceited; <1Cor 13:5> is not rude {unbecoming}, is not self-centered, is not easily provoked {inflamed; angered}, is not numbering wrongs {of others}; <1Cor 13:6> is not rejoicing in iniquity, but is rejoicing in the truth; <1Cor 13:7> covers all (sin), believes all (good), hopes all (good), perseveres all (good). <1Cor 13:8> Love never fails.

nm741 » The fruit of God's Spirit of love is "love, joy, peace, patience, kindness, goodness, faithfulness, gentleness and self-control. Against such things there is no law" (Gal 5:22-23). There is wisdom from this Spirit of love: "But the wisdom from above is first pure, then peaceable, gentle, reasonable, full of mercy and good fruits, unwavering, without hypocrisy" (James 3:17).

nm742 » What did Christ say when he gave His New Commandment? "A New Commandment I give unto you, *that you love one another, as I have loved you*" (John 13:34). Christ who had the Spirit of God inside of him behaved and acted one way – with Love. Everything Christ did was the living of the system of love, or the law of love. Every behavioral quality mentioned as belonging to the Spirit of God in the New Testament is also a description of love, the law or system of love. Let's look at scripture for further descriptions of love.

nm743 » The so-called sermon on the mount in Matthew, chapter five, was one of Christ's amplifications on the system of love. In chapter five Christ showed how deep the law of love goes; it goes to the very heart of man. In love you should not only not kill, but not be angry with your brothers (Mat 5:21-22; 1John 3:15).

nm744 » Love does not give evil for evil (Rom 12:17). Love does not bless and curse at the same time (James 3:10). But love is "peaceable, and easy to be entreated, full of mercy and good fruits, without partiality, and without hypocrisy" (James 3:17).

nm745 » Love does not worry or fear (Mat 6:25-29). Love, loves its enemies yet not their ways (Mat 5:44; Prov 8:13). Love does not hate his brother (the person himself), yet if his brother's ways are of evil he hates his brother's ways, yet not the person himself (Prov 8:13 & Luke 14:26).

nm746 » Love does in deeds what it utters in tongue (1John 3:18 & James 1:22). Love does not overtly tempt others with objects that might lead them away from the truth (Rom 14:20-21), yet Love knows no thing in itself is bad (Rom 14:14 & Titus 1:15).

nm747 » Those with love will clothe themselves "with compassion, kindness, humility, gentleness and patience. Bear with each other and forgive whatever grievances you may have against one another. Forgive as the Lord forgave you. And over all these virtues put on love, which binds them all together in perfect unity" (Col 3:12-14).

nm748 » "Finally, all of you, live in harmony with one another; be sympathetic, love as brothers, be compassionate and humble. Do not repay evil with evil or insult with insult, but with blessing" (1Peter 3:8-9).

nm749 » "And to put on the new self, created to be like God in true righteousness and holiness. Therefore each of you must put off falsehood and speak truthfully to his neighbor, for we are all members of one body. 'In your anger do not sin': Do not let the sun go down while you are still angry, and do not give the devil a foothold. He who has been stealing must steal no longer, but must work, doing something useful with his own hands, that he may have something to share with those in need ...

nm750 » Get rid of all bitterness, rage and anger, brawling and slander, along with every form of malice. Be kind and compassionate to one another, forgiving each other, just as in Christ God forgave you" (Eph 4:24-28, 31-32).

nm751 » "Brother, do not slander one another. Anyone who speaks against his brother or judges him, speaks against the law and judges it. When you judge the law, you are not keeping it, but sitting in judgment on it. There is only one Lawgiver and Judge, the one who is able to save and destroy. But you – who are you to judge your neighbor?" (James 4:11-12) Be slow to judge because only God has all the factors that enter into people's apparent misbehavior. This says nothing about obvious evil, where you have sound evidence of the evil. But we must be careful. Some people on one part of the earth believe one thing is wrong, while others on another part of the earth believe it is okay. Be careful. In areas of gray, it is better not to judge, than to make a mistake.

nm752 » "Do nothing out of selfish ambition or vain conceit, but in humility consider others better than yourselves. Each of you should look not to your own interests, but also to the interests of others" (Phil 2:3-4).

nm753 » "Therefore, as we have opportunity, let us do good to all people, especially to those who belong to the family of believers" (Gal 6:10).

nm754 » "If anyone has material possessions and sees his brother in need but has no pity on him, how can the love of God be in him? Dear children, let us not love with words or tongue but with actions and in truth" (1John 3:17-18).

Law of Love Is More Flexible

nm755 » In the kingdom of God when all people have the New Mind and the new immortal body, some kinds of behavior that are now evil, or considered evil by some, may not be evil in the New Cosmos. For example, you can jump off a high cliff without it being a sin (suicide) because you cannot get hurt. Your angel will glide you down safely.

nm756 » People with the New Mind and new body will have fewer social restrictions. Compared to today, their behavior will be more flexible because they do not see evil in as many places as those with the other-mind. Some of those of the other-mind see evil in the ankles of women, or in the wearing of red, or in having money, or in moderate drinking, or in other things that are not evil in, and of, themselves. Remember nothing God has made is evil in itself (Rom 14:14; Titus 1:15).

nm757 » People in the New Cosmos (new heavens and earth) with their new body of immortality will have fewer restrictions concerning their body because the body will be incapable of becoming diseased, will not age, cannot get pregnant, and will be truly beautiful to all. There will be no marriage in the New Cosmos between the new age people (Luke 20:35) because there will be no more child bearing. But if two agree to stay together as a couple for a million years or more, then this is, of course, alright. Relationships will last longer than any marriage ever lasted in the old age.

nm758 » Sexual intercourse in the old age foreshadowed two, the physical and spiritual, becoming one in the New Age. Sexual intercourse in the New Cosmos will be a memento of the creation, a reminder of the reason for the old age (see God Papers, Parts 5-7).

nm759 » Remember, "love works no harm to his neighbor." When people receive the New Mind and the new body, and begin to live in the new creation, the Spiritual law of love is flexible enough to take the new situation into account. But written law on stone is not as flexible.

What Law Did Christ's Spirit Free Us From?

nm760 » As shown above, those with the Spirit of God are freed from the Old Testament law and the curses in it. A Christian with the Spirit does not have to obey physically all those laws and rituals in order to be saved. But this does not mean a Christian can lie, or kill, commit adultery or do any other form of evil, for now they are under the law of love which goes deeper than the written laws in the Old Testament. But even though we are not under the law of the Old Testament, the law still projects to us what forms of behavior will harm us as individuals and as groups, and the law is an example to us and projects the antitype to us (see *God's Appointed Times [NM16]*).

Do Christians keep the Ten Commandments?

nm761 » Christians are not under the letter of the law, but they are under the Spirit of the law. In the New Testament scriptures we see the ten commandments reiterated in a deeper more Spiritual way in the Spiritual Church:

1. "We ... preach unto you that you should turn from these vanities unto the living God" (Acts 14:15).

2. "Little children, keep yourselves from idols" (1John 5:21).

3. "But above all things brethren, swear not, neither by heaven, neither by the earth, neither by any other oath" (James 5:12).

4. Paul taught on the Sabbath (Acts 13:14; 16:13) even though there were no references in the Bible after Christ was resurrected that said that Christians had to keep the physical Sabbath. Christians did come together on the Pentecost (Acts 2:1), which is an annual Sabbath. We who are Spiritual Christians keep the Sabbath Spiritually (See next section).

5. "Children obey your parents in the Lord: for this is right" (Eph 6:1).

6. "Whosoever hates his brother is a murderer: and you know that no murderer has eonian life abiding in him" (1John 3:15).

7. "Neither fornicators, nor idolaters, nor adulterers ... shall inherit the kingdom of God" (1Cor 6:9-10).

8. "Steal no more" (Eph 4:238).

9. "Lie not" (Col 3:9).

10. "Covetousness, let it not be named among you" (Eph 5:3).

According to Lewis Sperry Chafer, in his book called *Grace*, "Under the teachings of grace, the appeal of the first commandment is repeated no less than fifty times, the second twelve times, the third four times, the fourth (about the Sabbath day) not at all, the fifth six times, the eighth six times, the ninth four times, and the tenth nine times" (p. 156; I have not confirmed his count of the scriptures, but I know that the ten commandments are reiterated many times in the scriptures of Grace.).

nm762 » Christ taught a more Spiritual law (Mat 5:20-48; 6:1-7:29) because unlike physical Israel, he had the very Spirit of God in him so that his words and actions were Spiritual (John 4:24; 6:63). For example, Christ's words about eating his body can only be understood correctly in a Spiritual manner (John 6:55-56, 63). Those churches that try to make *physical* sense out of these scriptures become foolish in their doctrine. Christ just before his death, when he was still under the law (remember he was born under the law [Gal 4:4], for his mother was a Jew), began to teach his followers about the coming new Spiritual commandment, a system of love (John 13:34; 15:12). See "Keep the Commandments?" in the "Proof Paper" [NM 10] for more information.

Do Christians Keep the Sabbath?

nm763 » Yes. The only question is *how* do you keep it.

- If you have the Spirit you keep it Spiritually.

- *If you are under the law*, then to be saved you must keep *all* of it physically – you cannot keep it Spiritually since you don't have the Spirit (Rom 8:7-10; Gal 5:18).

Old Law Led to New Law

nm764 » Israel put themselves under the law when they promised to keep **all** the laws of Moses (Ex 24:3, 7; 19:8; James 2:10). One (Jesus Christ) did keep all of the physical laws. And we are saved through Him by our faith, our Spiritual faith (Gal 3:23-24; "Proof Paper" NM 10). But physical Israel did not keep the law even though they promised to do so (Acts 7:53). The law was set up to lead us to our true leader (Gal 3:19). We were given a new commandment by this new leader, Christ. That new commandment is the commandment of love on which all the laws of Moses hang (Mat 22:37-40). This new commandment only works with the new law's New Spirit. Those without the New Mind, the New Spirit, will say such things as, "It is okay to take these street drugs, I don't see anything in the Bible saying it is a sin to take them – so it is okay" (a person commenting to another about his street drug usage). Those of the *New Mind* will say, "I don't see any law in the Bible that tells me the street drug is wrong, but I know this drug will harm me, therefore I will not use it because not only do I not wish to hurt others, but also not to hurt myself." Therefore those with the New Mind do not need a library full of detailed laws to know how to behave; they know it intuitively, depending on their measure of the Spirit (Eph 4:7; see, nm336). This "love" is not sexual and it is not friendship love, but this New Love is a system of love, a system of behavior that Paul wrote about (Gal 5:22;

1Cor 13:4-8; etc). In this system of love there is no adultery, fornication, witchcraft, hatred, wrath, murders, drunkenness, and so forth (Gal 5:19-21).

New Way of Keeping the Sabbath

nm765 » We in the Spiritual Church do not have to keep all of the letter of the Old Testament law to be saved; we keep it Spiritually, which is a greater standard of morality. In reference to the Sabbath, we keep it always, we set each day aside to keep it holy, we seek to be holy always, not just on the seventh day. We fellowship, we congregate, and we, so to speak, are in church every day because we have the Spirit of Christ inside of us teaching us. But since we are also physical and need to fellowship with each other and need a day of rest, we gather when possible with others who have the New Spirit, on the seventh day and more often if possible, and at other days besides the seventh day if we are forced to by circumstance and state laws. Of course, if we controlled the laws in our country we would set aside the seventh day for rest and holiness. During the 1000 years the seventh day of the week will be the day of rest because this new age will be controlled by those of the New Spirit. See "Thousand Years and Beyond" paper [NM 15] and the "God's Appointed Times" paper [NM 16] to understand more about the Sabbath.

Do Christians Have To Follow the Laws of the Civil Government?

nm766 » Christians should attempt to follow all the laws and regulations of all nations on earth as long as the laws are not against the law of love. But if a government should try to force Christians by law to do things such as kill, or lie, or hate the truth, Christians need not and should not obey these laws. If laws are being applied wrongfully against us, we should try to correct the situation through the courts or in other ways.

nm767 » Real Christians can live under almost any kind of government including communism and dictatorships. All these governments are temporary. If you are not forced to kill, lie, hate, rape, bruise, and so forth, then Christians can live in these societies even if they forbid your Christianity. In such countries your example will teach. If such countries forbid you to teach, you may teach, howbeit in a more restricted matter, but be careful. If you teach in a discreet manner the authorities may let you be (Acts 4:18-20; 5:28-29). No country has the right to put you in jail for teaching Christ. But you must teach

Christ with respect towards the rights of others. You can't teach Christ and be rude at the same time. If they do put you in jail for teaching Christ, you may escape if you can. You have done no wrong. (But maybe God through predestination put you in jail to teach those in jail; maybe this is *your* mission.) But be careful. Why affront the authorities when with a little thinking you can teach, and not provoke the authorities. In countries in which you can vote, vote for the best and less corrupt representative. If your country allows you to be honest, allows family, allows liveable wages for your work, allows you to in some way to teach or at least speak about your faith, then you can live in such a country.

Hate In The System of Love?

nm768 » Yes, for real Christians who have the law or system of love in them, do *hate* their life in the present system of this world (Rev 12:11; John 12:25; Luke 14:26; James 4:4). "If any one come to me, and *hate* not his father, and mother, and wife, and children, and brethren, and sisters, yea, and his own life also, he cannot be my disciple" (Luke 12:26). This does not mean you hate your father, mother, wife, children and so on because they are your father, mother, wife, children and so on, but you hate their wrong behavior: "The fear of the LORD is to *hate* evil: pride, and arrogance, and the evil way, and the froward mouth, do I *hate*" (Prov 8:13). You cannot have the Spiritual law of love and at the same time love evil behavior. When you have true love, you hate evil. If your brother behaves evilly, you hate his evil behavior, not because of anything else. If you hate your life in this world, you hate it because of evil behavior in this world, not for anything else. Each and everything God has created is good in itself (Rom 14:14; Titus 1:15). It is merely the misuse of these things that we hate, not the thing itself. "You adulterous people, don't you know that love ['friendship'- KJV] of the world [system] is hatred toward God? Anyone who chooses to be a friend [or lover] of the world [system] becomes an enemy of God" (James 4:4). In this present age the world is evil, how can you love a system of evil? If you have the Spiritual law of God, you hate your life in this evil world. You do not hate life itself, you do not hate the few moments of joy in this world, but generally you hate the world because of its evil.

How Can You Love Your Enemy?

nm769 » When you have the Spiritual law of love in your heart, you can and do love your enemy, *but* you do not like him (his wrong behavior). The love Christ spoke of was the system or law of love. "Love is patient, love is kind. It does not envy, it does not boast" (1Cor 13:4). When you love your enemy you are patient with him, you are kind to him, you do not envy him, you do not boast to him, etc. This is how you love your enemy. You do not like your enemy, you love him, or that is, you practice the system of love on him.

Difference Between Biblical Love and Other Love?

nm770 » Yes! Greek is the language of the New Testament of the Bible. In Greek there are at least three words that can be translated into "love" in the English language: (1) *eros* (which means, love between the sexes); (2) *phileo* (cherishing or friendship or high regard or even sexual love depending on the context); (3) *agapao* (system of love). The last two Greek words were used in the New Testament. But it was mainly the Greek word, *agapao*, that was used in the New Testament to describe Christ's love. *Agapao* was the Greek word Christ used when he asked us to love our enemies (Mat 5:44). It was also the Greek word Paul used to describe love (Rom 13:9-10). Christ's love is the system of love.

NM 18: Other Papers On Christianity

NM18 Abstract

In this paper we are going to discuss various subjects including parables, the meaning of "flesh" in the New Testament, Christian's Warfare, Miracles, justification, and so forth.

Parable of the Sower

First Group (hears, understands not)

nm771 » Turn to the parable of the sower in Matthew 13:1-8. This parable is also explained in Mark 4:3-25 and Luke 8:5-18. Here are pictured four groups of people who are being called or invited to the kingdom of God. Jesus explains this parable in Matthew starting in verse 19: "when any one hears the word of the kingdom, and understands it not, then comes the wicked one, and catches away that which was sown in his heart. This is he which received seed by the way side."

nm772 » This first group hears about the kingdom of God but really does not perceive or understand the significance of the words being spoken about the kingdom. Why don't they understand? "Every man therefore that has heard, and has learned of the Father, comes unto me [Christ]" (John 6:45). Christ said that those who have heard and have learned do come to him. What is meant by having heard and learned? As Matthew 13:14-17 and other verses throughout the Bible show, there are people who hear physically, but not Spiritually. Those who hear physically the word about the kingdom, but do not understand Spiritually are those not chosen by God and are not being called by God's Spirit at the time they hear about the kingdom. (But they will understand later.) "We are of God: he that knows God hears us; he that is not of God [does not have the Spirit] hears not us. Hereby know we the Spirit of truth [if they hear], and the spirit of error [if they do not hear, Spiritually]" (1John 4:6).

Second Group (hears, but does not endure – no root)

nm773 » "But he that received the seed [the word, Mark 4:14, 15] into stony places [stones are dead things], the same is he that hears the word, and immediately with joy receives it; Yet has he no root [Christ is the true root, Rev 22:16] in himself, but endures for a while: for when tribulation or persecution arises because of the word, by and by he is offended" (Mat 13:20-21).

nm774 » This second group hears physically the word (seed) about the kingdom of God, the New Age, but the word comes into a stony heart. Even though these see physically the importance of the kingdom of God and take the word of this kingdom with great joy at first, they do not endure because they have not the Spirit or root of Christ which is of course God's Spirit since all in the Body (Church) have one kind of Spirit (1Cor 12:13). These can't endure the tribulation because they haven't God's Spirit that allows one to overcome (1John 5:4). "They [those without the Spirit] went out from us, but they were not of us; for if they had been of us, they would have continued with us; but that they might be made manifest [by their act of going out] that they were not all of us" (1John 2:19).

Third Group (hears, not fruitful)

nm775 » "He also that received seed among the thorns is he that hears the word [physically]; and the care of this world, and the deceitfulness of riches, choke the word, and he becomes unfruitful" (Mat 13:22).

nm776 » The third group is being called or invited to the kingdom of God, and they hear physically, but the cares of the world choke the word of the New Age and they do not produce the fruit. As shown in the paper, "Prove Paper" [NM 10], those who are indeed real Christians do produce much fruit. Thus, this is one proof that this third group who are being called are not really Christian. The third group is the group of people who are being called, but they are not of the chosen (Mat 22:14). Another proof that this third group isn't made up of Christians is that they let the cares of the world interfere with the word of the kingdom of God. One of the tests of being a true Christian is whether one hates the world's wrong ways (1John 2:15). In fact how could a Christian let the cares of the world get in their way when they are supposed to hate their very life in the world? (John 12:25)

Fourth Group (hears, understands, bears fruit)

nm777 » The fourth group are the real Christians, the called, chosen, and predestinated. "But he that received seed into the good ground is he that hears [Spiritually] the word, and understands it; which also bears fruit [John 15:5, 8, 16], and brings forth, some a hundredfold, some sixty, some thirty" (Mat 13:23).

Parable of the Ten Virgins

nm778 » The parable of the ten virgins is in Matthew 25:1-12: "Then the kingdom of heaven shall be compared to ten virgins." The word "virgin" means, one put aside. This Spiritually speaks of the set-apart ("holy") people, the Christians (see Rev. 14:4).

nm779 » "Then the kingdom of heaven shall be compared to ten virgins [Christians], who took their lamps." The word "lamp" is Spiritually speaking about God's word, "your word a lamp unto my feet" (Psa. 119:105).

nm780 » "Then the kingdom of heaven shall be compared to ten virgins [Christians], who took their lamps [God's word] and went out to meet the bridegroom." The word "bridegroom" is Spiritually speaking about Jesus Christ (see Rev 19:7).

nm781 » "Then the kingdom of heaven shall be compared to ten virgins [Christians], who took their lamps [God's word] and went out to meet the bridegroom [Jesus Christ]. And five of them were wise [with the Spirit], and five were foolish [without the Spirit]. When they took their lamps [God's word], the foolish ones [non-Spiritual] did not take oil [the Spirit, see 1John 2:20,27; 2Cor. 1:21] with them. But the wise took oil [the Spirit] in their vessels [bodies, see Rom. 9:21-23; 1Thes 4:4; Acts 9:15] with their lamps [God's word]. And as the bridegroom [J.C.] delayed, they all nodded and went to sleep. And in the middle of the night there was a cry, Look, the bridegroom [J.C.] is coming! Go out to meet him. Then all those virgins [Christians, with and without the Spirit] rose up and trimmed their lamps. And the foolish ones said to the wise, share your oil [Spirit] with us, for our lamps are going out. But the wise [with Spirit] answered and said, lest there should not be enough for us and for you. But rather go to those who sell, and buy oil for yourselves. But as they went away to buy, the bridegroom [J.C.] came. And those who were ready went in with him to the wedding feast. And the door was shut. And afterwards the other virgins [without the Spirit] also came, saying, Lord, Lord, open to us! But he [J.C.] answered and said, truly I say to you, I do not know you."

nm782 » In context of the verses around Matthew 25:1-12, where it is speaking of the end of the old age, we can see here that the virgins of this parable are Christians, waiting for the kingdom of God, those with the Spirit (oil) and those without the Spirit. Since those with the Spirit are the only true Christians, then the five virgins (Christians) with the oil (Spirit) are the ones that truly belong to Christ and will be in his kingdom. But the others who call themselves Christians, yet do not have the oil (Spirit), are not known by Christ and will not be in his kingdom during the 1000 year age.

nm783 » This paper like others again tells us that the only true Christian is the one with the Spirit of God, the New Mind. This parable also prophesies that just before Jesus Christ's return, one-half of those in the group with the Real Christians will not have the oil – the Spirit.

Flesh

nm784 » How does Paul use the word "flesh" in his scriptures? Notice that "the flesh lusts against the Spirit, and the Spirit against the flesh. And these are contrary to one another" (Gal. 5:17). The Spirit and flesh are contrary to each other. What does this mean?

nm785 » Paul is speaking to Christians and he says: "But you are not in the flesh but in the Spirit if the Spirit of God dwells in you" (Rom 8:9). Real Christians are "not in the flesh" when they have the Spirit of God in them, or that is, the New Mind in them.

nm786 » Those who have the Spirit are real Christians or sons of God: "For as many as are led by the Spirit of God, these are the sons of God ... you received a spirit of adoption in which we cry, Abba, Father. The very Spirit bears witness with our spirit that we are children of God" (Rom 8:14-16). Those who have the Spirit are the children of God, or sons of God, or the real Christians. Remember the Spirit is contrary or against the flesh (Gal 5:17), and Christians are not "in the flesh" (Rom 8:9).

nm787 » Notice, "that is, the children of the flesh are not the ones who are the children of God" (Rom 9:8). Those called the children of the flesh, those of the flesh, those in the flesh, are not Christians. They are not the New Age people because they do not have the Spirit of the New Age, the New Mind (Rom 8:14-16).

nm788 » Those of the Spirit are contrary to those of the flesh because one group has the Spirit of God that leads them toward the ways of God (Rom 8:14,6; Gal. 5:22-23). But the other group of the flesh does not have the Spirit of God, thus they follow in the ways of confusion (note Gal 5:19-21). The group of the flesh only has the other-mind, that old mind with the twisted spirit, in their minds misleading them. But the children of God have the Spirit of God, the New Mind, which is stronger than the other spirit in them (1John 4:4), and the New Spirit leads them to overcoming wrong (1John 5:4). Yet the children of God, because they still have the spirit of error in them in this the old age will sometimes still make mistakes. Therefore Christians or the New Age people are not completely out of the flesh, or the ways of the flesh. They are fighting the good warfare in their minds (see "Warfare Paper" [NM 18]). They will only be completely outside the ways of the flesh when they are in the New Age.

nm789 » Thus Galatians 5:17 is dual: First, it speaks of the "flesh" that is still in Christians, and it says that the Spirit is contrary and against the ways of the flesh. And second, it speaks of the people of the flesh, those without the Spirit of God, and says they are contrary to those of the Spirit.

Chapter Eight of Romans

nm790 » *"There is therefore, now no condemnation to those in Christ Jesus, who walk not according to the flesh, but according to the Spirit"* (Rom 8:1).

> Those in Christ, those with the Spirit or New Mind, have no condemnation. That is, they do not die for the thousand year judgement, but live in the kingdom of God during the thousand years (see "Reward for Christians Paper" [NM 11]).

nm791 » *"For the law of the spirit of life in Christ Jesus set me free from the law of sin and of death"* (Rom 8:2).

Through Jesus Christ we are dead to the law of sin and Satan (Rom 6:10), and we are set free from this law of bondage (Rom 8:15) or the law of sin and death.

nm792 » *"For what the law was not able to do, in that it was weak through the flesh, God, in sending his own son in the likeness of sinful flesh, and about sin condemned sin in the flesh"* (Rom 8:3).

Jesus came and overcame the present world which is the spiritual enemy's world (see John 16:33). Jesus judged the prince of the world (the other spirit) (John 16:11). The law of Moses was weak because those of the flesh, those without the Spirit of God, could not keep the law correctly. Thus, the law became for them (the flesh) the starting point for Satan (the other-mind) to mislead them. Thus, the law of Moses to the flesh, those without the Spirit, was a law of sin.

nm793 » *"In order that the righteous demand of the law should be fulfilled in us, who walk not according to the flesh but according to the Spirit"* (Rom. 8:4).

Those of the Spiritual law of God, of God's Spirit, have performed the requirement of the law through Jesus Christ (see "Freedom & Law Paper" [NM 17]).

nm794 » *"For they that are according to the flesh set their mind on the things of the flesh, and they who are according to the Spirit on the things of the Spirit"* (Rom 8:5).

The Spiritual walk according to the ways of the Spirit as opposed to the others who walk according to the ways of the flesh.

nm795 » *"For the mind of the flesh is death, but the mind of the Spirit is life and peace"* (Rom 8:6).

Those with the New Mind, those with the Spirit of God, think on life and peace as opposed to the others with their thoughts dwelling on death and destruction.

nm796 » *"Because the mind of the flesh is enmity towards God, for it is not subject to the law of God, for neither can it be"* (Rom 8:7).

The mind of the flesh is the mind that does not have the Spirit of God, the New Mind. The mind of the flesh has continuous flash-thoughts on death, fear, destruction, confusion, etc. Because of this, the mind of the flesh is an enemy against the ways of God. The mind of the flesh isn't subject to the flash-thoughts of the New Mind. The New Mind gives flash-thoughts of life, trust, peace, truth, etc. The old mind, the mind of the flesh, is not subject to the good thoughts of the New Mind.

nm797 » *"And they that are in the flesh are not able to please God"* (Rom 8:8).

This does not mean that Christians (New Age people) who live in a fleshly body can't please God. The way to make sense out of this verse is to take it in context with chapter eight as a whole and with Romans 7:5. That is, "they that are in the flesh" are not real Christians.

nm798 » *"But you are not in the flesh but in the Spirit if the Spirit of God dwells in you. But if anyone has not the Spirit of Christ, he is not His"* (Rom 8:9).

Real Christians are not "in the flesh." That is, they are not "in the flesh" in the way that Paul uses the expression. Real Christians are in the Spirit.

nm799 » *"But if Christ is in you, the body indeed is dead because of sin, but the Spirit is life because of righteousness. But if the Spirit of him who raised up Jesus from among the dead dwells in you, he who raised up the Christ from among the dead will also make your death-doomed bodies live because of His Spirit that dwells in you. So, then, brothers we are not debtors to the flesh to live according to the flesh. For if you live according to the flesh, you are going to die. But if you by the Spirit put to death the deeds of the body, you will live. For as many as are led by the Spirit of God, these are the sons of God"* (Rom 8:10-14).

Notice the "if" or the hypothetical statement in verse 13. Paul is saying that *if* you do the work of the flesh you are proving you do not have the Spirit because the Spirit does produce good works as John 15 and 1John manifest over and over again. When one does the works of the flesh he is proving he does not have the Spirit. One does good works: (1) to prove he has the Spirit and thus to prove that he will be saved or freed from the confusion; and (2) because when you have the Spirit you like to do good.

Christian's Warfare

nm800 » What kind of war should Christian's fight? "For though we walk in the flesh, we do not war according to the flesh: For the weapons of our warfare are not carnal, but mighty through God" (2Cor 10:3, 4).

nm801 » Christian's warfare is not a war of flesh and blood; their weapons are not those of the flesh. The Bible calls the Christian's warfare: "a good warfare" (1Tim 1:18).

nm802 » Christians are called and asked to "fight the good fight of faith, lay hold on aeonian life, whereunto you art also called, and has professed a good profession before many witnesses" (1Tim 6:12).

nm803 » Not only were Christians called (invited), but they were chosen to fight the good warfare: "You therefore endure hardness, as a good soldier of Jesus Christ. No man that wars entangles himself with the affairs of this life, that he may please him who has chosen him to be a soldier" (2Tim 2: 3-4).

nm804 » In verse 5 it adds importantly: "if a man also strive for masteries, yet is he not crowned, except he strive lawfully." No Christian will be crowned (with life, James 1:12) except if he fights lawfully. This means by God's laws not man-made laws, for it is speaking about God's soldiers, not soldiers of the world's nations. One of the laws of God tells man not to kill. God's soldiers do not kill, they fight lawfully. How can Christians win without killing? We need to know what kind of war Christians are fighting to answer this question.

nm805 » ***What kind of war are Christians fighting?*** Who are the Christians fighting?: "because your adversary the devil, as a roaring lion, walks about, seeking whom he may devour" (1Pet 5:8). "For we wrestle not against flesh and blood, but against principalities, against powers, against the rulers of the darkness of this world, against spiritual wickedness in heavenlies" (Eph 6:12). It is Satan and his spiritual angels that real Christians are fighting against. In fact the word Satan means: enemy. Further, Christians are warring against Satan's law in man's mind, the law of sin (see Rom 7:22-25).

nm806 » Christian's have two spiritual qualities in their minds – God's Spirit (the New Mind) and a satanic one (the other-mind). Christians are fighting against the satanic one, yet it is not the human-Christian who is really fighting, but God's Spirit in the Christian's mind which is doing the spiritual fighting against the satanic spirit or mind (see "Old Mind Paper" [NM 21]).

Overcome, How?

nm807 » How does a Christian overcome or subdue this enemy inside his mind? One overcomes by resisting through their Spiritual power (the New Mind) the other-mind in their head (note James 4:7). One must resist the suggestive power of this other-mind or other spirit. One suggestive power of this spiritual quality is envy: "the spirit that dwells in us lusts to envy" (James 4:5). But how does a Christian resist this other-mind or other spiritual power?

nm808 » "Finally, my brethren, be strong in the Lord, and in the power of his might. Put on the whole armor of God, that you may stand against the wiles of the devil" (Eph 6:10-11).

nm809 » What is the armor of God? "Stand therefore, having your loins girt about with truth, and having on the breastplate of righteousness; and your feet shod with the preparation of the gospel of peace; above all, taking the shield of faith ... and take the helmet of salvation, and the sword of the Spirit, which is the word of God: Praying always" (Eph 6:14-18, see 1Thes 5:8). Thus, the armor of God consists of such qualities as faith, righteousness, the good news of peace, salvation, the word of God, and prayers. All these qualities come from, or work best with, God's Spirit. Only real Christians have God's Spirit.

nm810 » **Winner, God's Spirit**. We should know that God's Spirit in real Christians' minds will win: "You are of God, little children; and have overcome them: because greater is he that is in you [God's Spirit], than he that is in the world [the other spirit]" (1John 4:4). God's Spirit is stronger in Christians, than their other spirit in their minds; thus, God is able to overcome.

nm811 » "For all that is begotten of God overcomes the world: and this is the victory that overcomes, our Faith" (1John 5:4). Thus, those begotten with God's Spirit will overcome by their faith which is a manifestation of God's Spirit (see Gal 5:22 & Eph 2:8). In other words, those who have God's Spirit, the New Mind, will have the Faith that will give victory. Christians will overcome as their example Jesus Christ did: "I have overcome the world" (John 16:33). Christians were called and chosen to conform to the image of Christ, thus, to overcome (see Rom 8:28-30 & "Predestination Paper" [NM 8]).

nm812 » Christians are fighting the good warfare and have the armor of God and God's Spirit to fight the spiritual war. Since God's Spirit is greater in power than the adversary's spirit in man's mind, and since with "the holy Spirit of God, whereby you are sealed unto the day of redemption [Eph 4:30]," then we know that Christians as individuals will win the good warfare, if they truly have God's Spirit in them, and thus are real Christians (Rom 8:11).

New Jerusalem

nm813 » Many look upon the book of Revelation's account of the New Jerusalem that comes out of heaven as being a physical entity only. But God tells us to look to the higher meaning (Phil 3:18-19; Col 3:1-2). The truth of the matter is that the Bible is dual and this prophecy in Revelation speaks of a Spiritual Jerusalem.

nm814 » In Revelation 21:2 & 10 we read, "and I John saw the holy city out of heaven, prepared as a bride adorned for her husband .... And he carried me in spirit to a great and high mountain, and showed me that great city, the holy Jerusalem, descending out of heaven from God. Having the glory of God: and her light like unto a stone most precious, even like a jasper stone, clear as crystal." The chapter goes on to describe it in fuller detail.

nm815 » But now let's turn to Revelation 3:12. Here Jesus Christ is speaking to the Philadelphia Church. "Behold I come quickly: hold that fast which you have, that no man take your crown. Him that overcomes will I make a pillar in the temple of my God, and he shall go no more out: and I will write upon him the name of my God, and the name of the city of my God, New Jerusalem, which comes down out of heaven from my God: and I will write upon him my new name."

Temple

nm816 » We see here that Christ will make the overcomers pillars in the temple of God. Now of course this does not mean being made a stone – what kind of a reward would that be to be made a dead, stone pillar? No this pillar is a spiritual pillar in the spiritual temple of God. But then it says he will never go out of the temple. Again if this verse was a physical temple what kind of reward would that be, to be confined to a temple forever? No, again it speaks of a spiritual temple.

nm817 » Paul speaking to Christians said, "you are the temple of the living God" (2Cor 6:16). And again, "for through him [Christ] we have access by one Spirit unto the Father. Now therefore you are no more strangers and foreigners, but fellow citizens with the saints, and of the household of God; and are built upon the foundation of the apostles and prophets, Jesus Christ himself being the chief corner stone; in whom all the building fitly framed together grows into a Holy *temple* in the Lord. In whom you also are built together for a habitation of God' through the Spirit" (Eph 2:18-22). And again in 1Peter 2:5, "you also, as lively stones, are built up a spiritual house." So the temple spoken about in Revelation 3:12 is a spiritual one – the Christians who overcome. And as there is a spiritual temple, so too is there a spiritual Jerusalem.

New Jerusalem and the Church

nm818 » Now we see in 1Peter 2:5 that it speaks of living stones that build-up to a spiritual house or temple. Peter calls the Christians, lively stones. Now turn to Malachi 3:16-17: "then they that feared the LORD spoke often one to another: and the LORD listened, and heard it, and a book of remembrance was written before him for them that feared the LORD, and that thought upon his name. And they shall be mine, says the LORD of hosts, in that day when I make up my JEWELS; and I will spare them, as a man spares his own son that serves him."

nm819 » With these two scriptures; and Malachi 3:3; Isaiah 54:11-13; Revelation 4:3; Ezek 28:13; and Isaiah 28:16 (Zion is the Church, Heb 12:22) taken in their context, we can conclude that the precious stones of Revelation 21:11, 19-21 are simply telling the reader that the new Jerusalem is Spiritual, for precious stones are symbolic of spiritual things. This Spiritual Jerusalem is the Church, for one proof that New Jerusalem is God's Church is revealed in Revelation 21:2, 9. New Jerusalem here is spoken of as a bride of the Lamb. Revelation 19:7-9 proves that the bride of the Lamb is the Church.

nm820 » For another proof note Hebrews 12:22 where it calls the Church "the city of the living God, THE HEAVENLY JERUSALEM." And in Galatians 4:26 it calls Jerusalem the "Jerusalem which is above is free, which is the mother of us all." Notice also the woman of Revelation 12:1 is clothed with the sun, and upon her head are twelve stars. Now we know that women are symbolic of the Church (Eph 5:22-25). And we know that the symbolic meaning of being clothed with the sun is to be clothed with the Spirit because (1) God is light (1John 1:5); (2) Christ the God is clothed with light (Mat 17:2; Psa 104:2) that makes him shine as the sun (Mark 9:3; Rev 1:16); and God is spirit (John 4:24). Thus, when one is clothed with light he is clothed with the Spirit (see Isa 30:1). The woman of Revelation 12:1 is God's Church.

nm821 » What are the twelve stars on her head? Stars are symbolic of angels (Rev 1:20). Notice the description of New Jerusalem – "and at the gates twelve angels, and names written thereon, which are the names of the twelve tribes of the children of Israel" (Rev 21:12). Thus, the stars or angels on the woman's (Church's) head are a tie-in with New Jerusalem (the Church) and its twelve angels of the tribes of Israel.

nm822 » But for a final proof that the New Jerusalem is the Church of God let's return to Revelation 3:12. Jesus speaking to the Church says he will write on them the NAME of the God, and the name of God's city – New Jerusalem. They will have the NAME of the God and New Jerusalem. Now we see God's Church in Revelation 14:1 having Christ's NAME written on their foreheads. New Jerusalem is the Church of God, either resurrected (Born of God), or, taken typically, those begotten of God (see "Begotten, Born Paper" [NM 5]).

Outward Show

nm823 »

- some do things for appearance so they may escape suffering. [Gal 6:12]

- But we do what is right even if it appears evil. [2Cor 13:7-8; 6:8; Mat 27:63]

- Christ who did everything right, (1) was called the deceiver [Mat 27:63], (2) was said by others that "he is beside himself" [Mark 3:21], (3) was called possessed by the prince of demons [Mark 3:22]

- Paul's speech was unpolished, but he was rich in knowledge. [2 Cor 10:10; 11:6]

- Paul did not speak in flattery. [1Thes 2:5]

- Christ did what was right even if it appeared wrong to others: (1) He did things against the traditions of the Jews [Mat 15:2]; (2) Christ rebuked the Jews even though they were offended by the reproof. [Mat 15:3-14]

- When Peter put on a show to satisfy some of the Jews, Paul rebuked Peter because he was being partial against the Gentile Christians. [Gal 2:11-14]

These verses and others indicate that we do what is right even if it may appear to others as evil. The verse, "abstain from all appearance of evil" (1Thes 5:22), is a bad translation from the Greek, it should read: "abstain from every form of evil."

Wisdom

nm824 »

- Real wisdom will rebuke all. [Luke 21:14-15]

- Man's wisdom is to be destroyed. [Isaiah 29:14; 1Cor 1:19]

- Those who reject God's word, reject the basis of wisdom. [Jer 8:9]

- Real wisdom is obtained through God's Spirit. [Eccl 8:1, 16-17; with 1Cor 2:9-14]

Reproof

nm825 »

- He that regards reproof shall be honored. [Prov 13:18]

- A fool despises his father's [God the Father] instruction, but he that regards reproof is prudent. [Prov 15:5]

- God asks us to turn at his reproof. [Prov 1:23-27]

- Instruction is grievous unto him that forsakes the way: and he that hates reproof shall die. [Prov 15:10]

- He that refuses instruction despises his own soul: but he that hears reproof gets understanding. [Prov 15:32]

- The ear that hears the reproof of life abides among the wise. He is one of the Spiritual wise. [Prov 15:31]

- Reprove one that has understanding [the Spirit of understanding], and he will understand knowledge. [Prov 19:25]

- A scorner loves not one that reproves him: neither will he go unto the wise. [Prov 15:12]

- Just because God is silent about the things one does, does not mean he approves. [Psalms 50:16-21]

- The reprover is hated, in the city a trap is laid for him. [Amos 5:10; Isa 29:21]

- One should not add to God's words, lest God reprove that one, and he be found a liar. [Prov 30:6]

- Open rebuke is better than secret love; he that rebukes a man, afterward shall find more favor than he that flatters with the tongue. [Prov 27:5; 28:23]

■ Those that do wrong rebuke before all. [1Tim 5:20; note context]

Miracles; Healing; Wonders; Signs

nm826 »

■ Miracles are performed through the power of the Spirit of God. [John 3:2; Acts 14:3; Acts 15:12; 19:11 Mat 12:28; 1Cor 12:9]

■ Miracles are given as a gift of the Spirit. [1Cor 12:9-10]

■ Miracles are given as God wishes them to be given. [1Cor 12:11]

■ Miracles are a sign of the Church. [Mark 16:17, 20]

■ Miracles or signs are indications of God's prophet. [Ex 4:1-9]

■ Signs, wonders, and mighty works are done by apostles. [2Cor 12:12]

■ The Spirit has power over *all* kinds of sickness and disease, and over the other spirit. [Mat 10:1]

■ Stephen did great wonders and miracles because he was full of grace and power. [Acts 6:8]

■ The Spirit of God can and shall cast out the other spirit from some people possessed by it, and eventually the whole world. [Mat 8:28-32; 12:28; Zech 13:2]

■ No man can do miracles, "except God be with him." [John 3:2; 9:16, 33; Mark 9:39-40; 3:22-23]

■ False miracles deceive the non-Spiritual. [Rev 19:20; 2Thes 2:9-12]

■ True miracles are undeniable. [Acts 4:16; John 11:47]

■ True miracles produce astonishment in those who see them performed. [Acts 3:1-10]

■ Such impossible things as making the blind see and raising the dead are true miracles. [John 9:1-8; 11:39-44]

■ Jesus Christ did his works in his Father's NAME [John 10:25, 38]

■ Jesus was in his Father's NAME because he had his Father's Spirit inside him. [John 14:9-10; see *God Papers*]

■ Healing, signs, and wonders are done through the NAME of Christ. [Acts 4:30]

Thus, one must be in the NAME of Christ in order for one to perform miracles, for miracles are performed through his name or through the power of being in his NAME.

- Healing sickness is like forgiving the sins of those of the Faith. [Mark 2:9-12; Luke 5:20; Mat 9:1-2]
- To have Faith is to have the Spirit of Faith, that is God's Spirit. [2Cor 4:13; Gal 5:22; Eph 2:8; 1Cor 12:9]
- Faith (true faith with the Spirit) is required in order to perform miracles, healings, signs, and wonders, etc. [Mat 17:20; 21:21; John 14:12; Acts 6:8]

nm827 » Faith (true faith with the Spirit) is required in those for whom the miracles are performed.

- "according to your faith" – Mat 9:29; "he had faith to be healed" – Acts 14:9; "your faith has saved you" – Luke 18:42, 43; "your faith has made you whole" – Mat 9:22; "I believe, help my unbelief" – Mark 9:22-24

Note: Those before the Pentecost did not have the Spirit, thus their "faith" was physical only, as were the miracles only physical: no one was spiritually healed before the Pentecostal events.

nm828 » Some signs that follow them that believe, thus those who have Faith of the Spirit, thus those who are in Christ's NAME are as follows:

- they cast out the other spirits or demons; they speak in new languages or tongues; they are sometimes not hurt by poison; they heal the sick by the laying on of the hands [Mark 16:17-18]

nm829 » In most cases the healer of a person touches the person being healed (for example Mat 8:15). Sometimes the healer indirectly heals the other person by sending pieces of cloth that he has touched to them, or the person to be healed touches the healer in Faith and then is healed (Acts 19:11-12; Mat 9:20-22; 14:36).

nm830 » In James 5:14 it speaks about anointing the sick with oil in the name of the Lord. Does this mean olive oil? Do we in the Spiritual Church, who worship God Spiritually (John 4:23-24), pour oil over those we are healing. No, we look to the higher sense of olive oil, the Spirit of God is the higher oil (cf 1John 2:20, 27; 1Sam 16:13). The elders of the Church anoint with the Spiritual oil – God's Spirit. It is God's Spirit that heals, not olive oil.

nm831 » It should be noted here that we are healed according to our Faith to be healed. Further we are given the measure of Faith to be healed. Sometimes this measure of Faith will not be given to us to be healed, for God does things that are, in the final analysis, best for us (Rom 8:28). If someone is sick, and dies because he didn't have the measure of Faith to be healed, then if he had the Spirit, it was best that he died. He is taken from the evil (note Isa 57:1); and thus we should be glad for he has run his race, and he is precious in God's eyes (Psa 116:15). But even though we should be glad that one has died from the wrongness of this world, we will be sad, for we will miss him. Yet we know he is away from the world's madness, thus we are glad for him.

Justification

nm832 » What does justification or being justified mean? In the Greek, which the New Testament was written in, the word translated justify means: to become right; to make right or just. In the inspired language justify means that those persons justified have been made right or just. Even the original meaning of the English word "justify" meant to make just. The English word has evolved to mean acquittal of past blame, but the word justify in its inspired language means to make right or just. The word itself says nothing about *how* one is made right or just. Just because a word through misuse has evolved to mean something does not mean we are to use its evolved meaning. "Justify" means to make right or just. We must ascertain how one is made just by the context the word is used in.

How Is One Justified?

nm833 » "Therefore having been justified by faith" (Rom 5:1). People are justified by faith. Again, "we conclude that a man is justified by faith" (Rom 3:28). People are justified by faith as the following verses also conclude: Gal. 2:16; 3:24; Rom 3:30; 4:5.

nm834 » People are justified by faith. But what kind of faith is the Bible speaking about? The true faith is the faith of the Spirit (1Cor. 12:9; 2Cor. 4:13; Gal. 5:22). "People are justified in the NAME of our Lord Jesus Christ, and in the Spirit of our God" (1Cor. 6:11). You are justified when you are in the NAME of Christ and when you are in the Spirit of God. When one has the Spirit they are in the NAME of Christ (see the "Baptism Paper" [NM 4]). When you are in the Spirit you have the true Spiritual faith. When you have this faith you are justified. What all this means is that when you have the Spirit of God you are justified, you are made right. You are made right because you have been given the good Spirit, the right Spirit, and with it you have the New Mind of love and harmony. With the New Mind you have been made right. You have put on the New Mind.

Richness

nm835 »

- "There is the one that makes himself rich, yet has nothing: there is the one that makes himself poor, yet has great riches." [Prov 13:7]

- "Give me neither poverty nor riches ... lest I be full, and deny you, and say, Who is the LORD [Jehovah]? or lest I be poor, and steal, and take the name of my God in vain." [Prov 30:8, 9]

- What good is riches to the owner, except to look at? [Eccl 5:11]

- The abundance of the riches will not permit the rich to sleep in peace. [Eccl 5:12]

- If you can't eat or use your riches what good are they? [Eccl 5:19; 6:1-2]

- "Take heed, and beware of covetousness [over-desire]: for a man's life consists not in the abundance of the things which he possesses." [Luke 12:15]

- "Now when Jesus heard these things, he said unto him, Yet you lack one thing: sell all that you have, and distribute unto the poor, and you shall have treasure in heaven: and come, follow me." [Luke 18:22]

- One should not glory in physical riches, but in the richness of knowing God. [Jer 9:23-24]

- You can't trust in riches and also get into the kingdom of God; it is very difficult for the rich (who trust in their physical wealth) to get into the Kingdom. [Mark 10:24-25]

- The rich are easily tempted to their destruction. [1Timothy 6:9]

- In order for the rich to make it into the Kingdom of God they must be willing in certain cases to sell their goods and give it to the poor of the Church. [Luke 18:22; Rom 12:13; 1Tim 6:17-18; Luke 14:33]

nm836 » In the Bible Spiritually speaking, when the rich are mentioned derogatorily, it signifies the children of the enemy; when the poor are mentioned positively, it signifies the children of the Spirit.

Joy

nm837 »

- Christian sorrows are daily as those of the others in the world. [1Pet 5:9; Job 15:20; 31:3; Psa 13:2; 31;10-11; 34:19; 43:2; 44:9-19, 22; 80:4-6; Rom 8:17-18; 1Thes 2:14; 2Tim 3:12; 1Pet 4:1]

- But the sorrows for Christians are only in the now; total Joy comes when Christ returns. [John 16:20-22; note Mat 5:4; & Isa 66:6-10 with Rev 12:1-2]

- The world rejoices now. [John 16:20]

- For folly is joy to those without wisdom. [Prov 15:21]

- The wicked *seem* happy, they *seem* to prosper. [Jer 12:1; Mal 3:15]

- But those with apparent joy *now* will mourn and weep at Christ's coming. [Luke 6:25 with Mat 25:30; 22:13; 24:51]

- Christians will be joyful in God's presence. [Psalms 16:11]

- We will have joy after we are freed from our captivity. [Psalms 53:6]

- We will have joy after God's return, then the sorrow will turn to joy. [Jeremiah 31:13]

- The sorrow shall flee away after God returns, then comes the songs of aeonian joy. [Isaiah 35:10]

- At Christ's physical return is the aeonian joy, at that time sorrow and mourning shall flee away. [Isaiah 51:11]

- Christians are recompensed at the resurrection of the just. [Luke 14:14]

- When Christians awake or are resurrected they will then be satisfied. [Psalms 17:15]

- Christian's joy is according to the joy of the harvest. [Isaiah 9:3; Rev 14:15; Mat 13:39]

- Christians will be glad in God's salvation after they have waited for him. [Isaiah 25:9]

- God will create Jerusalem or the Church (Rev 21:2, 9; Gal 4:26) a rejoicing, and her people a joy in the new heaven and earth. [Isaiah 65:17-19; Rev 21:1-4]

- Physical and Spiritual Israel will be happy when God returns to his people at his coming. [Psalms 53:6]

- At God's coming, then the mourning ends. [Isaiah 60:20]

- In God's salvation will our hearts rejoice. [Psalms 13:5]

- Now Christians sow in tears, but they shall reap in joy. [Psalms 126:5-6]

- The joy Christ left with Christians is the joy of the Holy Spirit. [Acts 13:52; 1Thes 1:6; one of the fruits of the Spirit is Joy, Gal 5:22]

- But this "joy" is not *full*, for the Spirit is given in measure (Eph 4:7, 16). The tribulation of the world (John 16:33) makes us suffer now, but full joy comes when Christ comes as the above scriptures indicate.

- The "joy of the Lord" is in the kingdom of God. [Mat 25:21]

- Rejoice because of the future hope. [Luke 6:22-23]

- The Hope of the righteous shall be gladness. [Prov 10:28]

- Christians rejoice for the Hope of the future great glory of God and his Kingdom. [Romans 5:2]

- Christians rejoice in Hope. [Romans 12:12]

- Christians rejoice now in their sufferings because of the hope of Christ's coming and the exceeding joy thereof. [1Peter 4:13]

Prayer

nm838 » The word "pray" from the Hebrew and Greek text of the Bible means: to ask; to wish for; to meditate; to pour out. Praying to God is pouring out of ones's self to God, and asking for something, or meditating about things, ideas, or ideals to God: it is communicating with God.

nm839 » All over the world today you see people "praying" to God. They get on their knees to pray; they lay flat on their faces to pray; they flog themselves to pray; they do penitence when praying; they squint their eyes and twist their faces when praying, the more they squint their eyes and twist their faces the more they think God will respond. What are they saying when they pray in this manner? Does the all powerful God need this kind of praying? The all knowing and all powerful God can read minds; He knows things you need *before* you ask for them (Mat 6:8). Is God like some kings of the old age who had a need for people to kneel before them, and to speak glowing words to them? Does God need our glowing words to help uphold His confidence in Himself? Does God need us to beg for help, when He knows we need His help? We are His children. Will He allow us to destroy ourselves permanently if we do not pray while squinting our eyes, twisting our faces, and flogging our bodies? Christ prayed in a physical way to teach us the Spiritual way of praying (John 11:41-42; etc.). There is a Spiritual way to pray.

Prayer Is Communication

nm840 » *In the physical or typical meaning of the Bible we learn the following.* We should admit our wrongs to him (Lev 5:5; Num 5:6-7; 1Sam 12:10; Psa 32:3, 5; Psa 51:3, 4; etc.). We should thank him for the present good and the coming Good (Phil 4:6; Acts 27:35; 1Cor 10:30-31; etc.). When we pray we should meditate on his Word (Joshua 1:8; Psa 1:2; 19:14; 104:34; 119:15-16; etc.). Prayer brings one closer to God, for it establishes a bond, or a relationship with him. Prayer is talking to God, is communicating with God. We can speak to God as if he is our friend (John 15:14-15).

What Do We Pray For?

nm841 » We ask only what God wills or wishes (Mat 26:39 & 1John 5:14). We can't receive what God has *not* prepared for us (Mat 20:20-23). We can find out about God's will through his Word, the Bible. So, in order to know what to ask for, we must know the Bible. To know the Bible we must read and study it. We should pray for the good of all, for others, and for us, not selfishly (Job 42:10; 1Kings 3:9-14; Mat 6:9-13). If we pray for ourselves it should be for strength to endure the world (Psa 31:3; 4:1), for wisdom to help others (1Kings 3:9-12), to overcome our weakness (Rom 12:21), and so forth. We do not pray for decaying physical wealth, for we know life is not the abundance of the things which we possess (Luke 12:15), for in this age wealth only brings worry and trials (Eccl 5:10-13; Mark 10:30). When we pray for physical things it is for what we need, such as our *daily* bread or food (Mat 6:11; Acts 2:44-46; 4:34-37).

Does God Hear Our Prayer?

nm842 » God hears the prayer of those who do his will, who are thus in the Spirit; He hears them always (1John 5:14; 3:22; John 9:31; 11:42).

When Does God Answer Prayer?

nm843 » The True God fulfills our prayer only if it is in harmony with the final Good. The good God does not fulfill prayer of harm to others, for we are to give good for evil, not evil for evil (Rom 12:14, 17). Many prayers in harmony with the word of God will ultimately be fulfilled beginning at Christ's return to the physical world (Psa 102:2, 13; Luke 14:14; Psa 17:15; Isa 25:9). The whole book of Psalms in its higher or Spiritual meaning, projects to us that most Christian's hope and prayer will be fulfilled beginning at God's return to earth. God answers our prayer if we have the Faith to believe he will fulfill our asking (James 1:5-7; Mark 11:24). This Faith comes from the Spirit of God (Gal 5:22). This Faith is given by measure (Rom 12:3, 6). Therefore we believe enough to receive an answer only when we have the given Faith to believe.

nm844 » *In Summary.* God answers prayer only when it is for the good, when it is within the rules of creation, when it is for the best of the person according to the predestinated plans for that person (Rom 8:28).

Pray Always

nm845 » Daniel prayed three times a day (Dan. 6:10), David prayed three times a day (Psa 55:17), some prayed seven times a day (Psa 119:164), but Christ said to pray always (Luke 18:1), and Paul also said to pray without ceasing (1Thes 5:17). We should pray always (Eph 6:18). The Spirit in Christians in a sense enables them to be a continual prayer (Rom 8:26;Heb 13:15-16; Rom 12:1). Because praying to God is communicating with God and because we love God, Christians consciously will pray often. Since prayer is talking to God, one can "talk" to God almost anywhere, and in any position (Luke 23:46; Luke 22:41; Psa 4:4; Neh 8:6; etc.). We should not pray just to be seen (Mat 6:5), for we can pray secretly (Mat 6:6) within our minds anywhere and at any time. This is not to say that praying in public is wrong. Jesus prayed openly in front of some people in order to teach them (John 11:41-42). We should not use worthless repetitions (Mat 6:7), but pray with all our hearts (Luke 22:44; Ho 7:14; James 5:17).

nm846 » Praying is not magical or repetitious (Mat 6:7). Praying is merely talking to God, rightly. Thus, talking within his will or wish. Therefore talking with God about the good, for the good, and thanking him for the good now, and for the Good to come. God is not ritualistic. There is no set position in which to pray. There are no set words to say. We pray with almost any words as long as they convey the meaning of what we want to talk with God about. There are no set number of minutes that we must pray to him. We think on the good, and talk about the good always with him everywhere within our minds. At times it may be easier to concentrate when we go to a spot in private and pray or communicate with Him (note Mark 1:35). Sometimes we might need to communicate all night as Christ did at times (Luke 6:12).

Who Do We Pray To?

nm847 » In the Old Testament they prayed to the Father, to the YHWH, the BeComingOne, also called Jehovah or Yehowah by some. Jesus taught the manner in which you should pray (Mat 6:9-13; 26:39). But near the end of his ministry Jesus told us that we could ask (pray) *in his name*, "that I will do, that the Father may be glorified in the Son" (John 14:13-14; 15:16; 16:23-26). Why did Jesus say that? Because Jesus was about to be given *all* God's power (Mat John 16:15; Mat 28:18), He would be going into the glory of the God (13:31-32), He would be given God's Name (John 17:11), which is Christ's New Name (Rev 3:12). God's name was shown to Moses in the Old Testament. God's Name is YHWH or the BeComingOne, or the "One (who) Will-Be" (See GP 1). "And whatsoever you shall ask in my name, that will I do, that the Father may be glorified in the Son" (John 14:13). Jesus will not relay these prayers to the Father (John 16:26). Why? Because Jesus is now in a sense the Father (Isa 9:6; see GP 5: ¶ gp487), sitting as the very right side of God (Acts 2:34). The Spirit for Christians, predestinated before the creation (NM 8), is now given through Jesus (John 20:22; Act 2:33). Thus, He is now in a sense our Spiritual Father (Isa 9:6). He has the Name of God; He represents the God, who will fill all in all (Note 1Cor 15:28; GP 6). , for He will fill all in all (Eph 1:10, 23; GP 6), but now, not all that will be in Christ, is in Christ (Heb 2:8; see *God Papers*, GP 5). Who do we pray to? We pray to Jesus, for the Father has glorified Himself in Jesus. Our God, who is the "Will-Be-One" (YHWH) is now represented by Jesus Christ, the Right Hand of the God, who will fill all in all (see the *God Papers*).

Prayer's Higher Meaning. With the New Mind: we pray always; we are always in contact with God because we are ONE in the Spirit of God, which is the Spirit of Christ, which is the Spirit of Christians. God does not need anyone to get down on their knees to Him, squinting their eyes, and doing penitence to get his attention. God is not a monster, or a pretentious king. God is/will-be a friend to all. In our minds we pray to God (Jesus was called: "my lord and my God") at any time, any where, because we are in the Spirit, and in contact or communication with God through His Spirit, which is the Spirit of the Father, Son, and Holy Spirit – the one same Spirit who is in all who will-be in Him (GP 6:gp483).

Living in Common

nm848 »

- Those who believed at first sold their possessions and goods and lived in common; each had only what he or she needed. [Acts 2:44-46; 4:32, 34-37]

- Christ said in order to be complete ("perfect") one must sell all and give to the poor. [Mat 19:20-21; Like 18:22; Mark 10:21]

- The Spiritual poor are Christians. [Isaiah 66:2; 14:32; Mat 5:3; Luke 6:20; Rev 2:9]

- To be a disciple of Christ one must forsake all. The higher meaning here is that we must forsake all of the old mind and its way in order to be a disciple of Christ in the truest sense. [Luke 14:33]

- Christ came that we might have abundant *life*. [John 10:10]

- But, "take heed, and beware of covetousness [desire to have more than one's share]: for a man's life consists not in abundance of the things which he possesses." [Luke 12:15]

- Sell your possessions and give, thus providing a treasure in heaven or in the Spiritual world. [Luke 12:33]

- For he that lays up treasures for himself is not rich towards God. [Luke 12:21]

- Notice the parable of the treasure in heaven. [Mat 6:19-21]

- Notice the parable of the treasure in the field and of selling all to buy it. [Mat 13:44]

- Notice the parable of the pearl and of selling all to buy it. [Mat 13:45-46]

- Notice a principle of sharing: "He that has two coats, let him impart to him that has none; and he that has meat, let him do likewise." [Luke 3:11]

- Notice another principle of sharing: "But by an equality, that now at this time your abundance may be a supply for their want, that their abundance also may be a supply for your want: that there may be equality: As it is written, He that had gathered much had nothing over; and he that had gathered little had no lack." [2Cor 8:14-15; note Ex 16:18]

- Christians labor in work that is good so they may have something to give to others in need in the Church. [Ephesians 4:28]

- Paul asked through Timothy that the physically rich of the Church do good so that they would be rich in good works; they must be ready to distribute, and must be willing to share. In this way they would be laying up in store for themselves a good foundation against the time to come, the time of the New Age, so that they may lay hold onto aeonian life. [1Timothy 6:18-19]

- Paul asked the Christians to do good and to share. [Hebrews 13:16]

- There is a difference between physical wealth and Spiritual wealth. [Revelation 3:17; 2:9]

- Those who make themselves poor for God are rich. [Prov 13:7]

- Wisdom and understanding are better than wealth. [Prov 16:16; 3:13-15]

- Better the poor that walk right, than the rich who do wrong. [Prov 28:6]

- The ungodly prosper in this age. [Psalms 73:12]

Book of Life

nm849 » What is the book of life? Whose names are in the book? The key to this truth is in Revelation 13:8. In the King James Version this verse reads: "and all that dwell upon the earth shall worship him [the beast], whose names are not written in the book of life of the lamb slain from the foundation of the world." So we see that all will worship the beast except those names written in the book of life of the lamb, Jesus Christ.

nm850 » This verse says that those written in the book of life were written into the book of the lamb (Jesus) who was as good as slain [Greek verb, perfect] before the foundation of the earth. This is confirmed in Revelation 17:8, "and they that dwell on the earth shall wonder, whose names were not written in the book of life from the foundation of the world, when they behold the beast." Thus, the book of life has names written in it since the foundation of the earth. But those who worship the beast haven't got their names in this book. Who are those with their names in the book of life?

Christians in The Book

nm851 » Those with their names in the book of life are Christians according to Paul: "and I entreat you also, true yoke-fellow, help those women which labored with me in the gospel, with Clement also, and with other my fellow laborers, whose names are in the book of life" (Phil 4:3). Thus, we see that the Christian's names are written in the book of life. And in Hebrews 12:23 we see that "the general assembly and church of the first-born" are written in heaven. Also in Luke 10:20 the seventy that were sent out two at a time were told to "rejoice because your names are written in heaven." Thus, we see that the followers of Christ have their names written in heaven. Being written in heaven is being written in the book of life.

nm852 » In 2Timothy 1:9 (in its Greek text) we see that those called were called "before the times of eons." And in Ephesians 1:4 we read "according as he has chosen us in Him before the foundation of the world, that we should be holy." Further, in Revelation 3:5 we read in Jesus Christ's message to the Sardis church: "he that overcomes, the same shall be clothed in white raiment: and I will not blot out his name out of the book of life." Surely, we can conclude from this that it is the true Christians, the called, chosen, and predestinated, who are the ones written in the book of life from and even before the world's foundation.

Good News

nm853 » Now here comes good news for real Christians. Notice in Revelation 3:5 Jesus says: "I will not blot out his name out of the book of life ... he that overcomes." True Christians are written in the book of life before the world began, and here Jesus said he would not blot out their names if they overcame. Please turn to Hebrews 10:39. There we see Paul speaking to true Christians and saying: "But we are not of them who draw back unto perdition; but of them that believe to the saving of the soul." And in 1John 5:4 we read, "for whatsoever is begotten of God overcomes the world." The reason for this is "because greater is he that is in you [the Spirit of God], than he that is in the world [the spirit of confusion]" (1John 4:4). God has predestinated real Christians "to be conformed to the image of his Son, that he might be first born among many brethren" (Rom 8:29).

nm854 » In Revelation 20:12 we read about the day of judgment: "and I saw the dead, small and great, stand before God; and the books [of the Bible] were opened: and another book was opened, which is the book of life: and the dead were judged out of those things which were written in the books [of the Bible], according to their works." Comparing this with verse 15 and other verses, we see that those of the "dead" during the day of judgement have not their names yet in the book of life. But they are to be put into the book of life when they are resurrected from their 1000 year judgment into the day of atonement (see, "Thousand Years and Beyond"). For all will be saved eventually as God clearly tells those who take God's word as truth.

nm855 » Go back to Revelation 13:8 and 17:8 and see that those who worshiped the beast were not in the book, for as we have shown above only those in the church of the first-born (Christians) are in the book of life now. Thus, those who worship the beast will, after the day of judgment, be put into the book.

nm856 » In Revelation 21:27, after describing the New Jerusalem it reads: "and there shall in no way enter into it any thing that defiles, neither works abomination, or a lie: but they which are written in the Lamb's book of life." So we see that no one can enter New Jerusalem except those written in the book of life (see "New Jerusalem Paper" [NM 18]). One must remember here, that all are under sin (Rom 3:9) and all have sinned (1John 1:8) except Christ (Heb 4:15). Thus, those who are written into the book of life have or will die to sin (Rom 6:10). The Christians are to die to sin through Spiritual baptism. The others will have died to sin by the time the millennium is through, then they too will be added to the book of life.

nm857 » One last proof that real children of God are those now written in the book of life is in Daniel 12:1. Here it says that "at that time your people shall be delivered, everyone that shall be found written in the book [of life] ... " The time setting of this verse is at Jesus Christ the Messiah's return.

nm858 » This book of life is the very "book of remembrance" (Mal 3:16-17).

NM 19: Reason Why

Why is there Evil?
Why know Evil?
Law of Knowledge
The Blind
God Created Evil?
Two Forces
Law of Knowledge Table

NM19 Abstract

*Why is there evil? If God is all powerful, if God is good and if he
created all things, then why is there evil? Could there be a reason for
evil? Yes, there is a reason for evil and it has something to do with the law
of knowledge. In fact, there cannot be good without evil. Good and evil
are comparative qualities that need each other in order for us to know
either quality.*

Why is there Evil?

nm859 » Why is there evil in this life or age? Why is the world the
way it is? Why is there disease? Why do children get sick? Why are
there natural catastrophes? Why is there war? Why is there death?
Why is there hunger? Why this world? Why the confusion and tears?
Why has God "allowed" evil? Or, to be more blunt, since the most
powerful being created the all, why has the Power, why has the God
(YHWH) created evil?: "forming light and creating darkness, making
peace and creating evil; I, the LORD [YHWH], do all these things" (Isa 45:7,
see Hebrew text). In the book many call God's book, the Bible, it says that
God created evil. The original text (Hebrew) says this, not some
translation of the text.

nm860 » "And the LORD said, Behold, the man is become as one *from*
us, to know good and evil" (Gen 3:22, see Hebrew; see Greek also). This
comment was made right after mankind had broken God's first
commandment by the influence of the serpent (see The "Old Mind" paper
[NM 20-22] for more details). Thus scripture says that man was getting to
know good and evil from the plurality ("us") of God (LORD or YHWH).

From the "us" of God man is learning good <u>and</u> evil. There was/is a plurality to God (See the *God Papers*).

nm861 » In the middle of the garden of Eden was "the tree of KNOWLEDGE of good and evil" (Gen 2:17). It was a tree of good and evil, not just a tree of good or not just a tree of evil. It was not just an ordinary tree, but a tree of *knowledge*. After mankind took from the forbidden fruit from the tree of knowledge of good and evil, God said man was getting to KNOW good and evil (Gen 3:22). God then took away the tree of life and placed the cherubs to guard the way to the tree of life (Gen 3:23-24). The Hebrew word translated "*from* us" in Genesis 3:22 can also be translated "*out of* us" or even "*of* us" as it is translated in most English Bibles. Because of Adam and Eve's behavior mankind did at this time go "out of" the God, but also, since the God knows all, including good and evil, then mankind was becoming like ONE *of* the God (of the "us" [His hidden plurality]) by learning good and evil. "One" here can be translated "whole" since in history the word one was more likely to mean "whole" or "unity" rather than just the number one (See the *God Papers* under "One Yehowah"). Consequently, as events manifested, man was mostly left under the influence of the evil spirit of Satan, who was symbolized by the serpent of Genesis (see "Old Mind" paper [NM 20-22]). In the New Testament Paul said we were and are under the influence of the devil/Satan/evil powers and so forth (Eph 6:12).

nm862 » In my studies it has become obvious to me that the one basic reason that mankind was left under the influence of Satan was to learn good *and* evil. To learn, not just good, not just evil, but good and evil. But why is God allowing this evil age to go on until the appointed time? (Mat 24:3 & Acts 1:6-7) Maybe God is evil or partly evil and wants us to suffer under evil? Or is God too weak and can't stop the evil or confusion of our existence? Why doesn't the God of love, the all powerful ONE, stop the evil and the general confusion of the present age? Maybe, just maybe there is a logical and reasonable reason?

nm863 » If you read the *God Papers* you will see the scriptures that indicate that the true God is ALL MIGHTY. Thus, He has the power to stop the evil, if that is what He wishes. But God has allowed this kind of world because He knows man *must* suffer or live in an age of confusion and unhappiness in order to be happy. Does this statement shock you? What are we saying? Man must suffer. As we will show, a purpose of creation is for man to develop the cognition of good *and* evil. But the reason we are learning good *and* evil is that we cannot truly learn good without also learning evil. For us to even understand what is good, we must know evil. Further, we must all learn evil by living it, for experience is the best teacher. Scripture and the idea and definition of God tells us that God is all powerful and thus could have created a non-changeable paradise-like-environment at first with each human being physically perfect and unable to die. But God did not do this because he understood that man must first suffer in order to be happy. God cut off the tree of life from mankind in order to allow billions of people to learn good *and* evil. Is is very important so do read on.

Why Know Evil

nm864 » Why is it important to know good *and* evil? Why know evil? Why live evil to know it? The main difference between a man and any other animal is his higher power to reason and know. So far, it is true he has misused this power, but, nevertheless, greater knowledge is what makes man greater than most other creatures of God.

nm865 » But why know evil at all? Why not just know good? Why do we need to know evil? Before we answer this we must know how one knows evil.

nm866 » ***Experience Teaches***. In order to know something, to truly know something, you must live it. It takes experience with evil to know evil. Our very life today teaches us that. How can you know pain if you had never felt it? How can anyone explain pain to you if you have never felt pain? Just stop and think for a moment. Try to imagine that you have never felt pain. If someone showed you someone else in pain, would you know what it was to be in pain, if you had never *felt* it? As you looked, you would see this person with an expression on his face like he was in pain. But how can you know pain through the face of a person in pain? Remember you have never *felt* pain. Any outward sign of a person in pain is just that, a sign or symbol of pain. Just because you see someone in pain, it does not mean you *know* pain for remember you have never *felt* pain, or *experienced* pain. You must *feel* pain to know it.

nm867 » The same applies with evil. To truly know evil, one must live it. How would you explain misery to one who never felt or lived misery? How would you explain the pain of losing a loved one to someone who has never felt such a feeling? Now on this latter example, you could compare it with some other form of misery or pain. But, what if the person who you were trying to explain this grief to, had never felt any grief, misery, or pain? You could never compare your grief of losing a loved one with anything that would allow that person to know of your misery. To obtain the knowledge of knowing evil, then, you must *live* it and *feel* it. To obtain the characteristic of knowing evil we must live in such a world as we now live in.

Know Evil To Know Good?

nm868 » But this is only a part of the overall picture. We must know evil to know good! Evil and good are inseparable! We must suffer evil to know good. Again, does that shock you? But why should it? Every day we live, we prove the principle that one cannot know good without real knowledge of evil. Every day that we obtain knowledge, we live this principle, and prove this principle. One cannot know good unless one know evil. You cannot separate the knowledge of good and evil. The very Law of Knowledge tells us that. What is that law?

Law of Knowledge

nm869 » **Basic Definition of the Law of Knowledge can be stated as:**
*Knowledge of **A** is equal to and dependent on the knowledge of **non-A**.*
  Where **A** can be any particular object, technique or belief;
  n**on-A** is anything but that particular object, technique or belief.
It follows —
  The depth of one's knowledge of **A** (and it truthfulness) is contingent upon the depth of one's knowledge of **non-A**; particularly, in the case of opposite qualities (light and darkness), you must know both qualities to know either; you must compare each with the other to know either.
In other words —
- To know **A** you must also know something to everything about **non-A**;
- The knowledge of **A** presupposes at least some knowledge of **non-A**;
- In order to know **A** you must compare **A** with **non-A**;
- the knowledge of **A** (and its truthfulness) is proportional to the knowledge of **non-A**.

nm870 » **True Knowledge through the law of knowledge:**
The continuum from incorrect knowledge —> to absolute true knowledge
- The less one knows about **non-A**, the less one knows about the truthfulness of **A** and the more likely one's knowledge is incorrect.
- The more one knows about **non-A**, the more certain one knows the truthfulness of **A**.

- If one knows all that is **non-A**, one knows absolutely the truthfulness of **A**.

    (An omniscient being would know the full truth; less than omniscient beings would not know the full truth.)

nm871 » In explaining the Law of Knowledge, we will first deal with how one obtains knowledge of opposite qualities. Next we will explain in a more general manner or it most broadest sense how one obtains knowledge of anything.

Knowledge of Opposite Qualities

Blind: Light & Darkness

nm872 » To amplify on this law we will use the example of a blind person. Try to empathize with a person that was totally blind from birth. Try to put yourself in such a person's mind. Close your eyes and imagine yourself as being blind. Now such a person has never seen light. Light is the quality that allows one's eyes to see objects. Without light no one would see even if they had perfect eyes. Light is the quality that the totally blind person cannot perceive or comprehend.

nm873 » If you had never seen light, how would someone explain light to you? What choice adjectives would describe light to someone who has never seen light? To explain anything to someone who has never seen it, you have to use comparison, and say it is like this or like that. But there is no comparative quality in the universe that compares with light. It would be impossible for someone to explain light to you, let alone sight, if you had never seen light.

Knowledge of Each Presupposes Knowledge of Both

nm874 » Yet at the same time one truly does not know what *darkness* is until one has seen light. The very definition of dark is: "without light." Darkness means without light as light means "without darkness." Each definition is dependent on its opposite quality. A definition of something is a statement of the knowledge of that thing. To know light or darkness by their very definition presupposes knowledge of each other. A blind person in order to know what darkness is, would have to see light. He knows darkness only if he sees light, for it is only then that he will understand what people were talking about when they spoke of darkness. The only reason that you can close your eyes, and call the result darkness, is because you have *seen* light. One cannot know darkness or light unless one has seen both and compared both qualities with each other.

nm875 » Thus, specifically in the case of opposite qualities, your knowledge of darkness ("A") is dependent upon your knowledge of light (opposite-"A"), and vice versa. Because they are opposite qualities, you must know both to know either quality, but in order to know either quality, you must compare each with the other.

nm876 » **Furthermore**, remembering that a blind person is blind because he cannot see light, it also follows that if there was only white light we would also be blind because we would not see or recognize any object, since in order to see anything, we need different shades of light and darkness, or more correctly since most of us see in color, in order to see anything, we need different shades of light and darkness and different hues of color.

Sound And Silence

nm877 » The same applies for sound and silence. If you had never heard sound, how would you know what silence was like? Sound and silence are opposite qualities as light and darkness are opposite qualities. You must know both to know either, and you must compare each with the other to know either. Since these two qualities are interrelated, one has to know both to know one. The very basic definition of sound ("without silence") and silence ("without sound") need the opposite quality to define it. To know sound or silence by their very basic definition presupposes knowledge of each other.

Hot and Cold

nm878 » The same can be said about hot and cold. "Hot" and "cold" are relative opposite qualities. One knows something is cold only so far as he has something hot to compare it with. You can place your hand into a container of water that is 90 degrees and it will feel warm to you. But if you place your hand into a container that is 110 degrees and keep it there for a while, and then place it again into the container of water of 90 degrees, the 90 degree water will then feel cool while before it felt warm. Your knowledge of hot or cold is obtained through contrast and comparison of both qualities. Knowledge of hot or cold presupposes knowledge of the other quality.

Life and Death

nm879 » Further, one does not know what life is until he has seen death. To have knowledge of life you must have knowledge of death. One is very aware of life only if one has seen or become aware of death.

nm880 » Adam and Eve didn't know death and that is one reason why they chose the tree of good and evil in the garden of Eden. Adam had never seen or felt the pain of losing a loved one. All he saw around him was life. This is very difficult for us to perceive today, for all around us are the living, the sick and dying as well as our remembrance of dead friends and relatives. Because of this we know a lot more about life and death than Adam and Eve. It is difficult for us to put ourselves into Adam's position.

Right and Left & More Examples

nm881 » The right side has no meaning unless there be a left side. You don't know what the meaning of right is until you know about left; you don't know what left is until you know what about right. You need knowledge about both to know either. You don't know something is "high" unless you know there is something "lower." You don't know something is "low" unless you know something is "higher." You don't know a "plus" quality until you know its "minus" quality. You don't know a "minus" quality unless you know its "plus" quality. You don't know light if you don't know darkness. But you can know light if you know darkness. You don't know or realize harmony, if you have never known confusion. Think on what is being said. If you had always lived in an environment where there was no confusion, where there was harmony, would you realize the goodness of that harmonic environment? Would harmony mean anything to you in such a harmonic environment? Can you really *appreciate* harmony if you have never lived in confusion?

nm882 » If you had good vision for forty years, and then lost your sight, you would truly know the value of sight, as does a blind person who miraculously gains his sight. But how does someone, after he loses his sight, come to appreciate the sight he once had?

Appreciation

nm883 » What does it mean to appreciate something? Webster's Dictionary says that to appreciate something one must: "recognize it gratefully; estimate its worth; estimate it rightly; be fully aware of it; and notice it with discrimination." Thus, when one comes to appreciate something (especially if it is good), one in fact comes to know that thing. To appreciate something is to really know it; to know something is to appreciate it.

nm884 » When one loses a loved one, one by the loss of the loved one knows the worth of the loved one. The same with good. One comes to know the worth of good only after he has lived in evil.

nm885 » How can we know joy, until we have lived sorrow? How can you really become happy unless you have been sad. How can we know good until we know evil? Opposite qualities need to be compared to each other to know either.

nm886 » The Law of Knowledge not only explains knowledge of opposite qualities, but also knowledge of everything capable of being known. The follow is a short explanation of how we learn, not only about opposite qualities, but about everything.

The General Law of Knowledge

How Children Learn

nm887 » One way to understand the Law of Knowledge is to understand how a child learns. Children's simple generalizations reflect lack of differentiation. That is, a child's wrong generalization about *A* (cow) reflects lack of knowledge of the difference between a cow and all that is not a cow (*non-A*) such as other four legged animals.

nm888 » A child when he is first learning about four legged animals sometimes may mix up a cow and a horse, or a cow and a deer, or even a cow and a dog. This is because the child does not know what a cow is not. When parents first begin telling their child what a cow is, they point to a cow and say, "that is a cow." The child with the aid of other knowledge in his memory and his senses "sees" this living animal with four legs. Depending on how many other four legged animals are pointed out to him, he may mix the cow up with any or all other four legged animals.

nm889 » After a cow is pointed out to him he may call a horse a cow, after all, to the child a horse is a four legged living animal (not a two legged animal or a toy animal or stuffed animal) just like the one pointed out earlier by his parents. But the child is wrong. This four legged animal is a horse, not a cow. The child fails to differentiate between a cow and a horse. How does the parent correct the child? The parent says, "no, it is not a cow, it is a horse." The parent is telling the child what a cow is not. The parent by telling the child what is not a cow is helping the child to learn what is a cow. Normally, after the child learns that a horse is not a cow, he doesn't call a horse a cow again. But the child may call a deer or other four legged animals a cow. When the child does this he is again corrected, "no, it is not a cow, it is a deer." The child has learned something else is not a cow (*A*); he has learned one more of the *non-A's* (all else besides cows). The more the child learns about other four legged animals not being cows, the better he is able to understand what a cow is. A cow is a four legged animal of a certain size (a cow is not a dog because for one thing a cow is bigger than a dog, etc.), but it is not any other four legged animal: it is not a dog, it is not a horse, it is not a deer, it is not an elephant, it is not a bear, etc.

nm890 » But further the child from other knowledge knows a living cow is not a mountain, it is not dead (not a dead toy, not a dead stuffed animal, etc.), it is not a rock, it is not the sky, it is not a two legged animal, it is not an ant, it is not a fish, it is not fog, it is not a color, it is not a quality like "good," it is not a plant, it is not water, etc. The child knows more what a cow is, by the more he knows what a cow is not. **Thus, the knowledge of a cow (*A*) is dependent on the knowledge of what a cow is not (*non-A*); or the child knows more about what is a cow (*A*), by the more he knows what is a cow is not (*non-A*).**

The Color Green

nm891 » Let's take another example, the color **green**. The more we know what the color green is *not* the more we know the uniqueness of the color green. The only way to point green out is to show what green is *not*. Since most of us know what the color green is (because we know what green is not), we will again try to understand how a child learns about the color green.

GREEN a color is "A"

nm892 » **The knowledge of GREEN (A) is dependent upon the knowledge of all that is not green (non-A).**

- First "green" is a subdivision of color. Before a child can learn what the color "green" is, he must know what is color. In order for a child to understand "color" his parents tell him, "that thing is the *color* red, that thing is the *color* blue, that thing is the *color* orange, that thing is the *color* green, that thing is the *color* ...." Along the line of learning "color" the child comes to understand (through comparison) what "color" is *not*: the color blue on a wall is not the wall, it is not the *material* that makes up the wall such as wall board, or wood studs, or nails, etc., but the quality on the wall that we call "color" is the *color* of the wall. A child learns what color is by understanding what color is not. So before a parent can make a child understand what the "color" green is, the child has to understand what "color" is, by understanding what "color" is not.

Now assuming that the child knows what "color" is we will continue:

- We know GREEN by knowing what is *not* green (non-A). Thus the child comes to know GREEN by knowing what is not green.

What the color green is not (non-A)

nm893 » **Green Is Not:**

- *More generally green is not*: a tree, a bush, a rock, an animal, a fish, a man, the universe, the sun, the moon, our parents, a car, a road, atoms, space, form or shape, relative position in space, time, a dimension, or any other thing or quality except for a quality we call "color."

- *More specifically green is not*: red, blue, orange, purple, or any other color, but the color we call green.

To summarize, *GREEN* is A; *GREEN* is not non-A. We know *GREEN* (A) because we know what *GREEN* is not (it is not non-A).

God Has Created Evil? ...

nm894 » Considering the above it is not difficult to see why God (YHWH) has *created* evil (Isa 45:7): it is so we can know good, to know good's worth, to appreciate good, and to enjoy good. The reason we must suffer the effects of evil is so we can know, to truly know good. To know what is good we must have something to compare good with. God through his wisdom has given mankind a time for good and a time for evil (Eccl 3:1-8), so as to know each. Thus in this way mankind comes to realize the value of good and harmony. God has given us joy to balance against adversity, so as to know joy (Eccl 7:14). To be able to know goodness, one must know evil: "For in much wisdom is much grief: and he that increases knowledge increases sorrow" (Eccl 1:18); "Sorrow is better than laughter: for by the sadness of the face the heart is made to be good" (Eccl 7:3).

Should We Then Seek Evil?

nm895 » Considering the above, then does this mean we should seek evil? No! Once we come to realize how bad evil is, then evil has served its purpose as the comparative quality to good. In good is where the happiness lives, not in evil. We in this age are mainly learning more about evil than good. There are moments of joy and happiness in this world which allow us to partially perceive just how bad evil is, and at the same time allow us to perceive how precious good is.

New Mind And True Knowledge

nm896 » As we are trying to communicate in this book, the best way to truly perceive good is only with God's Spirit – the New Mind. Through God's Spirit man begins to renew his knowledge and mind to the ways of good (Col 3:10; Rom 12:2). Before man receives God's Spirit, man is like a blind man: he lives in darkness, yet comprehends it not, for the blind do not know light. "And the light shines in the darkness; and the darkness comprehended it not" (John 1:5). Why? Because this world is Spiritually blind, this world or this age cannot perceive their sad state of affairs. This age and most people in it, do not and cannot know how bad this age really is until they receive God's Spirit – the New Mind, which is the Spirit of truth (John 14:17). This age only partially perceives how bad this age is, and this only because there is some joy in this age to compare with the average state of affairs. But those who have received God's Spirit know ever so much more just how bad this age is (Rev 12:11).

Two Forces

nm897 » Scripture project to us that there are two spiritual forces or mental forces in the world today: God's and Satan's. God's Spirit is "A" and Satan's is contrary or opposite to "A". Your knowledge of God ("A") is dependent upon your knowledge of Satan (opposite-"A"); To know God ("A") you must compare Him with Satan (opposite-"A"). Mankind will only have the knowledge of good and evil after they live under the bondage of Satan's rule and under the harmony of God's rule. That is why all who are eventually born of God will and **must** live under Satan's spiritual law of confusion *and* under God's Spiritual law of harmony.

nm898 » All must suffer evil. So that "they that sow in tears shall reap in joy" (Psa 126:5). The tears come first for man, the joy is the dessert of the creation. We learn unhappiness or the knowledge of sin through Satan's way. And it is through this knowledge of sin that we are able to truly know good, for then we have something to compare with God's way and his law of harmony. It is through God's Spirit and His law in our minds that we see the good (the light). And it is because of our former blindness (Spiritually speaking) concerning the good (light) that we are able to comprehend the worthiness of the good. Mankind is like a blind person who has lived in darkness (Satan's way) yet really didn't know how bad it was until he gained (or will gain) his sight (through God's Spirit) and was made able to comprehend the light (good), then all became understandable to him.

Two Forces Help Us to Distinguish and Know

nm899 » "Except they give a distinction in the sounds, how shall it be known what is piped or harped?" (1 Cor 14:7) Except that there be a period of time to distinguish between good and evil, how else would mankind learn or understand what is good?

nm900 » Since the knowledge of God depends upon the knowledge of Satan, then man must have a period under the way of Satan and a period under the way of God in order to understand the Goodness and worth of God and His way. "A time to love and a time to hate; a time of war and a time of peace" (Eccl 3:8). "Better is the end of a thing than the beginning thereof" (Eccl 7:8).

nm901 » **Mankind in School.** One could say that mankind is going through a learning process. Mankind is in school. Man is going through a process of discriminating between plus and minus qualities. Mankind is learning to discriminate between good and evil, by living each. Man is living each for it is impossible to teach it through words. How can you know pain through words? How can you teach a blind person what light is by words? No, man must *feel* pain to know pain, and the blind must *see* light to know light. But further, the blind must see light to know darkness, for our very definition of light ("without darkness") and our basic definition of darkness ("without light") projects to us that opposite qualities need each other to *know* either one of the qualities. A totally blind person even though he lives in darkness, does not know darkness until he sees light. We only know darkness because we have seen light. To know what is darkness one must have something to compare it with.

nm902 » We know something is "up" only because we see something below it in position. If everything were of the same height, there would be no "up" or "down."

nm903 » The same principle holds true for pain and non-pain, or sound and silence, or for that matter clean air and smog. But, what is important to us in this paper is that this principle holds true for good and for evil. If you only had lived in an environment of harmony, how would you know it was a good environment? You would have nothing to compare it with. You would be like a person who lived all his life at the top of a hundred story building in a room without any window or way to go downstairs. Even though you have 99 levels below you, you do not know you are at the top, for you do not know there is a down.

Law of Knowledge

(Pertaining to Opposite Qualities)

Both sides complement the other and give meaning to each other;
you must know both qualities to know either: you must compare each
with the other to know either

One Side	Opposite Side
love	hate
light	darkness
right	left
front	back
up	down
affection	contempt
good	evil
peace	war
kind	unkind
forgiving	unforgiving
thankful	unthankful
reconciliatory	revengeful
lawful	lawless
hope	hopeless
truthful	liar
fairness (impartial)	unfairness (partiality)
temperance	overindulgence
honorable	dishonorable
unpretentious	pretentious
elegant	crude
patient	impatient
harmony	disharmony
sympathetic	unsympathetic

NM 20: Other-Mind

NM20 Abstract

We all have positive thoughts, but are there negative flash thoughts that pop into people's minds? Why do people sometimes have inappropriate or strange thoughts that seem to just pop into their minds? Why does the mind have these unwanted/intrusive thoughts? Are people in control of all their thoughts? If not, why not?

White Bear and Unwanted Thoughts

nm904 » To start, let me introduce Richard Restak. Restak maintains a private medical practice in neurology and neuropsychiatry in Washington, D.C. where he is also a Clinical Professor of Neurology at George Washington Hospital University School of Medicine and Health. He has to date [2011] written 18 books on various aspects of the human brain; two were on The New York Times Best Sellers List. His first bestseller, *The Brain* (1984), was also the first companion book he wrote for a PBS series. *The Mind* (1988) was his second bestseller.

nm905 » This same Richard Restak wrote a review of Daniel M. Wegner's book about unwanted thoughts. Wegner is a professor of Psychology at Harvard University.[1] In this article Restak wrote:

> As a child, the Russian novelist Fyodor Dostoyevski "once challenged his younger brother to remain standing in a corner until he could stop thinking of a white bear. In this homespun experiment, the child learned something important about the human mind: We do not so much control our thoughts as we are controlled by thoughts that we don't want to think.
>
> Indeed, just about all mental illnesses – obsessions, compulsions, depressions, phobias, anxiety reactions, post-traumatic stress disorders, self-control problems such as addiction and eating disorders, schizophrenia and other psychoses – along with just

---

[1] http://www.wjh.harvard.edu/%7Ewegner/backbio.htm

plain everyday emotional distress – are marked by problems in the area of mental control.

There is a paradox here, too; namely, the more effort that one expends not to think something, oftentimes the more difficult it is to expel it from our consciousness."

("Honey of an approach to problems of the mind," review by Richard Restak of the book: *White Bears and Other Unwanted Thoughts: Suppression, Obsession, and the Psychology of Mental Control*, by Daniel M. Wegner, found in *Washington Times*, July 17, 1989, p. E9)

As Restak said, "we do not so much control our thoughts as we are controlled by thoughts that we don't want to think." And "just about all mental illnesses" are marked with problems of mental control. And in context of Wegner's book, this lack of control is the lack of control of *unwanted* thoughts. There are many thoughts each day that flash into people's minds: only some are unwanted.

Lately there is evidence that some mental problems have something to do with biochemical imbalances, as in the case of depression. But this factor has nothing to do with specific individualized unwanted thoughts. Depression is a *feeling* that comes from a certain part of the brain, and is unlike the thought or idea of a white bear. The white bear in the mind of Dostoyevski's brother was a concept, not a feeling. Although depression can be initiated by unwanted thoughts (death of a loved one), depression can just as well be initiated by a biochemical imbalance. There is a difference. The thought of white bear came before Dostoyevski's brother's unwanted thoughts of the white bear; the depression of a biochemical nature comes from an imbalance in the brain first, then the feeling of depression occurs.

Yes, good and positive thoughts enter our minds, from time to time, all day; other times, not so positive thoughts enter our minds. Sometimes these thoughts are like an intermittent breeze: lingering for awhile, disappearing for awhile. But sometimes the thoughts are like a fire that burns in the brain and cannot be extinguished. Like a simmering fire the thoughts may burn every so slightly in the back of people's minds, or the thoughts may rage like a wild fire that incapacitates the individual.

Wegner writes in his book about unwanted thoughts:

Most people report having at least one thought that won't go away. In a study conducted early in this century [1922], one psychologist found that many of the students in his classes admitted to having "fixed ideas" that could not be eliminated.[3] In a San Antonio study, when 180 people were asked to write down an unwanted thought, almost every person had one or more to mention.[4] They reported that their thought was "distressing," and occurred from once a day to every few minutes. Similarly, researchers in England report that people have "normal" obsessions that parallel in several ways the "abnormal" obsessions individuals seek psychotherapy to eliminate.[5] The fact that most people report such thoughts may provide a bit of solace to those of us who think we're odd for worrying. But this fact also indicates that there is indeed a general human problem in the area of mental control.

Unwanted thoughts turn up in a variety of psychological disorders. Of course, they are in center stage when people suffer from obsessions (recurrent unwanted thoughts) or compulsions (recurrent unwanted actions). But having trouble with thoughts that won't go away is characteristic also in many cases of depression, phobic or anxiety reactions, posttraumatic stress disorders, self-control problems such as addictions and eating disorders, and even in psychotic reactions such as schizophrenia. It is not surprising that mental control is rare when people have very severe problems, because the extremes of mental disorder are almost defined in terms of control lapses. However, unwanted thoughts themselves do not define a particular form of psychological disorder. Rather, they occur at all points in the spectrum from normal to abnormal, cutting across different kinds of disorders rather than distinguishing them from one another. (pp. 6-7)

...

What thoughts do people express the desire to avoid? The contents of such a list will vary, of course, with the time and customs of the people, with their sex and age and habitat. In 1903 in France, for example, the renowned psychiatrist Pierre Janet reported t he obsessions of his patients in five major groups: sacrilegious thoughts, urges to commit crimes, shame about one's behavior, shame about one's body, and hypochondria.[21] These obsessions are thoughts that the people were thinking *too much*, and so qualify as very unwanted. Many of these topics are still favorites today....

(*White Bears and Other Unwanted Thoughts: Suppression, Obsession, and the Psychology of Mental Control*, pp 6-7, 20)

Robert L. Leahy, Ph.D., who is a Clinical Professor of Psychology at Weill-Cornell Medical School and Director of the American Institute for

Cognitive Therapy, writes about unwanted thoughts and says everyone has these crazy thoughts:

> Thinking about your thoughts
>
> Three rules are important.　　.
>
> 1. Everyone has crazy and disgusting thoughts
>
> 2. Thoughts are not the same thing as reality
>
> 3. Thought-suppression doesn't work.
>
> Research on people without anxiety disorders shows that almost 90% of them have "bizarre" thoughts---thoughts about contamination, harm, religious impropriety, losing control, sexual "perversion"---you name it, we all have thought about it before." ("Those Damn Unwanted Thoughts," *Psychology Today*, June 1, 2009)

Unwanted Thoughts Are Intrusive Thoughts

From a well documented article in the free web encyclopedia called *Wikipedia* we see that "unwanted thoughts" are called "intrusive thoughts":

> Intrusive thoughts are unwelcome involuntary thoughts, images, or unpleasant ideas that may become obsessions, are upsetting or distressing, and can be difficult to manage or eliminate.[1]
>
> ...
>
> According to Lee Baer (a specialist at the OCD clinic of Massachusetts General Hospital), intrusive thoughts, urges, and images are of inappropriate things at inappropriate times, usually falling into three categories: "inappropriate aggressive thoughts, inappropriate sexual thoughts, or blasphemous religious thoughts."
>
> ...
>
> Many people experience the type of bad or unwanted thoughts that people with more troubling intrusive thoughts have, but

most people are able to dismiss these thoughts.[1] For most people, intrusive thoughts are a "fleeting annoyance."[5] London psychologist Stanley Rachman presented a questionnaire to healthy college students and found that virtually all said they had these thoughts from time to time, including thoughts of sexual violence, sexual punishment, "unnatural" sex acts, painful sexual practices, blasphemous or obscene images, thoughts of harming elderly people or someone close to them, violence against animals or towards children, and impulsive or abusive outbursts or utterances.[6] Such bad thoughts are universal among humans, and have "almost certainly always been a part of the human condition".[7]

...

When intrusive thoughts occur with obsessive-compulsive disorder (OCD), patients are less able to ignore the unpleasant thoughts and may pay undue attention to them, causing the thoughts to become more frequent and distressing.[1] The thoughts may become obsessions which are paralyzing, severe, and constantly present, and can range from thoughts of violence or sex to religious blasphemy.[5]

...

The possibility that most patients suffering from intrusive thoughts will ever act on those thoughts is low. Patients who are experiencing intense guilt, anxiety, shame, and upset over these thoughts are different from those who actually act on them. The history of violent crime is dominated by those who feel no guilt or remorse; the very fact that someone is tormented by intrusive thoughts and has never acted on them before is an excellent predictor that they will not act upon the thoughts.

...

Inappropriate aggressive thoughts

Intrusive thoughts may involve violent obsessions about hurting others or themselves.[16] They can include such thoughts as harming an innocent child, jumping from a bridge, mountain or the top of a tall building, urges to jump in front of a train or automobile, and urges to push another in front of a train or automobile.[4] Rachman's survey of healthy college students found that virtually all of them had intrusive thoughts from time to time, including:[6]

1. Causing harm to elderly people

2. Imagining or wishing harm upon someone close to one's self

3. Impulses to violently attack, hit, harm or kill a person, small child, or animal

4. Impulses to shout at or abuse someone, or attack and violently punish someone, or say something rude, inappropriate, nasty or violent to someone.

These thoughts are part of being human, and need not ruin the quality of life.[17] Treatment is available when the thoughts are associated with OCD and become persistent, severe, or distressing.

...

Inappropriate sexual thoughts

Sexual obsessions involve intrusive thoughts or images of "kissing, touching, fondling, oral sex, anal sex, intercourse, and rape" with "strangers, acquaintances, parents, children, family members, friends, coworkers, animals and religious figures", involving "heterosexual or homosexual content" with persons of any age.[18]

Like other unwanted intrusive thoughts or images, everyone has some inappropriate sexual thoughts at times, but people with OCD may attach significance to the unwanted sexual thoughts, generating anxiety and distress. The doubt that accompanies OCD leads to uncertainty regarding whether one might act on the intrusive thoughts, resulting in self-criticism or loathing.[18]

One of the more common sexual intrusive thoughts occurs when an obsessive person doubts his or her sexual identity. As in the case of most sexual obsessions, sufferers may feel shame and live in isolation, finding it hard to discuss their fears, doubts, and concerns about their sexual identity.[12]

...

Blasphemous religious thoughts

Blasphemous thoughts are a common component of OCD, documented throughout history; notable religious figures such as Martin Luther and St. Ignatius were known to be tormented by intrusive, blasphemous or religious thoughts and urges.[20] Martin Luther had urges to curse God and Jesus, and was obsessed with images of "the Devil's behind".[20][21] St. Ignatius had numerous obsessions, including the fear of stepping on pieces of straw forming a cross, fearing that it showed disrespect to Christ.[20][22] A study of 50 patients with a primary diagnosis of obsessive-compulsive disorder found that 40% had religious and blasphemous thoughts and doubts—a higher number than the 38% who had the obsessional thoughts related to dirt and contamination more commonly associated with OCD.[23] One study suggests that content of intrusive thoughts may vary depending on culture, and that blasphemous thoughts may be more common in men than in women.[24]

According to Fred Penzel, a New York psychologist, some common religious obsessions and intrusive thoughts are:[13]

1. sexual thoughts about God, saints, and religious figures such as Mary

2. bad thoughts or images during prayer or meditation

3. thoughts of being possessed

4. fears of sinning or breaking a religious law or performing a ritual incorrectly

5. fears of omitting prayers or reciting them incorrectly

6. repetitive and intrusive blasphemous thoughts

7. urges or impulses to say blasphemous words or commit blasphemous acts during religious services.

["Intrusive Thoughts," *Wikipedia*, Febrary 9, 2011]

Thoughts, Sometimes Negative

nm906 » Why do people sometimes get recurring thoughts which they can't seem to control? Why are people unreasonably afraid of some things? Why do we sometimes, in bitter arguments, say offensive things that we do not really mean? Why do people sometimes unreasonably criticize other people? If we do say something good about a person we may, in some situations, add something negative. Our thoughts are sometimes negative. And sadly from these negative thoughts come the confusion and misbehavior that makes for unhappiness. These thoughts, flash into people's minds in a split second, and some of them stay in our minds as unwanted thoughts because of the negative or persistent aspect of them. They are unwanted because of the way they affect us.

Flash Thoughts, Positive or Negative

nm907 » These unwanted thoughts pop into people's mind in a flash, a split second, and therefore can be called "flash-thoughts." A *positive* flash-thought is like when a great idea or thought pops into one's mind. A *negative* unwanted flash-thought is a thought that not only irritates, but *may* in certain cases lead to or result in behavior that hurts or harms our self or someone else.

But why do people get these flash-thoughts or ones like them? Do our parents teach them to us? Does society teach them to us? And the question must be asked, if people are actually in control of their minds, why do they get these thoughts, or why can't they rid themselves of these thoughts? Why can't people just order their brains to stop these thoughts as they order their brains to move their arms or fingers? Are we in control of our negative thoughts? Not too many positive thoughts are unwanted, if any. Why the unwanted thoughts?

More Examples: Sexual Fantasies Thrusts into the Open

nm908 » Many of these flash-thoughts may be embarrassing if revealed and so people generally don't talk about them. For example, erotic sexual fantasies were seldom talked about openly in most societies. Yet these fantasies existed and manifested themselves in the underground, in houses of prostitution and in banned pornographic writings, pictures, drawing or paintings. Due to the liberalization of the Western cultures and even in some of the religions, we now see books and magazines published with accounts of these sexual fantasies (*Forum* magazine; Nancy Friday's *My Secret Garden: Women's Sexual Fantasies*, or her *Forbidden Flowers*, and her *Beyond My Control: Forbidden Fantasies*. etc). The table of contents in Nancy Friday's *Beyond My Control: Forbidden Fantasies* list fantasies that pertain to: domination, masturbation, incest, exhibitionism/ voyeurism, S&M, threesomes and so forth (found on Amazon's "Look Inside" feature). The readers of Nancy Friday's books did not even know other women had sexual fantasies. Her female reader's thought their sexual fantasies were a manifestation of something wrong with them because they had erotic sexual fantasies. In Friday's own words from her book:

> I loved original work [research] and always had sexual fantasies.
> As I've noted before, when I approached several eminent
> therapists and psychoanalysts and asked their opinion of my
> research, I was repeatedly told: 'Women do not have sexual
> fantasies. Men do.

According to Friday, after reading her books women felt liberated
from guilt knowing other women also had them in one form or
another:

> But "we don't have to act on the fantasies to feel this way
> [liberated]. Some, fully realized, would become nightmares. Nor
> share them with our partners" ("Author to Reader" in *Beyond My
> Control*).

Why would they be nightmares? The nature of these sexual
fantasies can sometimes be unusual and even perverse in a religious
sense, or in the sense of decorum or propriety. So where do these
sexual fantasies come from? Do we teach our children sexual
fantasies? Or do we learn of these fantasies through books? Some of
these women according to Friday never saw a pornographic magazine.
They came up with these thoughts even though some came from
sheltered or conservative religious cultures. So where did these
thoughts come from? Where do other thoughts come from that could
be called negative or twisted? Some if acted out would be destructive
and could land the person to jail. Where do these thoughts come from?

Children and "No"

nm909 » Children are innocent little creatures, right? But the
caretakers of them see that they can be at times cunning, selfish, lying,
aggressive, violent, and so forth. Some say this is because they learn
from their parents' behavior and their environment. This is true to a
certain extent, but it is not the true answer.

nm910 » When children are very young parents notice that
sometimes they are very interested in doing things they were told not
to do. The parents say "no" to the child, and the "no" makes the child
want to do it even more. Now think about this. Do we teach our
children to do what we want them not to do? Do we set them aside
each day and tell them, "now Johnny, every time I tell you not to do
something, you should do it anyway and take great pleasure in doing
what I have told you not to do"? Of course not, we never teach our
children to disobey. We teach them to obey us and we back it up with

various forms of discipline. Yet, they continue at times to disobey us, even after we discipline them, and they, to judge by their facial expressions, take pleasure in disobeying us. Where do they learn this misbehavior? Who teaches them? We are not talking about children with neurological disorders; we are talking about healthy normal children.

In Control?

nm911 » Are we in FULL control of our minds and consequently our behavior? The psychologists, psychiatrists, priests, ministers, rabbis and so forth know people are *not* in full control of their minds or behavior, and that is the reason for occupations: their patrons come to them for guidance and help. If anyone wishes to move any part of their body, let's say a hand, they merely command their mind to move their hand when and where they want it to move. Only those who are physically impaired or disabled can't control their physical actions. If we are in control of our bodies, why are we not in control of our thoughts and our behavior? Some say we are in full control of our mind. If everyone is in full control of their mind then mankind could easily rid themselves of all falsehood, all guilt, all negativity in all forms. It would be easy to mold our children and our society. But it is not easy, is it? There *is* something more to all this.

The Dark Side of Man, "Devil within us"

nm912 » In *The Washington Times*, June 22, 1989, p. F4, Dr. Richard M. Restak, a neurologist and neuropsychiatrist, an author of "The Brain" and "The Mind," reviewed a book by Ronald Markman and Dominick Bosco, *Alone with the Devil: Famous Cases of a Courtroom Psychiatrist*, and in the review he writes:

- "Most crimes – even grisly murders – are not committed by mentally ill people, but by people just like you and me." He quotes with approval a statement by Linda Kasabian, a member of the Charles Manson "family," found guilty of the Sharon Tate-LaBianca murders: "I believe that we all have a part of the Devil within us – it's just a matter of bringing it out." Dr. Markman admits, "We all do have a willingness – even an appetite – to kill within us. All it takes is the right combination of factors to raise it to the surface."

This may seem like an extreme statement. But Dr. Restak is not an extremist, but an informed neuropsychiatrist. From others we hear, "The devil made me do it" excuses. Others speak of the "dark" side of man. The religious speak of the spiritual dark side. Mark Twain wanted very much to write the whole truth about his life, but even

Mark Twain couldn't bring himself to write about *his* dark side as the introduction of Mark Twain's new autobiography manifests. He tried to put off his autobiography for 100 years so he could write about his dark side. He never could write the truth about this side of him. (see Introduction, *Autobiography of Mark Twain*, Vol 1, Pub.: 2010)

The Imp of the Mind and "Bad Thoughts"

From a review in Publishers Weekly of a review of Lee Baer book, *The Imp of the Mind: Exploring the Silent Epidemic of Obsessive Bad Thoughts.*

> Specializing in the diagnosis and treatment of obsessive-compulsive disorder, psychologist Baer (an associate professor at Harvard) turns the spotlight on a little-known [by the general public] but common form of obsession, "bad thoughts." According to Baer, these "intrusive" thoughts fall into a few basic types: violent, sexual and blasphemous words, and images of a religious nature. Borrowing from Edgar Allan Poe, Baer blames such mental torment on "the imp of the perverse," that little devil inhabiting all human minds, cross-culturally and across time, "who makes you think the most inappropriate thoughts at the most inappropriate times." For most people, the imp proves no more than a "fleeting annoyance" most of the time, but for Baer's patients, these impish thoughts create extreme fear, guilt and worry. Attempting to suppress them only makes them stronger, leading the afflicted to avoid places, people and situations that provoke them. A new mother who obsessively thinks about harming her infant, for example, may increasingly avoid daily caretaking activities. Tending to be perfectionist and "overly conscientious," these people are highly unlikely ever to act on their bad thoughts, Baer explains. [From Publishers Weekly Jan. 15, 2000]

Professor Lee Baer calls these intrusive thoughts, "the imp of the perverse." But since the 1970s I've been calling these thoughts, the thoughts of the "other-mind."

Other-Mind

nm913 » Considering the above information, other studies, my observation and others' observations, since the early 1970s:

> I have come to the conclusion that *there is something like another mind in our brain feeding thoughts to our brain, many times unwanted thoughts. I call this the "other-mind."*

The other-mind is what I call the phenomena of those unwanted and many times negative thoughts that seem to annoy peoples' minds. Scientists do not know *why* people have them or *how* people get these unwanted thoughts, just like they don't know *why* there is gravity or *how* gravity works: science can only *describe* and list the unwanted thoughts and describe gravity in words or through mathematics.

Granted that in certain cases neurological disabilities or chemical imbalances can cause or lead to problems pertaining to mind and thoughts, but still the question remains: why don't these disabilities and chemical imbalances cause *positive* mental thoughts?

Lost of Control

Even though I believe that everyone has the "other-mind" feeding everyone unwanted thoughts, most people do not carry out these intrusive thoughts because most have some control over their behavior. But some do lose control. We see it every day in our newspapers. One example appears on CNN's web site today:

> (CNN Feb. 12, 2011) -- An unemployed New Yorker fatally stabbed three people, slashed at least four others, hit and killed one man with a car and hijacked two vehicles before being wrestled to the ground early Saturday while trying to break into the cab of a subway car, polic said.

> Maksim Gelman, 23, was arrested aboard a north-bound train in Manhattan around 9 a.m. Saturday, 28 hours after he allegedly began a spree across three New York City boroughs, Police Commissioner Ray Kelly said.

> "It's so horrendous and bizarre," Kelly told reporters Saturday afternoon. "We have no reason that we can give you as to why he did this."

When we come to understand that the unwanted thoughts of the "other-mind" cannot harm us, unless we allow it, and that by knowing that these thoughts do not radiate from our very selves, the shame and guilt can be mitigated. Also others with these unwanted thoughts can be understood and empathized with in a much more appropriate, if not tolerate manner.

NM 21: "Other-Mind" – Its Beginning

Spirit inside Mankind

Genesis: Chapters Two & Three

Serpent Tests Eve

Law and Sin

Other-Mind: Spirit & Power of Evil

Man's Heart & Other Mind

What is and Why is there the Phenomenon of the Other-mind?

nm914 » There is evidence through scripture and through human experience that there are supernatural phenomena. If the answer to the puzzlement of the other-mind comes from the supernatural, then science will not and cannot find the answer. Science has to do with nature, not the supernatural. If there are supernatural phenomena, if there is a God, then science, by its very definition, cannot find the answer.

nm915 » Through study I believe that there are supernatural phenomena and that there is a God being, who created the universe and who put some knowledge about himself into a text called the Holy Bible. Some of our other papers describe in detail more about this God Being and about the great debate of the genesis of the universe.

nm916 » From scripture, we believe that the *other-mind* is not physical; it is spiritual. That is, the *other-mind* is a mental phenomenon that does not belong to our physical body, but is an invisible (thus spiritual) power *in* our minds. Something that is spiritual is something that is not easily detectable by sight, touch, smell, or by our other senses. Spirit is analogous to air: you cannot see air but we see the effect of its wind; spirit is invisible but we see the effects on mankind's behavior. The spiritual is detectable mentally by many. Some of you believe in the spiritual. If you think of yourself as Christian, you believe in evil spirits and good spirits or angels. Some of you interested in the occult believe in the spiritual dimension also, although your perception of the spiritual is not like the Christian perception. The New Testament of the Bible speaks of demons doing harm to people. The Old Testament speaks of lying spirits. Some of you from other religions or backgrounds also believe in the spiritual or invisible world. Almost all peoples in history have had beliefs about the spiritual world. Even those who do not believe in the spiritual believe nevertheless in invisible forces that they call by such names as gravity, black holes, protons, etc. In the psyche of man there is knowledge of a spiritual dimension which is evil and affects mankind in various ways. So what does the Bible have to say about the subject of unwanted thoughts?

nm917 » Genesis is the first book of the Bible. In this first book is the Biblical story of the beginning of the universe ("heavens and earth") and the beginning of mankind. There were seven days of creation. On the sixth day of creation "God created man in his image, in the image of God created he him; male and female created he them" (Gen 1:27; see *God Papers* for information on the "Image of God").

Spirit Inside Mankind

nm918 » An amplification on the creation of mankind is mentioned in chapter 2 of Genesis. Here it tells us God created man out of the dust of the earth on the sixth day. The word translated as Adam or man is a Hebrew word meaning "to be red or reddish."

> "And Jehovah God [LORD God] formed the man, dust from the ground, and *breathed* into his nostrils (the) *breath* of life." [Gen 2:7]

Now notice that Jehovah "breathed" into man the "breath" of life. In the English version of the Old Testament the word "breath" is translated from either the Hebrew word *neshamah* or *ruah*. These words differ slightly in meaning, both signifying sometimes "wind" then sometimes "breath." The word translated into "breath" in Genesis 2:7 is the Hebrew word *neshamah*.

nm919 » Both Hebrew words, *neshamah* and *ruah*, are translated as "spirit" in various places in the English translations of the Bible. And in the book of John in the New Testament, Jesus Christ tries to explain spirit to some: "the wind blows where it wishes, and you hear the sound of it, but you do not know from where it comes and where it goes" (John 3:8). In other translations it has for John 3:8, the "spirit breathes" instead of the "wind blows." This is so because in the Greek New Testament the Greek word translated in English Bibles as "wind" or "spirit" is the same word. Thus in the Old Testament and the New Testament "wind" and "spirit" are interchangeable words. And Jesus

Christ tries to explain spirit by comparing it to the wind that blows. And in John 20:22 it reads:

- "and having said this he [Jesus] breathed on them and said to them, receive the Holy Spirit."

Notice the similarity between Jesus Christ breathing into his followers, which signifies them receiving the Holy Spirit, and Jehovah in Genesis breathing into man, which signifies them receiving the breath or spirit of life. We thus take Genesis 2:7 as indicating a dual sense. In one sense, the physical sense, Jehovah breathed into man the literal breath or air of life and man became a breathing and living life. In the second sense, the spiritual sense, Jehovah was putting a spirit into man after he created man. What spirit was put into man at that time? And what is meant by spirit? Also see information in NM 22.

Angels Are Spiritual Messengers

nm920 » Spirits and angels are connected because angels are spirits (Heb 1:7). And angels are messengers because the word "angel" is translated from a Hebrew word in the Old Testament and a Greek word in the New Testament which means messenger, or one who is sent. Not only do we know that angels are messengers by the meaning of the word, but also because of their activities in the Bible. Angels are spiritual beings sent to do the will of the God. They affect people and nations by putting thoughts into people's minds. The thoughts of confusion are administered by the angels of evil, or the other-minds, or shall we say the demons. (Do not jump to conclusions yet, do read on.) I do not care to use the word evil or demon because of the connotations these words create in some people's minds. But what I wish to communicate here is that the other-mind that works in each of us is a spiritual being or angel (messenger) who puts negative flash-thoughts into our minds, sometimes very subtle thoughts. An evil angel is a messenger of evil; he brings base thoughts to our brains. There are now some good angels or messengers who do bring good thoughts into some people's minds in this age, but for the most part most people in this age only have the other-mind inside their mind. This is the reason the present age is an evil age. Not only do we have to fight a hostile environment, we also must fight the negative thoughts from the other-mind.

nm921 » Now to answer the question above which was, "what spirit was put into man?" At the beginning of creation a spirit was put into the mind of man by Jehovah. (The word, Jehovah, is translated "LORD" in some English Bibles.) By looking around us today and by knowing something about the other-mind as I explained it previously, we know that the spirit or angel (messenger) that was placed in mankind's mind at the beginning was the other-mind, that confused and evil mind. We can begin to see the Biblical proof of this by reading chapters two and three of the book of Genesis. Let's go over the scripture in those chapters.

Genesis: Chapters Two and Three

nm922 » In Genesis 2:16-17 it reads,

- "And Jehovah God commanded the man saying, You may freely eat of every tree in the garden; but of the tree of knowledge of good and evil you may not eat, for in the day that you eat of it, dying you shall die."

In the day that man ate from the tree of knowledge of good and evil he would die according to God. Now next God created out of man a woman (in the beginning God created the man first before He created the woman) for God said that it wasn't good for man to be alone (Gen. 2:18-22). After God brought woman to man, the man said,

- "This now at last is bone from my bone, and flesh from my flesh. For this it shall be called Woman, because this has been taken out of man."

Then the story continues,

- "Therefore a man shall leave his father and his mother and shall cleave to his wife, and they shall become one flesh. And they were both naked, the man and his wife, and they were not ashamed."

Thus we see that they weren't ashamed, they had no shame even though they were naked. But next in chapter three of Genesis something happens.

First Lie

nm923 » In chapter three of Genesis it speaks of the "serpent" who deceived mankind into taking fruit from the "tree of knowledge of good and evil." Now in the book of Revelation (12:9) we see that this "serpent" is none other than the one called the Devil and Satan. He was the father of lies (John 8:44). We also see that in the Biblical rendition on this serpent in Genesis that this serpent spoke to Eve, the wife of Adam. Today we do not see any serpents or snakes talking to women. Because of such stories in the Bible some have come to think of the Bible as a book of tales with little or no truth. By reading our papers and by reading some of the books we recommend which document the soundness of the Bible as a true document, you will find out for yourself that the Bible is not a book of tales but a book of facts and true history with Spiritual insight and prophecy of future events.

Figures of Speech

How Satan Spoke to Eve

nm924 » What does the Bible mean when it says that a serpent spoke to the woman? Are we to take this literally that this serpent in the beginning spoke to mankind? I do not believe so just as we are not to take it literally that trees clap their hands or that mountains and hills shall break forth into singing (Isa 55:12). The Bible uses all kinds of figures of speech. The Bible uses similes, "his eyes were as a flame of fire" (Rev 1:14). The Bible uses metaphors, "tell that fox" (Luke 13:32). The Bible uses metonyms, "if the house be worthy" (Mat 10:13). The Bible uses synecdoches, "all the world should be taxed" (Luke 2:1). The Bible uses personifications, "the earth mourns and fades away" (Isa 24:4). The Bible uses apostrophes, "O death, where is thy sting?" (1Cor. 15:55) The Bible uses hyperboles, "the light of the sun shall be sevenfold" (Isa 30:26). The Bible uses allegories, "this Hagar is Mount Sinai in Arabia."(Gal 4:24) The Bible uses parables, "behold, a sower went forth to sow" (Mat 13:3). The Bible also uses irony, riddles, and fables (1Kings 18:27; Rev 13:18; and Judges 9:8 ff & 2Kings 14:9 ff). So we can see that the Bible is rich in its use of language (see *Figures of Speech Used in the Bible*, by Bullinger). The serpent did not literally speak to Eve, only in a figurative way did the serpent speak to Eve. I will now show you this.

Serpent Tests Eve

nm925 » In chapter three we see a serpent that

- "was crafty above every animal of the field which Jehovah God had made. And he said to the woman, Is it true that God has said, You shall not eat from any tree of the garden? And the woman said to the serpent, We may eat of the fruit of the trees of the garden, but of the fruit of the tree which is in the middle of the garden, God has said, You shall not eat of it, nor shall you touch it, lest you die. And the serpent said to the woman, Dying you shall not die, for God knows that in the day you eat of it, your eyes shall be opened and you shall be as God, knowing good and evil. And the woman saw that the tree was good for food, and that it was pleasant to the eyes, and that the tree was desirable to make wise, and she took of its fruit and ate; and

she also gave to her husband with her, and he ate. And the eyes
of both of them were opened, and they knew that they were
naked, and they sewed leaves of the fig-tree and made girdles
for themselves. And they heard the sound of Jehovah God
walking up and down in the garden at the breeze of the day.
And the man and his wife hid themselves from the face of
Jehovah God in the middle of the trees of the garden. And
Jehovah God called to the man and said to him, Where are you?
And he said, I have heard your sound in the garden, and I was
afraid, for I am naked, and I hid myself. And He [Jehovah] said,
Who told you[1] that you were naked? Have you eaten of the tree
of which I have commanded you not to eat? And the man said,
The woman whom you gave to be with me, she has given to me
of the tree, and I ate. And Jehovah God said to the woman, What
is this you have done? And the woman said, The serpent
deceived me and I ate." [Gen. 3:1-13]

Figuratively Speaking

nm926 » Notice what is revealed in these verses. First, *before*
mankind took from the tree of knowledge of good and evil, they had no
shame (Gen 2:25). Next a snake or serpent came along and spoke to the
woman. Now we do not have to take this literally. As I explained above
the Bible is very lively in its use of the language. The Bible uses many
different kinds of figures of speech. We know trees do not clap their
hands because for one reason trees do not have hands. Yet in Isaiah
55:12 it speaks of trees that will clap their hands. We also know that
serpents or snakes do not speak. At least they do not speak like
mankind. (Of course the serpent in the garden may have actually
spoken, for God can do that if he had wished it to be so. But because
the Old Testament is so filled with figures of speech, and because we
have no proof that serpents literally speak in the way mankind speaks,
we therefore won't take this part of the Bible literally just as we won't
take Isaiah 55:12 literally.)

nm927 » What happened was this: The woman was near the tree of
knowledge of good and evil when a physical serpent was winding itself
around the tree and through the serpent's various motions and
movements the serpent brought the woman's attention to the fruit on
the tree. But it was the spiritual serpent inside the head of Eve that

---

[1] Doesn't this seem to indicate that God knew an outsider
("who told you") influenced Adam and Eve?

spoke to her. In other words, what tempted Eve that day was the spirit that Jehovah put inside mankind (Gen 2:7). That spirit is the other-mind that even today is inside mankind's mind. It was the other-mind inside Eve that spoke to her that day. Notice in Revelation, chapter 12:9, it reads that "the old serpent, called the Devil, and Satan, which misleads the whole world." As explained in the "Duality Paper" we are to take the higher or spiritual meaning of the Bible in order to ascertain the Spiritual truths of the Bible. The higher meaning of the serpent in Genesis is the spiritual serpent which is the Devil or Satan. One can say that the spirit that Jehovah put into man in the beginning was the spirit of Satan or the Devil, or that is, the spirit of evil and confusion, or as we are calling it in this paper, the other-mind that now lives in mankind. The actual spirit ("breath") that God put into mankind was the spirit that started evil by testing Eve (See also NM 22). This is difficult to understand, but do read on to see more proof.

Law and Sin

nm928 » When mankind took from the tree of knowledge they were breaking the law that God had given to them. The law was simple, do not take any fruit from the tree of knowledge of good and evil. Mankind could take from all the other trees in the garden, but somehow they desired the forbidden tree very much. Even though God promised death as the reward for taking from the tree of knowledge of good and evil, mankind still took from that tree. The serpent lied to Eve about the death they would receive, "You shall not surely die" (Gen 3:4) The serpent mixed one lie with the truth to deceive Eve, a very subtle deception that played on Eve's desire for knowledge. And so as to not displease his wife, Adam listened to his wife and also sinned.

Romans Chapter Seven

nm929 » Notice the following statement that Paul made in Romans, chapter seven of the New Testament. What Paul said in chapter seven fits very well what happened in the Genesis' account:

- "**But sin, seizing the opportunity afforded by the commandment** [of Gen 2:17], **produced in me** [Paul represents mankind] **every kind of covetous desire** [for the tree]. **For apart from law, sin is dead. Once I was alive apart from law** [before Gen 2:17]; **but when the commandment** [Gen 2:17] **came, sin sprang to life** [the spiritual serpent sprang to life tempting Eve] **and I died.** [that is mankind was given death because they broke the law in Genesis 2:17] **I found that the very commandment that was intended to bring life actually brought death.** [God's warning to man was intended to keep man from death and bring him to life] **Did that**

which was good, then, become death to me? By no means!
But in order that sin might be recognized as sin, it
produced death in me through what was good, so that
through the commandment sin might become utterly
sinful. We know that the law is spiritual; but I am [mankind]
unspiritual, sold as a slave to sin. I do not know what I am
doing, For what I want to do I do not do, but what I hate I
do. And if I do what I do not want to do, I agree that the law
is good. As it is, it is no longer I myself who do it, but it is
sin living in me. I know that nothing good lives in me, that
is, in my sinful nature. For I have the desire to do what is
good, but I cannot carry it out. For what I do is not the good
I want to do; no, the evil I do not want to do – this I keep on
doing. Now if I do what I do not want to do, it is no longer I
who do it, but it is sin living in me that does it. So I find this
law at work: When I want to do good, evil is right there
with me. For in my inner being I delight in God's law; but I
see <u>another law</u> at work in the members of my body,
waging war against the law of my mind and making me a
prisoner of the <u>law of sin</u> at work within my members."
[Rom 7:8-23]

Law of Sin

nm930 » Paul in these verses can be substituted for mankind as a
whole with one exception. Paul had the good Spirit of God in him, but
in this age most people only have the evil spirit in them, for most
people will not receive their own good spirit until a later time. Yet we
see Paul fighting the *law of sin* inside him. Paul wants to do good, he
has the Spirit of God inside him leading him to good, but Paul finds
another law inside him, and that law is the law of sin. The other-mind
in mankind's head in this age works like a law of evil. The other-mind
is an evil angel or spiritual messenger inside man's mind misleading
man, and this other-mind operates like a law, that is, it operates like a
law of sin or evil.

Sin and Satan

nm931 » Sin is defined in the Bible as lawlessness (1John 3:4). As
Revelation 12:9 says the serpent in Genesis was Satan who has
deceived the whole world. Actually "sin" is just another name for
Satan. The words "sin" and "Satan" are interchangeable. As light, life,
and love are used in the Bible for God (John 1 & 1John 4:8) so too can
darkness, death, and sin be used for Satan. God is love, but Satan is sin.

Now when you transpose in Romans, chapter seven, the word Satan for sin, you can see more clearly how this chapter adds to the rendition in Genesis. It was the spirit of Satan that Jehovah put into mankind in the beginning(Gen 2:7). But this spirit didn't show himself evil until the commandment came (Gen 2:17). Then this spirit in mankind took as an occasion the commandment (Roman 7:8,11) and deceived man (Gen 3:1-5) and thereby killed man. As Jesus Christ said: "You belong to your father, the devil, and you want to carry out your father's desire. He was a murderer from the beginning [the spirit of Satan in a sense killed man by deceiving man in Genesis], not holding to the truth, for there is no truth in him" (John 8:44). It is the spirit of Satan inside mankind that is causing most of the problems in this age. It is the other-mind that is contrary to our eventual happiness and is the main cause of our present problems.

Other-Mind Is a Spirit and Power of Evil

Our struggle is not against flesh and blood

nm932 » It is Satan or the spiritual other-mind that misleads the whole world (Rev 12:9). It is the power of Satan or the power of the other-mind which we must turn from (Acts 26:18). It is the devil's schemes, deceiving spirits, and things taught by demons of which we must be careful (Eph 6:11; 1Tim 4:1). "Our struggle is not against flesh and blood, but against the rulers, against the authorities, against the powers of this dark world and against the spiritual forces of evil in the heavenly realms" (Eph 6:12). "He who does what is sinful is of the devil, because the devil has been sinning from the beginning" (1John 3:8). As we have shown you it was the spirit of Satan that put the thought in Eve's mind of breaking God's first law. This spirit of Satan is the spiritual other-mind that works in us.

Other-Mind also Called...

nm933 » The no-good thing living in man is that sin or Satan living and working in man (Romans 7:18,20). It is the spirit in us that lusts after evil (James 4:5). This spirit is also called the spirit of slumber (Rom 11:8), it is called the spirit of bondage (Rom 8:15), it is called the spirit of sleep (Isaiah 29:10), it is called the lying spirit (1Kings 22:21-23), it is called the unclean spirit (Zech 13:2), it is called the spirit of whoredoms and it causes people to err (Hosea 4:12; 5:4), it is called the spirit of this world (1Cor 2:12), it is called the haughty spirit (Prov 16:18), it is called the perverse spirit (Isa 19:14), it is called the troubled spirit (Gen 41:8), it is called the spirit of jealousy (Num 5:14), it is called the spirit of man (1Cor 2:11), and so on.

Spirit of Man

Satan in Peter?

nm934 » It is the spirit of man that is within mankind that knows the thoughts of man (1Cor 2:11). Since the Bible looks upon man in this age as evil, then this spirit of man must be evil. What is this spirit in man that thinks like man? "Out of my sight, Satan! You are a stumbling block to me; you do not have in mind the things of God, but the things of men" (Mat 16:23). Now in this last verse Jesus was speaking to Peter, for "Jesus turned and said to Peter, Out of my sight, Satan!" Jesus was talking to the physical Peter, but he called him Satan. Why? Jesus called Peter "Satan" because he was talking to the spirit of man which lived inside Peter and which was misleading Peter at that time.

Fight against Satan's Power

nm935 » In Luke 22:3 and John 13:27 we read where Satan even caused Judas to err. "The evening meal was being served, and the devil had already put it into the heart of Judas Iscariot, son of Simon, that he should betray Him." It wasn't Judas himself that conceived of the idea of betraying Jesus, it was the spirit of Satan inside him that did it. It is Satan's spiritual power that takes captive at his will, not mankind's nature (2Tim 2:26; Acts 26:18). It is the snare and wiles of the spirit of the devil that people must guard against, not human nature (Eph 6:11; 1Tim 4:1). It is the other-mind or Satan that we are fighting against, "not flesh and blood" (Eph 6:12). It is Satan who fills the heart to lie (Acts 5:3). There is a spirit in man that yearns to envy and this spirit is of the devil (James 4:5,7).

Worthless Mind

nm936 » Mankind was given the spirit of Satan in the beginning although it didn't show itself as evil until after God gave man a law. Because Satan's spirit is a law-breaking-spirit, it took the law to show the nature of Satan's spirit. Satan's spirit is the other-mind that works in us. It is the worthless mind described in Romans 1:28-31:

- "God gave them up to a mind that was not fit for any good, to do those things which were not right, being filled with all kinds of unrighteousness: fornication, wickedness, covetousness, malice, full of envy, murder, quarrels, deceit, evil habits, whisperers, slanderers, God-haters, insolent, proud, braggarts, deviser of evil things, disobedient to parents, without understanding, impossible to trust, without natural love, unforgiving and without mercy."

Man's Heart and the Other-Mind

Evil from Within

nm937 » It is because of the other-mind, that "man's heart is evil from his youth" (Gen 8:21). "For from within, out of the heart of men, proceed evil thoughts, adulteries, fornications, murders, thefts, covetousness, wickedness, deceit, lasciviousness, an evil eye, blasphemy, pride, foolishness" (Mark 7:21,22). "And an evil man out of the evil treasure of his heart brings out that which is evil. For out of the abundance of the heart his mouth speaks" (Luke 6:45). It is out of the abundance of the heart of mankind that man acts. And in man's mind is the other-spirit which continuously feeds man with unsound thoughts.

nm938 » This age is worse than many people think. False pride, false affections, false accusations, false documents, false theories, false love, false words, and so forth are so much a part of this age that most of us are somewhat unaware of the asininity and falsehood of this age. The great religions and theories of this age are built on the confusion of the other-mind and the falsehood of the other-mind.

Mind of this Age of Evil

nm939 » According to the Bible the people of this age are the children of the devil (1John 3:10), children of disobedience (Eph 2:2), children of the wicked one (Mat 13:38), children of the world (Luke 16:8; 20:34), and so forth. The father of these children is the devil according to Jesus Christ (John 8:42-44). The people of this age are the children of confusion because their spiritual father is the great other-mind that lives and feeds negative flash-thoughts into the mind of mankind. So this is why we must be careful:

- Beloved, **believe not every spirit**, but try the spirits whether they are of God. (1John 4:1a)

New Mind for New Age of God

nm940 » In the next age, the New Age, the spirit of the other-mind will be put out of man. For when the demons ("devils") or when the other-mind is cast out and locked up, "then the kingdom of God [the New Age] has come upon you" (Mat 12:28). "In that day" Jehovah will cause the unclean spirit or the other-mind to pass out of the land (Zech 13:2). "That day" is the New Age that is coming upon us. In the New Age people will be truly free from the other-mind because it will be put out of people's minds. The New Age begins at the physical return of the Messiah.

See the "Reason Why" paper in the *God Papers* [GP 7] for the reason God put this other-mind into man in the beginning. See the *God Papers* to understand who or what is God and what will happen to the spiritual other-mind.

Review

nm941 » There is a power of confusion and evil in our physical minds. We call this power the, "other-mind." It is a spiritual power that flashes negative thoughts into our minds. This spiritual power was placed in our minds at the beginning of the creation by the one called Jehovah. The "other-mind" didn't manifest itself as evil until a law was given by Jehovah, then the other-mind showed its evil nature. Ever since the beginning the other-mind has fed negative flash-thoughts into mankind's mind. Because of these invading thoughts, man has behaved often in a negative manner since the creation. But a New Age is coming when the other-mind will be put out of mankind's mind, and at that time an utopian system will begin.

nm942 » With the knowledge of the other-mind, we can better understand our misbehavior in this age, and through understanding it we can better control it. The best way to control our misbehavior is to have the New Mind. But better still is to rid ourselves of the other-mind – the old mind – and obtain the New Mind. We wait for this to happen to us all.

NM 22: Spirit of Man Given by God

Paradoxes of the Spirit of Man

Spirit put in Mankind

Who put the spirit in man?

NM22 Abstract

There is a "spirit in man." What kind of spirit is it? Where did it come from?

Paradoxes of the Spirit of Man

nm943 » It is hard to understand how God, who is good, can give mankind the **spirit of man** which has led to so much evil on the earth. This is yet another paradox of God. From the *God Papers* we read:

- How can God be love (1 John 4:8), and also a killer? In scripture the LORD says, "I kill and I make alive; I wound, and I heal" (Deut 32:39; 1Sam 2:6). Yet the Bible says that the God is good to all (Psa 145:9). How can God be good to all and also a killer? How can God predestinate some to wrath and destruction (Rom 9:21-23; Jude 4; Prov 16:4; 1Peter 2:8), and some to mercy and glory? (Rom 9:21-23; Eph 1:4-5; etc.) Not only is God love, but He is *all* powerful (Gen 17:1; Rev 1:8). In his all powerfulness He even *created* evil: "I make peace, and create evil: I the LORD do all these things" (Isa 45:7). These are some of the Biblical paradoxes of God. Just how can God be love and also a killer, or how or why has He created evil? According to the Biblical definition of love (1Cor 13:4-8), killing or evil isn't one of the qualities of love. Yet, according to the Bible, God is love and in someway has killed and in someway has created evil (From GP 1, ¶ gp10).

nm944 » Because of the paradoxes pertaining to God, some simply do not believe in God, or deny the Biblical God, or some are forced to not admit or not see the plentiful scriptures concerning God's "evil" side. As we find out in the *God Papers*, the secret to unlocking the paradoxes of God is the meaning of the NAME of God, the phenomenon of time, and the phenomenon of predestination. His NAME manifests to us *how* God can be good without actually doing evil in this old age. **Hint**: there is a left and right side of God. Satan, the left side of God (that is, the left cherub in the Holy of Holies [Ezek 28:14]; both cherubs were made from one piece; see *God Papers*, especially parts 8 and 9) is now doing all the evil in this age. The other hint is that God predestinated everything <u>before</u> the cosmos, thus before good, before evil, before law, and consequently before sin, so God's predestination is without sin. Soon the right side of God will take control of the earth away from Satan and bring good to the earth.

Spirit Put in Mankind

nm945 » Did God really put the **spirit of man** inside mankind? In the *Old Mind Papers* (PR21) we mention the spirit of man as being put into mankind at the beginning by God, that is, by Yehowah Elohim. In this paper we will show you the Biblical verses. We will also use the KJV with Mr. Strong's numbers behind each word or phrase. Strong's numbers are inclosed in "< >."

nm946 » Notice where the Bible first indicates **when** God gave man the spirit of man:

- KJV Genesis 2:7: And the LORD God formed man *of* the dust of the ground, and **breathed** into his nostrils the **breath** of life; and man became a living soul.

- KJV Genesis 2:7: And the LORD <03068> God <0430> formed <03335> (08799) man <0120> *of* the dust <06083> of <04480> the ground <0127>, and **breathed** <05301> (08799) into his nostrils <0639> the **breath** <05397> of life <02416>; and man <0120> became a living <02416> soul <05315>.

nm947 » Notice also that the "LORD God" **breathed** into man the **breath** of life. The Hebrew word translated "breathed" is Strong's number, 05301. The Hebrew word translated "breath" in "breath of life" is Strong's number, 05397.

nm948 » From Strong's concordance we see that the number 05301 means:

- **5301** נָפַח naphach {naw-fakh'} ... 1) to breathe, blow, sniff at, seethe, give up or lose (life) 1a) (Qal) to breathe, blow 1b) (Pual) to be blown 1c) (Hiphil) to cause to breathe out

nm949 » From Whittaker's Revised BDB lexicon, Strong's number 05301 means:

- וֹ conjunction נָפַח verb: qal imperf waw consec 3rd pers masc sing **B6438** [נָפַח] **vb. breath, blow -- Qal** *breath, blow*; sq. בְּ also *blow* into it (to scatter it); sq. עַל : אֵשׁ כָלָיו לְפַחַת *to blow fire upon* it (ore, for melting), so fig. *and I will blow upon you with* (בְ) *the fire of my wrath*; נ נַפְשָׁהּ *she hath breathed out her life* (of a mother, cf. **Hiph.**); abs. נָפוּחַ סִיר *a blown* (i.e. well-heated, boiling) *pot.* **Pu.** נֻפָּח לֹא אֵשׁ *a fire not blown* (by any human breath). **Hiph.** נֶפֶשׁ בְּעָלֶיהָ הִפַּחְתִּי *the life of its* (the land's) *owners I have caused them to breathe out*; אֹתוֹ וְהִפַּחְתֶּם *and ye have sniffed at* it (in contempt). **(pg 655)**

nm950 » Strong's number 05397 means:

- **5397** נְשָׁמָה n@shamah {nesh-aw-maw'} ... 1) breath, **spirit** 1a) breath (of God) 1b) breath (of man) 1c) every breathing thing 1d) **spirit** (of man)

nm951 » From Whittaker's Revised BDB lexicon Strong's number 05397 means:

- נְשָׁמָה common noun fem sing const **B6589** נְשָׁמָה **n.f. breath -- 1.** *breath* of God as hot wind kindling a flame; as destroying wind; as cold wind producing ice; as creative, giving breath to man. **2.** *breath of* man; breath of life חיים נשמת; as breathed in by God it is God's breath in man; and it is characteristic of man. **3.** syn. of נֶפֶשׁ in כָּל-נְשָׁמָה נפש *every breathing thing.* **4.** *spirit* of man. **(pg 675)**

Notice that one meaning of this word is "**spirit.**" The breath of life could have been translated the spirit of life.

nm952 » There was actually a dual sense to Genesis 2:7: one physical; one spiritual. Notice Genesis 2:7's close resemblance to John 20:22:

- KJV John 20:22: And when he had said this, he **breathed** on *them*, and saith unto them, Receive ye the Holy **Spirit**:

- KJV John 20:22: And <2532> when he had said <2036> (5631) this <5124>, he **breathed** on <1720> (5656) *them*, and <2532> saith <3004> (5719) unto them <846>, Receive ye <2983> (5628) the Holy <40> **Spirit** <4151>:

nm953 » Christ blew on them saying, "receive the Holy Spirit." The word "blew" or "breathed" is Strong's number 1720 which means:

- **1720** ἐμφυσάω

emphusao {em-foo-sah'-o} ... 1) to blow or breathe upon

nm954 » The word translated "**Spirit**" (# 4151) in John 20:22 means:

- **4151** πνεῦμα pneuma {pnyoo'-mah} ... 1) a movement of air (a gentle blast 1a) of the wind, hence the wind itself 1b) breath of nostrils or mouth 2) the **spirit**, i.e. the vital principal by which the body is animated 2a) the rational spirit, the power by which the human being feels, thinks, decides 2b) the soul 3) a **spirit**, i.e. a simple essence, devoid of all or at least all grosser matter, and possessed of the power of knowing, desiring, deciding, and acting 3a) a life giving **spirit** 3b) a human soul that has left the body 3c) a **spirit** higher than man but lower than God, i.e. an angel 3c1) used of demons, or evil **spirits**, who were conceived as inhabiting the bodies of men 3c2) the **spiritual** nature of Christ, higher than the highest angels and equal to God, the divine nature of Christ 4) of God 4a) God's power and agency distinguishable in thought from his essence in itself considered 4a1) manifest in the course of affairs 4a2) by its influence upon the souls productive in the theocratic body (the church) of all the higher spiritual gifts and blessings 4a3) the third person of the trinity, the God the **Holy Spirit** 5) the disposition or influence which fills and governs the soul of any one 5a) the efficient source of any power, affection, emotion, desire, etc.

nm955 » In Genesis 2:7 Yehowah Elohim (Jesus Christ's Father, see GP 2) breathed or blew into Adam's nostrils and thereby gave him the breath of life. The same word "breath" (Strong's number 05397) in "breath of life" is also translated **spirit** in Proverbs 20:27 ("spirit" of man) in the KJV. And as we saw above it can and does mean spirit.

nm956 » In John 3:8 **spirit** (Strong's # 4151) and **wind** (#4151) are used interchangeably depending on which English translation you use and in what context it is used:

- KJV John 3:8: The **wind** bloweth where it listeth, and thou hearest the sound thereof, but canst not tell whence it cometh, and whither it goeth: so is every one that is born of the **Spirit**.

- KJV John 3:8: The **wind** <4151> bloweth <4154> (5719) where <3699> it listeth <2309> (5719), and <2532> thou hearest <191> (5719) the sound <5456> thereof <846>, but <235> canst <1492> <0> not <3756> tell <1492> (5758) whence <4159> it cometh <2064> (5736), and <2532> whither <4226> it goeth <5217> (5719): so <3779> is <2076> (5748) every one <3956> that is born <1080> (5772) of <1537> the **Spirit** <4151>.

- YLT John 3:8: the **Spirit** where he willeth doth blow, and his voice thou dost hear, but thou hast not known whence he cometh, and whither he goeth; thus is every one who hath been born of the **Spirit**.'

- NAB John 3:8: "The **wind** blows where it wishes and you hear the sound of it, but do not know where it comes from and where it is going; so is everyone who is born of the **Spirit**."

nm957 » John 3:8 and 20:22 were put in the Bible by God for a reason. In context with Genesis 2:7, it is telling us that as Yehowah Elohim in the beginning put the spirit of man in mankind, but in the end times Jesus Christ (through the power of God given to him) will give mankind the new and better spirit, the Holy Spirit (John 20:28). The Holy Spirit was given to mankind on the first Pentecost after Jesus Christ was resurrected (Acts 1:5; 2:1-4). This was the Holy Spirit prophesied to be given to mankind (Isa 44:3; Ezek 11:19; 36:26; Joel 2:28). But before this Holy Spirit was given there was and is even today (1997) in mankind the spirit of man that God (Yehowah Elohim) gave to mankind in the beginning.

nm958 » There is a spirit of man that is in man (Job 32:8; Proverbs 20:27). It is man's spirit (Job 34:14; Eccl 3:21). This is an evil spirit (1Sam 16:16; see, "Old Mind Paper" [NM 21]).

Yehowah Elohim Gave the Evil Spirit to Mankind

nm959 » Yehowah Elohim, who created the heavens and the earth, he gives **breath** and **spirit** to them that walk on the earth (Isa 42:5).

- KJV Isaiah 42:5: Thus saith God the LORD, he that created the heavens, and stretched them out; he that spread forth the earth, and that which cometh out of it; he that giveth **breath** unto the people upon it, and **spirit** to them that walk therein:

- KJV Isaiah 42:5: Thus saith <0559> (08804) God <0410> the LORD <03068>, he that created <01254> (08802) the heavens <08064>, and stretched them out <05186> (08802); he that spread forth <07554> (08802) the earth <0776>, and that which cometh out <06631> of it; he that giveth <05414> (08802) **breath** <05397> unto the people <05971> upon it, and **spirit** <07307> to them that walk <01980> (08802) therein:

nm960 » The **spirit** and souls Yehowah Elohim made (Isa 57:16). God made the spirit. Yehowah (YHWH or the BeComingOne) formed or created the "**spirit** of man within him":

- KJV Zechariah 12:1: The burden of the word of the LORD for Israel, saith the LORD, which stretcheth forth the heavens, and layeth the foundation of the earth, and formeth the spirit of man within him.

Not only did God make the spirit he made the "spirit of man *within* him."

nm961 » It is the **spirit of man** that is within mankind that knows the thoughts of mankind, while the things pertaining to God no one can understand except they that have the Spirit of God (1Cor 2:11).

Battle Against the Spiritual, Not the Physical

nm962 » Since angels are spirits (Heb 1:7), since the meaning of "angel" is messenger, then the way evil entered the world is through the spirit of man within mankind (Also see "Old Mind" paper [NM 21]). That is why we fight against the spiritual world and not the physical world. Our battle with sin and evil on earth has to do with fighting a spiritual battle against the other-mind and its power, not against flesh and blood (Eph 6:12). That is, the flesh is neutral pertaining to good and evil, but the evil spirit or the spirit in man in this the old age is the evil we fight against. The good Spirit or the Holy Spirit or the Spirit of Christ is what is given to mankind to fight against evil. It is this good spirit that causes mankind to repent of its old ways.

Repentance

nm963 » The change of mind in **repentance** is the change from the ruling spirit of man to the new ruling Spirit of God. When we receive the Spirit of God we get a spirit that is stronger than the spirit of man inside of us; strong enough to overcome the old mind and its ways of sin (1John 4:4).

Go to the **"Old Mind Paper"** [NM 21] to read more about the spirit of man (¶ nm928ff).

NM 23: Judging

Judge Not

Christ Judges

Brothers not Fools

Who are Fools

Paul Judged Also

Christians to Judge the World

NM23 Abstract

What did the Bible mean when it said, "do not judge"? Does this mean we are not to judge anyone? If this is true, why did Jesus judge some people's behavior, and call them on their wrong behavior? Are we to have tolerance for the evil around us?

Judge Not

nm964 » There are scriptures that appear to some to say that Christians are not supposed to judge others at all. What do the scriptures say?

- Matthew 7:1: "Do not judge, so that you may not be judged. 2 For with the judgment you make you will be judged, and the measure you give will be the measure you get. 3 Why do you see the speck in your neighbor's eye, but do not notice the log in your own eye? 4 Or how can you say to your neighbor, 'Let me take the speck out of your eye,' while the log is in your own eye? 5 You hypocrite, first take the log out of your own eye, and then you will see clearly to take the speck out of your neighbor's eye."

nm965 » What this says is that you should be very careful how you judge. Do not be a hypocrite if you judge. But does this really say and mean, judge not at all, ever? These scriptures cannot possibly mean not to discriminate (judge) between good and evil because the whole Bible tells us to do so. So what is meant here?

nm966 » Let's look at Christ and Paul to see what Christ meant in Matthew 7.

- John 8:15: You judge by human standards; I judge no one. 16 Yet even if I do judge, my judgment is valid; for it is not I alone who judge, but I and the Father who sent me.

Christ here says that others judge by human standards, but he does not judge by human standards.

Christ Judges

nm967 » Christ does not say he never judges, for as we will see he did/does judge.

- John 8:26: I have much to say about you and **much to judge**;

- John 5:30: I can do nothing on my own. **As I hear, I judge**; and my judgment is just, because I seek to do not my own will but the will of him who sent me.

- John 7:24: Do not judge by appearances, but **judge with righteous judgment**.

- 2Timothy 4:1: In the presence of God and of **Christ Jesus, who is to judge** the living and the dead

Here it says that Christ does judge. But his judgment is righteous for one thing he does not seek his own gain (See "God's Wrath" papers to understand righteous judgment.).

Brothers not Fools

nm968 » Do not be angry with your brother or call him a fool:

- Matthew 5:22: **But I say to you that if you are angry with a brother or sister, you will be liable to judgment**; and if you insult a brother or sister, you will be liable to the council; **and if you say, 'You fool,' you will be liable to the hell of fire.**

nm969 » But Christ called people fools many times:

- Matthew 23:17: "You blind fools!" (See v. 19 & Luke 11:40)

nm970 » Christ judged people and called them hypocrites:

- Luke 12:56: "You hypocrites!" (Mat 15:7; 16:3; 22:18; 23:13) nm971 » Christ even called a few of his apostles, "O fools" (Luke 24:25).

nm972 » What did the scripture say about calling people fools?

- Matthew 5:22: **But I say to you that if you are angry with a brother or sister, you will be liable to judgment**; and if you insult a brother or sister, you will be liable to the council; **and if you say, 'You fool,' you will be liable to the hell of fire.**

Do not be angry with your brother, do not call him a fool.

nm973 » Now we know from scripture that Christ's "brothers" and "sisters" are those in the Spirit.

- Matthew 12:50: For whosoever shall do the will of my Father which is in heaven, the same is my **brother,** and sister, and mother.

- Matthew 7:21: Not every one that says unto me, Lord, Lord, shall enter into the kingdom of heaven; but he that does the will of my Father which is in heaven.

As we see in this book you can do the will of the Father only when you have the Spirit. When Christ called a few of his apostles fools (Luke 24:25) they had not yet received the Spirit. (They received it later at the first Pentecost after Christ's resurrection.) At the time Christ called them fools, they were not yet Christ's Spiritual brothers. Thus, Christ was not wrong when he called them fools, since anyone without the Spirit, in their behavior is a fool.

Who are Fools?

nm974 » Who are fools, who are the foolish?

- Matthew 7:26: And everyone who hears these words of mine and does not act on them will be like a foolish man who built his house on sand.

Those who do not Spiritually hear his words and thus cannot act on them are fools, are foolish, and anything they do is built on sand instead of the Rock.(¶ nm28)

Ten Virgins and who was Foolish

nm975 » In the parable of the ten virgins, which were foolish?

- Matthew 25:1: Then the kingdom of heaven will be like this. Ten bridesmaids took their lamps and went to meet the bridegroom. 2 **Five of them were foolish**, and **five were wise**.

3 When the foolish took their lamps, they took no oil with them; 4 but **the wise took flasks of oil with their lamps**. 5 As the bridegroom was delayed, all of them [all ten] became drowsy and slept. 6 But at midnight there was a shout, 'Look! Here is the bridegroom! Come out to meet him.' 7 Then all those bridesmaids got up and trimmed their lamps. 8 **The foolish said to the wise, 'Give us some of your oil, for our lamps are going out.'** 9 But the wise replied, 'No! there will not be enough for you and for us; you had better go to the dealers and buy some for yourselves.' 10 And while they went to buy it, the bridegroom came, and those who were ready went with him into the wedding banquet; and the door was shut. 11 Later the other bridesmaids came also, saying, 'Lord, lord, open to us.' 12 But he replied, 'Truly I tell you, I do not know you.'

nm976 » The foolish had no oil in their lamps, that is, they did not have the Spirit, and thus were "fools." The olive oil they used in the Old Testament to anoint their kings typified the new oil of the Spirit (1John 2:20, 27). The lamp is God's word, "Your word is a lamp to my feet, and a light unto my path" (Psa 119:105). The foolish do not have the Spirit to go with the word of God, and thus at Christ's coming the Lord will say to the foolish without the Spiritual oil, "I know you not" (Mat 25:12).

Paul Judged Also

nm977 » Paul judged obvious wrongs, and asked his physical churches to also judge against them:

- 1Corinthians 5:9: I wrote to you in my letter not to associate with sexually immoral persons – 10 not at all meaning the immoral of this world, or the greedy and robbers, or idolaters, since you would then need to go out of the world. 11 But now I am writing to you not to associate with anyone who bears the name of brother or sister who is sexually immoral or greedy, or is an idolater, reviler, drunkard, or robber. Do not even eat with such a one. 12 For what have I to do with judging those outside? Is it not those who are inside that you are to judge? 13 God will judge those outside. "Drive out the wicked person from among you."

Christians to Judge the World

nm978 » Paul also said that since Christians are to judge the world, why cannot they judge wrong among themselves instead of going to the outside:

- 1Corinthians 6:1: When any of you has a grievance against another, do you dare to take it to court before the unrighteous, instead of taking it before the saints? 2 Do you not know that the saints will judge the world? And if the world is to be judged by you, are you incompetent to try trivial cases? 3 Do you not know that we are to judge angels-- to say nothing of ordinary matters? 4 If you have ordinary cases, then, do you appoint as judges those who have no standing in the church? 5 I say this to your shame. Can it be that there is no one among you wise enough to decide between one believer and another, 6 but a believer goes to court against a believer-- and before unbelievers at that?

nm979 » Paul also cautioned others to be careful how they judged each other:

- Romans 14:10: Why do you pass judgment on your brother or sister? Or you, why do you despise your brother or sister? For we will all stand before the judgment seat of God.

- Romans 14:13: Let us not therefore judge one another any more: but judge this rather, that no man put a stumbling block or an occasion to fall in *his* brother's way.

In context Paul was speaking about so-called clean and unclean food. And so he said, "I know and am persuaded in the Lord Jesus that nothing is unclean in itself; but it is unclean for anyone who thinks it unclean" (Rom 14:14). There are some things that appear evil to some, but according to the law of love are not evil.

nm980 » Paul said we are to judge for ourselves what is right. We must be very careful how we do this:

- 1Corinthians 10:15: I speak as to sensible people; judge for yourselves what I say.

- 1Corinthians 11:13: Judge for yourselves: is it proper for a woman to pray to God with her head unveiled?

- Colossians 2:16: Therefore do not let anyone condemn you in matters of food and drink or of observing festivals, new moons, or sabbaths.

- James 5:9: Beloved, do not grumble against one another, so that you may not be judged. See, the Judge is standing at the doors!

nm981 » Some social customs that have no bearing on the law of love may be considered evil in some parts of the world, avoid appearing evil if you can (1Cor 10:23, 27-33). Always walk in love (Eph 5:2; Rom 13:8, 10, 13-14).

nm982 » Accusation against Spiritual elders should not be accepted except with two or three witnesses:

- 1Timothy 5:19: Never accept any accusation against an elder except on the evidence of two or three witnesses. 20 As for those who persist in sin, rebuke them in the presence of all, so that the rest also may stand in fear.

nm983 » When we think we find fault with a brother, we must bring our complaint first to the brother for clarification. We may have seen something that was not there.

nm984 » We must be careful how we judge, especially against a Spiritual brother. Why? Because **if** we call a real Spiritual brother a fool, it may be proof that we do not have the Spirit, and thus, we may be in danger of being destroyed in the fire to come (Mat 5:22; 1John 3:15; see "Last Judgment" paper [NM 24]). Those with the Spirit will recognize their brothers; those without the Spirit will not.

NM 24: Last Judgment

Day of Judgment: An Old Idea

Universal Salvation

Great White Throne Judgment

Biblical Teaching on Judgment

Two Groups

Lake of Fire

When is the Judgment?

Last Day

Gathering of the Nations

Hell Fire, Mankind, Real Judgment

Three Orders or Divisions

NM24 Abstract

In many religions there is a day of judgment, scales of Justice, a lake of fire, and hell. In this paper we are going to learn what the Bible says about judgment and hell. Is there a hell, and will people go to hell? Because of much confusion on these ideas, we will take a close look at these subjects.

nm985 » Before we see what the Bible says about the Judgment we will briefly examine some other ideas about it. We ourselves have heard various legends pertaining to hell and the judgment of the dead so we will recognize some of the following ideas. But the only ideas that count are the ones actually taught in the Bible, not the ideas that are alleged to be in the Bible.

Day of Judgment: An Old Idea

nm986 » The idea of the day of judgment has existed in most religions at least as far back as ancient Mesopotamia and Egypt. One book by S. Brandon, called *The Judgment of the Dead*, finds the idea of the judgment in ancient Egypt, Mesopotamia, the Greco-Roman culture, among Hebrews, among Christians, among Islamites, among Iranians, among Hindus and Buddhists, and among those in China and in Japan. Brandon believes that, "it is in Egypt that the earliest evidence is found of the idea that judgment awaited a man after death" (p. 6).

nm987 » Actually, this idea can be traced from the Biblical statement about not eating from the tree of knowledge of good and evil, "for in the day that you eat thereof, in dying, you will die" (see Hebrew text). Thus, If you sin, then when you die, you will really be dead, for you will be part of those called the "dead" in the Bible. The idea of the judgment of the dead is indeed very old, and not new.

Scales of Justice

nm988 » Brandon after expounding for pages about various ancient Egyptian writings about the weighing of good deeds and bad deeds of people at death writes about the tale of Senosiris, "Those whose misdeeds outweigh their good deeds are delivered to Amait, the bitch belonging to the lord of Amentit, so that their bodies and souls are utterly destroyed. Those who pass the awful test are conducted to heaven. The man, whose good and bad deeds equally balance, is placed among the dead furnished with amulets who serve Sokarosiris." Brandon goes on, "Belief in a judgment after death, symbolized by the balance or scales, can be traced on into the Roman period of Egyptian religion, and, as the curious *History of Joseph the Carpenter* shows, it passed in turn unto Coptic Christianity. The idea of weighing the deeds of men had already been adopted into Jewish apocryphal literature, and the variant concept of the weighing of souls had entered into Greek thought, as we shall see. Ultimately the idea found expression in mediaeval Christian art, with the archangel Michael assuming the role of 'Master of the Balance' which Thoth had held in ancient Egypt."(p. 45, *The Judgment of the Dead*)

Pit of Fire; Lake of Fire

nm989 » "In the *Amduat*, which purports to describe the underworld, these 'enemies,' represented either in human form or by hieroglyphs denoting 'shadows' or 'souls,' are shown in pits of fire" (p. 46). In the *Book of the Dead* it speaks of the " double Lake of Fire" (p. 186, 342 in Budge's Dover ed.).

nm990 » In *The Legends of the Jews*, Louis Ginzberg writes about what Enoch saw in hell, "He saw there all sorts of tortures, and impenetrable gloom, and there is no light there, but a gloomy fire is always burning. And all that place has fire on all sides, and on all sides cold and ice, thus it burns and freezes. And the angels, terrible and without pity, carry savage weapons, and their torture is unmerciful" (Vol. I, p. 132). In Ginzberg's books there are about 60 or more sections that speak about the Jewish legends concerning hell.

nm991 » The *Apocalypse of Peter*, a once popular book, which dates from approximately the early second century, shows the horrors of hell: "hanging by their tongues, and those were they that blasphemed the way of righteousness, and under them was laid fire flaming and tormenting them ... And in another place were gravel-stones sharper than swords or any spit, heated with fire, and men and women clad in filthy rags rolled upon them in torment" (Brandon, p. 116-117). These and other torments were to last forever, for the sinners, "shall be tormented eternally, for God willeth it so" (Brandon, p. 117).

Second Death

nm992 » "With these indications of the perpetual torments of the damned must also be set the idea of 'second death,' about which concern is shown in the *Book of the Dead*. From this conflict of eschatological imagery we can, accordingly, only safely deduce that the Egyptians believed that some awful fate awaited those whose hearts were found to be not right with *Maat* in the judgment after death" (p. 46-47). In the *Book of the Dead*, there are sections that deal with what one must do to escape the second death. These sections start out with the phrase, "chapter of not dying a second time [second death] in the netherworld." (p. 105, 184, 341 in Budge's Dover ed.)

Judgment After Death

nm993 » **Greek Thought.** In Brandon's opinion, "there was a significant body of opinion which affirmed that after death men would be judged on their conduct here. This belief was authorized by the

poetry of Homer, which was truly the 'Bible of the Greeks.'" (p. 87)
From Plato's *Republic* we see Socrates fearing what may come after his
death. At one time Socrates "laughed at the tales about those in Hades,
of punishment to be suffered there by him who here has done
injustice. But now his soul is tormented by the thought that these may
be true" (P. 87).

Are the above descriptions of a forever torture in a hell fire, and
other tales even worse, really what hell is all about?

Trial and the Thousand Years

nm994 » Among the Greeks, if Plato's writings are any indication,
was the idea of the judgment or trial of the souls after death: The souls
are "on the termination of their first life, brought to trial; and,
according to their sentence, some go to the prison-houses beneath the
earth, to suffer for their sins, while others, by virtue, of their trial, are
borne lightly upwards to some celestial spot, where they pass their
days in a manner worthy of the life they have lived in their mortal
form. But in the **thousandth year** both divisions come back again to
share and choose their second life, and they select that which they
severally please" (Plato, *Phaedrus*).

Notice that the idea of the millennium was also in Greek thought in
Plato's time. And notice that *after* 1000 years both divisions would
come back again (are resurrected) and do as they please.

Koran: Those on the Right and Left

nm995 » In the Islamic holy book, the Koran, the tales of hell and
judgment are told. "The sinners will be in punishment of hell, to dwell
therein" (Sura 43:74). At the end of the world, "when the earth will be
shaken to its depths, and the mountains shall crumble to atoms" there
will be those on the right and left of God, those on the right have "fruits
in abundance" they are given "shade," "thrones," and virgin
companions, but those on the left go off into "the midst of a fierce blast
of fire and in boiling water" (Sura 56:4, 8, 27ff, 41ff).

Universal Salvation

nm996 » Not all shared in the idea of the forever judgement to hell.
The great Alexandrian scholar Origen (about 185-254 AD) believed in
universal salvation. "According to his doctrine of *apokatastasis*, in the
end all souls, and even the demons, would be purified and reunited
with God. Although Origen's views greatly influenced many Eastern

Christians, Christians generally found it easier, and, it would seem, more congenial, to believe in both a Purgatory and a Hell where sinners would suffer physically the most horrible and revolting tortures that a morbid imagination could devise" (Brandon, p. 118).

nm997 » In Ginzberg's books on the legends of the Jews, he relates the legends of how God revealed to Enoch "that the duration of the world will be seven thousand years, and the eighth millennium will be a time when there is no computation, no end, neither years, nor months, nor weeks, nor days, nor hours" (Vol. I, p. 135).

nm998 » In some forms of Zoroastrianism all men are saved after the Good ultimately prevails over the Evil, "and all men become immortal for ever and everlasting" (Brandon, p. 163).

nm999 » Hosea Ballou in his book, *The Ancient History of Universalism*[1] attempts to show the belief in universal salvation from Titus Flavius Clemens (190 AD) to Origen (230 AD) and those who agreed with him , and onto the other traces of it in history to about 1498 AD. So the belief in universal salvation is not new. Some today who believe in it are called universalist. Ballou was pastor of the Universalist Church in Roxbury in the early 1800's.

Great White Throne Judgment

nm1000 » The popular Christian belief concerning the judgment of the dead is not new and can be stated as follows:

- At the return of Christ there will be a resurrection of the righteous and the wicked. (The Pre-millenarians teach a double resurrection: one of the just at the return of Christ, and another of the unjust a thousand years later.) Christ will judge those resurrected. This is called the great white throne judgment. All people will be judged at that time. This final judgment will be at the end of the world. Those judged the "wicked" will be consigned to hell or the lake of fire, and will suffer pains in body and soul for ever and ever. Those judged righteous will be given heaven as a reward. This heavenly state will be eternal. The resurrected will enjoy the fullness of life in communion with God for ever and ever.

---

[1] Published in Boston, 1828

Questions

nm1001 » Is there a judgment of the dead? What is the judgment of the dead? Does this judgment last forever? Is there a hell fire? Who goes into the hell fire? Are people tortured forever? Can people's flesh burn forever? Will people be tortured? When is the Judgment? What happens to Satan and his angels? Is there a heaven?

Biblical Teaching on Judgment

Know Three Things

nm1002 » In order to understand the real last judgment mentioned in the Bible you must know three things.

1. **That God judges righteously**. See "God's Wrath" [PR4] to understand God's righteous judgment. In short, "the LORD is known by the judgment which he executes: the wicked is snared in the work of his own hands" (Psalms 9:16). In short, God's wrath and judgment is righteous: he lets those who do evil destroy themselves.

2. **That the word translated "forever" or "everlasting" or "eternal"** in the English Bible literally means age or aeon or aeonian. See our "Age Paper" [NM 7] for proof on this matter. In short, there are ages in God's plan.

3. **There is a difference between immortal life and aeonian life.** Knowledge is distinguishing between facts that superficially may seem to be the same (see below & NM 11).

Resurrection of the Dead and the Judgment

nm1003 » There is Biblical doctrine pertaining to the resurrection and judgment (Heb 6:2).

-   "Indeed, just as **the Father raises the dead and gives them life, so also the Son gives life to whomever he wishes.** 22 The Father judges no one but has given all judgment to the Son, 23 so that all may honor the Son just as they honor the Father. Anyone who does not honor the Son does not honor the Father who sent him. 24 Very truly, I tell you, anyone who hears my word and believes him who sent me has aeonian life, and does not come under judgment, but has passed from death to life. 25 "Very truly, I tell you, the hour is coming, and is now here, when the dead will hear the voice of the Son of God, and those who hear will live. 26 For just as the Father has life in himself, so he has granted the Son also to have life in himself; 27 and he has given him authority to execute **judgment**, because he is the Son of Man. 28 Do not be astonished at this; for the hour is coming when all who are in their graves will hear his voice 29 and will come out-- those who have done good, to the **resurrection of life**, and those who have done evil, to the **resurrection of judgment**" (John 5:21-29).

Christ given the power of the Resurrection and Judgment

nm1004 » So in John 5 we have scripture that says the Father gave the authority to Christ ("Son of Man") to execute judgment. Remember the Father gave Christ *all* the power (Mat 28:18). One of these powers was to execute judgment and to give life to "whomever he wishes." In other words, Christ has the power to resurrect people. In verse 29 it speaks about the resurrection of life and the resurrection of judgment. Those who have done good will be in the resurrection of life, but those who have done evil will be in the resurrection of judgment. To be resurrected, you must have first died. So in the book of Acts 24:15 we see Paul saying "I have a hope in God – a hope that they themselves also accept – that there will be a resurrection of both the righteous and the unrighteous." Paul called this the resurrection of the dead (Acts 24:21; 1Cor 15:21). Jesus Christ himself was resurrected from the dead by the Father (1Pet 1:3; see GP 5). Daniel spoke about the resurrection of the dead, "And many of them that sleep in the dust of the earth shall awake, some to life of olam, and some to shame and contempt of olam." (Dan 12:2).

Two Groups; Two Destinies

One on the Right, One on the Left

nm1005 » Notice that there are two groups or divisions: one of the just and good, and one of the unjust and evil (John 5:29; Acts 24:15; Dan 12:2).

- "When the Son of Man comes in his glory, and all the angels with him, then he will sit on the throne of his glory. 32 All the nations will be gathered before him, and he will separate people one from another as a shepherd separates the sheep from the goats, 33 and he will put the sheep at his right hand and the goats at the left. 34 Then the king will say to **those at**

his right hand, 'Come, you that are blessed by my Father, **inherit the kingdom** prepared for you from the foundation of the world; 35 for I was hungry and you gave me food, I was thirsty and you gave me something to drink, I was a stranger and you welcomed me, 36 I was naked and you gave me clothing, I was sick and you took care of me, I was in prison and you visited me.' 37 Then the righteous will answer him, 'Lord, when was it that we saw you hungry and gave you food, or thirsty and gave you something to drink? 38 And when was it that we saw you a stranger and welcomed you, or naked and gave you clothing? 39 And when was it that we saw you sick or in prison and visited you?' 40 And the king will answer them, 'Truly I tell you, just as you did it to one of the least of these who are members of my family, you did it to me.' 41 Then he will say to those **at his left hand**, 'You that are accursed, depart from me into the **aeonian fire** prepared for the devil and his angels.' 46 And these will go away into aeonian punishment, but the righteous into aeonian life" (Mat 25:31-41, 46).

One group, the just, at Christ's right hand, is given the kingdom, the other group on the left hand side is sent to the aeonian fire.

Lake of Fire

Second Death is the Lake of Fire

nm1006 » Notice in the book of Revelation, 20:11-15:

■ "Then I saw a **great white throne** and the one who sat on it; the earth and the heaven fled from his presence, and no place was found for them. 12 And I saw the dead, great and small, standing before the throne, and books were opened. Also another book was opened, the book of life. And the dead were judged according to their works, as recorded in the books. 13 And the sea gave up the dead that were in it, Death and Hades gave up the dead that were in them, and all were judged according to their works. 14 Then Death and Hades were thrown into the **lake of fire**. This is the **second death**, the lake of fire; 15 and anyone whose name was not found written in the book of life was thrown into the lake of fire."

nm1007 » Those not written in the book of life are thrown into the lake of fire, and this is the second death – the lake of fire (Rev 20:14). Notice that all were judged according to their works (Rev 20:13; see NM 12). Those who overcome evil "shall inherit all things, and I will be his God, and he shall be my son. But the **fearful, and unbelieving**, and abominable, and murderers, fornicators, and sorcerers, and idolaters, and all liars, shall **have their part in the lake which burns with fire** and brimstone [lake of fire], which is the second death" (Rev 21:7-8). Thus the lake of fire is the second death.

Lake of Fire: More Information

nm1008 » As we have just seen in the book of Revelation, chapters 20 and 21, there is going to be a "lake of fire," and the lake of fire is the second death. The lake of fire is not a myth. This is not a myth. But at the beginning of this paper we wrote about the mythical *Book of the Dead* wherein a lake of fire is also mentioned. Also in many of the "myths" of ancient civilizations, pits of fire, hell of fire, lakes of fire, and other such descriptions are mentioned in connection with the fate of those judged evil in the day of judgement, or at the last judgment. There seems to be a collective-subconscious idea about some fiery fate for those who are evil, or for those who do not do enough good works while they are on earth. These myths are not the truth; they only have some aspects of the truth. The spirits of this age know something about a future judgment for them (Mat 8:28-29). Do they somehow project this subconsciously to mankind? (See, "Old Mind" paper [NM 21])

Scriptures that Point to the Last Judgment

nm1009 » The following verses, through type and antitype (NM15; Nm16; PR1; etc.), in their higher meaning all point to the real last judgment:

- 2Peter 3:10 But the **day of the Lord** will come like a thief, and then the heavens will pass away with a loud noise, and **the elements will be dissolved with fire**, and the earth and everything that is done on it will be disclosed.

- Zephaniah 1:18 Neither their silver nor their gold will be able to save them on the **day of the LORD's wrath**; in the **fire of his passion** the whole earth shall be consumed; for a full, a terrible end he will make of all the inhabitants of the earth.

- Malachi 4:1 See, the day is coming, burning like an oven, when all the arrogant and all evildoers will be stubble; the **day that comes shall burn them up**, says the LORD of hosts, so that it will leave them neither root nor branch.

- Isaiah 29:6 you will be visited by the LORD of hosts with thunder and earthquake and great noise, with whirlwind and tempest, and the **flame of a devouring fire.**

- Ezekiel 38:22 And I will judge against him with pestilence and with blood; and I will rain upon him, and upon his bands, and upon the many people that *are* with him, an overflowing rain, and **great hailstones, fire, and brimstone**.

- Isaiah 30:30 And the LORD will cause his majestic voice to be heard and the descending blow of his arm to be seen, in furious anger and a **flame of devouring fire**, with a cloudburst and tempest and **hailstones**.

- Ezekiel 13:13 Therefore thus says the Lord GOD: In my wrath I will make a stormy wind break out, and in my anger there shall be a deluge of rain, and **hailstones** in wrath to destroy it.

- Jeremiah 10:10 But the LORD is the true God; he is the living God and the everlasting King. At **his wrath the earth quakes**, and the nations cannot endure his indignation.

- Ezekiel 31:16 I made the nations quake at the sound of its fall, when I **cast it down to Sheol [hell] with those who go down to the Pit**; and all the trees of Eden, the choice and best of Lebanon, all that were well watered, were consoled in the world below.

- Revelation 16:18 And there came flashes of lightning, rumblings, peals of thunder, and a **violent earthquake**, such as had not occurred since people were upon the earth, so violent was that earthquake.

- Revelation 11:19 Then God's temple in heaven was opened, and the ark of his covenant was seen within his temple; and there were flashes of lightning, rumblings, peals of thunder, an **earthquake**, and **heavy hail**.

- Job 38:22 have you entered into the treasures of the snow? or have you seen the treasures of **the hail**, Job 38:23 Which **I have reserved against the time of trouble**, against the day of battle and war?

- Revelation 16:21 and huge **hailstones**, each **weighing about a hundred pounds**, dropped from heaven on people, until they cursed God for the plague of the hail, so fearful was that plague.

- Revelation 11:13 At that moment there was a **great earthquake**, and a tenth of the city fell; seven thousand people were killed in the earthquake, and the rest were terrified and gave glory to the God of heaven.

- Revelation 8:5 Then the angel took the **censer and filled it with fire** from the altar and threw it on the earth; and there were peals of thunder, rumblings, flashes of lightning, and an **earthquake**.

- Revelation 18:8 therefore her plagues will come in a single day-- pestilence and mourning and famine-- and she [spiritual Babylon] will be **burned with fire**; for mighty is the Lord God who judges her."

- Revelation 19:20 And the beast was captured, and with it the false prophet who had performed in its presence the signs by which he deceived those who had received the mark of the beast and those who worshiped its image. These two were thrown alive into the **lake of fire** that burns with sulfur.

- Revelation 20:10 And the devil who had deceived them was thrown into the **lake of fire** and sulfur, where the beast and the false prophet were, and they will be tormented day and night into the ages of ages [not, forever and ever].

- Revelation 21:8 But as for the cowardly, the faithless, the polluted, the murderers, the fornicators, the sorcerers, the idolaters, and all liars, their place will be in the **lake that burns with fire** and sulfur, which is the second death.

nm1010 » The scriptures above and others point to the great fire, great earthquake, great hailstones, great wind, great thunder, great lightning, thus, a **great tribulation**. This is the Last War. I write about in the "Last War and God's Wrath" paper [PR5]. See an outline of scripture concerning this Last War in "God's Wrath, An Outline" [PR6]. This Last War has to do with a great atomic war with a massive fiery wind storm caused by the abundance of weapons going off in close proximity to each other.

Hell Fire: Who is it For?

nm1011 » There is a lake of fire, but who is it for? Is the fire for humans? Myths say that humans in bodily form will be tortured in a hell fire forever and ever for the evil they committed on earth. Does the Bible teach this?

- "Then he will say to those at his left hand, You that are accursed, depart from me into the aeonian **fire prepared for the devil and his angels**" (Mat 25:41).

- "And **the devil** who had deceived them **was thrown into the lake of fire and sulfur**, where the beast and the false prophet are, and they will be tormented day and night into eons and eons" (Rev 20:10).

- "He seized the dragon, **that ancient serpent, who is the Devil and Satan**, and bound him **for a thousand years**, and **threw him into the pit**, and locked and sealed it over him, so that he would deceive the nations no more, until the thousand years were ended. After that he must be let out for a little while" (Rev 20:2-3).

Jesus Christ said that the fire of hell was prepared or made for the devil and his angels. In the book of Revelation it prophesies about the Devil (Satan that old serpent) being sent to a pit of fire for one thousand years.

nm1012 » Peter and Jude also wrote about Satan and his angels being reserved unto the day of judgment.

- 2PET 2:4: For if GOD spares not [the] angels who sin, but casts them chained into the hell [Tartarus] of darkness to be kept [there] for judgment;

- JUDE 1:6: And angels who had not kept their own original state, but had abandoned their beginning, for [the] judgment of [the] great day; chained perpetually[1] under gloomy darkness, he keeps [them].

And In Proverbs, "The LORD has made all things for a purpose, Yes, even the wicked for the day of evil" (Prov 16:4).

nm1013 » This is much like the heavens and earth being kept in store for the day of judgment:

- 2PET 3:7: But the present heavens and the earth by his word are laid up in store, kept for fire unto a **day of judgment** and destruction of ungodly men.

nm1014 » And this day of judgment will be with fire so hot the elements will melt:

- 2PET 3:12: waiting for and hastening the **coming of the day of the GOD**, by reason of which [the] heavens, being on fire, shall be dissolved, and [the] elements, burning with heat, shall melt?

---

[1] Strong's # 126 (from #104) = always, continual, perpetual, not necessarily "forever." See NM 24.

- Isa 64:1: Oh that you [God] would rip the heavens, that you would come down, that the mountains might flow down **at your presence**. Isa 64:2 As **when the melting fire burns**, the fire causes the waters to boil, to make your name known to your adversaries, that the nations may tremble at your presence! Isa 64:3 When you did terrible things which we looked not for, you came down, the mountains flowed down at your presence. Isa 64:4 For since olam past men have not heard, nor perceived by the ear, neither has the eye seen, O God, beside you, what he has prepared for him that waits for him.

- Psa 97:1 The BeComingOne [YHWH] reigns; let the earth rejoice; let the multitude of isles be glad thereof. Psa 97:2 Clouds and darkness are round about him: righteousness and judgment are the habitation of his throne. Psa 97:3 A **fire goes before him**, and burns up his enemies round about. Psa 97:4 His lightning enlightened the world: the earth saw, and trembled. Psa 97:5 The **hills melted like wax** at the presence of the BeComingOne, at the presence of the Lord of the whole earth. Psa 97:6 The heavens declare his righteousness, and all the people see his glory.

Names for the Judgment

nm1015 » A day will come when God will Judge the world. Various phrases are used in the Bible to describe it.

- Day of the LORD's anger (Zeph 2:2)
- Wrath of the LORD of hosts (Isa 13:13)
- Day of His fierce anger (Isa 13:13)
- Day of the LORD's wrath (Zeph 1:18)
- Great day of wrath (Rev 6:17; Psalms 110:5)
- Day of the Lord (2Pet 3:10; 1Thes 5:2)
- Day of judgment (Mat 10:15; 2Pet 2:9; 3:7)
- Day of the Lord Jesus (1Cor 1:8)
- Great and dreadful day of the LORD (Mal 4:5)
- Great day of the LORD (Zeph 1:14)
- Day of the Lord Yehowah [YHWH], a day of vengeance (Jer 46:10)
- Day of wrath and revelation of the righteous judgment of God (Rom 2:5)

There are many places in the Bible where it speaks about the day of judgment for the enemies of physical Israel. But in the Spiritual view or higher meaning they pertain to the Last War, and the Last Judgment against the enemies of Spiritual Israel.

When is the Judgment?

nm1016 » The next question is, *when* will this Judgment begin? "Jesus Christ, who shall judge the living and the dead at his appearing and his kingdom" (2Tim 4:1). At the appearance of his kingdom Christ will judge the living and the dead.

Right and Left Side

nm1017 »

- MAT 25:31 But **when the Son of man comes in his glory**, and all the angels with him, then shall he sit down upon his throne of glory, 32 and all the nations shall be gathered before him; and **he shall separate them** from one another, as the shepherd separates the sheep from the goats; 33 and he will set the sheep **on his right hand**, and the goats on his left. 34 Then shall the King say to those on his right hand, Come, blessed of my Father, inherit the kingdom prepared for you from the world's foundation: MAT 25:41 Then shall he say also to **those on the left**, Go from me, cursed, into aeonian fire, prepared for the devil and his angels: MAT 25:46 And these shall go away into aeonian punishment, and the righteous into life aeonian.

Last Trumpet

nm1018 » This judgement of the right and left side occurs when Christ comes with his angels at the last trumpet,

- "And he shall send his angels with a great sound of a **trumpet**, and they shall gather together his elect..." (Mat 24:31).

- "For the Lord himself, with a cry of command, with the archangel's call and with the sound of God's **trumpet**, will descend from heaven, and the dead in Christ will rise first" (1Thess 4:16).

- "In a moment, in the twinkling of an eye, at the **last trump**: for the trumpet shall sound, and the dead shall be raised incorruptible, and we shall all be changed, for this corruptible must put on incorruption, and this mortal put on immortality" (1Cor 15:52-52).

■ "Then the seventh angel blew his **trumpet** [last trumpet], and there were loud voices in heaven, saying, 'The kingdom of the world has become the kingdom of our Lord and of his Messiah, and he will reign into the ages of the ages.'" (Rev 11:15)

When are those on the right and left separated? When is the last trumpet, when the angels help gather the elect, when immortality is given, when the kingdoms of this world become the kingdom of God?

Last Day

nm1019 » The Bible mentions the *day* of the Lord, the *day* of wrath, the *day* of anger, the *day* of judgment. And the Bible also mentions the **last day**:

■ John 6:39 And this is the will of him who sent me, that I should lose nothing of all that he has given me, but raise it up on the **last day**.

■ John 6:40 This is indeed the will of my Father, that all who see the Son and believe in him may have aeonian life; and I will raise them up on the **last day**."

■ John 6:44 No one can come to me unless drawn by the Father who sent me; and I will raise that person up on the **last day**.

■ John 11:24 Martha said to him, "I know that he will rise again in the resurrection on the **last day**."

■ John 12:48 The one who rejects me and does not receive my word has a judge; on the **last day** the word that I have spoken will serve as judge,

nm1020 » What happens on this last day? There is a resurrection for those who are drawn Spiritually, who see Spiritually, and believe Spiritually. But those who reject Christ are judged by the words Christ spoke (John 12:48; Ho 6:5).

nm1021 » When is this resurrection? From the "last trumpet" section above we see that the resurrection is at the last trumpet, just as the kingdom of God begins its reign on earth. "Jesus Christ, who shall judge the living and the dead at his appearing and his kingdom" (2Tim 4:1).

How will Christ Judge?

nm1022 » At Christ coming in his kingdom he will judge (2Tim 4:1). He will let his words be the judge (John 12:48; Ho 6:5). One is judged according to their works (See NM 12). He judges righteously (PR4). Note the books (Bible) being opened in Revelation 20:12, "and the dead were judged out of those things which were written in the books, according to their works." In other words, those who are "just" according to their works and are on the right are given the kingdom and aeonian life (Mat 25:33-34, 46); those who are "unjust" according to their works and are on the left are sent away from the glory of the kingdom and given aeonian punishment (Mat 25:41, 46). This is the righteous judgment, you are judged according to your works. The evil other-minds will be destroyed in the lake of fire of their own creation – the results of the Last War (see "Last War and God's Wrath" paper [PR5]).

- ■ "The Lord Jesus is revealed from heaven with his mighty angels in flaming fire [caused by Satan's war], inflicting vengeance on those who do not know God and on those who do not obey the gospel of our Lord Jesus. These will suffer the punishment of aeonian destruction, separated from the presence of the Lord and from the glory of his might" (2Thess 1:7-9).

nm1023 » The judgment and the resurrection occur at the very time Christ comes with the power of his kingdom.

- ■ DAN 7:26 But the **judgment shall sit**, and they [Saints] shall take away his [Satan & Beast's] dominion, to consume and to destroy it unto the end. DAN 7:27 And the kingdom and dominion, and the greatness of the kingdom under the whole heaven, shall be given to the people of the saints of the most High, whose kingdom is a kingdom of olam, and all dominions shall serve and obey him.

nm1024 » This in context with Daniel 7:12-14, 21-22, pictures the time when Christ and his saints take the kingdom away from Satan, and when the judgment is set to happen, which is at the time the Beast and its kingdom are destroyed (See *Beast Papers*; PR2, PR3).

- ■ "And they went up on the breadth of the earth, and surrounded the camp of the saints and the beloved city: and fire came down and devoured them. And the Devil who deceived them was cast into the lake of fire and brimstone, and where the Beast and the false prophet [are]; and they shall be tormented day and night into the ages [aeons] of ages [aeons]. And I saw a great white throne, and him that sat on it, from whose face the earth and the heaven fled, and place was not found for them" (Rev 20:9-11; see Rev 20:15 & 19:19-21).

Last Day = Thousand Years

nm1025 » There are patterns in the Bible. One of them is the cycle of seven: Six similar units; the seventh different (See NM 15). In the beginning was the pattern of the week: six days of work; one day of rest (Gen 1:1-2:3; Exo 20:8-11). There is type and antitype in the Bible ("Duality Paper"). As Paul made much of the scriptures about Adam and Eve and Christ being the second Adam and the Church being the second Eve[1] (1Cor 15:45; Eph 5:23-32; etc), I will also make a great deal about the antitypical week of creation, in which each "day" equals 1000 years. When Peter was talking about the judgment, he wrote about a day for the Lord is as a thousand years (2Pet 3:7-8). Revelation 20:2-5 speaks about a rest from Satan lasting for 1000 years. Putting this together and knowing about type and antitype, we conclude that the "last day" Christ was speaking about in the book of John pertaining to the resurrection and judgment is the "day" of one-thousand years as mentioned in the book of Revelation.

When the Beast system is destroyed is when the judgment occurs, and when the kingdom of God takes over. This is also the time of the gathering of the nations to fight against Christ and his saints.

Gathering of the Nations

nm1026 » The following pertain to the time of the gathering of nations, Gog and Magog:

- EZE 38:2 Son of man, set your face against **Gog, the land of Magog**, the chief prince of Meshech and Tubal, and prophesy against him, EZE 38:14 Therefore, son of man, prophesy and say unto **Gog**, Thus says my Lords the BeComingOne; In that day when my people of Israel dwells safely, shall you not know it? EZE 38:15 And you shall come from your place out of the north parts, you, **and many people with you**, all of them riding upon horses, a great company, **and a mighty army**: EZE 38:16 And you **shall come up against my people of Israel**, as a cloud to cover the land; it shall be in the end of days, and I will bring you against my land, that the nations may know me, when I shall be sanctified in you, O Gog, before their eyes. EZE 38:17 Thus says my Lords the BeComingOne; are you he of whom I

---

[1] Christ the second Adam; the Church the second Eve returns and becomes one with her Husband: the marriage of the Bride and Lamb (Rev 21:2, 9). Etc.

have spoken in old days by my servants the prophets of Israel, which prophesied in those days many years that I would bring you against them? Eze 38:18 And **it shall come to pass at the same day when Gog shall come against the land of Israel**, says my Lords the BeComingOne, **that my fury shall come up in my face**. Eze 38:19 For in my jealousy and in the **fire of my wrath** have I spoken, Surely in that day there shall be a great **shaking** in the land of Israel; Eze 38:20 So that the fishes of the sea, and the fowls of the heaven, and the living creatures of the field, and all creeping things that creep upon the earth, and all the men that are upon the face of the earth, **shall shake at my presence**, and the mountains shall be thrown down, and the steep places shall fall, and every wall shall fall to the ground. Eze 38:21 And I will call for a sword against him throughout all my mountains, says my Lords the BeComingOne: every man's sword shall be against his brother. Eze 38:22 And **I will judge against him** with pestilence and with blood; and I will rain upon him, and upon his bands, and upon the many people that are with him, an overflowing rain, and **great hailstones, fire, and brimstone.** Eze 38:23 Thus will I magnify myself, and sanctify myself; and I will be known in the eyes of many nations, and they shall know that I am the BeComingOne.

- Rev 20:8 and [Satan] shall go out to deceive the nations which [are] in the four corners of the earth, **Gog and Magog**, to **gather** them together **to the war**, whose number [is] as the sand of the sea. Rev 20:9 And they went up on the breadth of the earth, and **surrounded the camp of the saints** and the beloved city: and fire came down and devoured them. Rev 20:10 And the **devil** who deceived them was **cast into the lake of fire and brimstone**, and where the beast and the false prophet; and they shall be tormented day and night into the ages [aeons] of ages [aeons] Rev 20:11 And I saw a **great white throne**, and him that sat on it, from whose face the earth and the heaven fled, and place was not found for them.

- Rev 19:19 And I saw the **Beast** and the **kings of the earth** and their **armies gathered** together **to make war** against him that sat upon the horse, and against his army. Rev 19:20 And the beast was taken, and the false prophet that [was] with him, who worked the signs before him by which he deceived them that received the mark of the beast, and those that worship his image. Alive were both **cast into the lake of fire** which burns with brimstone; Rev 19:21 and the rest were slain with the sword of him that sat upon the horse, which goes out of his mouth; and all the birds were filled with their flesh. Rᴇᴠ 20:2 And he [Christ] laid hold of the dragon, the ancient serpent who is [the] Devil and **Satan, and bound him a thousand years**, Rᴇᴠ 20:3 and cast him into the abyss, and shut [it] and sealed [it] over him, that he should not any more deceive the nations until the thousand years were completed; (after these things he must be loosed for a little time.) Rᴇᴠ 20:4 And I saw thrones; and they sat upon them, and **judgment was given to them** [Christ & Saints, Dan 7:22]; and the souls of those beheaded on account of the testimony of Jesus, and on account of the word of the GOD; and those who had not done homage to the Beast nor to his image, and had not received the mark on their forehead and hand; and they lived and reigned with the Christ a thousand years: Rᴇᴠ 20:5 (the rest of the dead did not live until the thousand years had been completed.) This [is] the first resurrection. Rᴇᴠ 20:6 Blessed and holy he who has part in the first resurrection: over these the second death has no power; but they shall be priests of the GOD and of the Christ, and shall reign with him a thousand years. Rᴇᴠ 20:7 And when the thousand years have been completed, Satan shall be loosed from his prison.

nm1027 » **Gathered Against Christ**. Here we have Gog and Magog, with the gathered nations and their armies going against Christ and his "army." Christ's army is, "And the armies which [are] in the heaven followed him upon white horses, clad in white, pure, fine linen" (Rev 19:14).

Who are those Dressed in White

nm1028 » And who are those dressed in white?

- Rᴇᴠ 7:13 And one of the elders answered, saying to me, These who are clothed with white robes, who are they, and whence came they? Rᴇᴠ 7:14 And I said to him, My lord, you know. And he said to me, These are **they who come out of the great tribulation**, and have washed their robes, and have made them white in the blood of the Lamb. Rᴇᴠ 7:15 Therefore are they before the throne of the GOD, and serve him day and night in his temple, and he that sits upon the throne shall spread his tabernacle over them. Rᴇᴠ 7:16 They shall not hunger any more, neither shall they thirst any more, nor shall the sun at all fall on them, nor any burning heat.

Thus, those clothed in white are the saints (Rev 3:5, 18; 6:11). They came out of the great tribulation.

Great Tribulation

nm1029 » There are two senses to this tribulation: (1) The greatest and last tribulation at the very end, and (2) the whole tribulation since the time of Adam (cf. Rom 8:22; Rev 1:9; 1Thess 3:4; 2Cor 7:4;). By reading our newspapers and by reading history, we know that the whole world has been in tribulation: and we know this is the result of sin.

To review. We see that the time of the last judgment is right at the time Christ comes to take over the kingdom or rulership from Satan. Christ does not destroy the world, the world destroys itself, for Christ comes to save not destroy (see God's Wrath papers [PR4, PR5, PR6]).

Hell-Fire; Mankind; Real Judgment

nm1030 » We know by various scriptures that the hell-fire will be for Satan and his angels (Mat 25:41; Rev 20:2-3, 10). But according to myth some of mankind will suffer **in** a fire forever for their sins. How can this be since physical bodies will burn-up in a fire? This whole idea is nonsense. They make God out to be sadistic. But our God is Love. (The *Parable of Lazarus* is logically explained in the "All Saved" paper [NM 13]) Yet Augustine in his book called, the *City of God*, quotes from John 5:29, Matthew 13:41-43, and Matthew 25:46 as proof of "the perpetual punishment of those condemned with the devil." In Augustine's answer to the question "whether bodies can survive in a burning fire," he says, "what proof then can I offer to convince unbelievers that it is possible for human bodies, endowed with soul and life, not merely never to be decomposed by death, but also to outlast the torments of eternal flames? They refuse to accept from us an appeal to the power of the Almighty, but press us to cite a precedent by way of argument. We can reply that there are animals, which are certainly liable to destruction, since they are mortal, but still survive in the midst of flames" (Book 21.1). This animal Augustine is speaking about is the so-called "fire-salamander" which never existed, except in myth. Later Augustine goes on and says, "we say that there will be living human bodies which will always burn and suffer, yet will never die" (21.5, Loeb Classical Lib, p. 31). He goes on about this, "In many things it is unclear to us what His will is. This [human bodies in hell, never dying], however, is very certain, that none of the things which He has willed is impossible, and we believe His predictions since we cannot question either his strength or his truth" (Loeb Lib, p. 31).

nm1031 » **God's Will**. Augustine tries to argue with things in nature, but fails, so he falls back on *his* corrupt idea of God's will. But what is God's will? "God our Savior, who wishes <u>all</u> to be saved, and to come to the knowledge of the truth" (1Tim 2:3-4). And the Lord is "not willing that any should perish, but that <u>all</u> should come to repentance" (2Pet 3:9). Because Christ does his Father's will (Heb 10:7; John 6:38), then what Christ wills is also what God wills. As shown in the paper called "All Saved" [NM 13], God willed that <u>all</u> will eventually be saved, and He will make this happen, irrespective if Augustine or you or anyone else believes otherwise. See "All Saved" paper [NM13] for details.

nm1032 » By his own arguments, we can see that Augustine knew that the word translated into "forever" in many Bibles can mean an "age" or "long period of time" and not an eternal period of time. In order to disprove that the Greek word *aionios* or the Latin word *aeternus* means forever and not aeonian, Augustine agues thus,

- Then what sort of reasoning is it, to take the eternal [*aionios*] punishment of the wicked as a fire of long duration and believe that eternal life is without end? For Christ said in the very same place, including both in one and the same sentence: "So these will go into eternal punishment, but the righteous into eternal life." If both are eternal, then surely both must be understood as "long," but having an end, or else as "everlasting," without an end. For they are matched with each other: in one clause eternal punishment, in the other eternal life. But to say in one and the same sentence: "Eternal life shall be without end, eternal punishment will have an end," is utterly absurd. Hence, since the eternal life of the saints will be without end, eternal punishment also will surely have not end, for those whose lot it is.

(See "Context Argument Two in the "Age Paper" [NM 7] for a fuller explanation of this.)

nm1033 » **What Augustine does here is mix-up two things**: (1) Christians are given <u>immortal life</u> when they are resurrected at Christ's coming; and (2), they are given <u>aeonian life</u> in the same age that the "dead" and Satan are given their <u>aeonian punishment</u>.

nm1034 » Notice that Paul in the so-called resurrection chapter in the first book of Corinthians, mentions Christian's immortality:

- 1Corinthians 15:42: So it is with the resurrection of the dead. What is sown is perishable, what is raised is imperishable [immortal].

- 1Corinthians 15:51: Listen, I will tell you a mystery! We will not all die, but we will all be changed, 52 in a moment, in the twinkling of an eye, at the last trumpet. For the trumpet will sound, and the dead will be raised imperishable, and we will be changed. 53 For this perishable body must put on imperishability, and this mortal body must put on immortality. 54 When this perishable body puts on imperishability, and this **mortal body puts on immortality**, then the saying that is written will be fulfilled: "Death has been swallowed up in victory."

Thus Christians will receive immortality as a gift. There is a difference between immortal life and aeonian life (NM11).

Three Orders or Divisions

nm1035 » **Three Orders:** This resurrection chapter is also talking about the sequential *order* in which mankind will be given immortal life.

- 1Corinthians 15:20 But in fact Christ has been raised from the dead, the first fruit of those who have died. 21 For since death came through a human being, the resurrection of the dead has also come through a human being; 22 for as all die in Adam, so **all will be made alive in Christ**. 23 But **each in his own order: Christ the first fruit, then at his coming those who belong to Christ. 24 Then comes the end**, when he hands over the kingdom to God the Father, after he has destroyed every ruler and every authority and power.

This thus pictures the three times that mankind will be resurrected from the dead and given immortal life. This fulfills the typical three times physical Israel was ordered by God to stand before him (See NM 16).

The first was Christ

nm1036 »

- 25 "Very truly, I tell you, the hour is coming, and is now here, when the dead will hear the voice of the Son of God, and those who hear will live. 26 **For just as the Father has life in himself, so he has granted the Son also to have life in himself**; 27 and he has given him authority to execute judgment, because he is the Son of Man. 28 Do not be astonished at this; for the hour is coming when all who are in their graves will hear his voice 29 and will come out-- those who have done good, to **the resurrection of life**, and those who have done evil, to the resurrection of judgment (John 5:25-29).

Christ was resurrected from the dead by the power of his Father (Rom 1:4; 1Pet 1:3; GP 5). He was first, "If then you see the Son of man ascending up where he was the first?" (John 6:62; see Greek text) Christ was the "beginning of the creation of God" or the *new* creation of God (Rev 3:14; Gal 6:15), "the first born of all creation" (Col 1:15), thus "first born of the dead" "who is the beginning" (Col 1:18) "He is the first-born among many brethren" (Rom 8:29).

Second Order

nm1037 » The second time mankind will be resurrected to immortal life is at Christ's coming (1Cor 15:23). This is the resurrection of life (John 5:29). This is the group on Christ's right at his coming who are given the kingdom and rule during the 1000 years (Rev 20:1-6). Satan and his angels, on the left side, are counted as unjust, and are put into the bottomless pit for 1000 years (Rev 20:2-3, 11-15; 21:8; 2Thess 1:9). Those counted as good are given immortal life and also the 1000 year aeonian life (Rom 2:7; NM 11). We explain the difference between the immortal life and the aeonian life in our paper called "Reward for Christians." [NM 11] They will rule with Christ during the 1000 years (Rev 2:26; 3:21; 5:10; Dan 7:27). This is the first of the last two resurrections to immortal life (Rev 20:5b).

Third Order

nm1038 » But the others "will suffer the punishment of aeonian destruction, separated from the presence of the Lord and from the glory of his power" (2Thess 1:9). While the "just" are enjoying the wonders of the kingdom during the 1000 years, the "unjust" will be taken from the kingdom for 1000 years. It is at the "end," after the 1000 years, when the "unjust" are resurrected (Rev 20:5a; 1Cor 15:24). This is the resurrection of the dead (John 5:29).

Conclusion:

nm1039 » The "just" are given immortal life and given the 1000 year aeonian life, but the "unjust" go for the 1000 year aeonian punishment (Mat 25:46 w/ Rev 20:1-5). This is the aeonian judgment (Heb 6:2). The judgment for sin is death (Ezek 18:11-13; Gen 2:17; Rom 6:23). "The wages of sin is death, but the gift of God is aeonian life, through Jesus Christ" (Rom 6:23). What God said in Genesis 2:17 was that if they ate from the forbidden tree they would in dying, be dead: "in dying, you will die" or "in dying, you will be dead" (see Hebrew text or BCB). What God was doing was projecting to us the group called the "dead" in the Bible (Luke 9:60; 2Tim 4:1; 1Pet 4:6).

In Short: Judgment is

nm1040 » Those who overcome will inherit all things (Rev 20:7; 1Cor 3:21-22; 2Pet 1:3). Those who do not overcome or are unjust or are evil are sent to the lake of fire to be destroyed from the presence of the Lord and his glory (Rev 20:10, 15; 21:8; Mat 13:41-42; 25:41; 1Pet 3:7, 10-11; 2Thess 1:9), for the 1000 years (Rev 20:4-5). Those who overcome eat from the tree of life, are not hurt by any second death, given a new Name, rule over nations in the 1000 years, will not be taken out of the book of life, will have God's Name, and will sit in/on Christ's throne (Rev 2:7, 11, 17; 26; 3:5, 12, 21 cf. 21:8). But after the 1000 year judgment there will be the coming together of all, so that God will be all in all (1Cor 15:28; NM15; NM16; GP6).

nm1041 » Christians will also judge, so to speak, the angels and the world at Christ's coming (1Cor 6:2-3; Dan 7:26-27). Their good works judge-down the evil works of the world, Satan, and his angels.

Remaining questions:

What happens to Satan and his angels? (See, NM 13,14, 15; GP 6, 7, 8) Is there a Heaven? (See, NM 25)

NM 25: Kingdom of God

What Others Say

nm1042 » *Is there a heaven?* In many churches members look upon going to heaven as going above the clouds and beholding God always while being in a state of heavenly bliss. Not too much detail is given, except it is a much better place to be than hell. According to many, if you go to hell, you are in a fire suffering forever (Last Judgment). But if you go to heaven you are blessed forever and you will live in one of the heavenly mansions in cities paved with gold. If you get to heaven there will be no work, no suffering, no day, no night. Everyone eats from the tree of life and worships God forever enjoying the beatific vision.

nm1043 » In the Koran, one description of heaven for the males is having a continuous supply of virgin "companions," with alcoholic drink and delicate food to eat – a continuous orgy and feast (Sura 56:4-41ff). This belief is not particular to the Koran, for many others also believe that the pleasures forbidden them on earth will be their permissible pleasure in heaven. But are the sinful "pleasures" denied on earth, the rewards of heaven? Or does this have more to do with the other-mind's pleasures being projected into mankind's physical mind in this age? (See "Old Mind" paper [NM 21])

What the Bible Says

But what does the Bible say about the "reward" for Christians? Do they go to heaven?

nm1044 » **Go to Heaven?** Now since the word "heaven" or "heavenly" is used interchangeably with "spirit" or "spiritual" (1Cor 15:44-49; see Duality Paper), then at Christ's coming, when we are infused into the spiritual dimension, we will, so to speak, go to heaven or go to the spiritual dimension. But at Christ's coming is also the end of the Beast of Revelation's rule ("Beast-System Paper" [PR2]), and the beginning of God's rule through his Christ and his saints (Dan 7:11-14, 24-27; Rev 19:20-20:4; 2Thes 1:7, 10). At Christ's coming there will be clouds in the sky (Dan 7:13; Mat 24:30; Rev 1:7; Ezek 32:7; Isa 13:10; Joel 2:31; 3:15; Amos 8:9; Rev 6:12-13; Zech 14:7) from the effects of the Last War [PR5], the two witnesses will be resurrected and ascend into heaven in a cloud (Rev 11:12), the other Christians also will ascend into heaven at that same time to meet Christ in the air (1Thes 4:13-17; 2Thes 2:1; 1Cor 15:23, 51-55) to be with Christ always, and because at that time Christ will come down to earth to rule, the Christians will bring Christ down (Rom 10:6) to rule on earth for the 1000 years (Rev 20:4; 5:10; 11:15), for Christ's kingdom will rule on the earth (Rev 5:10 Greek text; Psalm 37:29, 9; Mat 5:5). Thus, "heaven" as commonly thought of, is not the "reward" Christians receive, per se. Remember here that any "reward" Christians receive is not earned; we receive all from God as a gift (See NM 8-11).

nm1045 » In this book we have given you, here and there, some aspects of the heavenly "rewards." Let's review and put the facts together, so in one place we can see what these "rewards" will be:

1. **Aeonian Life**: This is life in the 1000 year period. This is explained in the "Reward for Christians" paper. [NM 11] This is different from the immortal life.

2. **Immortality**: This is explained also in the "Reward for Christians" paper and in the "Does All Mean All?" paper [NM11; NM 14]. Immortal life is life in an immortal physical body as a New Soul. It is different from the aeonian life, which is life with Christ in the 1000 year period during which others of the old age are in judgment (Last Judgment).

3. **Life in the Kingdom of God**: There are three orders of going into the Kingdom (1Cor 15:20-24). The first was Christ the man. The second "order" occurs at the return of Christ. The third order occurs *after* the 1000 year period. Life in the Kingdom of God is life under the rulership of God in peace and harmony. What the Kingdom of God will be like in the present universe is outlined in NM26.

4. **Life Forever in the New Heaven and Earth or New Universe**: Most fully this New Universe will start *after* the small age of 100 years which comes after the 1000 years of the Kingdom of God under Christ (NM 19). It may be as impossible to understand this as it would for a child in the womb to understand how it will be after he/she is born. Our lives up to the time of the creation of the New Universe are in preparation for life in the New Universe.

5. **Pleasure in the New Life**: We will have great pleasure in the New Life only because we have had great suffering in the old life. Pleasure and pain are comparative qualities: both need each other for either to exist (See "Reason Why" [NM 19], and GP 7 of

the *God Papers*). Our very bodies, our New Souls, will be in and of themselves pleasurable (See "New Body" in GP6). We will live both in the physical dimension and the spiritual dimension (GP 6). We will not need to travel by foot, or by car, or by plane, or by space ship, but by and through the spiritual dimension if we so choose ("New Body" in GP6).

6. **Happiness Forever in the New Life**: Because of the very law of knowledge, we will be happy in the New Life ("Reason Why" NM19). Happiness is a comparative quality. You cannot be happy, if you have never known unhappiness. Happiness and unhappiness are comparative qualities: both need each other for either to exist (See "Reason Why" [NM 19]).

7. **Love and Freedom in the New Life**: God will be all in all (1Cor 15:28). "God is love. Whoever lives in love, lives in God, and God in him" (1John 4:16). "God lives in us and his love is made complete in us" (1John 4:12). We will all live in the Freedom and Harmony of the System of Love (See "Freedom and Law" [NM 17]).

Jesus Christ: "You are my friends if you do what I command... My command is this: Love each other as I have loved you" (John 15:12, 14). "Yes, I am coming soon" (Rev 22:20).

NM 26: Plan of Creation, An Outline

NM26 Abstract

In this paper we will give a short outline of our main beliefs.

A Short Outline of Our Beliefs

Here follows an outline of our belief concerning the plan of creation, which we ascertained through scripture, patterns in scripture, and logic. Read Introduction to this book, to understand our premises and to better understand why we use the Bible and believe that the Bible reveals the truth. Better yet, read all of the many papers we offer for more details. It is almost impossible to understand this outline in full without studying all the *BeComingOne Papers*. Please do not jump to conclusions.

1. Before the Beginning the All Powerful God Predestinated Events.

nm1046 » Scripture indicated that God predestinated events *before* the creation. Christians were chosen before the foundation of the world (Eph 1:4). Jesus Christ, what he would do and what would happen to him, was foreordained before the foundation of the world or cosmos (1Pet 1:19-20; Act 2:23; 3:18; 4:27-28). God who is all powerful predestinated everything (NM 8; NM 9; etc.). Even evil was predestinated (Rom 9:21-23; Jude 1:4; Prov 16:4; 1Peter 2:8; etc.). God in his all powerfulness even commands Satan, the leader of evil (Job 1:12; 2:6). In his predestination God predestinated everything before the cosmos began, before good (as we know it), before evil (as we know it), before law (as we know it), and consequently, before sin (as we know it).

2. In The Beginning God Created The Cosmos; In The Six Literal Days God Created The First Cosmos From The Laws And Matter Created On The Very First Day.

nm1047 » In the beginning God created the heavens and the earth, that is, the cosmos (Gen 1:1; Isa 48:3, 13; Heb 4:3). After the creation of the heavens and the earth, or the cosmos (Gen 1:1), the earth was not yet finished: "the earth was without form and void" (Gen 1:2). God continued to create during the first six days of creation and rested on the seventh day (Gen 1: 3-2:3). It was only when the real God creates and finishes everything that it is pronounced good: "everything that he had made ... was very good" (Gen 1:31; 2:1). What the true God creates is good, not in confusion, for God is not the author of confusion (1Cor 14:33; see Isaiah 45:18; 1Tim 4:4; Deut 32:4). This creation week typified the longer spiritual creation of approximately 7,000 years. Peter called a day of God being equal to 1000 years (2Peter 3:8). The book of Revelation speaks of a 1000 year period when Satan is put away. This 1000 year period is like a rest period for mankind, a rest without evil (NM15; NM16).

3. Man Went Out of God To *learn* Good And Evil; The Kingdom of The Adversary Begins.

nm1048 » After man was created, a spiritual adversary misled man to break a law of God (Gen 2:16-17; 3:1-24). This spiritual adversary was "the old serpent, called the Devil, and Satan, which deceives the whole world" (Rev 12:9). See the "Old Mind Paper" [NM 21] for more information on this apparent myth concerning the "serpent." Mankind by breaking this first law of God was sent out of the Garden of Eden and, "Behold, the man is become as one out of [or from] us, to *know* good and evil" (Gen 3:22). After mankind sinned in the Garden they were sent out to learn good and evil (see the "Reason Why" paper [NM 19] and see GP 7 of the *God Papers* for the reason for evil). There is a great reason why the all powerful God allowed evil.

4. The Breaking of God's First Law Manifests the Other-Mind Inside Mankind.

nm1049 » In the "Old Mind Paper" [NM 21] we learn why man broke the first law of God and why this present age is an age of confusion and hate. It was the other-mind inside of man's mind that misled man into breaking God's first law. Because of this the world has been held in "the bondage of corruption" and "the whole creation groans and travails in pain" because of the other-mind's power (Rom 8:21, 22; Rev 12:9; 13:2,3; see the "Old Mind Paper" [NM 21]).

5. God Promised a Savior To Save Mankind

nm1050 » When God spoke to the "serpent" after he had misled man into taking the forbidden fruit, God said he would send a child of the woman ("her seed") and that he "shall bruise your [serpent's] head and you [serpent] shall bruise his [the seed's] heel" (Gen 3:14, 15). See the "Old Mind Paper" [NM 21] to understand the serpent of Genesis.

There was a child that was born of a woman (Gal 4:4) who will "bruise Satan," and he is Jesus Christ (Rom 16:20). "Jesus" is a word that means, Jehovah's *Savior*, and "Christ" is a word that means, anointed. Christ Jesus is the, "Anointed Savior of Jehovah." He is "the Savior of the cosmos" (1John 4:14).

Jesus Christ is the savior of the world, who is/will save the world from the spiritual adversary's influence that now is misleading mankind towards destruction. See the *God Papers* to understand who is Jesus Christ.

6. The Messiah Savior, Jesus Christ Came in the Flesh, and Died.

nm1051 » But Jesus Christ was a man ("the *man* Christ Jesus," 1Tim 2:5); he came in the flesh as a man (1John 4:1-3). Jesus Christ was a man born to be savior of the world, yet he did not save the world when he was alive. He died on a stake and was buried (John 19:16-17, 33, 40-41). While he was on earth, before his death, he had the Spirit of God in him, leading him and giving him power over evil (GP 4). In fact, this "Spirit of God" was the actual angel of God who helped Israel in the Old Testament (GP 3; GP 4; GP 5).

7. But Jesus Christ Was Resurrected and Became God.

nm1052 » After Jesus was resurrected, Thomas called him "My Lord and my God," for he was in God (John 20:28; see *God Papers*). Jesus who was born a man actually went into God and sits at God's right hand, as the right side of God (GP 5). The Bible talks about human beings actually becoming like God – that is, being *born* of God (1John 3:9; 5:18). If one is born of mankind, we know he is a man. If one is born of God, we know he is a God-like person – a son or daughter of God. The Bible actually calls man, Gods (John 10:33-35). In some way mankind will become God-like. See the *God Papers* to understand who or what is God, and in what way and how Jesus became God. It is by Jesus Christ's new life as God that He will save us (Rom 5:10).

8. Jesus Christ Promised to Return to Earth.

nm1053 » Time after time Christ promised to return to the earth (Mat 24:27; 30-31, 42; Mark 13:26; Luke 12:42-43; 13:28-29; 17:24; 18:8; 19:12; 21:27; John 14:3).

9. When Will Christ Return? – At The End of The Age.

nm1054 » Notice what Christ's students asked him: "Tell us, when shall these things be? and what shall be the sign of your coming, and the *end* of the age?" (Mat 24:3) What age is being spoken about here? It is the present age of confusion that is being spoken about. See *End of the Age* for more details.

10. Christ The God Will Come to *Save* Mankind at the End of the Age of the Adversary's Spiritual Rulership.

nm1055 » Christ will come as the savior of mankind; he will save man from destroying themselves: "for the son of man [Christ] is *not* come to destroy men's lives, but *to save them*" (Luke 9:56). There is going to be a great Last War at the end of the age, and if Christ does not come to save, then *no* flesh will be saved out of this war (Mark 13:20; see "Last War and God's Wrath" paper [PR4; PR5; PR6]).

11. At The Same Time Christ Will Judge Mankind.

nm1056 » The judgment of God is probably the most misunderstood doctrine of the Bible. What is God's judgement?: "The LORD is known by the judgment which he executes: the wicked is snared in the work of his *own* hands" (Psa 9:16). In other words, Christ the God will come to save the world after an atomic *Last War* has started before he returns to the physical dimension. And God's judgment is to let the works of man's OWN hands (their own weapons) begin to destroy mankind, then He saves mankind from their own madness. Man thus actually judges his own self, but God comes to save. See "Last War and God's Wrath" paper [PR5] for information on the Last War.

There will be a 1000 year judgment (see "Thousand Years and Beyond Paper"[NM 15]). This is the judgment of the dead. Some people have mixed this judgment up and turned it into a "hell" theory, or "lake of fire" theory.

12. Christ The God Will Come to Set Up The Kingdom of God *on* Earth.

nm1057 » Christ will return to set up the kingdom or rulership of God that will rule all the earth. Notice what prophecy shows: "the kingdoms of this world are become the kingdoms of our Lord, and of his Christ; and he shall reign into the ages of ages" (Rev 11:15). At His return the kingdoms of the world will be His. Since Christ is God, then these kingdoms will become the kingdoms of God.

nm1058 » Notice in Daniel 7:14 where it prophesies of Christ's return, "and there was given him dominion, and glory, and a *kingdom*, that *all* people, nations and languages, should serve him." The kingdom of God will rule people, *all* people. This is the time God will live with mankind and rule mankind (Rev 20:4). This kingdom of God will rule *on* earth with the saints, "and they shall reign ON the earth" (Rev 5:10). Notice that the symbolic stone, which is a symbol of Christ, smote the image, which represents the world's kingdoms, "and filled the whole earth" (Dan. 2:35).

nm1059 » The Messiah is coming to set up a kingdom *on* the earth to bring mankind into a utopia. God will then be King of kings (Rev 19:16).

13. But What Is The Kingdom of God?

nm1060 » A kingdom is a kingdom. It is a system of rulership. The expression, kingdom of God or the kingdom of heaven, is used about 150 times in the New Testament of the Bible. And tens of times in the Old Testament it speaks about God setting up a kingdom on earth. In the book of Isaiah it continually speaks of the LORD (BeComingOne, that is "Jehovah" or YHWH) coming to earth to save his people and setting up a utopian society.

nm1061 » Some think the Church is the kingdom of heaven or of God. But God's Bible says that when the kingdom is set up there will be no misery, no wrong, no tears (Isa 2:4; 11:9; Zeph 3:15; Rev 21:4). In the truest sense, the kingdom has not come to the earth. The Church now is merely a typical kingdom of God with only some of the world's people in it. Not until the Messiah comes with His peace, will there be true peace.

nm1062 » We know the kingdom of God is here only when we see Christ coming in clouds (the smoke of the Last War), for "every eye shall see him" (Rev 1:7). All will eventually *see* him. Since God is coming to save the world from cosmocide, and since he comes to set up a system of peace, and since everyone will literally see him; then we know he has not come yet and the kingdom is not set up on earth yet, for we still have war and we do not see anyone on earth like Christ. If you study the resurrected Christ you see pictured a person that could appear from nowhere and disappear out of sight. But when he appeared he was flesh and blood just like us. But he could change his body at will into an invisible body that could go through walls and any other matter. There is no one on earth who can walk through walls or appear and disappear at will; thus, Christ has not returned yet. If any one says to you that he is Christ, ask him to kindly walk through the wall (of course walk through the wall without harming it like Christ did). See the *God Papers* to understand who or what is God. Christ's main message throughout his ministry on earth was about the coming of the kingdom of God: "Now after that John was put in prison, Jesus came into Galilee, preaching the gospel of the kingdom of God" (Mark 1:14). He preached the gospel of the kingdom of God. The word "gospel" is translated from a Greek word that means *good news*. Christ was teaching people about the good news of the kingdom of God. It is good news because when the kingdom of God is set up there will be complete peace (Isa 2:4).

nm1063 » Paul the apostle also taught about the kingdom of God (Acts 19:8; 20:25; 28:23, 31).

nm1064 » Christ sent 70 men preaching the kingdom of God (Luke 10:9). He sent the apostles to preach the kingdom of God (Luke 9:1a-2). In fact one of the most important things that the Church has to do in this age is teach about the kingdom (Mat 24:14; Mark 16:15; Col 1:23).

14. What Will Happen During The Kingdom of God?

nm1065 » As Isaiah 2:4 says the first thing that will happen is "they shall beat their swords [weapons] into plowshares, and their spears into pruning hooks: nation shall not lift up sword against nation, neither shall they learn war any more" (Isa 2:4). This will happen because man's mind will change the instant Christ the God returns physically to earth. God will put away the spiritual adversary out of man's mind (Zech 13:2; Rev 20:1-3; see the "Old Mind Paper" [NM 21]). Man's attitude will change. He will no longer desire violence.

What Are Some of the Specific Changes God Will Make When He Returns?

nm1066 » **A.** *Cities Rebuilt*. Just before Christ the God's return there will be a Last War that will be destroying the earth (see "Last War and God's Wrath" paper [PR5]). The cities destroyed in this war will be rebuilt (Amos 9:14).

nm1067 » **B.** *The Earth Repopulated*. After this Last War many of the people alive now will be dead. The earth will be repopulated (Ezek 36:10-11).

nm1068 » **C.** *The Earth's Surface Renewed*. After the Last War the world will have atomic waste. But Christ the God will renew the surface of the world (Psa 104:30; Isa 61:4). This is the *typical* creation of the *new* heaven and earth.

nm1069 » **D. *Trees And Forests Will Be Everywhere*** even in the places where there are now deserts (compare Isa 41:19; 29:17; 60:13; 51:3).

nm1070 » **E. *Great Highways Will Be Built*** (Isa 19:23; 11:16; 40:3).

nm1071 » **F. *Children Will Play With Animals That Are Now Wild*.** Animals will all be tame in the kingdom of God (Isa 11:6-7).

nm1072 » **G. *Everyone Will Own His Own Land*** with the products of the land for their personal use (Amos 9:14; Isa 65:21-22; Micah 4:4).

nm1073 » **H. *Rain Will Fall At The Right Time In The Right Amounts*** so as to produce fantastic crops (Ezek 34:26; Isa 30:23; Jer 31:5, 12; Amos 9:13; Ezek 36:29-30).

nm1074 » **I. *A New Clear Language*** will be given to all mankind; there will be *one* language (Zeph 3:9).

nm1075 » **J. *There Will Be No More Sickness*;** all diseases will be cured (Isa 58:8; 33:24; 35:5-6; Jer 31:13-14). There will be no more sickness because Christ the God will heal them (Jer 30:17).

nm1076 » **K. *There Will Be True Freedom*.** When people speak of freedom they mean not total freedom, but freedom from things, activities, and restrictions that make them unhappy. What makes people unhappy is sin. Sin should be looked upon as a way of destruction. War is sin because in war people kill. Killing is against the laws of harmony and love. There will never be peace until people stop sinning, that is, stop making war. "Glory to God in the highest, and on earth peace among men of good will" (Luke 2:14). Peace will only come when men are of peace, that is, when men are of "good will." He that kills with the sword or weapon will be killed by the sword (Rev 13:10). Man kills, therefore man will die by the sword until he stops killing. Man will have true freedom in God's kingdom because God will automatically change man's attitude from conflict to peace.

nm1077 » **L. *All Men Will Be Prosperous During The Kingdom*.** Man will be prosperous because man during God's kingdom will be in harmony with the ways of harmony. Man will be putting his total output of work towards useful and constructive projects and thus will be in a much better economic situation than today when much energy is directed towards destruction (war) and towards the repairing of the destruction. There won't be any sick, mentally or physically, and this will allow more energy to be directed towards a prosperous economy.

15. 1000 Years of the Kingdom of God.

nm1078 » The Bible speaks about an "everlasting" kingdom of God (2Pet 1:11; Dan. 7:27). But the translators of the Bible have *mistranslated* such words as "forever," "everlasting," and "eternal." The Bible was written mostly in two languages – Hebrew and Greek. The original words that were translated into "forever," "everlasting," and "eternal" actually mean aeonian, not forever (see the "Age Paper" [NM 7]). In other words, almost everywhere in the Bible where you see "forever," "everlasting," and "eternal" should read aeonian, age, or ages. Aeonian is a far cry from forever, for in order for it to be aeonian it must have a beginning and it implies the possibility of an end. But the word everlasting means it has no possibility of an end. Thus, when scripture is correctly translated, God's kingdom is an aeonian kingdom, and there are ageS within it not everlastingS or eternitieS within it. But unlike most ages, God's great age does not end, yet within this great age there are other ages (see "Age Paper" [NM 7]). One age within the ages of the Kingdom of God is the 1000 years (Rev 20:3, 5). Also see *Ages in God's Plan* for more info on ages.

16. God's Kingdom *under* Christ, Who Is King of Kings (Rev 19:16), Will Last Through an Age of 1000 Years (Rev 20:4).

nm1079 » During this age some men "born" of God will rule as servants with Christ (Rev 20:4). These who are to be born of God, who were human beings during the time *before* Christ's physical return, can be labeled as true Christians. These real Christians will rule as *servants* of mankind, not as warlords (read Mat 20:25-28), during this 1000 year age.

17. But After the 1000 Year Age, The Kingdom of God Will Continue Into The Next Age – The Great Spiritual Last Day.

nm1080 » The next age in the kingdom of God is an age of 100 years, which we call the Great Last Spiritual Day of Creation. It is a spiritual day of unity with God. *ALL* people who ever lived will be resurrected and live during this 100 year period. This age is a period of typical equal rulership and authority between all peoples – "the God, all things in all" (1Cor 15:28).

This period after the millennium has been completely overlooked by most people. See "God's Appointed Times Paper" [NM 16] and the "Thousand Years and Beyond Paper" [NM 15] for more information on the 100 year period.

18. Then After The 1000 Year Age, And After The 100 Year Age, Comes The End of The Spiritual Creation When The Antitypical New Heaven And Earth Will Be Created (1Cor 15:24-28; Rev 21:5).

nm1081 » The antitypical creation is unlike the typical creation of the new heaven and earth. The typical creation of the new heaven and earth begins at Christ's physical return at the beginning of the 1000 year period (see 14 C above). The antitypical creation of the new heaven and earth happens at the time the totally *new* universe is created (note Rev 21:5). In that time everyone and everything will have been created new and will live in harmony and freedom from then and onward for God's age is an age without end (See "Age Paper" [NM 7]).

Index

INDEX

Acknowledgment

I thank my wife Shirley Clare for her help in correcting errors of grammar and supporting the thesis of this work as well as her patience over the years for the time I spent on my books. I also thank my daughter for her help in reading and correcting errors in grammar. I also thank all biblical scholars who wrote helps (concordances, interlinear Bibles, grammars, computer programs, creation v. evolution books, etc.) and critiques of doctrine, for they made my work easier. Lastly, I thank all scholars of serious works (religion, philosophy, science, etc) for their work for no one person can think through all opinions pertaining on subjects: we need to compare our knowledge with others in order to ascertain the truth of the matter.

Walter R. Dolen

September 2012

About the Author

Walter Dolen is an author who uses the scientific method[1] to research the material for his books. He has researched and written on science, chronology, philosophy, psychology, theology, religion, sex differences, feminism and so forth. The author questions everything and from this he writes his books. For more info on the author see:

www.walterdolen.com or www.walterdolen.ws

May Grace Abound to All

---

[1] (1)Perceive a problem; (2) examine and analyze all the available evidence; (3) examine and imagine different hypotheses in attempt to solve the problem in a logical manner, (4) form a theory that answers the problem; (5) test the theory; (6) always have an open mind for better theories or answers to the problem; (7) change the theory if new evidence is inconsistent to your prior theory

Notes

* 9 7 8 1 6 1 9 1 8 0 2 4 6 *